El

Pa are

International Practical Theology

edited by

Prof. Dr. Chris Hermans (Nijmegen),
Prof. Dr. Maureen Junker-Kenny (Dublin),
Prof. Dr. Richard Osmer (Princeton),
Prof. Dr. Friedrich Schweitzer (Tübingen),
Prof. Dr. Hans-Georg Ziebertz (Würzburg)

in cooperation with the
International Academy of Practical Theology (IAPT),

represented by

Daniel Louw (President)
and Elaine Graham (Vice President)

Volume 1

LIT

Pathways to the Public Square

Practical Theology in an Age of Pluralism

International Academy of Practical Theology, Manchester 2003

edited by

Elaine Graham and Anna Rowlands

LIT

Cover Picture: The University of Edinburgh Library Special Collections

Bibliographic information published by Die Deutsche Bibliothek
Die Deutsche Bibliothek lists this publication in the Deutsche
Nationalbibliografie; detailed bibliographic data are available in the
Internet at http://dnb.ddb.de.

ISBN 3-8258-8423-6

A catalogue record for this book is available from the British library

© LIT VERLAG Münster   2005
Grevener Str./Fresnostr. 2   48159 Münster
Tel. 0251-62 03 20   Fax 0251-23 19 72
e-Mail: lit@lit-verlag.de   http://www.lit-verlag.de

Distributed in North America by:

Transaction Publishers
New Brunswick (U.S.A.) and London (U.K.)

Transaction Publishers   Tel.: (732) 445 - 2280
Rutgers University   Fax: (732) 445 - 3138
35 Berrue Circle   for orders (U. S. only):
Piscataway, NJ 08854   toll free (888) 999 - 6778

Contents

Preface

With the first volume "Pathways to the Public Square", the new series, International Studies in Practical Theology, is established. This book collects papers and presentations from an international conference held in Manchester in 2003. Scholars from all parts of the world reflect on Practical Theology in the public sphere, with contributions refering to the local and global level. Therefore this book is a programmatic start of the new series: it has an international authorship, it focuses on a world-wide relevant topic, and it is a good representation of practical-theological reflections around the globe. The editors are happy to begin their series with this book.

What is the general approach of the series? In a globalized world, academic disciplines need international exchange and debate, which reflects a range of cross-cultural and religious developments, theories and models, research topics, and methods. This series will establish a forum for researchers who are working across cultural, disciplinary and theoretical boundaries, either through international collaborations or engagement with topics of international relevance. Contributions from diverse cultural and national theological contexts will explore how current religious practice can be explained, understood, and developed. The series will also reflect on the nature and academic standards of practical-theological research, seeking to stimulate the sharpening of methodological issues and procedures. The series will publish books mainly in the English language. The editorial board is linked to the International Academy of Practical Theology, and many of the publications will reflect continuing collaboration within the Academy, although the editors welcome other high-quality contributions from researchers in Practical Theology.

The editors acknowledge the stimulation of Dr. Rainer from the LIT-Publishing house in Münster (Germany) to establish this series.

Chris Hermans (Nijmegen, The Netherlands)
Maureen Junker-Kenny (Dublin, Ireland)
Richard Osmer (Princeton, USA)
Friedrich Schweitzer (Tübingen, Germany)
Hans-Georg Ziebertz (Würzburg, Germany)

Pathways to the Public Square: Proceedings of the 2003 IAPT Conference, Manchester UK

Introduction

Elaine Graham and Anna Rowlands

Our conference theme for 2003 explored the relationship between the concerns of Practical Theology and the category of 'public theology'. In exploring this wide ranging theme we drew inspiration from our local context – the twin UK cities of Manchester and Salford. Over the past decade the urban landscape of Manchester and Salford has been transformed: the first British industrial city of the nineteenth century, which saw its pre-eminence decline during the twentieth, is undergoing a dramatic rejuvenation as a twenty-first century metropolis. And theological themes are writ large across its landscape. From the ethnic pluralism of Manchester, representing cultures in which religion, far from declining, persists as a vital source of community life and identity, to involvement of faith communities in the process of regeneration and the re-working of religious images and narratives in aspects of urban design and economic renewal, we were confronted with the question: how can we 'speak of God in public'? This question becomes all the more urgent and complex amidst the vernacular spiritualities and secular temples of the built environment.

Christian 'talk about God' is inescapably 'public'. Theological discourse can never be simply the internal conversations of a group set apart. So long as Christians are called to be light of the world, salt of the earth, then they will be involved in worldly matters; and their faith will have some kind of 'public' impact. Nevertheless, the ways in which that public dimension takes shape, and the precise boundaries between 'church' and 'world', have been a matter of debate and disagreement since the time of the earliest Christians. A classic text in this respect might be H. Richard Niebuhr's *Christ and Culture* (1951) which stands in an important sociological tradition of analysis which admits to a range of different formulations of the relationship between 'Christ' on the one hand and 'Culture' on the other: from complete identity, to total separation (if that is ever possible). To be 'in' the world but not 'of' it is clearly a perennial tension, made all the more acute by the difficulties and compromises inherent in deciding in any given context what kind of church, what kind of theology, what kind of Christian practice and vocation – and indeed what kind of society – is actually called for.

But this is about more than simply the extent to which Christians can identify the signs of the times as also containing signs of the Gospel, and the extent to which the culture in which we find ourselves must be subject to the transformations of Christ. We must also ask what we mean by 'public' as a category: is it synonymous (identical) with 'political'? And political at what level, to what degree? Clearly, there are time-honoured models of public theology which assume that the institutional church will be an integral part of the constitutional processes and structures of the State, such as the traditions of establishment of the Churches of England and Scotland (despite their contemporary and historical differences from one another).

However, the task of 'speaking truth to power' brings opportunities and challenges. At a deeper cultural level, too, this kind of model of establishment may assume a fair degree of harmony and consensus – that one privileged religious body can be held to represent, in an almost organic fashion, the character of the wider body politic. Yet the dominance of one theological or even ecclesial tradition may come to be regarded as an unacceptable imposition, a position exemplified in the constitutional separation of Church and State in countries such as the United States and France, a stance characterised by a modernist, post-Enlightenment conviction that the public domain must be kept separate from matters of faith. Yet this boundary between sacred and secular, private and public, constitutional and confessional, is one which is coming under increasing pressure throughout the world, as many of the contributions to this volume make plain.

Alongside these models of establishment and separation, however, we might also find examples of societies which are attempting to build up traditions of civil society and political participation, in which one or many traditions of religious faith provide shared moral values which undergird in procedural or substantive fashion, agreed principles of justice, law and citizenship. This is more in tune with Charles Villa-Vicencio's (1992) 'reconstructive' function of public theology, although it also relates closely to contemporary debates about communities of faith as sources of 'social capital' (see for example, Putnam, 2000), providing some of the material as well as ideological resources – such as buildings, expertise, voluntary labour energy – by which civil society is maintained.

These questions, of whether a 'public theology' is possible in a globalizing, secular and pluralist world, and the shape it will take in any particular context, form the central thread to this volume, and elicit a rich and diverse response. In the papers that follow we see many familiar conversations re-emerging: rich exchanges between practical theologies and practical philosophies, practical theologies and modern psychologies, between practical theologies and liberal (Protestant) theologies. The dominant discourses of twentieth century practical theologies – modern psychologies, ethics, Christian education, theologies of liberation and empirical research – find their place anew in this collection, and they are well-represented here. Equally, new life is breathed into much older patterns of homiletics, spirituality and liturgy as urgent and renewed expressions of practical and public theology. For that reason, it is encouraging to see that this collection creates spaces for significant new (renewed) and challenging exchanges: for example, between practical theologies and the arts (Nadeau, Couture), practical theologies and law (Reed, Kennedy), practical theologies and social philosophy (Mager), practical theology and 'media society' (Graeb, Lefebvre) and (most timely) practical theologies and the dialogue of religions (Webb, Hall).

Inevitably in the first IAPT gathering since September 11th 2001, the weight of recent world events is felt throughout this text. This is approached most systematically in Duncan Forrester's contribution. Forrester argues powerfully that the terrain of the old dialogue between secular reason and religious practice has been radically (and tragically) reconfigured; that the way in which we address the question – what does public theology look like in a post-Christian, post-secular world – changes and we find ourselves called to new practices of theological interpretation. The dramatic demonstration that the state, however powerful, cannot set the limits of political (or religious) discourse raises an urgent set of questions about the role that a (Christian) public theology might play in our world. Forrester points (as other contemporary theorists do), towards a reconfiguration of the borders between civil religion, political theology and public theology; a renewed configuration in which the relation between state, civil society and religion conceived according to Liberal, Enlightenment models is displaced. This is the theological and cultural centre that no longer holds in which the identity, role and relation of practical theology and its ability to 'speak of God in public' is itself at issue.

We might also want to highlight the convergence of both renewed practical theologies and public theologies upon the ground of 'civil society'. As we hinted earlier, in the past decade discourses of civil society have become significant in both academic life and public policy and as Max Stackhouse has argued, the urgent task of public theology is the reconfiguration of the assumed relation of state, civil society and religion in modernity (Stackhouse, 2004). He critiques the Erastian role of religion understood as 'subservient subordination

to and ideological support of cultural identity and national interest.' Instead
he is interested in speculating about the resources which might be offered 'as
a public theology for a world situation in which a civil society is now being
formed – without a clear and centred political order.' For a renewed public
theology to begin to generate such resources requires, amongst other tasks,
attention to the complex processes of contemporary globalisation and its intel-
ligent analysis.

The distinction for Stackhouse between a political and a public theology
lies in public theology's view of the political order as 'subject over time to
the more primary powers in society – those spheres of life that embody those
moral and spiritual orientations that become embodied in social and ethical
tissues and associations of the common life and that are prior to the formation
of political orders'. So the argument seems to be that, the (old) *centre* no longer
holds, to borrow Tracy's phrase; and yet because of this, the *middle* is already
at least partly healed – the healed middle being found in pre-existent civil
societies which exist as 'convictional-commitment-incarnate multiple centers
in the lives of the public' these being 'the most decisive core of civilizational
life'. With proper cultivation these centres work not bottom up, or top down but
'from the centre out'. This renewed *middle* is a comprehending one – the free
associations of civil society comprehend at least as much as the state. With
some nuance this is an insight which many practical theologians will share.
As Chris Hermans argues in this volume, drawing on the work of Johannes
Van der Ven, a new consensus has now emerged, stressing a practical theology
'broadened in its co-ordinates' which takes such an understanding of society
as the starting point for the study of theologically disclosive practice.

There is therefore much in this volume that could be brought into fruitful dialogue with such a public theology. Storrar's call for a public theology
understood in both contemporary and historical context as 'a Christian humanist discipline of moral cartography' stands out in this regard. He argues that
practical theology is inherently public and must be placed in the context of
an adequately historicized understanding of globalisation. He offers a broad,
theologically informed definition of globalisation as 'human interconnections
which have assumed global proportions and transformed themselves'. This is
a process which has always been with us; but as historian Robbie Robertson
argues, has had three distinct waves. This has resonance with Stackhouse's
insistence that public *theological* discourse requires a much broader concept
of globalisation than has been dominant in recent social and political theory.
Such a broadening is essential if, as Storrar – drawing on Jurgen Habermas –
argues, theologians are to contribute effectively to the 'social space' generated
by 'communicative action'.

Writing collaboratively in this volume, John Atherton, Chris Baker and Elaine Graham are also keen to advocate a move towards a renewed '*ad extra*' focus for public, practical theology with an emphasis on relevance, reason and relationship. Practical theology itself exists as part of the web of relationships which form, to draw on Stackhouse again, a 'comprehending civil society'. As such, as Atherton, Baker and Graham suggest, it has a responsibility to speak meaningfully, to address concrete concerns and to bring carefully discerned positive resources from Tradition which must be communicated intelligibly. This echoes much in Duncan Forrester's recent writings on Practical Theology as 'Truthful Action' (2000). The advocacy of such an approach is met richly in the diverse and wide ranging chapters which follow, engaging themes from law, media, violence and popular culture, to theological conversation, theologies of action, the challenge of naming God in post-modernity to reflections on metaphor and liturgy and much more. This volume offers significant 'fragments' (in Forrester's words) towards a contextual reworking of both the role and relation of twenty-first century practical theology.

References

Forrester, Duncan B. (2000) *Truthful Action: Explorations in Practical Theology.* Edinburgh: T&T Clark.

Herbert, David (2003) *Religion and Civil Society: Rethinking Public Religion in the Contemporary World.* London: Ashgate.

Putnam, R. (2000) *Bowling Alone: The Collapse and Revival of American Community.* New York: Simon and Shuster.

Stackhouse, Max (2004) Civil Religion, Political Theology and Public Theology: What's the Difference? *Political Theology* 5:3, 275 - 93.

Villa-Vicencio, Charles (1992) *A Theology of Reconstruction: Nation-building and Human Rights.* Cambridge Univ. Press.

PART I: RELIGIOUS DISCOURSE AND SECULAR REASON IN AN AGE OF PLURALISM

It is the task of practical theology to mediate between text and context, tradition and contemporary practice; and the impact of changing global conditions shapes the contributions in this first section, as they reflect on the changing balance of power between 'faith' and 'reason' after 9/11, the task of practical theology in an age of religious pluralism, and the role of religious discourse and faith-communities in shaping understandings of political legitimacy and civil society.

Engaging with the challenge of pluralism for public God-talk, Viau enters a plea for an engaged and productive public theology. Focussing on the theologian as artisan and the range of theological discourses – from authoritative texts, and high art to postmodern film – as artefacts, he recasts public, practical theology as a self-critical 'Fides Quarens Verbum'. Exploring his encounters with the built environments of the Abbey of *Maillezais* and Dresden's *Frauenkirche* he suggests a theology of presence which is able to generate renewed and reconnected artefacts animated, via the person of the theologian, into powerfully resonant public speech.

Duncan Forrester's starting point is with reflection on the kind of questions that have structured the work of public theologians in recent years. He suggests that their discourse has been centrally concerned with "the conditions on which religious arguments and reasons might be legitimately admitted to the public forum." He notes the tensions inherent in a debate in which the Rawlsian gatekeepers of the public square permit religious access to public discourse on narrow and exclusive criteria of 'reasonableness'. For Forrester, however, this difficult paradigm is blown apart in a post-September 11th world. Challenging problematic theories of 'overlapping consensus' – where religion gains legitimate public voice by endorsing what is shared between secular and religious viewpoints – Forrester calls for a distinct theological voice which offers a unique contribution to questions about the rebirth of living apocalyptic in our modern world. Arguing for both the difficulty and yet the necessity of re-finding a theological engagement with emergent apocalyptic, he suggests a threefold framework for aiding public understanding. For Forrester, apocalyptic might be understood firstly, as a powerful interpretation of contemporary 'inner reality', secondly, as a refusal to accept the existing order as final, and thirdly, as a narrative which stresses the *inevitability* of a radically alternative future.

Tracing the contours, theoretical and practical, of Roman Catholic-Muslim dialogue in the USA, Raymond Webb offers a particularly timely and resonant contribution to this volume. Exploring dialogue as conversation and text, Webb weaves Tracy and Ricoeur into an urgent account which advocates the *habitus* of interreligious dialogue as a rich form of contemporary religious experience and public theology.

Friedrich Schweitzer takes the expansion of the European Union, and current debates about a common constitution for the EU, as a case study in the relationship between civil society and religion. At present, the underlying assumptions informing understandings of the role of religion within the new Constitution seems to be that peace and tolerance in European only be achieved if religion is confined to the private sphere. At the same time, the fear of conflicts between the different adherents of different religions as well as the issue of including Islamic Turkey within the Union have made people aware of a hidden Eurocentric religious dimension and of the complexities of articulating a shared European identity. Schweitzer considers what the role of practical theology might be in this context, and whether it can contribute constructively to the debate.

Doing Practical Theology in an Age of Pluralism

Marcel Viau

Does the pluralism of contemporary culture make discourse about God impossible? This is indeed our greatest fear, anguish, even, which is brought to light by this redoubtable question. Not so much that we fear the isolation of our discourse. After all, haven't we gotten used to it since the modern era? According to several, we are experts in preaching in the desert, a sort of John the Baptist in city clothes. No! Solitude in itself does not frighten us. But the indifference shown by the people we talk to, yes! Doubting the relevance of our remarks: even more! What if the Message no longer had a *raison d'être*? What if the deep compassion of Christ for the world was no longer welcomed because of us, pitiful angels with broken wings?

I would really like to reassure you by bringing you a few words of comfort, something of the kind: 'Let's be united first of all with humankind, and theology will come abundantly'. Rather, I would like to bring you today one of my deepest convictions: 'Theology is still possible if we work hard to make our discourse about God relevant.' For me, a theologian is first and foremost a worker or a craftsman, or (the term that I prefer), an artisan. Isn't the idea of considering the theologian as a worker or an artisan attractive? [1] But s/he's not just any old artisan, because s/he's making a world rather than objects. Thus, we are going to examine the state and the function of the theologian under this operating principle: doing theology is first of all to exercise one's creative function. Are we able to take the spiritual measurements of our contemporary era, all of its spiritual dimensions? Above all, do we have the precious tools that permit us to make relevant theological discourses, discourses which I prefer to call 'artifacts'? [2]

In general, the artifact is any product 'made by human hands', which includes a large number of works spanning from a book of the Bible to '*The*

---

[1]   This idea has already been outlined by Audinet (1988) in his article 'De l'artisanat théologique'.

[2]   I owe the inspiration of using the term 'artifact' to Langer (1942). Authors who support the new rhetoric also took on this terminology. For an overview, see Foss (1989). See also my article 'Les discours sur Dieu comme artefacts' in Beaude & Fantino (1998).

Madonna and Child' by Giotto, even including the *Uffizi* that exhibits it. This definition, however, excludes the Highlands and the Thames, although ... ! I prefer the word 'artifact' to the word 'discourse' applied to Practical Theology because it leaves several possibilities of creation open. Of course, Saint Thomas' *Summa Theologiae* is a theological artifact. This is clear for all theologians worthy of this name. But the Florentine San Lorenzo Church is equally one, and also the *Journal d'un curé de campagne* by Bernanos, and even (why not?) the movie trilogy *Bleu-Blanc-Rouge* by Krzysztof Kieslowsky, movies full of religious allusions.

My definition of Practical Theology meets the more traditional one of Anselm of Canterbury: *Fides Quaerens Intellectum*, the faith that seeks to understand. However, the *Intellectus* seems to become real today under a specific form in which the language, this same *Verbum* of ancient times, holds a dominating role. In contemporary culture, the production of discourse and the conflicts brought about by their diversity often take precedence over pure rationality and ideology. Even human practices can only be understood if they are put into discourse. In this sense, a discourse is not hollow verbiage but *Intellectus* which is spoken in and by the practice of it.

From now on, the function of Theology consists of mainly producing discourses on faith in relation to the diverse human practices in the culture. In brief, Theology would be more a *Fides Quaerens Verbum*, a faith that seeks to speak, or, more precisely, to discourse with effectiveness. However, it is important to not take for granted the effectiveness of this discourse. We must therefore ask the following questions: Can we make it so that Theology becomes relevant again for our contemporaries? If so, how can Practical Theology play a role in this process?

So, then, our work is cut out for us. The theologian must exercise a creative function, which will get him or her away from certain caricatures, which would make him or her into no more than a sophisticated parrot. The theologian's job is colored by urgency, because it is accomplished in the contemporary culture of today, and this culture decodes less and less of our cryptic language. Let's exclude for the moment the possibility that we no longer have anything to say, that we are like empty wineskins or, even worse, full of hot air. Would we have simply lost our ancestors' touch? If it's the case, is it possible not to try to retrieve it, but to invent a new touch, which is better suited for today?

This idea will be examined starting from two examples of theological artifacts, two examples which seem to resemble each other a lot at first glance, but which will reveal their extraordinary diversity with use.

Part I: The Function of the Theological Artifact

1. Maillezais

A few years ago, I had a chance to visit a historical site that was out of the ordinary: it was the Abbey of *Maillezais* in the Department of *Vendée* in France.
The old monument, born shortly after the year One Thousand, is at the origin
of the boom of the *Bas-Poitou* region, a hostile, marshy region which, once it
was dried out, formed the marvelous marsh that is there now. I was first of all
struck by the harmony and the majesty of the place, its calm and serenity. It
was at the beginning of the summer, and the sun was bursting out at us with
all its strength. Going through the outer wall, I was seized by deep emotions
when I saw the north wall of the Abbey, all that remains of the original Abbey.
This immense solitary wall appeared to me like a great sailing ship crossing
over time, an impression reinforced when I found out that the hill on which the
Abbey had been constructed had been an island for a long time.

While coming close to the wall, I was able to discern easily its contours. As
the inner wall was the one which appeared at first glance, I could clearly read
on it the different architectural strata, a little like reading a cut-away picture
in an illustrated dictionary. That brought about a second shock. Here was a
monument almost in ruins of which only one wall remains, a poor vestige
of the past, a souvenir of ancient times. In their destitution, these stones still
showed what the majesty of the building must have been, and its ultimate goal
as well, what the skills of the artisans of that time must have been.

Built firstly in the Romanesque era, nothing is left of this period but a few
fragments of a nave flung out to the West by an imposing masonry mounting
that is half ruined. The Gothic stratum shows more, because it sets the tone
for the whole structure. One can still see there the remains of the seven bays
with side aisles and galleries above. Columns with Corinthian Capitals meet
up with groined vaults. Above, the high windows lit up the galleries. One can
still see where the toothing-stone of the cradle vaults was. We know that a fire
broke out during the works, which obliged the workers to modify their plans
quite a bit. To the West, the architects built a powerful entrance which had the
effect of darkening the ancient facade. To the East, they constructed a chancel
with a deambulatory and radiating chapels, characteristic of the great Churches
of pilgrimage of the eleventh century. As well, it is possible to see what is left
of a Gothic transept with elliptical arches leaning on small gallery which dates
from the thirteen-hundreds.

The question which troubles me about *Maillezais*, and everything in relation to it, is this: How many human beings, poor and rich, nobles and serfs,
all mixed together, died to keep this building going, to mark the stones with

their fragile stylus? Touching these walls, it seemed to me that the presence of these mystic artisans almost emanates from the limestone. One after another, they found and constructed material signs there: sculptures in the stone, shapes and colors. Their God seemed so powerful that they were ready to die for Him. Compared to their God, ours seems very artificial, don't you think?

2. Dresden Frauenkirche

Let's hold that thought for a minute, like fallow land, and go on to another monument which is also as intriguing. It's the Dresden *Frauenkirche* in German Saxony. Imagine for an instant a traveler at the end of the 1980s. Let's say, for the sake of hypothesis, that this tourist is sensitive to religious things: a theologian, maybe, or a believer who appreciates aesthetics. Whoever s/he may be, s/he has decided to only visit these two monuments, and hurried over to *Poitou* first of all, and then drove right over to Dresden without stopping (which, I must say, would require good health, a solid vehicle, and visas that were already in order because Dresden was then still in the German Democratic Republic). Imagine, I say, that s/he took the time to let himself be moved (as I was) by *Maillezais*, and that s/he is now examining the *Frauenkirche*. What does s/he see? As strange as it may seem, s/he sees about the same thing, a few sections of wall that were once tailored, but are now dilapidated. However, the *Frauenkirche* is much more recent, constructed in the middle of the eighteenth century. It's now nothing but a pile of stones from which a few walls stick out to let one see the splendor of the workmanship. What happened?

If time has inexorably worn down the Abbey of *Maillezais*, the folly of humanity has destroyed the *Frauenkirche*. On day in February 1945, a few months before the end of the war, the Allies bombed the city of Dresden, the 'Florence on the Elbe River', as it was called at the time. This bombardment had as its unique objective to break the Germans' morale. It had no strategic goal, as Dresden wasn't an industrial city, outside of a few porcelain factories. In fact, this was why they had assembled thousands of refugees there, coming mostly from East Germany to escape the advance of the Soviet soldiers. There were, we know for certain, at least 35 thousand inhabitants of Dresden killed, but certain people bring the numbers up more accurately to 100 thousand dead, and this in one night of terror. 90% of the old city was destroyed, leaving nothing of the beautiful Baroque monuments (constructed on impulse by Saxon Prince Augustus the Strong) but blackened, smoking ruins. The *Frauenkirche*, however, held up ... for 24 hours. It then caved in, the foundation stones having crumbled under the effect of the intense heat.

For more than 40 years, the Church was left in the state that it was in after the bombing. Several reasons determined this deliberate choice: on the one hand, the Soviets have always shown more zeal for reconstructing opera houses and museums than churches and, on the other hand, the inhabitants of Dresden wanted to make the burned rubble into a symbol of the absurdity of war.

Let's get back to our traveling theologian, who is silently looking at the ruins of the *Frauenkirche*. What does s/he feel when s/he sees this limestone debris? Disgust and horror are probably rising up in his/her throat; s/he feels like shouting, 'Never again!' S/he is maybe thinking of the thousands of human beings sacrificed to the logic of war. Then, s/he gets close to the ruins themselves and slowly goes around them, and looks at the mosaic of the limestone, some parts of which are completely blackened, while others have almost kept their clear colour. S/he examines closely the remains of the columns and capitals, and recognizes in them the curves and grooves typical of this architectural period. S/he tries to imagine the decorative forms apparently illogical, the flying buttresses, the wall bracket, the lining done in trompe-l'œil, the gesticulating statues, the broken pediments. Another emotion then comes to him or her: 'What beauty and grandeur!'

Well, s/he will remain touched by this spectacle for a long time after leaving this place. Still in shock, s/he will think first of all about this God who lets human beings kill each other without intervening. Certain images of the Holocaust will come maybe to his or her mind. S/he will also tell himself that God did not want such a catastrophe to happen, that God had given multiple signs, but that humanity did not listen. Then, calmer, s/he will see the Church again in his or her mind, this time thrilled by its magnificence. S/he will remember the importance of the Protestantism of this era, of the gargantuan effort made by thousands of workers to show the faithful that the Lutherans could construct monuments that were as imposing as the Catholic ones. S/he will hold in high esteem the creativity of the architects who made the *Frauenkirche* into a rather unique work of art that is at the service of the State religion. S/he will remind him/herself, the Catholic theologian, that God is also Lutheran.

First fragments of reflection

What can we get out of these first fragments of reflection about the stakes of our Conference?

First of all, we must affirm that time would have no meaning for humans if they weren't surrounded by material objects [3]. We know that time exists because we see the things around us erode (and also things that are built). What

---

[3]   The relationship between meaning and materiality can seem insignificant at first glance, but it is, however, very difficult philosophically speaking. One has just to think of the incredible mass of work invested by the Empiricists on this question to be convinced of this. From John Locke and his *Essay concerning Human understanding* up to John Stuart Mills'

is left of these fragile objects are the only means at our disposition to make our mark in time. The artifacts that the Abbey of *Maillezais* and the *Frauenkirche* are offer themselves to our perception as they are. At first glance, we are struck by their similarities. After all, they are only heaps of stone whose shapes strangely resemble each other. We are also struck by their incompleteness. There is no longer anything but bits of objects, vestiges, useless leftovers. Time has done its work, it has forever marked them.

A history and culture buff will maybe discover a few differences. The *Frauenkirche* is planted in the heart of a city marked by great contemporary disruptions, while *Maillezais* is easy to forget, lost in the French countryside. The former comes from a Baroque architecture, while the latter is Gothic. *Maillezais* was constructed at the moment of the re-christianisation of *Bas-Poitou* while the *Frauenkirche*, a Lutheran Church, was ended under the reign of Frederic-August II, a Saxon prince who was Catholic ... but tolerant.

Moreover, a distracted visitor seeking objective differences would have a lot of trouble to find any. The ruins understood as material objects can almost be confused. They are both made of stones whose colours resemble each other strangely. The same sun hits the same scorched sections of walls. The same debris is strewn out over the same soil. In a certain sense, these are objects which are not worth anything but their presence, in the sense that it is only possible to appreciate them in the present. [4]

The theological consequences are unexpected. A theological artifact has neither a past nor a future when it shows itself to our eyes. It is present, fully present, so present that it seems impossible to make it be anything else than what it is. Its very materiality demands our respect, constrains us to put up with its limits. The artifact inflicts on us a Law of the Medes and Persians in

---

System of Logic and including George Berkeley's *The Principles of Human Knowledge* and especially David Hume's *An enquiry concerning human understanding*. All the Empiricists more or less agree on the problem of the importance of the physical object. This reflection is continued today by several American philosophers. Here, we're talking about the tenants of Realism like Quine (*Word and Object*) or Kripke (*Naming and Necessity*) who oppose Anti-Realists like Rorty (*Philosophy and the Mirror of Nature*) without mentioning those seeking a compromise position like Putnam (*Representation and Reality*) or Davidson (*Inquiry into Truth and Interpretation*). These philosophers are all seeking a way through this problem which would better sum up the tension between 'the word and the thing'.

[4] For a long time, Analytic Aesthetics leaned on this question: What makes a material object into a work of art, and, therefore, an object that has meaning? The problem was brought up even more bluntly when Marcel Duchamp exhibited a urinal in a New York Museum, presenting it as a work of art. Andy Warhol's Brillo boxes had the same effect in the 1960s. To see the problem more clearly, it is worth looking at Shusterman (1989). See also Beardsley (1981), Danto (1989), Dickie (1997), Margolis (1980). Several French authors have been interested for several years in this trend of Aesthetics. Lories (1988), Pouivet (1996), Château (1994), Vouilloux (1997), Genette (1994 & 1997).

terms of its corporal reality, despite all the efforts that we deploy to get away from it.

But then, if *Maillezais* and the *Frauenkirche* are nothing more than piles of stones, what use is there of being interested in them? What can they teach us about God and God's action in the world? In and of itself, absolutely nothing, like all theological artifacts, actually. Artifacts cannot communicate anything or, as we like to repeat today, are incapable of 'giving a meaning'. [5] Let's never lose sight of the fact that the artifacts are inert objects, whether we are in front of an Abbey in ruins or a work of theology. They are nothing more than piled up rocks or rough scrawling.

But it doesn't stop at this. From all evidence, these stones or inscriptions are set up in a certain way. Someone somewhere thought to put them in a certain order. They made the decision to shape the stone in this way, and not another; they sometimes sweated blood and water to transform the material into an original curve. The theologian-artisan imposed other rules onto the material, which was well contained until the rules imposed by nature took over.

Thus, the theological artifact would be seen as having no meaning other than in virtue of the ordering of the material used to make it. [6] All that would be left for us to do is to learn to decipher the rules which presided over the making of an artifact in order to understand its meaning, as we would do to learn a foreign language, for example. Unfortunately, things are not so simple. Every artifact keeps its secret jealously, in spite of what it offers to the eye (rather, I would say, especially because of what it offers to the eye). Our translation tools seem as poor as those that we sometimes find on the Internet. I don't know if you have ever had the experience of translating a sentence, be it the

---

[5] Thus, the language used in theology is not a simple vehicle of 'meaning' which is supposed to be produced elsewhere, it becomes an activity. The definition of language is no longer substantial, but genetic. It's Ernst Cassirer who first insisted on this particular perspective. See his monumental work *Philosophy of Symbolic Forms* in three volumes: *Language, Mythical Thought and The Phenomenology of Knowledge*.

[6] The history of western thought has gotten us used to thinking of discourse as a construction made according to strict rules: rules which are logical, first of all, and then grammatical. Aristotle is often cited as the first one to form these rules. Certainly, we know him for the study of Analytical Reasoning, which gave place to syllogisms and to deduction. These methods of reasoning deal with truth and are impersonal where the conditions of truth are true and independent of opinion. He especially dealt with these methods of reasoning in the first part of *Organon*, particularly in the *First* and *Second Analytics*. However, we tend to forget that Dialectic Reasoning gained a place that was just as important in his work. Reasoning is Dialectic if it leans on premises that are made up of generally accepted or plausible opinions. Reasoning is no longer impersonal, because it depends on opinion. Its aim is not to establish a truth, but to persuade someone that an opinion is well-founded. We find these reflections especially in his *Rhetoric* and his *Poetic*.

simplest one possible, using one of these tools. The results are often appalling. The translation tool seems to understand the rules well, but it really lacks the keys that would permit it to capture the genius of the language.

In the presence of an artifact like the Abbey of *Maillezais*, I feel a little like one of these translation tools. I am quite capable of reading the Gothic configuration of the north wall, but with the unpleasant feeling in my heart that I will never be able really to understand it in the end. It seems obvious that, in interpreting these ruins, we look 'through' the stones too quickly. We say, for example, while contemplating a capital, 'There is no doubt that the people of this era were in permanent contact with the Transcendent'. But that's false! The medieval artisans were in contact with stones which represented for them the only way to make a mark in this world. And these are the marks which we have so much trouble to decipher today.

A few objections

In the light of what was just said, we could legitimately ask the following question: 'Are we saying that, in talking about God, it's nothing but noises or strokes of a stylus with no meaning other than the sound emitted by our mouths or the line cut by the chisel?' The answer is obvious: 'Of course not, because these noises or stylus strokes are placed in a certain order.' Another question immediately follows: 'Well, then, what use is it to us since we are not able to decipher the rules of its ordering?'

Let's recognize that each artifact is a sort of puzzle as we are placed in its presence. But then, how is it that we can feel so exalted or troubled before it? What happens, then, inside us (spectator or listener) that an inanimate object brings out so many emotions? We could easily stay with this statement which is rather 'contagious' without being any the worse for it. The problem comes up the moment when, after reflection, we notice that our whole being has been changed by our proximity to the artifact. Didn't I start believing a little bit more after my meeting with the remains of *Maillezais*? Didn't I change my view of Christianity after passing through Dresden?[7]

Pushing the argument a little farther, I can without contest affirm that the theological artifacts made me into the believer that I am today. Without them,

---

[7] The problem posed here is that of the true function of the artifact. Neither strictly logical and rational discourse, nor a pure emotional and affective product, it also touches the existential dimension of our being. By itself, it would seem, art is able to reach all these levels at once. For this occasion, it would be necessary to reread the works of Gombrich (1977). For him, image is illusion, a substitute for life, that is to say, that it is able to replace life more efficiently in certain circumstances, even if this image doesn't resemble life. The 'illusory' image is apt to produce a beneficial effect on the receiver, a true *catharsis* in the Aristotelian sense of the term.

the effectiveness of Jesus Christ's salvation would have been null and void. However, these artifacts are only matter which is rough-hewn, tacked onto a 'ball that rolls around in infinity', as the song says. However, there is still a mystery there that we are going to have to solve.

Part II: The Structure of the Theological Artifact

Now that we've arrived at the second part of the reflection, it is time to unveil a tiny bit of the mystery of the structure of the artifact, which will put the theologian-artisan in the presence of a theoretical apparatus likely to help him or her to construct (or reconstruct) a world.

The three universes

1. The aesthetic universe

What have we discovered in examining the two artifacts that *Maillezais* and the *Frauenkirche* are? First and foremost, the appearance is what hit us with full force. These artifacts are visible to our eyes, able to be sensed by our hands. We have heard the wind sweeping through the dilapidated walls; we have smelled the scent of the flowers that were growing between the rocks. Appearance is mostly related to perception, and perception comes from the senses. An artifact, because it's a material object, is sensual. An observer, educated or not, receives a physical impact from this object. This is inevitable. He is reached in his body by this tangible reality whatever his level of sensitivity or the quality of his senses may be.

As a result, I affirm that the theological artifact is composed of a first dimension, the one that is most immediately perceptible by a receiver, that I call the *aesthetic universe* (see Viau, 2002). In order to talk about aesthetics, I like to refer to the definition that Baumgarten (1750), the inventor of the modern concept, gives: it would be the 'science of knowing what is able to be sensed'.

A theological artifact is a polymorphous one, subject to being perceived in diverse ways. However, only one face is presented to a particular observer, at least one at a time. Whatever we may think of it, this manifestation of the object is always a construction. There are no artifacts existing that are unintentional or simply shaped by nature. I do not wish to develop this idea more, knowing that the debate over this is becoming a big deal these days in the Philosophy of Art circles (Schaeffer, 1996). Let's be content, for now, with this affirmation: the theological artifact is a human construction coming from a certain stylistic art.

Between the lines of any artifact, one finds a theory of aesthetics, that is, a certain way of organizing the subject in terms of its presentation. Cicero (55

BC) talked about it already in his time, as the 'colour' of discourse. For example, everyone knows that there's nothing innocent about painting a wall green instead of white. And let nobody come and tell me, 'That's not important', or even, 'It's only a question of aesthetics' (in the pejorative sense of the word, of course). It's enough to spend a few days in a hospital room painted in unwashed green to understand the significance of this colour. There is much more in the aesthetic universe than we suppose. One finds there an infinity varying from words, lines, sizes, and colors that take the form of specific figures. These figures have their own rhythm and particular tones. They can be rapid and jerky or the opposite, slow and peaceful, with vivid colors or faded, sharp like a word from Voltaire, or soft like the watch in the Dali painting. [8]

Behind these variations is found an artist that is aware of his means. Swimming against the tide of established common ground, I affirm that the artifact is the result of a controlled aim on the part of a producer. Nothing is farther away from the aesthetic universe than the preconceived ideas on 'instinctive creation' or the 'spontaneity of a gesture'. Stylistic composition is a voluntary act on the part of a creator who seeks to reach an audience as adequately as possible. He owes it to himself to put into place a theory of aesthetics that is adapted to the ways and customs of the audience. The Ancients called this important component of discourse *prepon* (appropriateness) [9]; they made it into the pivot of any discourse of argumentation.

The aesthetic universe uses inscriptions and prints as a language, but it uses them in an unusual manner. The words, lines, colors, and their arrangements are evaluated in virtue of their expressive quality and not their intrinsic value. [10] Before this raw material, the artisan will wonder how s/he can combine these elements in order to touch the senses of the eventual receptor even more. When it comes down to it, the creator of a theological artifact is put in the same position as the poet looking for the best tone for his sentence. The famous words *'les sanglots longs des violins de l'automne'* that Verlaine wrote have

---

[8]   Of course, we recognise here elements which belong to what is commonly called Stylistic in our days, quite an imperfect name according to my definition. I prefer to refer to it by invoking the ancient concept of *elocution*. Quintilian is the ancient author who is still the point of reference in this domain. In this regard, reread books VIII, XIX, and X of his *Institutio oratoria*. Hermogenes, his Greek contemporary, also deserves to be reread; see particularily his*Peri ideôn logou*. A modern work remain a classic: Lausberg (1960).

[9]   Quintilian devoted an entire book to the concept of *prepon* (Book XI of the Institutio Oratoria).

[10] Concerning this particular dimension of the range of words and images, we must get to know a remarkable work by Georges Didi-Huberman (1990) brings up the fact that this way of playing paintings and poetry against each other comes from the famous words by Horace (in his *De Arte Poetica*, 361): *Ut Pictura Poesis*, 'Poetry is like painting' Numerous authors have glossed over this famous saying, sometimes in a beautiful way (Lichtenstein, 1989), sometimes without any real insight (Lee, 1967).

no sense rationally, but they make us feel in an effective way the state of mind of someone who spends several months in the fog of London.

2. The rhetorical universe

If the aesthetic universe is of major importance for the makeup of a theological artifact, it is not the only one, as you probably suspected. As we saw for *Maillezais* and the *Frauenkirche*, even the dizziest observer can't help but be struck by the vaults, the capitals, or the sculpted images. S/he will therefore be interested in the rules of composition of the object itself even if s/he is incapable of deciphering its meaning. This dimension of the crafted object is what I call the *rhetorical universe* (see Viau, 1997).

This rhetorical universe is equally part of the makeup of the theological artifact. It comes from rules of composition that are as old as the history of thought and of Western discourse. It is amazing that we forgot the existence of these rules for a time (Fumaroli, 1999). Well, 'forget' is a strong word; 'conceal' would be more exact. Several people laughed this formidable linguistic tool to scorn until the day when we noticed its return with a vengeance in certain domains of social and business life. Like aesthetics, rhetoric must overcome numerous prejudices, the least of which is not that of the manipulation of the masses. This is not the time or place to justify a domain which has less and less need of it anyway. I say to my students that one of the few politicians who never used rhetoric was Stalin. He didn't need to because s/he was content with simply eliminating his opponents.

So, the theological artifact is composed of a rhetorical universe to which rules of composition are applied. [11] Let's try for a moment to get into the skin of the artisans of the Abbey of *Maillezais* in the 12th century. They had before them a ruin which someone hired them to reconstruct. How to go about it? Probably, one of their first tasks was to make a sort of inquiry to get up to date on the latest architectural developments of the era. Certain ones left for Paris, others for Italy. They came back from there with panoply of shapes and colors. Few of them brought back new ways of doing things, others drew from their newly acquired experiences. In other words, a rather large palette of processes was offered to the master builder.

---

[11] Rhetoric is as old as the history of Western language. Nothing better than returning to the great classics to know it: Aristotle, Cicero, Quintilian, Hermogenes, etc. But, it is interesting to notice that the contemporary works dealing with rhetoric are becoming more and more numerous. I can't help but quickly name a few titles: Bitzer & Black (1971), Black (1992), Barilli (1983), Booth (1974), Connors (1984), Cunningham (1990), Ehninger (1972), Foss (1985), Golden (1978), Kennedy (1994), Kinneavy (1987), Mason (1989), McKeon (1987), Perelman (1958), Richards (1936), Vickers (1988).

Let's try to represent how our builder must have proceeded to this step of the process. Let's imagine that he's a Monk from the region, proud of his home, whose aim was to adapt the architecture to local populations. He knew well the Anglo-Norman churches on both coasts of the English Channel. He had visited the churches of *Saint-Michel-en-l'Hern* and *Saint-Maxient*. He believed, for example, that the arches had to be sharper or that there had to be a double elevation. To sum up, he made a choice among the processes that his assistants had brought back to him or her. And this choice was not silly because, for the most part, it came from 'convention' to the ways and customs of the era.

But why on earth would our Monk is not contented with faithfully reproducing what was being done elsewhere? That is the great question underlying the production of the theological artifact. Why is one obliged to recreate without ceasing? Because we seek by our works to reach that which makes each human a survivor on this earth. I call 'belief' this dynamic part of our being. [12] Belief is not a simple subjective opinion or an idea that is somewhat backed up, that would need irrefutable proof to be taken seriously. It is much more powerful, because it provokes in us feeling that is stronger and more stable than an idea. The psychic act that brings it to light is of a radical, absolute nature, of an all-or-nothing order. We either believe or we don't believe in this or that. In this matter, there's no half-way point (about this idea, see Newman, 1870).

However, an important problem comes up before the one who, like our Monk, wants to reach this active principle: the belief hidden in the depths of the human being is literally unfathomable. Certainly, we generally concede that we are made up of a web of beliefs. I believe that God exists. I also believe that the earth is round, and that the plane will take me back to Canada. But, you who are listening to me don't know anything about my beliefs. You have to trust me, to 'take my word on it'. What's more, I am not even sure myself to really know my own beliefs, as Grandfather Freud would say. The only concrete clues of belief are held entirely in what the others who bring it to us allege. There you have what's at stake in the theological artifact: how do we come to reach the beliefs of another in order to transform him or her, when we know almost nothing of his reality?

Now let's go back to our craftsman. In order to try to modify the beliefs of those who will visit his Abbey, he is content to draw from his old rhetorical tool box, using the best arguments possible. For example, he raises the walls of the church and makes the windows bigger, hoping that the light will be able

---

[12] The concept of belief takes here a special connotation which has a clearly philosophical meaning. We must look for it first in the writings of Hume, then among the American Pragmatists and Neo-Pragmatists to trace its development. Let's remind ourselves of a few basic works here: Davidson (1984), Dennett (1987), Dewey (1938), Hume (1751), James (1907), Peirce (1981), Putnam (1987), Ricoeur (1977), Rorty (1979).

to penetrate into the wall more. From then on, even miscreants will come away more convinced of the existence of the Light with a capital 'L'.

3. The epistemological universe

This last remark leads us to the third and last stratum which makes up the theological artifact. This is the stratum that brought me to say, 'Oh! These people must have lived close to transcendence'. As I stated this opinion out loud before the building in ruins, a nearby tourist looked at me, taken aback, maybe saying to himself in his mind, 'and yet, that guy LOOKS normal!' This particular level of discourse isn't necessarily accessible to all who come across it. As you see, one can easily pass by that stratum without suffering unduly. This tourist had no doubt felt something similar to my own emotions because s/he was also hanging back to take a closer look at the work. But, in all probability, s/he was not interested in this particular universe of the artifact which I name the *epistemological universe* (see Viau 1999a).

Any theological artifact involves an epistemological universe. Our builder-Monk of the Abbey of *Maillezais* was surely more aware of it than others. Let's work our imagination one more time. Suppose that our contractor had studied in Paris, and that, from then on, s/he had been placed in contact with the Classical Scholastic. It is not certain that the builders of Gothic churches would all have read the works of Thomas, but they would all have been touched in one way or another by his influence. Thus, their activity put them in regular contact with the liturgical and iconographic programs of the day. They had been to School, had heard sermons or had probably attended the *disputationes de quodlibet* that made difficult theological questions accessible to the general public.

In this context, what hinders us from thinking that our architect was subjected to the same influences? Thus, s/he would have come home envisaging the possibility of putting the Classical trends (in logical levels) into relationship with the multiple subdivisions in the great Gothic churches. For example, the first principle of the Classical Scholastic is the *manifestatio*, that is, the idea that faith can be made clear by reason in a complete and autonomous system of thought. Reason has, then, a function of making clear which pushes into a deductive *modus operandi* founded on division and subdivision. Is it really the result of chance if this principle is shown in architecture? The First Gothic, that which was nothing but main pillars and networks of windows or ribs and arches, is subdivided from now on into major and minor columns, mullions, or primary, secondary, or tertiary profiles, series of moldings multiplied to infinity (see Panovsky, 1951).

But, let us not be mistaken. The epistemological universe is not the content of which the aesthetic universe is the form, nor is it the theory of rhetorical practice. Such a distinction between content and form doesn't exist, because an artifact is always presented to an observer in its totality. If there is a distinction, it comes from art criticism, from the theoretician or the artisan who makes it legitimately for the sake of his analysis. But the act of contemplating a work of art is first and foremost a global experience. [13] An artifact, even if it is very ancient, really becomes one starting from the moment when it lives in the experience of a human being. The material is still the same, of course, but the way in which an individual interacts with it makes it into something radically new which didn't exist beforehand. As an arrangement of old, varnished stones, the Abbey stays identical all through its history (outside the changes that the ravages of time bring, of course). But as an artifact, it is recreated each time that it is experienced by someone.

As a result, it is useless to ask what a producer of an artifact might have wanted to say through it. Our old architect would probably have happily responded, 'What you see is what you see!' *Maillezais* is universal, because it continues to inspire new experiences in the individuals who contemplate it. Even if it is impossible to live the same experience before this church as the medieval believer, the fact that a contemporary observer is capable of new experiences before it probably comes from the intensity of the experience of those who 'modeled' the material in the past. The artifact becomes from then on a material formed by a producer for the construction of an adequate experience on the part of those who will contemplate it.

In order for this vision of the artifact to be realized, it is important not to consider the epistemological universe as a stable and unchanging foundation on which lies the Truth in opposition to the universe of the ephemeral, and of appearances. The creator also creates his or her epistemological universe. Or rather, s/he sets it down, rather than uncovering it. This universe belongs *de facto* and entirely to the artifact itself, which is nothing but the sum of any material object worked upon by the hand of man. The theological artifact is never a creation *ex nihilo*, and the epistemological universe that is inherent in it is always a human fabrication.

---

[13]   The concept of experience goes a lot farther here that what we are used to understanding, as used as we are to the Kantian and post-Kantian definitions. It comes, rather, from American Pragmatism. You will find in the bibliography of my book (Viau, 1999a) a few reference works on this subject. Let's remember that John Dewey, a pragmatist from the very start, was interested in the relationship between experience and art. We find the essence of his thoughts on this subject in Dewey (1929) and Dewey (1934).

The theologian-artisan

It is high time now to answer the question that we began with: Is it possible to have a discourse on God in the context of today's pluralism? After an examination which mostly consisted of an imaginary trip into the past, I would like to come back to the present situation, maybe because the future is at stake.

Let's state in one sentence what our last reflection led us to suspect: *artifacts truly exist only when human beings take hold of them and model them.* In any case, we are phagocytes of artifacts. We seize all those that surround us, devour them in part, and digest them in order to make new ones out of them. It's the law of survival on this earth. Sometimes the destruction jumps out at us, and God knows that the twentieth century hasn't been spared in this regard. Sometimes, though, and luckily I say this, production comes to the forefront. At that moment, we put into place more or less the same mechanisms as our artisan ancestors.

We must come back to our two examples at the beginning. At first glance, the Abbey of *Maillezais* would be a good example of a destroyed artifact that no longer is worth much, other than its testimony of days gone by. That's what I thought, too, standing before these vestiges, until the guard warned me not to touch one of the sculptures. I suddenly understood that I was in the presence of a construction that couldn't be more up-to-date, and not a ruin from the past. A whole group of ethnologists, historians, and architects from University X united their efforts at the request of Departmental Council Y to come to this very simple result: leave things in the state they're in, and, whatever you do, don't modify anything on the site. They probably met for a long time to criticize the work of the preceding team. Then they took an inventory of all that was published at that moment about the conservation of heritage. Then, they made a choice among several alternatives, their option based on a solid museological perspective (the latest), which consisted in avoiding the reproduction of the original monument, because this isn't realizable anyway.

So then, would the approach of our intellectuals seem to look down on that of our friend the Monk-Architect of the Middle Ages? A small difference, maybe: *Maillezais* is now a Museum and no longer a church. From all evidence, the religious dimension was evacuated, or at least relegated to a historical fact. Back in the Middle Age, the faithful celebrated the Liturgy regularly in its chapels that had no roof and whose walls were dilapidated. Today, such a proceeding would be seen as scandalous. At least it would be necessary to ask for a bunch of permits to do it. This is precisely what makes the originality of an artifact. Someone takes hold of it, and phagocytes it, with the intent of making something else out of it.

The other artifact of which I spoke, the *Frauenkirche* of Dresden seems to me an example that sheds even more light on this subject because its ending is more complex. In the 1990s, a few years after the fall of the Berlin Wall, a group of citizens of Dresden undertook to reconstruct the church. The idea had been in the air for a long time already, but the realization of it was only possible after reunification. After a multitude of debates of all kinds, they arrived at the conclusion that they had to reconstruct the *Frauenkirche* exactly as it appeared before the bombing. It was feasible because they had on hand more than 40,000 photos taken following an important renovation that had been made a few months before the disaster.

Can we conclude that this decision was the right one? We would in fact have an artifact that would present itself as it was in the past, an object springing up intact from the past. Assuredly, this is perfectly inconceivable, even when the work seems to be reproduced to the smallest detail. For example, the architects conceded to modernizing the electricity and plumbing, which already makes the work different than what it was before the war. Of course, they will use the same stone as the original church, but they will conserve all the stones blackened by the bombs. The mosaic of beige and black will present a monochrome image that will have more of a contrast than the image painted by Canaletto in the 18th century. I don't think that we will see an exact reproduction of the building when it is unveiled in 2004.

Unlike *Maillezais*, however, the 'new' church will serve to celebrate services. It will be a witness again to a Christian faith that is anchored in German culture. But, as the prospectus says, it will be a monument called to promote peace and tolerance for all peoples. If this church was from the start a bone of contention between Catholics and Protestants, it will be today a symbol of reconciliation. A new theological artifact is born out of the leftovers of an old one, and nothing will ever be as it was.

Conclusion

Standing in front of the immense scaffolding that completely hid the colossal enterprise of reconstructing the *Frauenkirche*, I started to reflect on our poor state as artisans in Practical Theology. We live surrounded by monuments, more than others, perhaps. There are some immense ones which almost touch the sky; there are also some small ones, poor ones, and even grotesque ones. These monuments have all shaped our Christian faith in their own way. We are the worthy products of the theological artifacts which surround us.

Today, I have the feeling of standing in front of the ruins of the theology of days gone by. In itself, it is not so terrible when we know that these remains brought many people distressing experiences. But I still prefer the position of the artisan of the old days who is asked to reconsider the theological enterprise in light of current sensibilities. This is what I wish for all Practical Theologians. It's true that the scaffoldings are going to block our view of the work for a certain time. Is it not the price we need to pay so that our contemporaries can learn to read our theological artifacts in another way? We will then become true builders, creators of worlds capable once again of letting others catch a glimpse of the Infinite.

References

Audinet, Jacques Audinet *et al.* (1988), *Essais de théologie pratique, L'institution et le transmettre.* Paris : Beauchesne.

Beaude, Pierre-Marie and Fantino, Jacques (dir.) (1998). *Le christianisme dans la société. Actes du colloque international de Metz,* Québec/Metz : Presses de l'Université Laval/Université de Metz.

Barilli, Renato (1983) *Rhetoric.* Minneapolis: University of Minnesota Press.

Baumgarten, Alexander Gottlieb [1750] (1988) *Esthétique,* Paris : L'Herne.

Beardsley, Monroe [1958] (1981) *Aesthetic. Problems in the Philosophy of Criticism.* Indianapolis: Hackett Publishing Co.

Bitzer, Lloyd F. and Black, Edwin (eds) (1971) *The Prospect of Rhetoric.* Englewood Cliffs (NJ): Prentice-Hall.

Black, Edwin (1992) *Rhetorical Questions: Studies of Public Discourse.* Chicago: University of Chicago Press.

Booth, Wayne (1974) *Modern Dogma and the Rhetoric of Assent.* Notre-Dame (Ind.): University of Notre-Dame Press.

Château, Dominique (1994) *La Question de la question de l'art.* Paris : Presses universitaires de Vincennes.

Connors, Robert J. (1984) 'The Revival of Rhetoric in America' in Robert J. Connors (ed.), *Essays on Classical Rhetoric and Modern Discourse.* Carbondale/ Edwardsville: Southern Illinois University Press, 1 - 15.

Cunningham, David S. (1990) *Faithful Persuasion. In Aid of a Rhetoric of Christian Theology.* Notre Dame (Ind.): University of Notre Dame Press.

Cicero [55 BC] (1988), *De Oratore, Book III,* Paris: Belles-Lettres, 199 - 209.

Danto, Arthur [1981] (1989) *La transfiguration du banal.* Paris: Seuil.

Davidson, Donald (1984) *Inquiries into truth and interpretation,* Oxford / Clarendon Press; New York / Oxford University Press.

Dennett, Daniel C. (1987) *The intentional stance,* Cambridge, Mass., MIT Press.

Dewey, John [1934] (1980) *Art as Experience.* New York, G.P. Putnam's Sons.

Dewey, John [1929] (1989) *Experience and Nature,* LaSalle, Ill., Open Court.

Dewey, John (1938) *Logic. The theory of inquiry.* New York, H. Holt and Co.

Dickie, George [1984] (1997) *The Art Circle, A theory of Art.* Evanston (IL.): Spectrum Press.

Didi-Huberman, Georges [1990] (1995) *Fra Angelico, Dissemblance et figuration.* Paris: Flammarion.

Ehninger, Douglas (ed.) (1972) *Contemporary Rhetoric. A Reader's Coursebook,* Glenview (Il.): Scott, Foresman & Co.

Foss, Sonja [1985] (1991) *Contemporary perspectives on Rhetoric.* Prospect Heights: Waveland Press.

Foss, Sonja (ed.) (1989), *Rhetorical Criticism: Exploration and practice.* Prospect Heights (Il): Waveland Press.

Fumaroli, Marc (1999) 'Preface' in Marc Fumaroli (ed.) *Histoire de la rhétorique dans l'Europe moderne (1450 - 1950).* Paris : Presses Universitaires de France, 1 - 16.

Genette, Gérard (1994) *L'œuvre de l'art. Tome 1. Immanence et transcendance.* Paris: Seuil.

Genette, Gérard (1997) *L'œuvre de l'art. Tome II: La relation esthétique.* Paris : Seuil.

Golden, James L. *et al.* (1978) *Rhetoric of Western Tought.* Dubuque (IW): Kendall / Hunt Publishers Co.

Gombrich, Ernst (1977) *Art and Illusion.* London: Phaidon,

Hume, David [1751] (1955) *An Inquiry concerning Human Understanding,* Indianapolis, Bobbs-Merrill Educational Pub.

James, William (1907) *Pragmatism: a new name for some old ways of thinking: popular lectures on philosophy,* London; New York, Longmans, Green.

Kennedy, George A. (1994) *A new history of Classical Rhetoric.* Princeton: Princeton University Press.

Kinneavy, James L. (1987) *Greek Rhetorical Origins of Christian Faith.* New York: Oxford University Press.

Langer, Susan (1942). *Philosophy in a new key. A study in the Symbolism of Reason, Rite, and Art.* Cambridge (Mass): Harvard University Press.

Lausberg, Heinrich [1960] (1998) *Handbook of literary rhetoric: a foundation for literary study,* Leiden: Brill.

Lee, Rensselaer W. (1967) *Ut pictura poesis: the humanistic theory of painting.* New York: Norton.

Lichtenstein, Jacqueline (1989) *La couleur éloquante.* Paris : Flammarion.

Lories, Danielle (1988) *Philosophie analytique et esthétique.* Paris : Méridiens/Klincksieck.

Margolis, Joseph (1980) *Art and Philosophy.* Brighton:The Harvester Press, 1980.

Mason, Jeff (1989) *Philosophical Rhetoric.* London / New York: Routledge.

McKeon, Richard (1987) *Rhetoric. Essays in Invention and Discovery.* Woodbridge: Ox Bow Press.

Newman, John Henry [1870] (1992) *Essay in Aid of Grammar of Assent.* Notre-Dame (Ind.): University of Notre-Dame Press.

Panofsky, Erwin (1951) *Gothic Architecture and Scholasticism.* Latrobe (Pa.): Archabbey Press.

Peirce, Charles Sanders (1981) *Writings of Charles S. Peirce: a chronological edition.* Bloomington: Indiana University Press.

Perelman, Chaim [1958] (1979)*The new rhetoric and the humanities: essays on rhetoric and its applications.* Dordrecht (Holland)/ Boston: D. Reidel Pub. Co.

Pouivet, Roger (1996) *Esthétique et logique.* Bruxelles : Mardaga.

Putnam, Hilary (1987) *The many faces of realism.* La Salle (Ill.): Open Court.

Richards, I. A. [1936] (1965) *The Philosophy of Rhetoric*. Oxford: Oxford University Press.

Ricoeur, Paul (1977) *The rule of metaphor: Multi-disciplinary studies of the creation of meaning in language*. Toronto: University of Toronto Press.

Rorty, Richard (1979) *Philosophy and the mirror of nature*. Princeton: Princeton University Press.

Schaeffer, Jean-Marie (1996) *Les célibataires de l'art. Pour une esthétique sans mythe*. Paris : Gallimard.

Shusterman, Richard (1989) 'Introduction: Analyzing Analytic Aesthetics' in Richard Shusterman (ed.) *Analytic Aesthetics*. Oxford: Basil Blackwell.

Viau, Marcel (1997) *Le Dieu du verbe*. Montréal/ Paris : Médiaspaul/ Édiitons du Cerf.

Viau, Marcel (1999a) 'Actualité de l'*elocutio*' in Gilles Routhier (ed.), *Faire écho au Verbe: réinvestir dans l'homélie: Hommage à Lucien Robitaille*. Montreal : Médiaspaul.

Viau, Marcel (1999b) *Practical Theology. A New Approach*. Leiden : Brill.

Viau, Marcel (2002) *L'univers esthétique de la théologie*. Montréal : Médiaspaul.

Vickers, Brian (1988) *In Defence of Rhetoric*. Oxford: Clarendon Press.

Vouilloux, Bernard (1997) *Langages de l'art et relations transesthétiques*. Paris : Éditions de l'éclat.

Theological and Secular Discourse in an Age of Terror

Two monuments, two worlds

Duncan B. Forrester

Religious Reasons in the Public Forum

For some time I have been concerned with the debate in the West, and particularly in the United States, about the conditions on which religious arguments and religious reasons might be legitimately admitted to the public forum. This debate is not only important and interesting in itself, but it has some perplexing features and ironies. In the first place, the way it is outlined and pursued reflects the rapid and radical secularization among liberal American intellectuals in the last few decades. We now have predominantly skeptical or agnostic intellectuals operating in a society in which, unlike Western Europe, most people profess religious belief, and religious observance continues to flourish exceedingly – some would say excessively. And these secular intellectuals, with the support of a series of court decisions on 'the wall of separation between church and state', have constituted themselves the gatekeepers of the public forum, determining which arguments may be entertained in public deliberation, and on what conditions.

Their consensus is that only *rational* arguments which do not rely on any other source of wisdom than human reason may be admitted. Rationality is often left rather loosely defined. And it is often assumed, rather than demonstrated, that religious reasons and religious arguments are irrational and have no place in public discourse unless they can be translated without remainder into secular language, and meet modern secular standards of truth. Behind this there lies, of course, a raft of assumptions about religion as something primitive which is doomed to disappear with the advance of enlightenment, or even as a malign, divisive and threatening form of irrationality.

John Rawls is perhaps the most open and influential of the social theorists I have in mind at this point. It has been argued fairly convincingly that in his last years Rawls moved from a position where he regarded religion in all its forms as simply divisive, arbitrary and irrational, and thus to be excluded as far as possible from the public realm and confined to private life. Now his view seems to be slightly more sympathetic in relation to religion. In his later writings he seemed to be saying that religious views may be admitted to the public forum provided they meet the commonly accepted criteria of 'public reasoning', and can be expressed in secular, non-religious terms. He instances the Roman Catholic understanding of natural law as just such a transposition of religious views into secular form to qualify them for entrance into public debate. [1]

Furthermore, Rawls, in developing the idea of what he calls the 'overlapping consensus' among 'reasonable comprehensive doctrines', locates public political reasoning in the *overlap* between these comprehensive world-views. In a democratic society, he argues, there will be a variety of reasonable world-views which nevertheless converge in supporting a common understanding of justice, and the fundamental principles of social order.

There are two important issues here. In the first place, how and who decides whether a comprehensive religious or other doctrine is 'reasonable', and thus admitted to the public sphere? Is the introduction of the criterion of reasonability a way of excluding from the discussion overconfident religious or ideological systems that wish to reshape the society, or which challenge the existing order of things, or indeed which ask fundamental critical questions? Such systems are often only too 'reasonable' and intellectually coherent! According to Rawls, the common religious 'zeal to embody the whole truth in politics is incompatible with an idea of public reason that belongs with democratic citizenship.' (Rawls, 1999: 132 - 3) Is it possible that comprehensive positions which modern secular western intellectuals find peculiarly difficult to understand and appreciate are, on that ground, dismissed as unreasonable, almost out of intellectual laziness?

The second issue is this: what are we to do with that part of a comprehensive doctrine which lies outside the consensus? Is it not possible that the most interesting, challenging, distinctive and important things that the believers in a reasonable comprehensive doctrine feel they have to offer in the public sphere may be resolutely relegated to the private and ecclesiastical spheres by Rawls and his ilk because they do not lie in the consensual overlap? Religion in general, in Rawls's scheme, is still for the most part confined to the private realm, and its voice is not welcome in the public sphere unless it comes to endorse the existing overlapping consensus. In the public sphere one should refrain from using religious language, or references to the distinctive resources of a particular tradition. Beyond that, Rawls now recognises that religion is a part of

---

[1] 'Political liberalism also admits ... Catholic views of the common good and solidarity when they are expressed in terms of political values.' (Rawls, 1999: 142)

civil society which may, or may not, strengthen the civic virtues and encourage attachment to democracy.

This whole debate seems strangely parochial, and isolated from what is happening in the rest of the world, let alone in the heartland of America. In a world that is so full of strongly held and powerful religious beliefs, we surely need a far broader and more hospitable forum if religious views are to be understood and challenged, and positive religious insights enabled to contribute to public debate, and enrich the life of society. What would the world today be like if Gandhi's sometimes eccentric religio-political views had been disallowed, and as a consequence unable to influence Martin Luther King, or Desmond Tutu, or many another? And more threatening and violent religious notions call out for understanding and interpretation before they are responded to.

Public Theology after 11 September 2001

The events of 11 September 2001 transformed in a moment the whole scenario, and made it impossible for me to continue an earlier project on the claims of contemporary Christian theology to a hearing in the secular public arenas of the North Atlantic countries. The issue is no longer how to gain and sustain a constructive Christian theological presence in the Western public sphere; it is now the urgent life and death question of how to understand, discipline, channel and criticize the powerful ideological forces of religion which in fact today dominate the global political scene, for better and for worse. In the liberal West these voices are for the most part disguised and enter the public forum as something else, or they are excluded altogether from the public forum. What we now need is not so much a forum for more academic and good mannered discourse about conflicting truth claims, but an arena in which rage, frustration, hatred and fear are in play, and the actual reasons that motivate people and shape their understanding of the world, even when these seem bizarre and extreme, are seriously attended to.

Acts of radical evil, apparently motivated by religion, exposed the unreality of the western debate about religious reasons in the public forum. Whether we allow them or not, or like them or not, religious reasons bulk hugely in global politics today. As John Gray has written: 'Al-Qaeda did more than demolish a familiar landmark and kill thousands of civilians. It shattered an entire view of the world.' He continues:

If progressives are aghast at the turn of events, they are not alone. The western intelligentsia as a whole is more confused and marginal than it has been for generations. [In the past Marx, Keynes, Dewey, Popper or Hayek gave] illumination. None of these thinkers has anything of interest to say about the circumstances we face today. All of them subscribed to the Enlightenment faith that as societies became more modern, they became more alike, accepting the same secular values and the same view of the world. That faith was always questionable. Today it is incredible. If now we reach to our shelves for books that can help us to understand what happened on 11 September, we find almost nothing. (Gray, 2002:50)

But perhaps, if the book we reach down to consult is the Revelation of St John the Divine, or the thirteenth chapter of the Gospel of St Mark, or the Book of Daniel, we may find some enlightenment and help! This type of apocalyptic writing is hard for most modern Westerners to understand, respond and relate to. But theologians should perhaps be able to mediate and relate to living apocalyptic in the modern world. Certainly they should be able to suggest some reasons why it is so influential in the modern world, and perhaps enter into dialogue with those for whom apocalyptic is wildly alive today.

I first heard of the attacks on the World Trade Center and the Pentagon when I was boarding a bus in Edinburgh. The driver had a radio on, and told me what was happening as we spoke. My first reaction was that this was unreal, a fantasy generated by a diseased mind, a rerun, perhaps of the broadcasting of H.G.Wells's *War of the Worlds* that caused panic in New York in the late 1930s. In both cases something totally unexpected, out of the ordinary, alien and disastrous was at issue. But quickly it became clear that this time the horrifying events in New York and Washington were for real. The twin towers of the World Trade Center and the Pentagon were, of course, immensely powerful symbolic edifices, shrines of economic and military power. That was precisely why they were chosen for attack by assailants who were well aware of the language of symbolism.

When I reached home and switched on the TV and saw the horror of what was really happening, an apocalyptic passage from the Bible came immediately to mind, about the predicted destruction of another great building charged with powerful symbolism. The passage was Mark 13. I read this and other apocalyptic passages from the Bible with a new kind of fascination and a degree of puzzlement. They did not speak of the world I inhabit, and much in them I find quite inaccessible. But it seemed both to be challenging to me as one who tries to be a disciple, and to take the Bible seriously, and to provide some kind of clues to the thought world that the hijackers, and bin Laden and many other religious believers today, as in the past, inhabit. My puzzlement and horror was surely part of the more general problem for us of understanding and relating to forms and expressions of religion that we see as bizarre and dangerous.

There was a great deal of unabashedly and irreducibly religious language used about the events of 11 September, on both sides. The hijackers received a kind of perverse spiritual discipline as they prepared for what they understood as martyrdom, a way of witnessing with one's life to the truth. Bin Laden's broadcasts and statements reflected a characteristically apocalyptic dualism between absolute good and absolute evil, and an extraordinary confidence that supernatural agency would ensure the rapid destruction of America. And on the other side the language of a war against absolute evil, a crusade, and 'God bless America' was on the lips of President Bush and many another.

And then there was also the deeply moving religious language of love, spoken through mobile phones by people about to die. Rowan Williams points to the contrast between the two kinds of language:

The religious words are, in the cold light of day, the words that murderers are saying to themselves to make a martyr's drama out of a crime, the non-religious words are testimony to what religious language is supposed to be about – the triumph of pointless, gratuitous love, the affirming of faithfulness even when there is nothing to be done or salvaged. (Williams, 2002: 1 - 2)

The modern liberal dialogue about religious reasons in public debate has been, at least for a time, bypassed. We now see huge religious movements – not only al Qaeda and Osama bin Laden – whose world-view and activity is dominated by religious, often apocalyptic imagery. This may be dangerous territory, full of mines and traps and unpredictable hazards. But it has to be traversed.

The Rebirth of Apocalyptic

Events such as those of September 11 2001 seem to demand religious, even apocalyptic, language if they are to be adequately described and understood. It is virtually impossible to understand them within the context of our normal frameworks of meaning. Apocalyptic images and symbols are again and again, to borrow Austin Farrer's term, 'reborn'.

The language with which the Bible, particularly the New Testament, is peppered about principalities and powers, angels and demons, thrones and dominions, seemed for long to many liberal exegetes to be 'obscure mythology' which should and must be dispensed with. But when Christians had to struggle with the manifest evil of Nazism, they turned to these themes in the Bible and found in them clues and guidance as to how to respond faithfully and well to Hitler's evil tyranny. This particular symbolic structure had sprung back to life. It seemed to provide meaning. It was a symbolic structure in which many people found they could live.

Great issues, events that 'cut history in two like a knife', turning points and encounters with radical evil or with authentic holiness in history seem to demand religious symbols and religious, even apocalyptic, language for their adequate interpretation and description. More conventional language tools seem quite inadequate for handling such portentous matters, for here we are pressing against the limits of humanity's ability to comprehend and order the world; we are moving into new and uncharted territory. Our modern maps often seem inadequate; we turn perforce to older charts. People return, sometimes instinctively, sometimes in desperation or in anger, to the ancient symbolic systems of religion, and long for the rebirth of religious images which have for centuries lain dormant and forgotten, particularly in the secular West.

Ancient systems of interpretation and 'discerning the signs of the times' carry with them risks of which we should be aware. The straining for the recovery of old keys for the interpretation of what is radically new and threatening has its dangers, of course. A turning to religious language and religious symbols may indicate a recognition that the issues are grave and unusual resources are needed to cope with them, but it does not guarantee that these matters will be handled wisely. Religious symbols may inflame rather than illumine, and religious rhetoric excite rather than clarify. Such religious rhetoric may be a powerful agency for recruitment, especially among those in the West who have 'grown weary of their non-religious upbringing', so that they feel no sense of purpose, and believe that they are not being allowed to contribute to some great cause. [2] Osama bin Laden, to point to the most striking example, constantly uses the rhetoric of apocalyptic to justify his outrages and place them in a particular apocalyptic frame. Apocalyptic characteristically divides the world into the absolute good and the absolute evil.

This is precisely the point at which a major theological responsibility comes into view: theologians are, or ought to be, people trained in the disciplined and critical investigation of religious symbolic structures, and the careful and responsible use of religious language – skills much needed today, with the new explosion of religious rhetoric and religious language around the world. But theologians have their problems too, the most relevant of which is how we can analyze and describe religious symbolic structures from the outside, as it were. Modern liberal intellectuals and believers are more or less excluded from the realm of apocalyptic. We find it hard to understand why and how people inhabit such structures, and allow them to shape their faith and life, for good or ill. And we presume, perhaps too quickly, that apocalyptic is both primitive and evil.

---

[2] 'Suleyman tells me he grew weary of his non-religious upbringing: "I felt like I had no sense of purpose. I felt as if I wasn't being allowed to contribute to anything."' (Wazir, 2002: 33).

Understanding Apocalyptic Today

Perhaps modern scholarship can help us to understand. A leading biblical scholar gives an account of the major features of apocalyptic literature, especially as represented by the Book of Revelation. This strange book, he writes, expresses 'alternative conceptions of the world, its history and its future' through:

... a concern with the contradiction between God's rule over creation and the apparently unchecked dominance of evil in the world, the hope of an impending final history in which God will bring eternal good out of all the evils of this world and renew his creation...

It draws [us] into different ways of seeing things... It speaks to a world whose imaginative view of the world is controlled by the power and propaganda of the dominant political and economic system. By envisioning the same world from the perspective of God's kingdom... *Revelation liberates its readers from the dominant world-view. It exposes the idolatry which from top to bottom infuses and inspires the political, economic and social realities in which its readers live, and calls them to an uncompromising Christian witness to the true God who despite earthly appearances is sovereign.* By seeing the world differently, readers are enabled to live and to die differently... They are empowered... to live in hope of the coming of God's kingdom as the ultimate truth of the world which must prevail over all that presently opposes God" rule. (Bauckham, 2001: 1287 - 8, emphasis mine).

This kind of scholarship helps us to understand the attraction of apocalyptic today, and why it as it were comes to life, or is reborn, in times of crisis (Rowley, 1947: 8). Characteristically apocalyptic arises among groups that despair about the conditions of the present world order, and believe in its imminent destruction or overthrow (Rowland, 1982: 1 - 2). It has, I suggest, three particular functions which are particularly relevant to our present context. In the first place, apocalyptic claims to reveal, unveil, make manifest the inner reality of what is actually happening in the world today. It is concerned to understand things as they are now, not simply to predict the future (Rowland, 1982: 2). It seeks to discern what is happening in history, and what God is calling his people to do. The powers of evil that have presented themselves as angels of light are unmasked, and believers are enabled to discern what is really happening.

Apocalyptic denies the finality and acceptability of the existing order of things (*pace* Francis Fukuyama!). The pretensions of rulers and dominant authorities are cut down to size and relativized. Apocalyptic declares that the existing powers that be are not the final manifestation of God's purposes; their days are numbered. An alternative order, in which the weak and the excluded will have an honoured place is not only possible, but it is promised, and it will break in and disrupt the existing order... In the third place, apocalyptic nourishes a confident hope not only that things *can* be different, but that they *will* be different, for if believers are faithful God will bring out of the present disorder a new era which will be characterized by peace and justice and the vindication of the oppressed.

In much apocalyptic, as in the book of Revelation, alongside a radical political critique there is much bloody imagery of a holy war. In this war, martyrs despite appearances are the real conquerors. The holy war may be a spiritual or a real conflict; God may take the initiative, or call on the saints to wage war on his behalf. And 'waging war' may simply be a metaphor for keeping the faith in times of persecution. But the Christian nature of authentically Christian apocalyptic is represented by the centrality in Revelation of the triumphant Lamb that has been slain and who has absorbed in his own body the wrath and rage and violence of the world. This Lamb is praised by the faithful, singing a new song, those who are the first-fruits of the new humanity. [3]

There are, of course, specific problems associated with a lively apocalyptic world view. The dualism characteristic of apocalyptic thought presents as central to its radical political critique a polarization between absolute evil and absolute good, which is at the least a colossal simplification of any actual situation in the world. It can breed a very dangerous and unqualified self-righteousness. And these distortions can have a malign effect on political judgements – as can a relativism which hesitates to make a clear distinction between good and evil. A second major problem is that, while much apocalyptic encourages the saints to be patient until God brings their deliverance, other forms encourage the faithful to take things into their own hands, so that they understand themselves as saints combating and destroying unqualified evil in the name of God and at the direct command of God. This is not something that I find prominent in the Book of Revelation or as a dominant element in Jewish and Christian apocalyptic generally. But it is certainly prominent in some varieties of apocalyptic which are dangerously influential in today's world.

More positively, apocalyptic holds out an open future and offers hope to the poor, the powerless and the excluded. Its message to the powerful, the prosperous and the complacent is a word of judgement, and a challenge to hear the uncomfortable word that the Spirit is saying to the churches. And for us this demands careful attention to the question why young men will blow themselves to death and destroy multitudes of innocent lives in the process believing that this is the will of God, and that their act is heroic. For until we understand it is hard to respond intelligently and creatively.

Apocalyptic language is language of people who feel themselves weak,

---

[3]   See Yoder, 1988.

marginalized, oppressed and forgotten. [4] It is a language of hope for change, and it is language of judgement. It is language that motivates powerfully, for good or ill, and it is language which polarizes between the good and the evil, the saints and the wicked in a quite Manichaean way. This kind of polarization is always, of course, a huge simplification at the very least. In the real world we have always to deal in subtle shades of grey rather than a contrast between black and white. But sometimes we need to highlight the awfulness of evil or the wonder of goodness.

Apocalyptic is thus a major way of sustaining hope, the kind of hope that keeps people going when all around seems hopeless. But the central thing about Christian apocalyptic, as I read the Book of Revelation, is this: at the heart of all the struggles, all the sufferings, all the anger and rage is not so much the victory of the saints in a bloody battle as the worship by the 144,000 who are the first-fruits of God's great harvest, and who sing a new song in honour of the Lamb who has been slain and has absorbed into himself the rage and fear and violence of the world.

The temptation simply to dismiss apocalyptic – or even all religious language in the public forum – as irrational and pathological should be resisted, as should the temptation of simply reversing the polarization of radical evil and radical good, characteristic of apocalyptic. We have to attend to and deal with this reborn and powerful language discerningly and sensitively, if we are to respond wisely. For the global public forum in an age of terror is full of religious, often extravagant and dangerous, ideas and evocative religious symbols and narratives. Religious reasons cannot be exorcised from the public forum. And attempted exclusion from the debate of the public square only makes matters worse, for there is no longer pressure to explain and to vindicate or modify one's understanding. In this new, post 9/11 age, there are fresh and urgent responsibilities laid on the shoulders of public theologians to engage with, interpret and respond to, the powerful and often destructive religious ideas which are now rampant in the public forum.

References

Bauckham, Richard (2001) 'Revelation' in Barton, John and Muddiman, John, (eds.), *The Oxford Bible Commentary*. Oxford: Oxford University Press.
Cohn, Norman (1970) *The Pursuit of the Millennium*. London: Paladin.
Gray, John (2002) 'Why terrorism is unbeatable', *New Statesman* 25 February.
Rawls, John (1999) *The Law of Peoples, with 'The Idea of Public Reason Revisited'*. Cambridge, Mass., Harvard University Press.
Rowley, H.H., (1947) *The Relevance of Apocalyptic*. London: Lutterworth.

---

4   On this see especially the sociological literature on millenarianism, such as Cohn, 1970.

Rowland, Christopher (1982), *The Open Heaven: A Study of Apocalyptic in Judaism and Early Christianity*. London: SPCK, 1982.

Wazir, Burhan (2002) 'The Talibanisation of Britain proceeds', *New Statesman* 11 February.

Williams, Rowan (2002) *Writing in the Dust: Reflections on 11*[th]*September and its Aftermath* London: Hodder and Stoughton.

Yoder, John Howard (1988) 'To Serve our God and to Rule the World', *The Annual of the Society of Christian Ethics*, 3 - 14.

Roman Catholic-Muslim Dialogue

Alternate Pathways to the Public Square

Raymond J. Webb

Interreligious dialogue is a developing form of public theology. After presenting selected descriptive examples of Roman Catholic-Muslim dialogue from global, national (U.S.A.), and local (Chicago) perspectives, this paper will offer some sociocultural interpretive comments, a theological and hermeneutical perspective, and practical theological strategic suggestions.

Description

There are about 1.2 billion Muslims in the world, slightly more than the number of Roman Catholics. In 1965, encouraged by the Second Vatican Council, Pope Paul VI set up a department of the Vatican, the Secretariat for Non-Christians (since 1989, the Pontifical Council for Interreligious Dialogue). Roman Catholic-Muslim dialogue has existed worldwide, frequently sponsored by the Vatican and appropriate Muslim groups, for almost thirty years. Muslim-Catholic contacts are well documented in the Pontifical Council's journal, *Pro Dialogo*. Pope John Paul II has addressed Muslims in 200 talks and statements. Scholars from the Vatican and Al-Azhar University in Cairo meet in formal conferences. Ramadan greetings are sent annually. Vatican and Islamic country representatives have cooperated on issues of mutual concern at international meetings, including United Nations sponsored conferences on population and family. Religious leaders prayed in each others' presence at gatherings convened at Assisi in 1986 and 2002 and in Rome in 1999.

Muslims in the United States number about seven million. (Catholics are about 63 million.) Converts to Islam are reported to be numerous. The two dominant Muslim groups are African Americans (40 per cent) and immigrants or descendants of immigrants. These latter come from many areas, including the Middle East, Africa, India, Pakistan, and Indonesia. Many immigrant Muslims join the Islamic Society of North America, their largest umbrella group.

Annual meetings draw about 35,000 participants. Employment of immigrant Muslims spans the range from entry-level jobs to highly educated professionals. African American Muslims have returned to the Islamic mainstream after a period of divergent views, which lasted into the 1960s. They represent an inculturated way of living Islam in America. Many unite in the American Society of Muslims, under the leadership of Imam Warith Deen Mohammed.

In the United States, a variety of dialogic contacts exist, including those between the United States Conference of Catholic Bishops and the Islamic Society of North America and the American Society of Muslims. Important is the Midwestern regional dialogue of religious experts, which has addressed the issue of the "Word of God" as understood by Muslims and Catholics and the question of the religious understanding of violence. Notable academic dialogue centers are found at Georgetown University and Catholic Theological Union in Chicago.

Frustrated for some time about certain aspects of U.S. foreign policy and realizing that political influence in the U.S. means uniting, voting together, and making financial contributions, Muslims voted 72 per cent for George W. Bush in 2000. Although he has celebrated the end of Ramadan with Muslims and invited Muslim leaders to the White House, President Bush has disappointed many Muslims with his postelection policies. Repeatedly, he has professed that current "anti-terrorist" measures should not be seen as casting aspersions on Muslims. But many Muslims feel discrimination from the U. S. government in the policies being enacted or followed, specifically in antiterrorism legislation, new immigrant registration requirements and attendant arrests, and surveillance of mosques and worshippers. Certain Islamic charities have been accused of funding terrorism or engaging in activities inconsistent with laws governing charities. Instances of anti-Muslim rhetoric, even by public officials; acts of vandalism against Muslim institutions; and occasional controversies over the wearing of the Muslim head-covering, the *hejab*, are all part of this climate. Political contributions often are returned to contributors as being linked though "chains of acquaintance" to "terrorist sympathizers." Accepting Muslim financial contributions is a political liability few politicians risk. Access to the realities of power in the American system is far from being realized.

In my local area, Chicago, there are an estimated 400,000 Muslims (as compared with 2.6 million Roman Catholics). 65 mosques and Islamic centers are found in the Chicago area, along with seven Islamic day schools. A variety of dialogical and cooperative efforts exist between Muslims and Catholics in the Chicago area. When Francis George became Roman Catholic Archbishop of Chicago in 1997, he was welcomed to Chicago with a dinner given by the Muslim community. When he was called to Rome to become a cardinal, he took a Muslim with him in the delegation of religious leaders that accompanied him. He annually attends and speaks at a special *iftar* (breaking the Ramadan fast) dinner. He gave the welcome at the national convention of the Islamic Society of North America in 1999 and has participated in discussion of issues with Muslim and Catholic leadership.

A bimonthly dialogue group with representatives of the Chicago Roman Catholic Archdiocese and of the Council of Islamic Organizations of Greater Chicago, a member organization of ISNA, has met for more than five years. Muslims participate in the Council of Religious Leaders of Chicago and a large interfaith Chicago area community organizing effort. Catholic–Muslim women's groups, formed by neighboring mosques and churches, have had significant durability and report a warm, informal atmosphere. A recent celebratory luncheon drew 250 Muslim and Catholic women. A joint Catholic-Muslim project to speak about each other's religion in their respective religious schools has had some success. A Catholic church offered worship and meeting space to a local Muslim congregation during the renovation of their Islamic Center. Many Catholic churches extended invitations both to Muslims and to persons knowledgeable about Islam to speak. Immediately after September 11, 2001, there were many interfaith prayer services involving Muslims. The interfaith community has responded to many problems encountered by Muslims.

Socio-cultural Interpretations

Though somewhat secularized, the U.S. can certainly still be called a Protestant country in origins and values. The Deism and Calvinism of the founders is still in evidence (Dolan, 2002). The pre-eminence of the individual is dominant, and achievement, once treated as a sign of salvation, maintains its importance. The official disestablishment of religion has been an opportunity for the various religions to work out their own interrelationship without any officially stronger and weaker participants. But this also presents the challenge of a "secular" set of values becoming the dominant "religion" by default. In the midst of this, there is a "religious establishment" in the public square – a variety of places of worship adjacent to the classical town square, networks and organizations of religious groups and leaders, and the varied attempts to have religious attitudes and values find a place at the table of public discussion.

Catholics and Muslims, both from religions highly structured though in different ways, find themselves as minority participants in a constitutional democracy with still influential Protestant roots. At the end of the nineteenth century, Catholic leadership promoted assimilation into mainstream society. For instance, Irish-Americans, who are largely Catholic, have become the second most successful ethnic group in the U.S., but it can be argued that they are more American than Catholic. A Catholic was elected president in 1960, saying that his religion would remain private. It is said that, at the present time, a Catholic politician espousing certain important Catholic ideals – opposition to abortion and capital punishment as well as advocacy of strong social justice positions – would find a home in neither major political party (Hagen, 2003).

The *umma* (Muslim community) in the United States draws from more than 55 ethnic groups, who work to see how their own internal relationship will develop. In addition Muslims will be forced to develop new understandings of the complex relationships between religion, government, politics, citizenship, and charity. Islam in the U.S. has been relieved of the governmental tensions and pressures found in predominantly Islamic countries. Not having authoritative worldwide structures, Muslim have developed several national American-style voluntary organizations. Interestingly, Farid Esack (2003) cautions that "'fitting in' is profoundly unprophetic. It is not the task of Muslims or Christians or of any prophetic community."

Roman Catholics and Muslims engage in the multi-leveled relationship found in the United States for many reasons. Catholics have been encouraged by the Second Vatican Council, papal statements, and other Vatican initiatives to engage in dialogue in a variety of ways with religious bodies throughout the world. The United States, the land of pluralism, seems well-suited to dialogue, which, in fact, is one of the kinds of activities engaged in by religions in the United States. Most of the groups involved in the public life of religion in the United States engage in this conversation. Public events, such as gatherings after the World Trade Center destruction, anti-war protests, and Thanksgiving Day community celebrations, are largely ecumenical/interreligious. A weekly religion page is found in most newspapers. Major religious feasts receive media coverage. A dialogue connection brings with it the acceptance and respectability that the dialogue partner may have gained over time.

Theology, Hermeneutics, and Public Theology

In this section I will present some Roman Catholic and Muslim theological and anthropological perspectives on dialogue; offer a Roman Catholic typology of dialogue; discuss hermeneutical considerations regarding "conversation" and "text"; and name some of the issues dialogue has raised for the publics of theology.

Islam and Roman Catholicism are both universal and missionary religions, professing that the best possible expression of the relationship of God and humankind is to be found in their particular traditions. *Da'wa* (the presentation of Islam leading to conversion) is the duty of every Muslim. Catholics believe that salvation is possible for all, though this is through the action of

God's grace somehow mediated through the church. Catholics have a duty to proclaim this. Muslims seem to hold out the possibility of other "people of the book" reaching paradise. Both religions may be seen as "inclusivist", claiming their own religious tradition as privileged but recognizing the possibility of religious truth in other traditions (Griffiths, 2001, 56 - 57).

"Dialogue," though distinct from "proclamation," is an aspect of evangelization for the Catholic Church. The Pontifical Council for Interreligious Dialogue (1991) has presented a useful framework for understanding interreligious dialogue, describing four types of interaction. In the foundational dialogue of life, people as neighbors share the joys, sorrows, problems and concerns of daily life. In the dialogue of action, there is collaboration for the development and liberation of peoples, including a commitment to action, social justice, human rights, advocacy for victims of injustice, and the promotion of spiritual and human values. In the dialogue of theological exchange, specialists and non-specialists seek to deepen their understanding of their respective religions, heritages, values and practices. In the dialogue of religious experience, spiritual traditions, faith, ways of searching for God and traditions of prayer are discussed. At times one may be present during the prayer of the other. The concern for holiness can be a strong bond.

Roman Catholic Perspectives

Franz Jozef van Beeck (1994) has developed a Christian rationale for dialogue with non-Christians. He stresses that Christian truth claims are "proximately" validated by how Christians live their lives. A living Tradition integrates "foreign" elements. "Even as they interpret the other, interpreters will find themselves interpreted to themselves; familiarity with the unfamiliar other turns out to be inseparable from familiarization with a yet-unfamiliar self ... " (1994: 49). Discernment combines constructiveness and receptiveness. Constructiveness ideally discerns, sympathetically interprets, commends and even integrates foreign elements of religion and humanity. Receptiveness involves a hermeneutical process in which Christian identity is reinterpreted.

Archbishop Michael Fitzgerald, the president of the Pontifical Council for Interreligious Dialogue, has written about "... the dialogical character of the Christian life that is founded on the eternal dialogue at the heart of the Trinity and shapes from within the conversation between God and the human creature, giving a new shape to interpersonal relations .... We can say that there is in the Church a profound faith in the dialogue that God carries on with every human being and in the final design of salvation. This conviction must guide each one of our meetings. But one can dialogue fruitfully only if our identity is clear ... " (2002: 8)

Muslim Perspectives

Mahmoud Ayoub finds in Catholic-Muslim dialogue since Vatican II an end to hostilities, a new era of relationships, and an appreciation of Muslim piety. But there is no acceptance of Islam as a belief system. Ayoub wonders, "Is this openness true dialogue, or could it be simply condescending tolerance aimed at facilitating evangelization?" (1999: 179) Since Catholics believe that humanity is saved in Jesus Christ, there is not room left for "a genuine fellowship of faith, which must be the ultimate goal of interreligious dialogue" (1999: 181). Ibrahim M. Abu-Rabi sees in John Paul's II's doctrine of dialogue "engagement, appreciation, sacrifice, patience, spiritual enrichment, and fighting on behalf of the underprivileged in society" (1999: 199). One goal of dialogue is reconciliation between Muslims and Catholics in public life, leading to the building of a better world. Abdullah Noorudeen Durkee (1998) calls for a dialogue of good works, in which we move from talking to action, with Allah being the judge of it all.

Muzammil Siddiqi (1998) describes Islam as recommending dialogue as one of the best ways to communicate with others, to remove stereotypes, to benefit communities and humanity, to promote justice and peace and goodness in society and harmony in the world, and to face moral breakdown in the world. Dr. Ghulam-Haider Aasi, a scholar of Islam long active in interreligious dialogue, raises practical concerns about dialogical activities of which he is aware. He feels that the Muslim participants are ill-prepared and confuse da'wa, Islamic activism, and dialogue. They may not be representative of the Muslim community. "Their interest is in dispelling stereotypes about Islam, explaining Muslim positions on international political crises and forging personal, local and national friendships with Catholic leaders. ... [T]heir lack of knowledge and qualifications hinders real progress in serious interreligious issues; whether related to theology, spirituality, socio-economic justice, law or morality" (2002: 181).

Dialogue as Conversation and Text

David Tracy (1987) describes conversation as a willingness to follow a question wherever it may go – dialogue. Allowing for difference and otherness, one is open to finding similarity amid difference in what has already been experienced, hence the value of what Tracy calls the "analogical imagination." (Real difference in this case is seen as similar to what one already knows.) Authentic conversation contains openness to mutual transformation. Tracy (1991) asserts that interreligious dialogue in itself is religious experience, one which is likely to lead to revision and rediscovery in one's own tradition.

Paul Ricoeur's application of his description of "text" to the concept of meaningful action widens the significance of dialogue. Meaningful action can have a kind of objectification similar to a text. Actions are detached from their authors and have their own consequences. The importance of an action goes beyond its original situation. "... [T]he meaning of human action is also something which is *addressed* to an indefinite range of possible 'readers'." (1991: 208) Interreligious dialogue has a dimension of importance for our shared future which may far exceed the particular dialogical events.

Dialogue as conversation is an event, a series of events, an attitude, even a way of life. The very dialogue itself is to be interpreted. Considering dialogue as "text" allows us to investigate the dialectical relationship between understanding and explanation (Ricoeur, 1981). Using Ricoeur's foundational understanding of the dialectical interplay between understanding and explanation, let us see what we might expect in Muslim-Christian dialogue. We guess at the meaning of the dialogue in the first understanding. We explain what happened in dialogue – the particulars, structures, effects, consequences. We look at the exchange of information and the attempts to understand the other and be understood. We speak out about the experience of dialogue. There are psychological processes involved: curiosity, assumption, generosity, apprehension, defensiveness, perhaps anger, changes in our mental schemata. Then we come to a second understanding, a new comprehension, and hopefully, the will to continue the conversation. For a person who becomes aware of the dialogue but has not directly participated, the same process of understanding-explanation-understanding can occur. The impact, consequences, and meaning go beyond the particular dialogical event and the consciousness of the participants.

Dialogue as Public Theology

David Tracy (1981) identifies the three publics which theology must address – the church, the society, and the academy. The four types of dialogue (life, action, theology, prayer) sometimes overlap and are all ways to the public square, given that church and now mosque, the greater society, and the academy have addresses there.

Dialogue is a conversation in which persons both say something about something to others and then listen to what the others say to them about something and then discuss both the content and the exchange. If one accepts Tracy's analysis, the search for truth in the matters of the practical theology here is the effort to overcome human division, antagonism, hostility, and their sorry history in the relationship between Muslims and Christians (Armour, 2002). The dialogue will encourage Christians and Muslims both to look within their own traditions for elements neglected or under emphasized. This will further illuminate the dialogue and the relationship between the religions, leading to a kind of movement toward unity in human relations; solidarity for the common good of humanity; and awareness of similarities in understanding the relationship of God and humanity and other religious dimensions of life (Tracy, 1983).

I will examine contributions and questions from the four types of dialogue to the three "publics" of theology.

1. Academy

Several issues are available to the academy from dialogue. How is the success of women's groups to be understood in light of feminist theory? Certainly, the dialogue of life indicates that the paradigm of "clash of civilizations" is open to serious challenge from the fact that this dialogue exists and grows (Alexander, 2002). "Action" dialogue comes to the academy with questions. What is real development? Is technological progress to be accompanied by Western ideas, by controversial "modernity"? When is development not "progress"?

The "Word of God" conversation invites further exploration of the traditions. The issue of the relationship of religion and violence will draw on theological and philosophical ethics, understandings of Islamic and church law, issues of symbol and culture, and many practical theological considerations. One can also continue to look at the place of the believer in the academy. Belief can be studied as a theological reality and as a psychological phenomenon. The relationship between specifically Muslim and specifically Catholic spirituality would promise to be a fruitful object of study. Qualitative research and other postmodern approaches may be significant here. The dialogue itself warrants study, both as a sociological phenomenon and in its theological significance.

2. Society

The dialogue of life invites consideration of what it means to be a religious person and to participate in the greater society. How are Catholics and Muslims accepted in neighborhoods; as visible participants in public life; and when bringing concerns which are affected by public policy? The dialogue must address the fact that Muslims have met resistance in attempting to engage themselves in the American political process of votes, lobbies, and contributions.

In regard to the dialogue of action and development, Muslims consult with Catholics in regard to religious schools, charities, and social agencies. Muslims participate in Catholic universities abroad and benefit from charitable projects in many countries. In the greater society, there is cooperation around issues of mutual concern regarding public policy, including family, population, and just distribution of resources issues. In the United States, issues of prayer in public schools, chaplains in the military and prisons, even anti-war protests and other public events have dialogical components. Does solidarity as a concept offer a way forward in dialogue and action? (George, 2002) How successful can Muslims and Catholics be in a lobby system in regard to domestic issues, foreign policy concerns, and real self-determination for peoples, which imposes neither totalitarianism nor Western-controlled democratic schemes?

3. Church

The wonderful durability of women's groups raises questions for both church and mosque about the particular roles and actual influence of women in religious activity. Church and mosque social institutions have implications both in the greater society and in church and mosque themselves. The existence of theological/religious dialogue has implications as well. In regard to the dialogue of sharing of religious experience and prayer, one notes the Assisi and Rome gatherings, where religious leaders prayed in each others' company. Similarly, throughout the United States, praying in each others' company was the mode of prayer services following the World Trade Center attack.

As universal and missionary religions, dialogue questions of theological significance include the questions of salvation for outsiders, dialogue as distinct from evangelization and *da'wa*, conversion, and ideals of religious freedom. Would adherents of either religion agree with the claim that through knowing the other better they have come to understand their own religious tradition in new ways? Will dialogue with Muslims paradoxically be helpful in the conversations of the Christian churches with each other?

Conclusion

Interreligious dialogue in itself is an act of public theology. It has implications for the three publics of theology. In several ways it brings the participants to the public square in the United States. The willingness to engage in dialogue will shape church and mosque themselves, affecting their place in the public square and the public square itself. Consideration of dialogue as conversation and text well describe its present reality and its potential for a future impact beyond the original dialogue and its participants.

The American shape of Islam is now taking form. Muslims will profit from learning about the experience of other religious groups. How Catholics support the shaping of the relationship in appropriate ways will affect future dialogue.

References

Aasi, Ghulam-Haider (2002) 'A Muslim Participant's Reflections' in Ghulam-Haider Aasi and Rita George Tvertkovic, (eds.), *Catholic-Muslim Relations in Chicago.* *Chicago Studies* 41: 2, 169 - 182.

Abu-Rabi, Ibrahim M. (1999) 'John Paul II and Islam' in Byron L. Sherwin and Harold Kasimow (eds.), *John Paul II and interreligious dialogue.* Maryknoll, N.Y.: Orbis, 185 - 204.

Alexander, Scott C. (2002) 'The "Clash of Civilizations" and the Dialogic Imperative.' *Chicago Studies* 41:2, 192 - 208.

Armour, Rollin, Sr. (2002) *Islam, Christianity, and the West: A Troubled History.* Maryknoll, NY: Orbis.

Ayoub, Mahmoud (1999) 'Pope John Paul II on Islam' in Byron L. Sherwin and Harold Kasimow (eds), *John Paul II and Interreligious dialogue.* Maryknoll, N.Y.: Orbis, 169 - 184.

Dolan, Jay (2002) *In Search of an American Catholicism.* New York: Oxford University Press.

Durkee, Abdullah Noorudeen (1998) 'Personal Thoughts on Muslim-Christian Dialogue' in M. Darrol Bryant and S.A. Ali (eds), *Muslim-Christian dialogue: promise and problems.* St. Paul, MN: Paragon, 111 - 124.

Esack, Fardid (2003) Unpublished Lecture, Catholic Theological Union, Chicago, Illinois, April 2, 2003.

Fitzgerald, Michael (2003) 'Dialogical Nature of Christianity Calls for Faith and Listening Ability.' *Osservatore Romano*, N. 10 (1783), 7 - 8.

George, Francis Cardinal (2002) 'Public morality in a global society: Catholics and Muslims in dialogue.' *Theology Digest* 49:4, 319 - 332.

Griffiths, Paul J. (2001) *Problems of Religious Diversity.* Malden, MA: Blackwell.

Hagen, John D., Jr. (2003) Pro-life Democrats.*Commonweal*, 103:1, 11 - 12.

Ricoeur, Paul (1981) 'The Model of the Text: Meaningful Action Considered as a Text' in John B. Thompson (ed, trans, intro), *Hermeneutics and the Human Sciences.* Cambridge, U.K: Cambridge University Press, 197 - 221.

Siddiqi, Muzzamil (2001) 'How an Islamic Leader Views Dialogue.' *Origins* 30: 38, 662 - 663.

Tracy, David (1981) *The Analogical Imagination.* New York: Crossroad.

Tracy, David (1983) 'The context: the public character of theological language' in David Tracy and John B. Cobb, Jr. (eds.), *Talking about God.* New York: Seabury, 1 - 16.

Tracy, David (1987) *Pluralism and Ambiguity.* San Francisco: Harper and Row.

Tracy, David (1991) *Dialogue with the Other: The Interreligious Dialogue.* Grand Rapids: William B. Eerdmans.

van Beeck, F.J. (1994) 'Christian Faith and Theology in Encounter with Non-Christians: Profession? Protestation? Self-Maintenance? Abandon?' *Theological Studies* 55, 46 - 65.

Civil Society Without Religion?

The Role of Theology in Multicultural Europe

Friedrich Schweitzer

Most theologians would probably say that it makes sense to speak of the public relevance of theology and religion. Yet many others, especially in politics, do not share this conviction. So we must be aware of the fact that the prevailing view of religion does not attribute any public relevance to religion or to theology. In this essay I want to use the changing shape of Europe in general and especially of the European Union as a case study for the relationship between civil society and religion.

At present, the leading assumption of European politicians seems to be that peace and tolerance in Europe can only be achieved if religion is confined to the private sphere. At the same time, the fear of conflicts between the adherents of different religions as well as the issue of including Turkey as a Muslim country withiin the Union have made people aware of the possibility that Europe may have something like a hidden religious (Christian) identity as well as of the need for a European civil religion. I will start with a few comments on how religion is treated, especially in European politics, before looking into what I consider the public relevance of religion and theology and the contribution of theology.

My writing comes from a practical context. Aside from my academic responsibilities I am in charge of the internationalisation of my faculty which, at this point, involves creating a European network of theological faculties and departments of religious studies. In addition to this, I am part of a political initiative which aims at making religious education more visible as a topic of European scope.

The Prevailing View: The Ambivalence of Religion

Religion has not been a central issue in European politics. Within the European Union religious topics are explicitly left to the member states, and the political institutions of the larger Europe have rarely addressed issues of this kind. The few statements which can be mentioned in this context, most notably two recommendations of the Council of Europe, recommendation 1202 on *Religious Tolerance in a Democratic Society* adopted in February 1993 and recommendation 1396 on *Religion and Democracy* adopted in January 1999 (documented in Schreiner et al., 2002), indicate that religion is most often associated with fundamentalism and with other forms of politicized religion. Therefore religion is considered a source of intolerance and violence, of divisiveness and of separatism. There is a deep fear that religious communities might attempt to lay their hands on political power and to interfere with democratic procedures. Or, as the 1999 recommendation puts it:

... even in a democracy, there are still certain tensions between religious expression and political power. There is a religious aspect to many of the problems that contemporary society faces, such as intolerant fundamentalist movements and terrorist acts, racism and xenophobia and ethnic conflicts; consideration should also be given to inequality between sexes in religion. (Schreiner et al., 2002:45 - 46)

The recommendation acknowledges that "extremism is not religion itself" and that a "humanist path" is the true mission of what is called the "great age-old religions". Nevertheless the recommendation continues:

As for religions they must not try to take the place of democracy or grasp political power... (2002: 46).

The recommendation also includes some more hopeful and encouraging signs for religion and even for theology. The Council sees the potential of a constructive role for religion in democracy:

Democracy has proved to be the best framework for freedom of conscience, the exercise of faith and religious pluralism. For its part, religion, through its moral and ethical commitment, the values it upholds, its critical approach and its cultural expression, can be a valid partner of democratic society. (ibid.)

And among the suggestions for the governments of the member states we even find a brief reference to theology. The governments of the member states are invited:

to promote better relations with and between religions and in particular... [to] promote regular dialogue between theologians, philosophers and historians, as well as with representatives of other branches of knowledge... (2002:47).

Summarizing these observations it is probably fair to say that, among European politicians, the prevailing view of religion is ambivalent. On the one hand, there is a strong fear of a religious threat to democracy, and on the other hand there is a certain acknowledgement of the political importance of the values supported by the major religious traditions. The fears are clearly stronger than the positive expectations vis-à-vis religion which can also be seen from how the recommendation gives preference to the teaching *about* religion rather than the teaching *of* religion in public schools (Schreiner, 2002:47). Teaching *about* religion traditionally is not associated with theology but with the social scientific study of religion or with religious studies. On the whole, the Council of Europe does not foresee a public role which religion or theology should play within democracy. It seems that the Council considers religious neutrality of the public sphere one of the most important presuppositions of democracy.

It is important to note that theology is at least mentioned in the recommendation. Yet we should also not overlook the dominant tendency of supporting religion and religious freedom only to the extent that religious communities do not strive for a public role or for political influence. Many European politicians seem to adhere to a model of the separation between state and religion which turns religion into a private matter. According to this view, religion is to be confined to the private sphere while the public has to be religiously neutral.

As we all know, the events of September 11, 2001 represent a deep challenge to this understanding. Many people have come to ask themselves if the privatisation of religion will indeed be a sufficient basis for peace and tolerance or if there is a need for a public place for religion in Europe.

One of the most telling and, given the tradition of French *laicisme*, also one of the most surprising statements on this can be found in the recent report of Régis Debray on the *Teaching about Religions in the Laicist School* – a report which was commissioned by the former French Minister of Education (Debray, 2002). In his plea for this kind of teaching, Debray is very outspoken about the detrimental effects which the exclusion of religious topics from the school curriculum has had in France and beyond: lack of understanding of European history and culture, an increasing shallowness of everyday life, weakening of all social ties, increase of prejudice, esoteric religion and irrationalism. And he also points out that the future of European culture and the future of religion are closely connected. For him, culture is a cumulative process which is premised on the continuity of traditions. This is why he maintains that there is a very close relationship between the religious traditions and the future of the humanities.

Challenging the Prevailing View: The Constructive Public Role of Religion

In this section, I want to briefly state what, from my point of view, religion can contribute to the future of European societies as well as to the future of Europe as a whole. For the sake of space I will limit myself to three core aspects: solidarity, peace, and identity.

One of the most pressing questions of the present is about the *sources and the maintenance of social solidarity*. Sociologists of different persuasion have left little doubt that the structure of modern or postmodern societies cannot be relied upon as sources of solidarity. Rather, these structures are premised on a high degree of differentiation and individualization, and they put a premium on successful competition among individuals. Given this situation, there obviously is a need for social values which must come from a source which is different from the market place or from technology. Many will agree that at least the Christian tradition and faith have operated in this manner and that they hold the potential of serving as sources of solidarity in the future as well. Yet this potential will certainly not be realized if religion is not even allowed to assume the public role which is required, for example, by the Christian self-understanding. You cannot have both, privatised religion and the public fruits of religion in ethics.

I am quite aware that this point of view will probably lead to an argument with those who are convinced that the plurality of religious convictions only breeds intolerance and, if allowed into the public realm, will not result in solidarity but only in aggression. Yet it is also easy to see that tolerance and peace in a multicultural and multireligious Europe can hardly be achieved where cultural and religious ignorance prevails. Living together peacefully requires *dialogical relationships between the religions*. It requires *mutual respect and acceptance* which are achieved on the basis of knowing the other and on the awareness of cultural and religious difference. Rather than keeping the religions out of the public sphere, we should encourage the development of public dialogue and cooperation between the religions wherever there is a chance to do so. At a time when people are rightfully becoming more self-confident about their personal autonomy and about expressing themselves in public, the future of Europe cannot be premised on religiously neutralizing public life.

This brings me to the last aspect in this section: the question of *European identity*, which must be more than a "Euro-Identity", the identity afforded by the 'Euro' (€), the common currency of the European Union. "*Giving a Soul to Europe*" was one of the catch-phrases of European politics in the 1990s. Leading politicians came to recognize that a democratic Europe will not be achieved by economic cooperation alone and also not by technological innovations or by the introduction of a single currency. Rather, a democratic Europe requires something like a shared identity of people who feel that, while coming from different traditions and while not giving up their particular identities, they can still share some of their deep convictions about life: convictions, that is, which inevitably have to do with social and moral orientations, with the values and worldviews which have emerged in the history of Europe. Quite independently of one's own religious or political convictions there can be no doubt that this history has been influenced and, in many instances, shaped by the religions present in Europe – most of all by Christianity and Judaism but, at certain times, also by Islam. Unless one considers it possible artificially to create a "European Soul", there will be no such identity without including its religious roots. And since we can only speak of such roots in the plural, European identity must be a pluralistic and dialogical identity which takes on a dynamic shape and is able to combine unity with diversity.

The Contribution of Theology: Towards a Public Practical Theology

So far I have limited myself to religion because religious life is where the need for theology arises. However, I am also convinced that the constructive public role of religion is premised on the availability of academic theology, especially of a practical theology which makes the public role of religion one of its central topics. In other words, at least in our contemporary situation, religion can only contribute to social values, to peace and tolerance, and to a European identity, if it is informed by theology. Without theology, religion will not be able to achieve the reflective and dialogical orientations and the skills which are needed for religion to play a public role. From this external point of view (which is not the only possible one because theology also has important internal tasks), the major contribution of theology is the reflective rendering of a religious tradition and community through academic research. Theological research and teaching serve the religious community by supporting its future existence through considered advice, but research and teaching also serve society in that they enable religion to make its contribution to the future of society. Consequently I am convinced that theology has a legitimate place within any academic context, be it in a university funded by the state or a religious institution.

I know that this may sound like a theologian praising himself for his work – a suspicion which we probably cannot avoid altogether when we, as theologians, have to advocate theology. But even if this is true, we should also be aware of not just defending what we have achieved in theology so far. This is why I want to conclude by pointing out three different directions for future work in theology, with a special focus on practical theology.

First, we must become much more intentional about extending the idea of *public theology* towards a *public practical theology* – a concept which Richard Osmer and I have developed in more detail in our recent book on *Religious*

Education between Modernization and Globalization (Osmer and Schweitzer, 2003). Public theology means that theology must intentionally address an audience which is much broader than the church and which also extends beyond Christianity in the widest sense. In a multi-religious society, theology can only be public to the degree that it also has a non-Christian audience in mind, for example, the Muslim citizens in Europe, but also non-believers and even atheists. Moreover, public theology should become aware of at least two more requirements. It must be cast in a language which is understandable outside the Christian community, and it must refer to issues which are of importance to people outside the church as well. Saying this I am aware of the growing number of theologians who have advocated the need for a public theology (for a clear statement and additional references cf. Thiemann, 1996, also see Osmer and Schweitzer, 2003). But I am also convinced that we still have a long way to go if we really want to become public theologians and if theological faculties should really become places of public discourse. A public practical theology should not only address society as one of its genuine audiences – a requirement which, once more, affirms the need for moving beyond the so-called clerical and ecclesial paradigms. It should also be able to show how theology contributes to solving problems of general societal concern. My next two points will hopefully shed some light on what such problems could be.

Second, theology must become more intentional about the *dialogue between different worldviews and religions*. This demand is more unusual than the first. The existing models of public theology tend to focus on ethics as their main topic. They seem to assume that public agreement can be achieved over questions of ethics while faith topics will remain divisive. From the perspective of a public practical theology this is not enough or not even helpful because it may further increase the tendency of privatising religion which clearly works against the claims of any public theology. Treating religious views as a private matter also fails to do justice to the achievements of ecumenical and interreligious dialogue. Despite all open questions or even controversies, the twentieth century has been a time of ecumenical and interdenominational dialogue and progress, and we should make sure that we will not fall back behind of what has been achieved in this respect. However, if we want the plea for a public role of religion to become plausible, if we want it to be convincing or even attractive to others, theology must demonstrate its ability of facilitating civilized forms of intercultural and interreligious encounter and cooperation. By this I do not mean that theology should pretend that there is only harmony between the different religious faiths. Quite the opposite holds true: academic dialogue is only helpful if it does not circumvent the many unresolved questions or the numerous conflicts around cultural and religious issues arising in society.

Therefore theology's attempts of facilitating civilized forms of interreligious encounter and cooperation must include theoretical as well as practical issues. It must be located within a broad circle of theory and praxis or, to put it differently, they must include all of the theological sub-disciplines – from exegesis and dogmatics all the way to practical theology. Dialogue about philosophical and credal topics is necessary but will certainly not be sufficient vis-à-vis the political challenges of a pluralistic society which has to resolve practical issues like the development of prejudice and aggression, conflicts over religious norms in education, the acknowledgement of women's rights within the family and the public presence of Muslim monuments like mosques and minarets with loudspeakers. Public theology must come to include a public practical theology which offers models for dealing with such issues in a civilized manner and without taking refuge in neutralizing the public sphere from all religious influences. By developing such models theology could clearly contribute to the solution of problems which are high on the agenda of politics as well as of society in general.

My last point fits very well with the aims of our International Academy of Practical Theology (cf. Schweitzer and van der Ven, 1999). It refers to the need for theology to become *more international* and, in the context of my present topic, to become *more European*. By speaking of "European theology" I am not arguing for a new division between theologies from the different parts of the world. Even if the need for indigenous and contextualized theologies is obvious, we should not strive for having separate national theologies as self-sufficient entities. Rather, trying to internationalise and to Europeanize theology is an immediate consequence and implication of its public character. Increasingly, the public is no longer organized according to national boundaries. Civil society can no longer be restricted to local or even national levels. There clearly is a need for international networks which some observers consider the roots of an emerging international civil society. The process of European unification takes place within the context of globalization. It does not only transform the political public but also affects many other dimensions of public life – in culture and education but also in terms of values and religion. The challenge ahead of us is to work towards a Europe which is more unified, just and peaceful, more open and more democratic because it allows religion to play its public role. And this includes the model of a Europe which does not only focus on its own needs and which will not limit its attention and commitment to its own interests. With the idea or ideal of *ecumene* – the concern for life in the one world – theology has much to contribute to the task of shaping the processes of globalization, be it on a limited level within European internationalization or be it on a worldwide level.

References

Debray, Régis (2002) *Rapport à Monsieur le Ministre de l'Éducation nationale " L'enseignement du fait religieux dans l'École laïque "*. Paris : Odile Jacob.

Osmer, Richard R. and Schweitzer, Friedrich (2003) *Religious Education between Modernization and Globalization: New Perspectives on the United States and Germany*. Grand Rapids: W.B Eerdmans.

Schreiner, Peter et al. (eds.) (2002) *Committed to Europe's Future: Contributions from Education and Religious Education*. Münster: Comenius-Institute.

Schweitzer, Friedrich and van der Ven, Johannes A. (1999) *Practical Theology – International Perspectives*. Frankfurt/M.: P. Lang.

Thiemann, Ronald F. (1996) *Religion in Public Life: A Dilemma for Democracy*. Washington: Georgetown University Press.

PART II: PUBLIC THEOLOGY IN GLOBAL AND LOCAL PERSPECTIVES

In this section, contributors offer a series of reflections on the diverse nature of public theology from a variety of local, national, cultural and political contexts. In a historically and culturally rich engagement with the IAPT host city of Manchester, John Atherton, Chris Baker and Elaine Graham offer a collaborative paper which explores Manchester – from the industrial 'Cottonopolis', to post-industrial 'Ideopolis' and the utopian vision of 'Cosmopolis' – as archetypal case study in public theology. They explore a model of practical, public theology attentive to the threefold critical issues of economy, marginalisation and urban context, which unfolds into a call for "a profoundly performative [public] theology, judged in its effectiveness and authenticity by its capacity to mobilize faithful witness for the good of the city".

Taking contemporary Dutch culture as her context, Riet Bons-Storm argues that violence is deep seated and takes many forms, from coercion of the powerless to physical aggression. Such violence is mapped onto the hierarchies of gender, race, class and dis/ability, and sanctioned by theological traditions that understand God as Almighty and all-powerful. She considers what resources are available in the Christian pastoral care tradition to address and heal the symptoms and causes of violence in our society. She draws on new models and metaphors for God found in the work of feminist theologian Sallie McFague and medieval theologian Hadewich to propose a public theology that promotes equality and mutuality.

Tracing the bias in American Public Theology towards a more cognitive and less practical conceptual orientation Bonnie Miller McLemore offers a comprehensive survey of the interface of public and practical theologies in the United States. Writing from an Australian perspective, Gerard Hall explores the possibilities for a new, dialogical Christian rhetoric which addresses the challenges of finding truth in a postmodern, pluralist context. Advocating a relation of direct proportion between the polarities of spirituality and theology, mythos and logos, and finally diverse religious traditions, Hall highlights the mediating and healing power of narrative, finally refocusing the Christian

practical and public task as that of a 'remembering and storytelling community'.

In the context of the United Kingdom, Esther Reed addresses the issues
surrounding the representation of the Church of England in a reformed House
of Lords. Exploring current proposals and their limitations Reed also engages
with the deeper and broader theological questions of Christian responsibility
and legitimate law in modern plural societies. Wilhelm Graeb's contribution is
the first of a number in this volume to reflect on the task of practical theology
in relation to the media and mass communications – and thus taking us into
the realm of realities such as 'public opinion' and 'popular culture'. Graeb discusses the construction of a virtual public space which is both constructed and
mediated by communications technology. He assesses theologically the media's "almost transcendental function for the constitution of our knowledge".
Graeb weaves the connections between media culture, modernity and the logic
of capitalism whose politics of novelty are then contrasted with the redundancy, repetition and remembrance of Christian ecclesial practice. For Graeb metaphor, symbol and narrative, explored hermeneutically, constitute alternative
and abiding technologies of communication.

Reflecting on her experiences as a media commentator on religious affairs in Canada, Solange Lefebvre offers a diagnosis of the paradoxes running
throughout Canadian society in terms of religion as 'public truth'. Faced with
what Arendt terms the 'three pillars of modernity' – doubt, political salvation
and intra-worldliness – academic theologians and church figures have esche-
wed explicit testimonies of faith or claims to religious particularism in favour
of a 'spirituality of discretion' which avoids public proclamations of faith in
favour of a kind of social activism. Paradoxically, however, this may actually
fuel the trends towards the evacuation of the public sphere of any references to
faith, value or transcendence, at the same time as other counter-movements are
challenging the very precepts of modernity. Lefebvre offers no easy solutions,
but suggests that those who have traditionally sought such an accommodation to modernity may fail to respond adequately both to the logic of secular
modernity and to the resurgence of anti-modern and conservative expressions
of religion. Given the extent to which the discipline of practical theology has
been associated with the emergence of Western modernity, this highlights the
continuing dilemmas for those seeking to make theologically-grounded interventions in the public sphere in ways which respect both the particularity of
faith and the pluralism of society.

Abraham Berinyuu argues that representations of Africa, and theology in
Africa, have tended to be formed in the image of Western preconceptions. In
tracing the prospects for the emergence of a genuinely 'contextual' public theo-

logy in Africa, there is a need to appreciate the diversity of different 'Africas' and indeed of African theological perspectives. An African-centred hermeneutics capable of representing the complexities of its cultures and perspectives will be oriented towards a practical theology capable of engaging with that continent's struggles to overcome human suffering.

From a French Canadian perspective Jean-Guy Nadeau reflects on 'public talk about God and relationship to God in rock music'. His paper engages the implicit and explicit theology found in the way rock music uses the Bible, and provides intriguing insights into the ways religious language remains as a residual point of reference in an ostensibly secular culture. For Nadeau the very form of rock music facilitates the sort of correlational and hermeneutic-experimental process which practical, public theologies appear to advocate. In exploring this terrain he reopens the question of the relationship between public theology, practical theology and the arts as a key cultural form.

A 'Genius of Place'?

Manchester as a Case Study in Public Theology

John Atherton, Chris Baker and Elaine Graham

Eamon Duffy's account of the small village of Morebath with thirty three families in South West England in the sixteenth century is the dramatic story of local engagement with religious change in the context of social, political and economic transition (Duffy, 2001). It is an account which powerfully resonates with the story of Manchester's journey through even greater processes of change from the late 18th century to the present. For as Max Weber reminds us, the emergence and development of urban-industrial societies represented a phenomenon 'differing not merely in degree but in kind from the social order preceding it' (Weber, 1970:4). What also connects Morebath and Manchester is the continuing 'genius of place' which 'proves the assertion, that the great forces of the world can best be understood in terms of their local effects.' (Ackroyd, 2000).

Using Manchester as representative case study of a fulcrum of social, economic and political change, we want to comment on the implications of trying to do public theology in three dimensions, drawing on David Tracy's threefold characterisation of what being public means for theology in terms of its needing to engage constructively and critically with voices from academy, society and church (Tracy, 1981). In taking Manchester as a case study of what it means to do theology 'in public', we identify three ways in which it provides, if not a totally unique context, then a strikingly archetypical example of the key factors to which public theology must attend:

i) Realities of economic growth, political economy

ii) Human dimensions in terms of marginalisation

iii) Church as implicated in changing fortunes of urban life

Firstly, the economic and social realities. As arguably the 'Ur city' (Soja, 2000: 78) of industrial and urban change, and thus of modernity/postmodernity as definitive currents of Western society, set amidst a globalised economic and cultural order, then Manchester offers keys to understanding something of the socio-economic contexts in which theologians must locate themselves – the lived experience of massed populations, mobility such as the world has never seen, the growth of great cities as the norm rather than the exception of human living.

Secondly, however, these forces of material, technological, economic and demographic change bring with them the challenges generated by reflection upon their human dimensions. How are those who observe the phenomenon of the urban condition to communicate and assimilate its significance? Is it an occasion for exhilaration and wonder; or something which calls forth dismay at the diminution of the quality of life it produces? What if the experience of city living is, as even the most casual stroll through the streets of any global city may reveal, a deeply polarised phenomenon? Can the fruits of wealth and innovation compensate for the poverty and deprivation that often seems to accompany it; is the latter, indeed, a *necessary* price to pay for the former?

So Manchester may be regarded as a fulcrum of debate about how to understand and analyse society, especially the dynamics of exclusion/inclusion, power/powerlessness, and wealth/poverty. In this, it also connects with Schreiter's global theological flows of liberation, feminism, ecology and human rights (Schreiter, 1997:15 - 20), all powerfully linked to the dynamics and processes of *marginalisation* and its discontents (Atherton, 2003).

Thirdly, we have the question of how such a city as Manchester is informed by, and makes an impact on, the theological and practical imagination of the churches. It is these factors which should inform Elaine Graham's definition of this emerging public theology as essentially a performative discipline, measured for example, by the effectiveness of its engagement with marginalisation (Graham, 1999: 82 - 83).

And it is this specific problematic of marginalisation which is of particular interest because:

– it recognises the connections between modernisation processes and marginalisation, the paradox of wealth-creating processes originating in Manchester.
– it links the local, national and global dimensions of living today
– it invites public theology to be problematic-based and contextually-located, for it is in relation to that, that we now best develop critical theories: like Karen Lebacqz, 'In order to understand the meaning of justice we need to listen to the experiences of those who are suffering injustice.' (Lebacqz, 1987; cited in Jarl, 2000)

This article will reflect on how the specificities of Manchester, its past, present and future, might have relevance for practical theology. We begin with some reflections on Manchester's particular history as first industrial city: christened 'Cottonopolis' by commentators in the nineteenth century, it embodied the best and worst of the economic, political and cultural transformations associated with the birth of capitalism. Following a period of economic decline in the twentieth century, the past decade has witnessed a remarkable urban renaissance. Once again, however, the story of Manchester's reinvention as 'Ideopolis' is one of exclusion and marginalisation as well as innovation and promise. It is important to ask what kinds of values underpin the organization of space, place, movements and populations in these great narratives of urban growth and change. Finally, we consider the possibilities of Manchester as 'Cosmopolis', an idea which continues to stress the importance of space and place, the dynamics of material wealth and distribution, but which also explicitly addresses ethical, participative and democratic ideals.

Cottonopolis

Any contemporary reflection, however, needs to be located in Manchester's historical context, as the very crucible of the industrial world, and thus of capitalism and modernity themselves. For it was in this location that these processes first emerged in the late eighteenth century in this small township of a Manchester of 20,000 people in 1776 – demographically exploding ten-fold, to 240,000 by 1841 and 316,213 by 1851 (Kidd, 2002:14). Manchester, first industrial city of modernity, with an astonishing wealth creating capacity based on new sources of power, technologies, and forms of industrial organisation. Manchester, the globalising city of Cottonopolis, transforming the world through manufacturing and free trade (Atherton, 1997).

Yet the centre of wealth creation was also the location of profound marginalisation processes, such as those identified by Engels in his 1845 *Condition of the Working Class in England*, which was researched in Manchester. By virtue of his industrialist father's wealth Engels was a member of the bourgeoisie, the capitalist class; but his political and emotional loyalties lay elsewhere, with the working people of the city. He was one of the first social researchers to document the geopolitical character of the emergent modern city, by drawing attention to the vast gulf not only of material wealth, but of consciousness and shared experience between the classes, as manifested in the physical segregations between rich and poor (Engels, 1969). Urban life as both microcosm and demonstration of the ambiguities of industrial capitalism was later to be confirmed by the Salford study of Robert Roberts' *Classic Slum*, relating to the earlier twentieth century (Roberts, 1971), and then by the William Temple Foundation research in Ordsall, in Salford, in the late 1970s, splendidly subtitled 'Engels knew a slum when he saw one' (Markall, 1980).

No wonder this new phenomenon of Manchester also became known as the 'shock city' (Briggs, 1968); and for Engels, the 'hypocritical city', where the degradations of poverty, ill-health and poor housing were justified in the name of wealth-creation and progress. In *The Condition of the Working Class in England* he uses the tale of an encounter with a wealthy acquaintance of the entrepreneurial class to launch an attack on what he regarded as the intolerable complacency of the middle classes:

'I have never seen a class so deeply demoralized, so incurably debased by selfishness, so corroded within, so incapable of progress, as the English bourgeoisie ... For it nothing exists in this world, except for the sake of money, itself not excluded. In the presence of this avarice and lust of gain, it is not possible for a single human sentiment or opinion to remain untainted ... I once went into Manchester with such a bourgeois, and spoke to him of the bad, unwholesome method of building, the frightful condition of the working-people's quarters, and asserted that I had never seen so ill-built a city. The man listened quietly to the end, and said at the corner where we parted: "And yet there is a great deal of money made here; good morning sir." It is utterly indifferent to the English bourgeois whether his working-men starve or not.' (Engels, 1969: 301 - 2)

And that sense of shock over marginalisation, as a reminder of the 'underside' of economic well-being, continues into the present with the national government's *Indices of Multiple Deprivation* (2000), revealing that 36% of Greater Manchester is numbered in the most deprived 10% of communities nationally, including the poorest community in England, Wythenshawe, a garden city in South Manchester, adjacent to the great international airport, symbol of prosperity in a now globalised city (Dicken, 2002). And that, of course, reminds us that these marginalised communities of Manchester, as Giddens recognises, are 'not just pockets of deprivation within national societies, they are fault lines along which the Third World rubs up against the First.' (Giddens,, 1994:148) In finding traces of the broader logic of history embedded in the specific conditions around him, Engels argued that the contradictions of abject poverty amidst such opulence would lead inevitably to the very collapse of capitalism. Yet whilst we can see how Ackroyd's 'genius of place' functioned for Engels, it is important to realise that it still operates for us too: for the immediate and concrete continues to be a microcosm of wider forces of global change, migration, class, poverty and power.

An emergent post-industrial and post-modern society is paradoxically encouraging the growth of *both* religious and secular forces, emerging from the context of globalisation. This situation compels us to engage with diversity, and to recognise the contribution of tradition to that engagement, including the formation of identity. The task of developing public theology as an integral part of that Christian engagement with an increasingly hybrid and fragmented world relates profoundly to recognising and developing the contribution of theological traditions, including a recognition of Tracy's second understanding of the public area, as the role of the academy. This will be elaborated with reference to three explanations of marginalisation processes (Atherton, 2003:79 - 92) and how they are informed in turn by particular theological traditions.

First, economic growth is essential for resourcing people's capabilities to function effectively in contemporary societies. Without it, people and nations face endemic marginalisation. Manchester lay at the heart of the astonishing emergence of a virtuous cycle of economic growth in the 19th century. The Malthusian nightmare was never realised because the fourfold population increase in Britain in the 19th century was outpaced by the fourteenfold increase in Gross National Product. It was these processes which the theological tradition of Christian political economy sought to engage at their very outset in the late 18th and early 19th centuries (Waterman, 1992). Essentially, this movement represented an innovatory linking of theology with the emerging new discipline of economics, increasingly at the heart of modernisation processes. What Manchester does, therefore, is to add the significance of political economy and our engagement with it. For in deciding what to call its great public space in the nineteenth century, 'The Free Trade Hall[1], it decisively rejected traditional resorts to Kings, politicians, or saints, but chose a central principle of political economy, free trade. Engagement with that is what, in Manchester, public theology is about!

Equally important, it recognises the value of connecting political and economic tasks, in the discipline of political economy. A major contribution to these endeavours was made by John Bird Sumner, Bishop for this area from 1828 - 1848, and his theological engagement with the clergyman-economist Thomas Malthus' seminal work on population and economics (still at the heart of the contemporary marginalisation problematic) (Atherton, 1994: 333 - 352). That broadening of economics into effective dialogue with ethics and politics remains a central part of the contemporary engagement with the marginalisation problematic. As a continuing tradition, it formed the basis of Ronald Preston's theological contribution in Manchester from 1948 to 2001, is central to our work, and feeds into current moves to establish a Centre for Public Theo-

---

[1] Originally a centre for political gatherings, the Free Trade Hall was a concert hall for most of the twentieth century, home of the Halle Orchestra. It is now a commercial hotel.

logy in the Department of Religions and Theology in Manchester University, launched in May 2004 (Baker and Graham, 2004).

Second, explaining marginalisation and how to overcome it also relates to growing international recognition of the importance of good governance for social and economic prosperity. Maintaining order, law and corrupt free government is also now complemented by the drive for inclusive democracy and supportive health and educational systems (representative of the post 1989 coordination of the civil and political liberties of the West with the economic and social rights of communism). Theologically speaking, it was the formative contribution of William Temple, leader of the ecumenical movement and Bishop of Manchester in the 1920s which addressed these matters through his embodying of the Anglo-Saxon tradition of incarnational theology in debates for a modern welfare state and Keynesian economics (Temple, 1942). That tradition continues to inform contemporary British public theologies including the seminal Anglican report, *Faith in the City*, in 1985.

Third, the absence or presence of economic growth and good governance are necessary but not sufficient explanations of contemporary marginalisation. For example, there is an understandable growing suspicion that modernisation processes generate not simply economic growth but also marginalisation. De Tocqueville, commenting on his visit to the shock city of Manchester in 1835, expressed the paradox much more pithily, that from the 'filthy sewer' of Manchester 'pure gold' flowed (Briggs, 1968: 70). The remarkable statistical correlation between economic growth and increasing marginalisation from the early 19th century to the present confirms that likely connection, a connection only exacerbated by the rapid acceleration of these divisions since the 1960s, the period witnessing the emergence of the global economy itself. That systemic problem is further exacerbated by a dimension of structural injustice, as in the recognition powerfully expressed by R. H. Tawney, Anglican lay theologian, economic historian and socialist philosopher. Representing a radical Christian socialist development of incarnational theology, from his base in early twentieth century Manchester he was clear that 'there is a unity underlying the individual cases of poverty . . . . they are connected with social institutions, specimens of a type, pieces of a system' (Tawney, 1972: 45). It is an explanation of marginalisation which goes beyond the distributional justice of Rawls' Difference principle, to recognise with Iris Young that 'the predominant approaches to justice tend to presuppose and uncritically accept the relations of production that define an economic system' (Young, 1990: 90). Theologically speaking, therefore, this represents a challenge to consider how questions of social justice are underpinned by foundational, structural processes (Hollenbach, 2002: 201 - 3, 225 - 30) – increasingly so in an era of globalisation.

Ideopolis

Engels' memorable critique of the polarisation and marginalisation processes of industrial capitalism he saw shaping the 'hypocritical city' of nineteenth century Manchester has set the tone of much of the public theology debate surrounding the city. Observing the new and gleaming temples to retail, culture, entertainment, research and finance, and the 'loft-style' apartment housing now encircling its medieval cathedral, one is aware that the Manchester of the 21st century has been substantially rebranded. A 'new' Manchester is swiftly rising from the ashes of the de-industrialised wastelands of Cottonopolis in and around the city centre, but a public, performative theology will still be orientated towards asking the 'questions behind the questions' not least in respect to issues of marginalisation and exclusion. Is the 'new' Manchester still a 'hypocritical' city in terms that Engels would recognise, or is the rebranding and regeneration of Manchester a brave step into a more inclusive and sustainable form of urban community? We shall attempt to answer this question by looking at two key theories of urban change as they apply to Manchester at the present time, and by studying some of the geopolitical forces that are reshaping the southern periphery closest to its rapidly-expanding airport. We shall then reflect on the dilemmas for the church presented by these forces of rapid urban and social change.

First, there is Manuel Castells' theory of space as flows, developed in two seminal books, *The Informational City* (1989) and *The Rise of the Network Society* (1996). Here, Castells outlines how urban space and manufacturing during the mid 70s shifted from what has classically been called the Fordist monocentres to post-fordist multicentres. In economic terms this meant the ability of capital, investment and the new service economy to connect in ways which no longer 'depend on the characteristics of any specific locale for the fulfilment of their fundamental goals' (Castells, 1989: 348). Rather these new forms of wealth generation require merely the 'dynamics of information-generating units, while connecting their different functions to disparate spaces assigned to each task to be performed' (Castells, 1989: 349).

The logical outcome of this new economy, based on nodes of communication, high-tech infrastructure and the enormous speed and quantities of knowledge and capital that can be handled by information technology is that people also have to follow the flow of this economy, either as managers for the new processes of production, or as workers, forced to uproot themselves and follow global patterns of migration in search of employment in newly re-structured industries. Castells notes, 'The new professional managerial class colonizes exclusive spatial segments that connect one another with one another across the city, the country and the world; they isolate themselves from the fragments of local societies, which in consequence become destructured in the process of selective reorganisation of work and residence.' (Castells, 1989: 348)

In spatial terms, the relocation of industries away from the centre to the periphery has produced what in effect is an urban carpet, as people flow out to the decentred industrial and commercial nodes in the suburbs, to beyond the suburbs, what Garreau (1991) calls Edge City, what Soja (2000) calls 'Post-metropolis' (short hand for the post-modern, post-industrialised space), what others call the 100 miles city; regions of hundreds of square miles of mainly low density, suburban housing, retail malls, entertainment zones, hi-tech in-dustry and retail and distribution nodes – and of course endless freeways, dual carriageways.

What is clear is that in the decentred postmetroplis there is a far less-defined sense of what constitutes the local – at least the local in terms of public space. Rather, we flow towards the nodes of hubs of our existence; usually the shopping mall, the health club or our places of work now four or five hours away. Networks of acquaintances may be local, but are more likely to be ba-sed on communities of association or interest which will be city-wide or more likely located in the virtual geography of the world-wide web. Those with eco-nomic spending power spend less and less time in the local – only those who cannot afford to choose or travel inhabit a local space, but that space will now have been fragmented and changed, be it by redevelopment or relocation.

In order to compete in a world now based on flows, European regional ci-ties like Manchester have had to position themselves in a global league table or hierarchy which has increasingly little to do with national agendas. Rather, city regions are now competing directly with each other for a share of inward glo-bal investment (in other words trying to divert some of the flow their way), and in order to do *that*, they have had to pioneer the art of self-reinvention. Man-chester is claiming to be at the forefront of this kind of urban renaissance, a story which is being written as we speak. It tells the heroic tale of how the first city built on the processes of industrial capitalism (i.e. a city based on produc-tion) and *the* globalising city of the early-to-mid 19th century, is also the first city in the UK consciously to reinvent itself on the processes of *post*-industrial capitalism (namely consumption) as a result of huge deindustrialisation in the 1960s to the 1980s which saw one in three jobs in manufacturing lost and one in four factories closed.

A succinct definition of this transformation is to name it the shift from 'Cottonopolis' (a city based on textile factories and heavy manufacturing) to 'Ideopolis'. Ideopolis is an American urban theory based on a 21st century version of the Italian renaissance city-states (Westwood and Nathan, 2002).

The theory is that cities are vital to economic growth and competitiveness, but that a vibrant economy is fundamentally driven by the quality of its human resources – and especially the skills that will foster high productivity and innovation – as well as a good transport and communications infrastructure. This, so the argument runs, helps to create a city 'where people want to live, to learn, to generate and exchange ideas and to do business.' (Hutton, in Nathan and Woodward, 2002). Key requisites of Ideopolis are thus an international airport, thriving cultural industries, a substantial higher education/research and development sector and the capacity to generate new ideas. In response to international debate about cities' role in economic regeneration, the 'Core Cities Group' [2] identified ten key indicators of urban competitiveness:

– Effective communications and transport infrastructure, including international airport and IT connections
– A distinctive city centre, including strong architectural heritage and iconic new physical development
– Nationally and internationally recognized facilities
– Facilities for research, development and innovation involving good links between higher education and the commercial sector
– Large numbers of highly-skilled professionals and a well-educated work force
– An inclusive and diverse population
– A reputation for excellence in culture and the arts; a strong service sector
– Good local governance and policy/political autonomy
– Commitment to environmental responsibility and investment
– A good stock of high-quality residential options

Whereas many of the ten factors listed above concern governance, physical environment and infrastructure – elements that have perennially been crucial to economic growth – what lies at the core of the notion of Ideopolis is undoubtedly that of skills and human resources. Where once land, minerals or mass industrialisation were primary sources of economic capital for cities, now it is so-called *knowledge capital* which creates the buoyant demand, intellectual capacity and business self-confidence essential for the flourishing of the postmodern global city.

Manchester's aspiration to becoming the UK's exemplary Ideopolis can be traced back to the city council's decision to abandon municipal socialism in the late 1980s in favour of a pragmatic acceptance of property-led strategies for urban regeneration and the need to introduce business competition into its

---

[2] A lobby of representatives from English regional cities (Manchester, Birmingham, Bristol, Nottingham, Newcastle, Leeds, Sheffield and Liverpool) in an attempt to counteract the predominance of London and the South-East of England.

operations. Thus the 'Manchester Mafia' was born; an alliance between a Labour council and the city's business community which constructed successful bids for both private and public money for physical regeneration schemes such as City Challenge and Olympic and Commonwealth Games bids. This process of 'boosterism' was carefully marketed and orchestrated to convey the story of Manchester's rebirth to local, national and international audiences and was epitomised in the swift response to the IRA bomb in the city centre in 1996 (Peck and Ward, 2002). According to the Manchester script, the city has been reborn as a post-modern, post-industrial and cosmopolitan city standing in Europe's premier league. New Manchester is vibrant and culturally diverse – well connected to take advantage of the emerging information economy.

'The ideopolis can become a world-class brand for Manchester, a collective watchword for the city's economic prosperity, cultural capital and can-do approach. Manchester, the world's first industrial city which split the atom and created the computer would re-invent itself as the ideopolis; a place for ideas, vitality, creativity, and diversity ... More broadly, Manchester's strengths provide the basis for an alternative centre of gravity for the UK – a Northern hub of economic, social and cultural activity.' (Westwood and Nathan, 2002:73)

This means bidding farewell to the old, industrial Manchester of factories and mills – a city built on manufacturing and production – and ushering in the brave new world of café-bars, nightclubs, huge retailing hubs, cultural and heritage industries, urban lifestyle apartments, university mergers attracting 74,000 fulltime students, cutting-edge research and small-business incubators. This is a city making its living through the thriving 'knowledge industries' and a 24/7 party culture, and representing a decisive shift from production to consumption. The attempt to create a city of 'liveability' based on cultural diversity, leisure and high-quality architecture and design thus reflects significant economic and urban shifts. 11% of all jobs in Manchester are now retailing based, with thousands more employed in bars, restaurants, hotels, cultural industries and fitness clubs. Sankey's Soap factory in Ancoats (once Manchester's industrial heartland) is now a state-of-the-art dance club; Canal Street, (as its name suggests), once the hub of industrial transportation for Cottonopolis, is for Ideopolis now the heart of the thriving gay and lesbian village. Other former factories are now trendy apartment blocks for young single professionals, named after that 60s movie epitomising urban chic, *La Dolce Vita*.

Most dramatic of all, however, is the shift from manual skills to what has been called 'aesthetic labour' required by Ideopolis. Not only do 'Ideopolis' employees need to look good and sound right. They are also exhibiting high standards of confidence, motivation, communication, inter-personal skills and teamworking. These new jobs will be accessed by workers who are prepared to be highly mobile, learn new skills and be part-time or contingent, such as students. One of the most painful mismatches between Cottonopolis and Ideopolis is the gulf between those communities with a preponderance of older male workers, long-term unemployed or poorly skilled, or with the wrong sort of work or cultural experience behind them. So behind the cosmetic presentation of Manchester's city centre as a post-modern 'liveability' environment is 'poor Manchester' – a city of uncertain employment, lifetime poverty, chronic ill-health and educational disadvantage' (Herd and Patterson, 2002). Some wards surrounding the newly regenerated city centre have unemployment levels as high as 19%; Manchester has the worst male mortality rate in England (Peck and Ward, 2002: 194), and high levels of long-term poverty. The suicide rate for Manchester is over 50% higher than the national average, while the infant mortality rate is nearly double the national average (Manchester City Council, 2003).

One area of Manchester which epitomises the turbulence and inequality caused by new Manchester's attempts to reposition itself in a globalised market as an Ideopolis is a suburb called Wythenshawe. It is a huge public housing development estate for 50,000 built from the 1930s onwards on the borders of Cheshire, nine miles from the city centre. It was designed to be a self-contained garden-city for the newly aspiring working class created by Barry Parker (who co-designed Letchworth Garden City) with well-built housing in the neo-cottage vernacular, generous gardens, green spaces and wide, curvilinear street design. It continued to develop up to the 1970s, but by then housing specifications were higher density and prefabricated; a collapse of spatial and housing standards which unfortunately coincided with the deindustrialisation of Manchester's manufacturing sector, particularly within Trafford Park, where many Wythenshawe residents once worked. The 1980s and 1990s saw steady further decline with high unemployment, decaying infrastructure, crime (and the fear of crime) and drug abuse problems. Yet since the mid 1990s, new energy has been placed into regeneration: replacing decayed housing stock with newer estates, many of them private and gated; addressing poor school and health statistics with Education and Health Action Zones; improved transport infrastructure with a new proposed tram system and rebuilding some of the depressed 1960s shopping centre in its midst.

What Wythenshawe now crystallises so powerfully is the global/local divides currently affecting urban space and which public theology needs to address. Wythenshawe contains the poorest electoral ward in England – Benchill – and yet lies only one mile from the source of New Manchester's wealth and its portal to the global market: its International Airport. An observable dynamic of globalisation is the way economic benefits created by global nodes or hubs (such as airports) are almost immediately conducted away to the adjoining city, region, national economy or elsewhere in the international market. The local community is effectively bypassed, except possibly to provide a pool of cheap labour. Thus Manchester's airport and its new second runway will expand its passenger traffic from 18 to 60 million per year in 2025, with access to 175 global destinations. It is now the third largest UK airport (behind Gatwick and Heathrow), employs 18,000 people directly and a further 16,500 indirectly. It injected last year £1.7 billion into the national economy, of which £600 million went to the North-West region. But in terms of its contribution to the local economy its effect is neglible. In 2002, only 11% of employees lived within six miles of the airport. 89% lived between seven and over 30 miles away, while estimates of people from Wythenshawe directly employed by the airport was a mere 25 (Wythenshawe Partnership, 2002).

Meanwhile, within Benchill, a new private estate built in the last two years on the back of the airport expansion, proposed tram link and cheap land is offering a new three bedroomed semi-detached starter home for £125,000. The average price of a three bedroomed council house (same size and with as much garden) across the road is £23,000; a price ratio of more than 4:1. In the 'old' Manchester of the 19th and 20th centuries one had to journey two or three miles out of the city slums to find that sort of differential. In the new 21st century Manchester it is a matter of a few yards. The new estate, called the Kensington Estate, has a high wall running round it, with luxury cars such as BMWs and Porsches on the driveways. Thanks to globalising pressures, the widening gap between rich and poor is now expressed locally by extreme proximity; and yet, as in Engels' day, the two groups may as well be inhabiting different universes.

Urban space in Manchester is being rapidly reconfigured as a direct result of its attempts to reposition itself as a global city. Urban space is being fragmented and gentrified with rich and poor living closer together, but in many ways further apart. The fragmentation of urban space into smaller enclaves, often ethnically monochrome and defended, not only makes poverty and marginalisation more difficult to engage with, but strikes at the heart of the churches' cherished notions of being at the heart of identifiable and strong communities.

Performative Theology: the Churches and Marginalisation

We return to earlier points about the changing nature of public theology and the processes of marginalisation that it is having to address, including the struggle of many institutional church communities to engage with evolving forms of urban space and the 'communities' that now live in them. We will argue that we can see it as a case study of the churches' attempts to develop theology that is both *public* and 'performative' (Graham, 2002). Yet it also concerns the importance of local *church* – and urban church strategy amongst marginalised communities – as a location for developing public theology.

Running alongside local and global experiences of marginalisation is the story of marginalised *churches* in Manchester. The gradual decline of most mainstream denominations in Britain and Western Europe through the 20th century suddenly accelerated dramatically in that historic generation from the 1960s to the present. The Anglican diocese of Manchester lost 60% of its membership, and if present trends continue, it will cease to exist in any effective way by 2040. Many churches in Manchester therefore now face great difficulties, including questions of sheer survival. So just as we can identify communities facing severe difficulties through the Index of Multiple Deprivation, so we can identify local churches facing severe difficulties. Indeed, what is particularly informative is the profound overlap between them. So two thirds of these churches fall within the most deprived 10% of communities. It suggests profound linkages between marginalised churches in marginalised communities in a nation deeply divided by such processes, and a Church and Christianity increasingly disconnected from public as well as private relevance. And that is matter of profound concern for public theology, because, as Tracy recognises, the church is one of three essential locations for promoting such theology. So, learning from the church's engagement with marginalisation processes must therefore contribute to developing contemporary public theology. For example, in Manchester, two ways of being church illustrate this potential source for public theology formation.

On the one hand, there is the emerging understanding of the church as 'networking' (Atherton, 2003:132 - 8). In the diocese of Manchester this is particularly evidenced by an evolving strategic engagement with a conurbation marked by a multifaceted marginalisation. Beginning in 1998, with the report *Changing Church and Society*, this developed a strategy of promoting more effective churches in more effective communities as targeted response to the vicious cycle of marginalised churches in marginalised communities, recognition that their regeneration was therefore intimately linked to their partnership in a common task through a series of collaborations and networking. It has led to a prioritising intervention in the most difficult communities and churches as embodiment of the theological principle of a 'bias for inclusivity' (Atherton, 2003: 117 - 122).

On the other hand, that strategic approach is also embodied in the "local" church as locations for multistrategy programmes promoting the community's development, and through that its own: a profoundly interactive relationship between theology and society for their mutual benefit. It is powerfully productive of a whole series of rich insights into urban living, which represents churches as both testing ground for, but also contributor to, a performative public theology. And that process will be enriched by the equally essential contribution to the formation of public theology by contextual analysis and the traditioning of the academy. And that multifaceted, multidimensional approach to building up public theology today reflects, of course, the multifaceted, multidimensional and multicausal nature of contemporary problematics such as marginalisation within the emerging contemporary global context. It is a powerful embodiment of the connection of local through national into global but then proceeding into a whole series of other interconnections.

The generation from the 1960s to the present has transformed Manchester and increasingly the world from an industrial society of mills, mines and factories to a post-industrial society of technological theme parks and out-of-town shopping complexes. This transition from more production-oriented to more consumption-oriented context affects every area of life, from family and personal relationships to the practice of politics and an increasingly post-modern culture. It profoundly relates to plurality and choice, not least in religious life, and is powerfully symbolised by the embedding of faiths in what has historically been a one faith society. But equally it is a plurality which informs the public responses of Christianity in terms of its implications for interdisciplinary studies and practical partnerships between government, business, and voluntary sector (Atherton, 2002).

The coming of Cosmopolis?

The final image of the city for the twenty-first century, that of Cosmopolis, illuminates the same issues of how social analysis is deployed to help us understand its foundations and dynamics; offers a metaphor for the human and moral values underpinning patterns of inclusion and exclusion; and helps us consider what a public theology might bring in terms of a performative presence and witness of faith by the churches.

The meaning of Cosmopolis is exemplified in the work of radical urban planner and geographer Leonie Sandercock (1998; 2003). She envisages a heterogeneous, culturally diverse city of the future that is fully the product of global economic and demographic forces, yet also embodies progressive values of inclusivity, pluralism and tolerance. The coming to birth of Cosmopolis depends on recognition of those in power of the frequently exclusive function of hegemonic discourses of urban planning, integration and development, and seeks instead to develop an entirely new kind of democratic process within which voices of diversity can flourish. Whereas Cottonopolis and Ideopolis seem to be cities whose narratives are told by the victors, however, Sandercock's Cosmopolis embodies two radically different principles. The first is that this is a city whose future is premised not on exclusion or the polarisation of social groups, but on what Sandercock terms 'the politics of inclusion' (2003: 47). The task of the urban planner, in particular, is that of facilitating spaces and places in which the multiple histories of many communities can flourish, which respect cultural diversity and incorporate into the body politic former-ly excluded groups such as women, indigenous communities and gay/lesbian/ transgendered people.

'The future multicultural city – *cosmopolis* – cannot be imagined without an acknowledgement of the politics of difference; ... a belief in inclusive democracy; and the diversity of the social justice claims of the disempowered communities in our existing cities. If we want to work towards a politics of inclusion, then we had better have a good understanding of the exclusionary effects of planning's past practices. And if we want to plan in the future for multiple publics, acknowledging and nurturing the full diversity of the many social groups in the multicultural city, then we need to develop a new kind of multicultural literacy.' (Sandercock, 2003: 47)

Urban Planning is therefore a vital process, and not only a matter of the design of the built environment, but a one of engineering political spaces in which the scope of citizenship, participation and governance are negotiated. These are decisions about the management of space, goods and services, po-pulations and power; and the planner can either help or hinder processes of emancipation and empowerment.

The second dimension of Cosmopolis' radical conceptualisation of the ur-ban is the extent to which it eschews the modernist project of rational city planning in which technical urban design is the panacea for all social problems. Such planning theory rests on universalised, centralist provision, in which the authority of the planning process is derived from its perceived status as posi-tivist, value-neutral science. Instead, it is committed to a more complex, more democratic process of consultation and advocacy, in which planners acknow-ledge the necessity of a heterogeneity of provision, of interventions founded on local partnerships, and where planners' interventions are acknowledged as explicitly geared to community empowerment:

'I want a city where people can cartwheel across pedestrian crossings wi-thout being arrested for playfulness; where everyone can paint the sidewalks, and address passers-by without fear of being shot; where there are places of stimulus and places of meditation; where there is music in public squares, and street performers don't have to have a portfolio and a permit, and street vendors co-exist with shopkeepers. I want a city where people take pleasure in shaping and caring for their environment and are encouraged to do so; where neighbours plant bokchoy and taro and broad beans in community gardens. I want a city where my profession contributes to all of the above, where city planning is a war of liberation fought against dumb, featureless public space; against STARchitecture, speculators, and benchmarkers; against the multiple sources of oppression, domination and violence; where citizens wrest from space new possibilities, and immerse themselves in their cultures while respecting those of their neighbours, collectively forging new hybrid cultures and spaces.' (Sandercock, 2003: 208)

Sandercock's writing may appear utopian, even over-romantic; perhaps she should recognise the ambivalence, even danger, of urban life, and acknowledge that the 'underside' will always be with us. Critics may justifiably challenge Sandercock for her comparative neglect of the necessity of economic uplift, and especially the importance of wealth creation leading to sustainable employment, as necessary, if not sufficient, criteria, for urban well-being. Yet Sandercock's celebration of the heterogeneity and spontaneity of Cosmopolis must be seen as in part a protest against the traditions of urban planning and policy which embodies a kind of 'environmental determinism' (Amin, Massey and Thrift, 2000:3) which over-rides the interests of its human inhabitants, and which ignores conflicts of interest which bear no relation to lived reality. It is also an eschewal of the assumptions of planning processes founded on top-down, means-end rationality in favour of more participative, democratic models based on practical wisdom (Sandercock, 2003: 209).

'"The public realm" is too often evoked as a neutral space where all can come together unproblematically. Yet we know this not to be the case. Public space at its worst can be the site of one group's dominance over others. At its best it can be a place of active engagement and debate. The city is a place of difference, and that includes different interests. A policy which does not square up to that will not address the underlying problems.' (Amin, Massey and Thrift, 2000:4)

If the first two themes of urban growth and regeneration – social theories of change, and patterns of power and exclusion – figure prominently in Sandercock's vision of Cosmopolis, then the role of public theology – or, more precisely, perhaps, religion or *spirituality* – is also present. Sandercock advances a positive role of religion in Cosmopolis, as a significant source of community cohesion, and as a wellspring of resistance to the technical-instrumental values of modernist planning schemes. At its best, too, religion as a source of what other authors term 'social capital' (Morisy, 2004), also provides resources for important dialogue between faith-communities, and thus holds the potential to be a tool of greater tolerance and multi-culturalism (Sandercock, 2003: 125). If the condition of Cosmopolis is to be one of pluralism and heterogeneity, then Sandercock has high hopes for religious practices and values to function, at a sociological level, as a kind of 'moral infrastructure' of belonging and integrating. For Sandercock, it is part of the task of nourishing a new, creative imagination of city life, informed and sustained by narrative, ritual, art and spirituality (2003: 225 - 228).

Certainly Sandercock's analysis chimes in with empirical research carried out in parts of Britain in recent years, which draws similar conclusions as to the integrative power of religion, of its (perhaps unique) capacity to mobilise its membership into wider service within the community (Farnell *et al*, 2003; Devine, 2003): faith-communities as extraordinarily committed to the *long-term* regeneration of the city; as providers of social support services, as unrivalled sources of volunteer labour, and as bearers of positive values of active citizenship. Nevertheless, it is important that Sandercock's valorization of faith, or spirituality, is not confined simply to an oppositional form of affective values which are seen as only representing ethnic minority or first-peoples/indigenous communities, yet in other ways fall short of engaging with 'mainstream' culture. In contemporary, postmodern, regenerating cities, faith-communities must be wary of either being co-opted by governments to provide token representation for minority or marginalised communities, or simply as compliant providers of pastoral care or superficial demonstrations of multiculturalism. They can also be forces of social dysfunction as well as cohesion within the wider community, as attested to in recent British research on regeneration and renewal in UK cities and towns (Farnell, 2003).

The church in Cosmopolis

More research is needed to identify the emerging patterns of church that are engaging with the post-modern pluralism identified in Sandercock's Cosmopolis. However, current research by the William Temple Foundation (William Temple Foundation, 2003) into contributions by churches to local civil society in parts of Manchester, perhaps begins to define early contours. The Foundation is working with four different church communities in East Manchester, once the industrial heartland of the city but now host to the Commonwealth Games stadium and a new Asda-Walmart hypermarket.

The first church is a traditional Anglican parish which includes a mixture of existing unemployed or low-wage families alongside young professionals living in city-style apartments surrounded by new leisure and shopping outlets and eateries. Reflecting on the continuing presence of the church and its Catholic-oriented liturgy, the vicar says its vision is not to 'do', but to 'be', and incarnate 'the value of a different rhythm and a sense of quiet, a healing space and long-term sustainability.'

A few hundred metres away, an independent charismatic church has been working for five years out of borrowed premises with the youngsters of the area. This experience has opened the eyes of the church members to the complexity of the poverty and drug-related issues they are living amongst. They have learned the value of working in partnership (including, for example, liberal churches and secular agencies) and being open and accountable for what they do. They are valued as a key contributor to the future fortunes of the community. Their evangelical faith is now mixed with a strong engagement in political change, albeit with humour, toughness and growing subtlety.

A stone's throw away is a tiny Baptist church, meeting in a soon to be demolished mission hall. Comprised of a dozen elderly residents, with a leadership influenced by liberation theology techniques such as participatory Bible study and narrative sharing, the church space opens its doors to asylum seekers and those struggling with poor mental health. The building is used as a complementary therapy centre, and a thick piece of buttered toast and mug of sweet tea cost 10 pence (15 €uro cents). When the building is demolished, the congregation will invest its money in partnership with local doctors to build a healthy living centre which will combine health care with community facilities. The church will meet in the 'multi-faith' space that will be part of the new complex.

Fourthly, a church-based project has recently emerged with the specific purpose of operating within a 'network' model. It has been at the forefront in creating a unique participatory budgeting exercise with the local authority, as well as setting up a wide range of networks across the city, designed to inform local communities of government regeneration opportunities, support grassroots responses and offer specialised support (for example, disability and gender perspectives). Its employees include both faith and non-faith based personnel.

The significance of these case studies is threefold. Firstly, no one model meets the totality of need. Instead, each offers a specialist contribution to the needs of a rapidly changing urban locality. Secondly, each church is prepared to work in partnership with others, but not to the detriment of their essential identity and belief. It is a pragmatic, multi-disciplinary approach that prefers to work with a grass-roots ecumenism. Thirdly, these churches reflect a spectrum between institutional and non-institutional forms, which reflects the balanced approach required between different forms of governance as advocated by political theorists such as Wainwright (2003) and Young (2000). The church of the Cosmopolis is a mixed economy of methodologies and theologies that holds a vision for simultaneous macro and micro-levels of change.

Conclusion

Sandercock's celebration of the multicultural vision of Cosmopolis confirms many of the themes already identified, not only in terms of important factors affecting our understanding of urban change and development, but also the very contours of public, practical theology. Firstly, there is the centrality of political economy, of understanding the very dynamics of urban growth and wealth-creation; but this reveals itself to be a multi-faceted phenomenon, depending not only on the crude materialism of capital and labour, but other factors to do with adequate transport, thriving and innovative city cultures, good governance and availability of an educated, motivated workforce. Secondly, we have pinpointed the necessity of exercising a kind of *hermeneutics of suspicion* in relation to these very processes: is the success, even the self-image, of a thriving city premised on the impoverishment or marginalisation of many of its citizens? In which case, what strategies of empowerment and participation can be developed to tell the stories of the 'underside' of our great cities as well as those of the victors? And thirdly, we have developed some proposals for the shape of public theology: that it is a profoundly *performative* theology, judged in its effectiveness and authenticity by its capacity to mobilise faithful witness for the good of the city, and embodied in the local presence of congregations and communities which actively practise their values in programmes of personal care, active citizenship, neighbourhood renewal, partnership and social transformation.

References

Ackroyd, P. (2000) 'Review: The Voices of Morebath' *The Times*. 15 August.
Amin, A., Massey, D. and Thrift, N. (2000) *Cities for the Many, Not the Few*. London: The Policy Press.
Atherton, J.R. (1994) *Social Christianity: A Reader*. London: SPCK.
Atherton, J.R. (1997) 'Church and Society in the North West, 1760-1997', in Ford, C., Powell, M., and Wyke, T., (eds.) *The Church in Cottonopolis*. Lancashire and Cheshire Antiquarian Society.
Atherton, J.R (2002) *Public Theology for Changing Times*. London: SPCK.
Atherton, J.R. (2003) *Marginalisation*. London: SCM Press.
Baker, C. and Graham, E.L. (eds) (2004) *Religious Capital in a Regenerating Community*. Manchester: William Temple Foundation.
Briggs, A. (1968) *Victorian Cities*. Harmondsworth: Penguin.
Castells, Manuel (1989) *The Informational City*. Oxford: Blackwell.
Devine, J. (2003) *Faith in England's Northwest*. Warrington: North-west Development Agency.

Dicken, P. (2002) 'Global Manchester: from Globaliser to Globalised', in Peck, J. and Ward, K. (eds) *City of Revolution: Restructuring Manchester*. Manchester University Press.

Duffy, E. (2001) *The Voices of Morebath: Reformation and Rebellion in an English Village*. Yale University Press.

Engels, F. [1845] (1969) *The Condition of the Working Class in England*. London: Panther.

Farnell, R., Furbey, R., Hills, Shams Al-Haqq, S., Macey, M. and Smith, G. (2003) *"Faith" in Urban Regeneration? Engaging faith communities in urban regeneration*. London: Polity Press.

Garreau, J. (1991) *Edge City: Life on the New Frontier*. London: Doubleday.

Giddens, A. (1994) *Beyond Left and Right*. London: Polity Press.

Graham, E.L. (1999) 'Towards a Practical Theology of Embodiment', in Ballard, P., and Couture, P., eds., *Globalisation and Difference: Practical Theology in a World Context*. Cardiff Academic Press.

Graham, E.L. (2002) *Transforming Practice: Pastoral Theology in an Age of Uncertainty*. 2nd edition, Eugene, OR: Wipf & Stock.

Herd, D. and Patterson, T. (2002) 'Poor Manchester: old problems and new deals' in Peck, J. and Ward, K. (eds) *City of Revolution – Restructuring Manchester*. Manchester University Press.

Hollenbach, D. (2002) *The Common Good and Christian Ethics*. Cambridge University Press.

Jarl, A-C. (2000) *Women and Economic Justice*. Uppsala University Press.

Kidd, A.J. (2002) *Manchester*. 3rd edition, Edinburgh University Press.

Lebacqz, K. (1987) *Justice in an Unjust World*. Augsburg Publishing House.

Manchester City Council (2003), Key Health Statistics for Manchester [online], available at: www.manchester.gov.uk/health/jhu/intelligence/city.htm (accessed 22/07/04).

Markall, G. (1980) *The Best Years of Their Lives*. Manchester: William Temple Foundation.

Morisy, A. (2004) *Journeying Out: A New Approach to Christian Mission*. London: Continuum.

Roberts, R. (1971) *The Classic Slum*. Manchester University Press.

Sandercock, L. (1998) *Towards Cosmopolis: Planning for Multicultural Cities*. Chichester: Wiley.

Sandercock, L. (2003) *Cosmopolis II: Mongrel Cities in the 21st Century*. London: Continuum.

Schreiter, R. (1997) *The New Catholicity: Theology Between the Global and the Local*. New York: Orbis.

Soja, E. (2000) *Postmetropolis: Critical Studies of Cities and Regions*. Oxford: Blackwell.

Temple, W. (1942) *Christianity and Social Order*. Harmondsworth: Penguin.

Tawney, R.H. (1972) *Commonplace Book*. Cambridge University Press.

Tracy, D. (1981) *The Analogical Imagination*. New York: Crossroad.

Wainwright, H. (2003) *Reclaim the State*. London: Verso.

Waterman, A. (1992) *Revolution, Economics and Religion: Christian Political Economy, 1793 - 1833*. Cambridge University Press.

Weber, M. [1905] (1970) *The Protestant Ethic and the Spirit of Capitalism*. London: Unwin.

Westwood, A. and Nathan, M. (2002) *Manchester: Ideopolis? – Developing a knowledge capital*. London: The Work Foundation.

William Temple Foundation (2003) *Regenerating Communities: A Theological and Strategic Critique – Mapping the Boundaries*. Manchester: William Temple Foundation (www.wtf.org.uk).

Wythenshawe Partnership (2002) *Wythenshawe Partnership Evaluation 2002*.

Young, I.M. (1990) *Justice and the Politics of Difference*. Princeton University Press.

Young, I.M (2000) *Inclusion and Democracy*. Oxford University Press.

From the Lord and His Servants to God and Her Friends

The importance of 'equality' in a world of violence

Riet Bons-Storm

Introduction: the template of inequality

Daily the media show violence everywhere: in homes, on the streets, in schools and in the wide world. One cannot avoid being shocked by this abundance of violence. In our society violence is often considered a justified means to achieve one's goal: war to achieve peace, security and prosperity for some. Violence occurs when a person or a group of persons induce pain, eliminate or diminish the possibility of people to live in order to get what is wanted. Violence is related to power-relations. On the one hand we see the violence of the powerful, forcing the people considered dependent to think or act according to the will of the powerful. On the other hand there is the violence of people who are made or kept dependent: the violence of impotence, born out of frustration and anger. The powerful confiscate the logic to justify their behaviour: the master owns the tools to build and maintain his own house.

Many attempts are made to end violence of all sorts. Psychologists, counsellors and ambassadors do their best to solve conflicts leading to violence, trying to establish reconciliations and peace, but often to little avail. Often conflicts end by reversing the positions of power. The oppressed become the new oppressors and new violence may occur. Nothing really is changed. The same system is just put upside down. This makes me think that we have to dig deeper to end violence in society. As violence is associated with power I assume we have to think deeper about power. The problem is not 'Who is in power?', but ultimately: 'Which system, which images about power guide our thinking?'. In this article I focus on this question.

In our culture, but also in our dominant theologies, I detect a certain 'template' that molds human relationships. Throughout his classic book *The Interpretation of Cultures* (1973), Clifford Geertz uses this idea of a template, typical for a certain culture, that sets limits for behaviour and guides thought, emotions and practices along predictable paths.

Earlier in my work (Bons-Storm, 1992, 46-68) I argued that in Western patriarchal culture the template for power is understood as a *ladder*, constituting a hierarchy. The ladder is much wider at the base than at the top. It is rather difficult to imagine, but one has to combine the image of a ladder with the image of a pyramid (Schüssler Fiorenza, 1992, 114-118). Each higher rung is narrower than the lower. At the top there is only room for one: the almighty, the supreme power.

The ladder/pyramid-template for relationships is marked by *inequality*. Inequality means that in a relationship the one is considered to be more powerful than the other. The template for relationships we live by induces competition, striving for' higher' positions, more status, keeping others in dependence and obedience, if needed by violence. Inequality breeds violence: violence from the powerful and the violence of impotence.

This template of inequality is found also in dominant Christian traditions. The deeply rooted patterns of thinking and behaviour in society and religion reflect and strengthen each other. I argue that the template of inequality stays so strong in our societies because the basic inequality, typical for our dominant hierarchical Christian tradition, has achieved the status of norm for human relationships. Often violence, rooted in inequality, is sanctioned by religious arguments. In Christian tradition God is the One Almighty, the All-Powerful. He sits at the summit of the power-pyramid. The highest virtue is obedience to those who are considered 'above' oneself, ultimately God and those who are considered to know his will: theologians and the ordained. Many governments in our world still maintain that they reign 'by the grace of God', as all power comes ultimately from God. The likeness to this almighty ladder-God – being male for instance – helps people to attain to relatively high rungs. Culture and religion are intertwined at this point.

In this article I will explore this template of inequality in Christian tradition and look for means to change it, so room is created for a more equal society, assuming that this could be a means to diminish the need for violence in our lives.

Ladder and circle in society and Christian tradition

Power can be described as the possibility to influence and alter the thoughts, emotions and actions of others. This possibility can used in a negative or in a positive sense. Power is used in a positive sense when the possibility to influence the other is emancipative. In a relationship where positive power is used, power is always temporal and attached to certain domains of life. The goal is to end the power-relationship that was temporally inequal and achieve a relationship that is more equal. When the – temporally dependent – other has acknowledged her/his possibilities, her/his strong and weak points, the temporally inequal relationship becomes an equal one. Positive power is possible in a template of equality, where people can be imagined as equals, where mutuality is a rule, where people with just a few possibilities are not considered weak in a negative sense, they are not' losers'. The image of the template of equality is the circle. The ladder-template induces people to use power in a negative sense as it means coercing people – who are considered to be on lower rungs – to think, feel and act in a way, in which people do not have the freedom – or are aware of their possibility – to think and to act according to their own gifts and insights. Violence is there, where the one overrules the other, belittles the other or 'puts the other down' with words, jokes, gestures, or hurts the other's body, psyche, soul or cherished possessions. Violence is power used either to coerce the other to identify with the ideas and emotions of the one, or, if this proves to be impossible, to weaken, remove or kill the other. Violence is always aimed at victory over and against the other in order to obtain or come nearer to a place at the top, ultimately being the one who is on top. Power in ladder-thinking tends to focus not only on the possibilities, projected to a person or group on a certain rung, but also on the person her/himself. One's place on a certain rung tends to cling to the person, whatever her/his possibilities and gifts may be. Conflicts are avoided if everybody knows his or her place, and does not think or act 'above her or his station'. One can see in our society that the conditions of being on a high rung of the power-ladder are having a great quantity of the following qualities:

– being male/fatherly,
– being born into a prestigious family,
– being tall (men only) or attractive (women),
– being White,
– having properties or embody the promise to achieve them by being strong, young or able bodied,
– having formal education.

According to the Western ladder-template for human relations the result of the (quantity of) these qualities determines the rung a person attains on the ladder of power. Sex, class, race/ethnicity, and the amount of possessions and education determine the amount of somebody's power.

Even if more persons sit on the same rung of the ladder, there is a great risk of inequality. Competition is always present. Consciously or half consciously questions arise: who is the best, the most clever, the strongest of us? Who has the highest status? Who has the best opportunity to go higher? The predicta-

ble paths ingrained in the Christian/Western template of power and authority
make it very difficult to imagine more people sharing one rung of the ladder
comfortably.

It is, for instance, for Israel and the Palestinians very difficult to think about
sharing the land and sharing the status of citizen with all its rights. Sharing a
status is unthinkable in the dominant template of power, so competition and
violence are always near. In this conflict Israel is the more powerful, with the
super-power U.S.A. as its ally. God the Almighty sanctions its claims on the
whole land. Violence is considered legal, because the Almighty God promised
the land to the people of Israel thousands of years ago. The Palestinian Authority is the less powerful. Even in the Arabic world it is often not considered
opportune to antagonize the wishes of Israel/the U.S.A. The Palestinians have
fewer resources, their water supply is far worse than that of the state of Israel.
The recent building of the Wall, not on the 'Green Line' of the situation of
1967, but far inland, not only takes away a great part of Palestinian land, but
also causes a humanitarian disaster, taking away important life resources from
Palestinians. Palestinians answer this violence with the violence of impotence,
often called 'terrorism'. Even many secularized Dutch people are pro-Israel,
because they know it as the Promised Land. According to the ladder-template
there can only be one god. He can only be trusted to be and stay on the highest point because He is considered to be male, a father, the whole world his,
he is the fount of wisdom and not coloured. To imagine God as female would
destroy the leading image, it is outside the boundaries of the template. In the
ladder-template with its strong patriarchal bias it is impossible to have as much
reveration and respect for a God imaged as female as it is for a male God.

The reality of violence

My own context, the Netherlands, is a thoroughly secularized country. Many
women and men are not so much atheist, as agnostic. God-talk is almost totally absent in public debates. A deep individualism shapes their consciousness.
One could say that they are very modern in their outlook on life: navigating on
their own private compass. From modernity however they plunged into postmodernity, into the elusiveness of truth and into diversity in all sections of life:
racial, cultural, religious. This breeds insecurity. Individualistic as the Dutch
may be, most of them are no anarchists, so they have to construct their attitude towards authorities. Being more and more aware of economic and political
ties with the rest of Europe and the world, this attitude to authorities becomes
more urgent and complex. Dutch people feel dependent on the bigger nations
of this world. In the crisis around Iraq for instance many people were as much
against Saddam Hussain as against President Bush, because they opposed Sad-

dam Hussain's dictatorship and oppression of many Iraqis on the one hand, but on the other hand they opposed president Bush and his assumption to be the only super-power in the world.

There is violence on the streets, shootings in schools, violence against coloured people, violence against Muslims, violence against women inside and outside the family. We have a Christian Democratic government acting along conservative lines: the weak and poor have a very low status, the strong and rich are rewarded.

Disturbed by the growing violence in society the prime minister promotes more attention to 'values and norms', meaning the Christian ones, emphasizing 'family values'. Traditional family values mirror the ladder-template: the man may assume that he is entitled to a better job and a higher status than his wife. Ethnicity is an important issue. For women – the more for Black women – it is difficult to break the glass ceiling in all kinds of institutions – especially the churches and the academy – and to achieve leadership positions. More and more women are becoming pastors in the Protestant churches. "Men are searching for other arenas" is the title of an article in a leading newspaper, *Trouw*, read mostly by Christian people (February 3, 2004). Women are still considered unequal to men in tasks that lack prestige. "To be exempted from caring tasks is a sign of male power," said Joan C. Tronto in a lecture in the Netherlands in 1994 (see Tronto, 1993). This inequality reigning inside and outside the family, gives possibilities for violence. I assume the template for relationships, including the relationship to authority, is still a rudimentary Christian one in the Netherlands. This helps the ladder-template to stay strong. On billboards at the side of roads and at railway stations an attractive young woman is pictured lying down in a graceful position, wearing scanty but beautiful lingery. "Forever Eve" is the text advertizing underwear. The Grand Narrative of Christianity may have gone underground, it still strongly influences the discourse and imagery in everyday life, constructing the template of power and as such constructing the common sense or the common order of things which are ideologically constructed yet have assumed a natural and almost biological presence in our life (Althaus-Reid, 2000, 11 and Gramsci, 1971, 33).

The two voices of Christianity

Christianity speaks with two voices. On the one hand Christian theology developed messages like: "Blessed are the poor", "Who does not receive me – Jesus – like a child, shall not enter the Kingdom of Heaven", "The last will be the first". In my opinion these messages are very important in the gospel. One could say: they *are* the gospel. Nevertheless these messages are in our societies not more than a weak counter-voice, overruled and lost in the Christian symphony of dominant theology. In this theology the main themes are: inequality is unavoidable; only one can be the boss, victory through battle, albeit bloody, slaying enemies, with words mainly, but if need be, with arms. Onward Christian soldiers. Having means and properties became mostly understood as a just reward for the righteous and able bodied industrious people, a sign of God's blessing, giving the rich the upper hand.

I would argue that this theology, deeply influenced by what is most common in most cultures, has shaped Western thinking for so long that it has had a devastating influence on public thought, public actions and decisions and public theology. Sometimes church and academy explicitly voice this dominant Christian message, justifying war, inequality in relations between the sexes, justifying tax-cuts for the rich, opposing healthcare for the poor, and so on.

Thinking about God outside the ladder-template

Sallie McFague's project to design new models of God is akin to my project. She emphasizes the importance of the willingness to change theological constructions, for instance God-imagery like 'father' and 'king'.

Theological constructions are 'houses' to live in for a while, with windows partly open and doors ajar; they become prisons when they no longer allow us to come and go, to add a room or take one away – or if necessary, to move on and build a new house (McFague, 1987, 27).

The medieval theologian, mystic and poetess Hadewich, who lived in the 12th century, understood the relationship between the Divine and human beings as equal. In her ninth letter she writes:

Where the depth of his wisdom is, there he shall teach you who he is and how sweet the one lover dwells in the other in such a way that none of them knows her/himself anymore. They enjoy one another mutually, mouth in mouth and heart in heart and body in body and soul in soul, while one sweet divine nature flows through both of them. (Van Bladel, 2002, 28, translation from the Dutch by Bons-Storm)

In Hadewich's thinking God's power is understood as positive, its aim to bring God and a human being in all-absorbing mutual love, as equals. The starting-point for Hadewich's theology was not guilt and salvation through cross and blood, but creation. She used such a different theological construction from the dominant theologies of our time, mostly based on sin, guilt and redemption by substitution.

I agree with Sallie McFague who contends that the imagery, the metaphors used for God are right if they have salvific power: the possibility to liberate people from every oppression, from within and from without to open them up for the mystery of God's love and inspiration. If the heart of the gospel is the salvific power of God, triumphalist metaphors cannot express that reality in our time, whatever the appropriateness may have been in the past. And this is so even if God's power is seen as benevolence rather than domination. (McFague, 1987, 69)

In his book about sexual abuse, The Abuse of Power (1991) James Poling writes that the imagery of God as a powerful figure, who has the freedom to be wrathful or compassionate, characterized by lack of mutuality and accounta- bility, has no incentive to end the abuse of power among human beings. "Like the perpetrator of sexual violence, such images of God assume prerogatives of unilateral power over those who are unprotected." (Poling, 1991, 174) Poling opts for an image of a God "who lives within the relational web as a fully active and interdependent partner" (ibidem). Such a God-image has salvific power.

Thinking about God and human beings as equals does not mean that God and humans are alike. Within the boundaries of the ladder-template the holi- ness of God is imaged as being the One who is special because He is at the top. Within the circle-template God is holy because God, female/male, mo- ther/father, is in the centre, the focus of all who are standing in the circle, in- spiring them all. An image of God outside the ladder-template can have female and/or male traits. Feminist theology, a theology of persons for centuries socia- lized into the idea that their place was on the lower rungs, but touched by the liberating love of the Divine, does not lightly use names for God such as Lord, King or Almighty Father. Feminist theology even looks at the imagery of the shepherd with suspicion, because it makes the believers into sheep. Dorothee Soelle writes about "God and her friends" (Soelle, 1988, 13). This imagery is totally different from "The Lord and his servants". It affects us differently, it in- spires us to a new attitude towards God: an attitude of intimacy and respect, as is usual among friends. A new imagery of equality brings about an attitude of mutual responsibility, of dialogue about serious matters and laughing together about what is good in life. In this light Elisabeth Schüssler Fiorenza descri- bes the early Christian movement as a "discipleship of equals", as "equality in the spirit", as ekklesia, that is, "the democratic decision-making assembly of equals". This assembly of equals is conceptualized as counter-term to the struc- tures of exclusion and domination that were institutionalized in Greco-Roman patriarchy (Schüssler Fiorenza, 1993: 105 - 106). The notion of a discipleship of equals is still a counter-term to our patriarchal ladder-template, but it can still inspire to change.

The long road towards another template

As the ladder-template is dominant is our religion and culture we are all socia- lized into thinking within its boundaries. It can be assumed that not the urge to win is typical for human beings of all times, but the urge to survive with dignity. The conditions of what brings forth a sense of dignity can be changed. Dignity need not only be attached to winning, succeeding at all costs, being rich, being (like a) male, being White. In order to change the template the value-system has to be changed. Deliberately people have to be trained to hold mutuality and sharing, mutual dependency and emancipating others in high regard. 'The neighbour' has to recapture its true meaning: it is somebody *next* to us, not above or under us. People have to be aware where their power lies: the possibility to influence others, to use it in a deliberate way. The choice between positive and negative power has to be highlighted. Every charisma, even the smallest one, can be used in positive power. The highest value will not longer be to be in control of everything, but a shared life of equal opportunities. This can be heard as synonymous with the biblical idea of justice and peace for all.

The idea of positive power, limited, focused on equality, mutual respect and emancipation, has to be further explored. When there is no ladder, no pyramid, whose top has place for only one, competition may become less necessary, and with it aggression and violence. Sharing power becomes possible. The other is less threatening. In such a relationship the power shifts from the one to the other, back and forth. Sometimes the one is the strongest one on some point and educates the other, sometimes the other educates and leads the one. The goal is a society – in all its constituencies, from marriage, family to university and state where people come to see what they are worth, what they can achieve and what their limitations are. Limitations do not necessarily put people on a lower rung, as the ladder is no more. All people are entitled to respect.

Changing a template is changing a culture. The enormity of the endeavour can lame us, only the conviction of the necessity of change can keep us going. Theologians working at the university, and pastors trained by them, are key persons. Religious education, preaching and pastoral work are the means. A precise and deliberate use of words and images is needed. Sustained and guided by a Christian community, gradually more used to new imagery and language about the Divine, individual people can be trained to rear their children using positive power and the ideal of equality. Socialization in and outside the home can be guided, constructed. The value of equality, emancipation and respect for so-called losers can be introduced consciously into the education of the young, practised in our daily life in great and small decisions and practices. No prize-winning contests anymore. No more official rewards for the best this or the best that, re-thinking of real democracy and voting practices. No glorification of winning or of violence anymore. This may be a long road, but worth exploring.

In our attempts to overcome the template of inequality and its inherent hierarchical images it helps perhaps to use – for the time being – non-andromorphic images for the Divine. The Divine can be understood as Holy Spirit, Creative and Redemptive Energy blowing through the world and all its societies and constituencies. The Spirit touches people and aims at their emancipation: the situation where they know what their strengths are and where their weaknesses lie. Giving them courage to develop their strengths and to bear their weaknesses without shame. This Creative Energy can do nothing on its own. It has to work together with human beings in order to fulfil its desire: a world of togetherness in respect and love. The kingdom of God can be thought of a world according to God's desire and longing.

A new template: a vision, far away? I look at it as something to work and think for. This needs a lot of honest thinking, of critique of our daily practices in family, academy, politics and religion. It requests of us a perpetual vigilance when we speak of God in church and in society as a whole."We are responsible at least for the language we engrave on the minds and prayers of others." (Ramshaw, 1990, 169) I am convinced that unless we change the basic ideas of our theology, peace will never come.

References

Althaus-Reid, Marcella (2000) *Indecent Theology: Theological Perversions in Sex, Gender and Politics*. London/New York: Routledge.

Bladel, Frans van (2002) *Hadewich. Die Minne es Al*. Leuven: Davidsfonds/Literair.

Bons-Storm, Riet (1992) *Pastoraat als Bondgenootschap*. Kampen: Kok.

Geertz, Clifford (1973) *The Interpretation of Cultures*. New York: Basic Books.

Gramsci, A. (1971) *Selections from the Prison Notebooks*. London: Lawrence and Wishart.

Mcfague, Sallie (1987) *Models of God: Theology for an Ecological Nuclear Age*. London: SCM Press.

Schüssler Fiorenza, Elisabeth (1992) *But She Said: Feminist Practices of Biblical Interpretation*. Boston: Beacon Press.

Schüssler Fiorenza, Elisabeth (1993) Discipleship of Equals. A Critical Feminist Ekklesia-logy of Liberation. London: SCM Press.

Poling, James Newton (1991) *The Abuse of Power: A Theological Problem*. Nashville: Abingdon Press.

Ramshaw, Gail (1990) 'The Gender of God' in Ann Loades (ed.) *Feminist Theology: A Reader*. London: SPCK, 168-180.

Soelle, Dorothee (1988) God is meer dan een man, feministisch theologische teksten. Baarn: Ten Have.

Tronto, Joan C. (1993) *Moral Boundaries: a Political Argument For an Ethic of Care*. New York/London: Routledge.

Pastoral Theology and Public Theology

Developments in the U.S.

Bonnie J. Miller-McLemore

When pastoral theologians in the United States talk about "public theology," they often have something different in mind than their colleagues in other countries. Broadly speaking, they lean toward more cognitive than practical, hands-on forms of public theology. Distinctive factors, internal and external to theological scholarship, have affected this conceptual orientation. The following essay identifies some of these factors. It draws on research on pastoral theology as public theology for a supplement of Abingdon Press's *Dictionary of Pastoral Care and Counseling* (Hunter, 1990) and incorporates observations from the International Academy of Practical Theology's 2003 Conference on public theology in Manchester, UK.

The 1990 *Dictionary* did not even include an entry on public theology. The only entry under "public" – "Public/private Interface" – directs users to other entries: "*See* Personal, Sense of. *See also* Prophetic/Pastoral Tension in Ministry; Shame." Pastoral theologians and counselors of the mid-twentieth century were remarkably invested in the personal. Enamored by amazing strides made by new psychologies, pastoral theologians correlated fresh understandings of the internal dynamics behind individual behavior with theological ideas about sin, love, and redemption and offered this package to a receptive U.S. population. This approach enlivened abstract, systematic espousal of doctrine from which many laity and some theologians were alienated. In claiming the "living human document" as primary text, rather than written documents, pastoral theologians brought to theory-bound doctrinal theology a wealth of vivid human experiences. The case study or verbatim, developed in clinical programs in the medical and social sciences, focused closely on particular interchanges and emotional, theological forces between and within individuals and a caregivers.

Over the past few decades, U.S. pastoral theologians have gradually shifted metaphor and emphasis. Several years ago I named the "living human web" a notable mutation of the "living human document" and one of the key developments in the field (1993; 1996; 1999). Other scholars also called attention to this (Graham, L., 1992; Patton, 1993; Gill-Austern, 1995; Couture, 1996). Today one rarely finds pastoral theological reflection that does not include some kind of "case" material. What has changed, however, is the way in which it is understood, analyzed, and positioned. Pastoral theologians now work hard to locate the case publicly, as part of a wider social and cultural web.

Pastoral theology's credibility as public theology will rest on clarity about the origins of this new orientation and conscientiousness about its implications. How far will this new direction carry the field? Will the focus be primarily on conceptual influence or political and social activism? Or are these two foci complementary to each other? Understanding trends behind the change in pastoral theology as public theology provides an initial step toward answering these questions.

General Trends Behind the Push for Public Theology

The constitutional separation of church and state in the U.S. has had considerable effect on the interplay between religion and the wider public. Public theology looks different in other countries where a Church is either established by the state (as in Britain) or disenfranchised (as in China). In the U.S., religion is allowed, even protected, from the state's encroachment. But great fear surrounds the reverse: the intrusion of religion into government. As a rule, the public is skittish about religion in the public sphere, not simply because modern science and technology undermine its validity, but also because historical claims about religious freedom seem to forbid its presence.

Evangelical and fundamentalist Christianity has heightened this anxiety. The media and the uninformed person on the street often equate a Christian view on any subject, whether family, abortion, or terrorism, with the Christian Right. Although many practical theologians in Western Europe bemoan Christianity's decline, the situation is more ambiguous in the U.S. Conservative forms of Christianity continue to grow in influence and numbers. Even among the former mainline, church attendance varies across the country. Meanwhile, since new immigration laws in the 1960s Islam, Hinduism, Buddhism, and other religions have grown. So, in contrast to countries where churches have moved from a dominant to a minority position (Heitink, 1999, 139, 142), pastoral theologians must negotiate a religiously pluralistic public in which certain forms of Christianity still prevail.

Several specific economic, political, and cultural developments have renewed interest in public theology. Under current market conditions, theological study does not attract resources since it does not directly promote capitalism's infrastructures. Divinity schools and seminaries lack the kind of wealthy constituencies that often support comparable institutions of professional education, such as medicine, law, and business. The constituency with which many theological schools associate – mainline Protestant denominations – have suffered financial hardships of their own. Newer conservative seminaries do not have long-standing resources. Hence, foundations that offer resources have had increasing influence on academic priorities. A variety of grants have propelled theologians to engage questions of Christianity's public role.

Major organizations, such as Lilly Endowment, Pew Charitable Trusts, and Henry R. Luce Foundation, have made Christianity's public role a funding initiative. Over the last decade, for example, several Lilly programs have engaged public problems, such as political conflict over the family. More generally, these organizations have funded innumerable conferences, projects, publications, and university centers aimed at bridging academy, church, and the wider public (see Miller-McLemore, 2000).

In part, Lilly, Pew, Luce, and other foundations worry about the post-civil rights decline in Christianity's social activism and, as troubling, the Christian Right's increased ability to influence society through large conglomerate operations, such as Focus on the Family or Promise Keepers. Christianity, the implication seems to be, has more to offer the public than simplified proclamations about "family values", for example, or prayer in school. The desire is not to return to mainline hegemony but for greater understanding of Christianity's proper role in an increasingly diverse and religiously pluralistic society.

Interest in public theology arises on another more political front. In recent years, "faith-based organization" and "faith-based initiative" have become common catch phrases. In developing these concepts, politicians have renegotiated the delicate lines of state and church separation established by the First Amendment in order to direct tax monies to religious groups for the delivery of social services and community outreach programs. Even more surprising, some spokespersons express a relatively fresh openness to bringing faith perspectives to bear on national moral issues, such as overcoming racism or strengthening the family. Faced with ineffective governmental efforts to improve the welfare of the poor or to influence cultural norms, government looks afresh upon religious congregations as viable mediating institutions equipped to provide programs and values.

Finally, religion's de-privatization is also related to intellectual shifts. Public intellectuals question the value-free objectivity of science, Enlightenment's rationalistic disdain for particular traditions, and technology's ability to solve all dilemmas (Rorty, 1991; Kuhn, 1996; Keller, 1996; and Harding, 1991). Contrary to modern assumptions, some people argue that particular religious beliefs are not arbitrary, unimportant, or irrational but instead have a legitimate, even if necessarily delimited, place in public discourse and decisions (see Carter, 1994). People are more skeptical not only about science but also about the state and the market's ability to solve looming national and international problems, such as the increasing disparity between rich and poor with capitalism's expansion or the ongoing violence around gender, race, sexual orientation, and religion. Many people have begun to affirm the importance of community, tradition, and belief in sustaining democracy and addressing problems of the common good (Bellah, et al., 1985; Putnam, 2000). In the mid-1990s people began to talk about the essential resources of "civil society," the sphere standing between state and market, inclusive of organizations such as religious congregations (see Wolfe, 1989).

Interest in public theology is not just another way to talk about civil religion, however. The latter refers to a generic, watered-down fusion of democratic values and Christian belief or the influence upon political process of religious symbols with universal appeal and without ties to any denomination or group. Public religion instead involves religious beliefs and practices in all their particularities. And public theology, as distinct from public religion, means critical and constructive reflection upon particular religions (see Cady, 1993, 21-25).

Theological Trends

Factors internal to theological study have also kindled interest in public theology. The study of religion has not had a secure place in the U.S. academy, especially in state universities where even the shadow of faith commitments in the classroom comes under suspicion. Many previously religious-identified colleges have also gradually lost or purposively moved away from explicit religious confession or affiliation with denominational structures. This situation has led scholars to debate the proper public role of religion in the university (Schwehn, 1993; Sloan, 1994; Cherry, 1995; Marsden, 1997; and Burtchaell, 1998) and in a pluralistic society (Weitham, 1997; Audi and Wolterstorff, 1997; Thiemann, 1991, 1996; Pasewark and Paul, 1999).

From where, however, comes the term "public theology"? Theologians throughout history, such as Augustine and Martin Luther, have called Christianity a political force. What special meaning has the term acquired today in the postmodern context of the U.S.? Although the term appears earlier, it entered common usage in the mid-1980s. In particular, debates between University of Chicago's David Tracy and Yale's George Lindbeck codified the term and, in the process, pushed pastoral theology toward more cognitive modes of public theology. Liberation theology provided a counterweight to this conceptual leaning. Although the Chicago school primarily affected central individuals who came directly within its orbit, liberation theology's transformation of pastoral theology was more widespread. Although I do not intend to describe the Chicago-Yale controversy in detail or catalogue liberation theology's major spokespersons, it is important to explore how one side, the Chicago school, modified pastoral theology, and to identify how liberation theology suggests alternative directions.

The Influence of the Chicago School

When I use the phrase "Chicago school," I do not refer to University of Chicago's mid-century emphasis on process philosophy or its earlier 1890s' manifesto on pragmatism. I simply use it to capture how several prominent scholars influenced pastoral theology toward public theology through their sway over doctoral students. While I will focus on the impact of Tillich, Tracy, James Gustafson, and, Don Browning, other early twentieth century Chicago scholars, such as Shailer Mathews, and more recent figures, such as Martin Marty (1981), Robin Lovin (1986), and Clark Gilpin (1990, 1996), have all been part of a gestalt of interest in the public church, public ministry, and public intellectuals.

Tillich had a fundamental impact as early as the 1950s and 1960s through his influence on his colleague, Seward Hiltner, on Hiltner's students, such as Browning, and even on Browning's students, such as Pamela Couture and myself. Tillich lays a foundation for pastoral theology as public theology through three conceptual moves: his correlational method, his devotion to a theology of culture, and his view of practical theology. He describes his correlation of the "questions implied in the [secular] situation with the answers implied in the [Christian] message" (1951, 8) as "apologetic" explicitly over against Karl Barth's kerygmatic neo-orthodoxy. The latter stands at such distance from secular society, Tillich believes, that the gospel has to be literally "thrown like a stone" at the modern world (1951, 7). He seeks to relate the Christian message to society so that "neither of them is obliterated" and both may potentially be transformed (8). In short, apologetic theology picks up liberal theology's longstanding public agenda, hoping to establish the modern validity of Christianity as Schleiermacher had done a century before. Most pastoral theologians today employ some version of this liberal model, however modified by revisionist, liberation, or postmodern theology.

A similar notion reached pastoral studies via H. Richard Niebuhr and the work of theological ethicist James Gustafson, another later Chicago scholar who affected Browning and his students. Niebuhr formulated a now-classic1950s typology of Christian and world engagement. Although debate continues about the fairness of his characterization (see Gathje, 2002),

Niebuhr, like Tillich, favors a Christ that transforms rather than stands over, against, immersed within, or in tension with culture (1956). While Niebuhr's emphasis on reclaiming the narrative "internal history" of particular faith communities (1941) inspired Hauerwas' postliberal advocacy for the church as a distinct, even alien community (1989), Gustafson championed Niebuhr's commitment to making Christianity intelligible to the general public. He, like Tillich and Tracy, is invested in a genuine conversation between church and public, often using social science and philosophy as guides (1961, x). Confining study of the church to traditional doctrinal categories "oversimplifies and distorts" the church's public role, he contends, just as a strict sociology fails to grasp completely the meaning of religion (1961, ix). The "earthen" church – of this world even if its mission originates from sources transcendent to it – cannot be adequately understood "only in its own private language" (1961, 100).

In fondness for what he called a "theology of culture," Tillich made a second contribution. Simply put, a theology of culture attempts to "analyze the theology behind all cultural expressions" (1951, 39; 1959, 42). It is a rather short step from this idea to Browning's well-established evaluation of the quasi-religious and ethical claims behind the "cultures of psychology" from Freud to behavioral science (1987). Much recent pastoral theology takes up this job of analyzing culture's religious presumptions, assuming responsibility for the "lacuna" that Edward Farley later says systematic theology has overlooked – the "theological interpretation of situations" (1987, 1, 11).

Finally, when Tillich outlined theology's organization, he bequeathed an ambiguous legacy to pastoral theology's development as public theology. On the one hand, he described practical theology in a quintessentially public way as a "bridge" between systematic and historical theology and the world, concerned with how theology is realized within church and society. Practical theology "can put new questions" before theologians that arise out of public life, preserving the church from the perils of both "traditionalism and dogmatism." Inversely, it "can induce society to take the church seriously" (1951, 33 - 34).

Yet in almost the same breath Tillich reduces practical theology's range. It is not really the crown of the sciences that Schleiermacher imagined. Rather it is simply the "technical theory" through which historical and systematic theology get "applied to" the church (1951, 32). In short, on the one hand, he sees practical theology as concerned with the public visibility of Christian norms. On the other hand, he empties practical theology of substance as merely the application of theory to clerical practice, a means to an end without its own tangible contributions.

Impetus to see pastoral theology as public theology, however, finally emanates from Tracy. Of all the Chicago figures, he stands out as most concerned – even obsessed – with the various publics that theologians must address. He is acutely aware of the challenges of pluralism and religious privatization. Stated simply, he believes "all theology is public discourse" (1981, 3). When he turns to practical theology, he is most concerned with establishing schema by which it functions "as public theology" (1983, 61).

Fundamental and systematic theology become public by using common categories of philosophical and metaphysical reasoning or by expressing the particular Christian symbols in a classic way. Practical theology's public voice emanates from its ability to transform daily practices in response to "cultural, political, social, or pastoral need bearing genuine religious import" (1981, 57). Especially elucidating is Tracy's portrait of theology's three different publics of church, academy, and society. Practical theology's primary public is society. In a technology-driven world, practical theologians must recover the richer "symbolic expressions of our culture," such as the contributions of Calvin's notion of covenant to the Constitution or Martin Luther King's appropriation of Christian ideals of social justice in the call for civil rights (1981, 13, 31).

Tracy's influence, however, is also slightly contradictory. On the one hand, he offers a richer conceptualization of practical theology's agenda than one finds among postliberal theologians. It is one of the three central subdisciplines, alongside fundamental and systematic theology. Practical theology correlates interpretations of practical wisdom in secular and religious efforts to affect human change. Its more concrete and confessional focus, in contrast to fundamental theology's abstraction from personal experience, does not make it any less accountable to the general public.

Yet Tracy leaves his own project incomplete. He authored an initial book on the public nature of fundamental theology (1975), a second book on systematic theology (1981), but never wrapped up his efforts with a book on practical theology. This leaves undeveloped an exploration of Christian communities, practices, and moral wisdom, an oversight for which postliberal theologians rightly criticize him. Moreover, as in the two illustrations above, he emphasizes practical theology's cerebral contribution to discourse more than its relevance to social practice per se. In short, Tracy yields immense conceptual clarity about practical theology's public role but ultimately fails to establish its relevance to congregational and communal activity and to challenge its position as subordinate to fundamental and systematic theology.

The Influence of Liberation Theology

Liberation theologians, such as Rebecca Chopp (1987, 123), have challenged the liberal and cognitive orientation of Tracy's public rendition of practical theology. In Latin America and beyond, liberation theology gave a whole new meaning to the personal and its relationship to the public. Theology is not just public. "Every theology is political," Juan Luis Segundo declares, "even one that does not speak or think in political terms" (1976, 74). He wholly agrees with Gustavo Gutiérrez that "nothing lies outside the political sphere." In such a context, "personal relationships themselves acquire an ever-increasing political dimension" (1973, 47).

The public is no longer the "cultured despisers" that troubled Schleiermacher and later liberal theologians but instead what one theologian calls the "nonperson" or those who have heretofore been deprived public presence and recognition (Fulkerson, 1994, 36). Where liberal theology worried about convincing either a modern scientific audience (Tillich) or a scientifically disenchanted postmodern audience (Tracy), liberation theologians address those previously marginalized, silenced, and erased from social history, political voice, and theological mediation. In Chopp's words, "while liberal-revisionist theologians respond to the theoretical challenge of the nonbelievers among the small minority of the world's population who control the wealth and resources in history, liberation theologians respond to the practical challenge of the large majority of global residents who control neither their victimization nor their survival" (1987, 121, 128).

Having redefined the personal and the public, liberation theology demands a prophetic reorienttation. If the personal is political and if the public now includes those most oppressed and not just the dominant voices, then genuine improvement in one's personal plight means collective change in economic and political relationships and structures. Concrete change is required not just in the more obvious economic and political realms but in realms heretofore considered private, such as congregation, family life, and the arts.

Liberation theology sees critical reflection as the "second step" coming after the more primary step of commitment to public service and political action. Public theology then does not just mean making cognitive sense of Christian claims. Rather, it demands radical social reformation of the "practical crisis of the victims of history" (Chopp, 1987, 131). This cry for justice and freedom can sometimes wax idealistic, utopian, and even eschatological. Moreover, it is unclear whether Chopp or many others who identify themselves within the liberationist realm, have followed through on these mandates. Nonetheless, liberationist public theology does at least issue a grassroots cry for social activism and public transformation

What does all this mean for pastoral theology as public theology today? Broadly speaking, two primary factors distinguish the most recent move toward public theology: concern about the silence of mainstream Christianity on key social issues and awareness of the serious limitations of pastoral focus on the individual alone. Recent pastoral theologians have attempted to alter public discourse on a wide range of dilemmas that have important social and political implications, such as Western economic imperialism and domestic violence. This emphasis goes against the grain of the stereotypical understanding of pastoral theology as merely focused on clerical skills. However, in attempting to avoid what Farley called the focus on the "clerical paradigm" (or pastoral care defined around the skills of individual clergy) (1983a, 26; 1983b, 85), pastoral theologians have concentrated more on conceptual strategies to transform culture than on practical tactics to build social ministries.

Despite liberation theology's influence, U.S. pastoral theologians have focused primarily on influencing public discourse and need to move toward a more service- or action-oriented approach that considers congregations and non-profit organizations central sites for study and participation. From another perspective, however, one might also argue that U.S. pastoral theologians are well positioned to reap the benefits of both approaches. For, neither social ministry nor ideological examination can be sustained for long without the energy of the other. If the Christian conceptual understanding of belief and practice languishes, so also will the many social programs it initially spawned. Inversely, intellectual exploration of Christianity becomes a hollow shell without social purpose and practice.

References

Audi, R. and Wolterstorff, N. (1997) *Religion in the public square: The place of religious convictions in political debate.* Landam, Md.: Rowman& Littlefield.

Bellah, R. N., Madsen, R., Sullivan, W. M., Swidler, A. and Tipton, S. M. (1985) *Habits of the heart: Individualism and Commitment in American Life.* Berkeley, Calif.: Univ. of California Press.

Boff, L. and Boff, C. (1987) *Introducing Liberation Theology.* Maryknoll, NY: Orbis Books.

Browning, D. S. (1987) *Religious Thought and the Modern Psychologies.* Minneapolis: Fortress.

Burtchaell, J. (1998) *The dying of the light: The disengagement of colleges and universities from their Christian churches.* Grand Rapids: Eerdmans.

Cady, L. E. (1993) *Religion, theology, and American public life.* Albany: State University of New York Press.

Carter, Stephen L. (1994) *The culture of disbelief: How American law and politics trivialize religious devotion.* New York: Anchor.

Cherry, C. (1995) *Hurrying toward Zion: Universities, divinity schools, and American Protestantism.* Bloomington, IN: Indiana University Press.

Chopp, R. S. (1987) Practical theology and liberation. in L. S. Mudge and J. N. Poling (eds), *Formation and reflection: The promise of practical theology*. Philadelphia: Fortress, 120 - 138.

Couture, P. D. (1996) Weaving the web: Pastoral care in an individualistic society. in J. S. Moessner (ed.), *Through the eyes of women: Insights for pastoral care*. Philadelphia: Westminster John Knox, 94 - 104.

Farley, E. (1983a) Theology and practice outside the clerical paradigm. in D. S. Browning (ed.), *Practical theology: The emerging field in theology, church, and world*. San Francisco: Harper & Row, 21 - 41.

Farley, E. (1983b) *Theologia*. Philadelphia: Fortress.

Farley, E. (1987) Interpreting situations: An inquiry into the nature of practical theology. in L. S. Mudge and J. N. Poling (eds), *Formation and reflection: The promise of practical theology*. Philadelphia: Fortress.

Fulkerson, M. M. (1994) *Changing the subject: Women's discourses and feminist theology*. Minneapolis: Augsburg Fortress.

Gathje, P. R. (2002, June) A Contest Classic: Critics ask Whose Christ? Which Culture? *Christian Century*, 28 - 32.

Gill-Austern, B. (1995) Rediscovering hidden treasures for pastoral care. *Pastoral Psychology* 43: 4, 233 - 53.

Gilpin, W. C. (ed.). (1990) *Public faith: Reflections on the political role of American churches*. St. Louis: CBP Press.

Gilpin, W. C. (1996) *A Preface to Theology*. Chicago: University of Chicago Press.

Graham, L. K. (1992) *Care of persons, care of worlds: A Psychosystems Approach to Pastoral Care and Counseling*. Nashville: Abingdon

Gustafson, J. M. (1961) *Treasure in earthen vessels: The church as a human community*. Chicago: University of Chicago Press.

Gutiérrez, G. (1973) *A theology of liberation: History, politics, and salavation*, C. Inda & J. Eagleson (eds. & trans.). Maryknoll, NY: Orbis Books.

Keller, E. F. (1996) *Reflections on gender and science*. New Haven: Yale University Press.

Harding, S. (1991) *Whose science? Whose knowledge?: Thinking from women's lives*. Cornell: Cornell University Press.

Hauerwas, S. and Willimon, W. H. (1989) *Resident aliens: Life in the Christian colony*. Nashville: Abingdon.

Heitink, G. (1999) Developments in practical theology in the Netherlands. *International Journal of Practical Theology* 3: 1, 127 - 44.

Hunter, R. J. (1990) (ed.). *Dictionary of Pastoral Counseling and Care*. Nashville: Abingdon.

Kuhn, T. S. (1996) *The Structure of Scientific Revolutions*. Chicago: University of Chicago Press.

Lovin, R. (1986) (ed.). *Religion and American public life*. New York: Paulist.

Marsden, G. M. (1997) *The outrageous idea of Christian scholarship*. New York: Oxford University Press.

Marty, M. E. (1981) *The public church: Mainline, Evangelical, Catholic*. New York: Crossroad.

Miller-McLemore, B. J. (1993, April) The human web and the state of pastoral theology. *Christian Century*, 366 - 69.

Miller-McLemore, B. J. (1996) The living human web: Pastoral theology at the turn of the century. In J. S. Moessner (ed.), *Through the eyes of women: Insights for pastoral care*. Philadelphia: Westminster John Knox, 9 - 26.

Miller-McLemore, B. J. and Gill-Austern, B. (1999) (eds), *Feminist and womanist pastoral theology*. Nashville: Abingdon.

Miller-McLemore, B. J. (2000) The public character of the university-related divinity school. *Theological Education* 37:1, 49 - 61.

Niebuhr, H. R. (1941) *The meaning of revelation*. New York: Harper.

Niebuhr, H. R. (1956) *Christ and culture*. New York: Harper.

Pasewark, K. A. and Paul, G. E. (1999) *The emphatic Christian center: Reforming Christian political practice*. Nashville: Abingdon.

Putnam, R. (2000) *Bowling Alone: The Collapse and Revival of American Community*. New York: Simon and Shuster.

Rorty, R. (1991) *Objectivity, relativism, and truth*. Cambridge: Cambridge University Press.

Segundo, J. L. (1976) *The liberation of theology*, trans. by J. Drury. Maryknoll, N.Y.: Orbis.

Schwehn, M. (1993) *Exiles from Eden: Religion and the academic vocation in American*. New York: Oxford University Press.

Sloan, D. (1994) *Faith and knowledge: Mainline Protestantism and American higher education*. Louisville: Westminster John Knox.

Thiemann, R. F. (1991) *Constructing a public theology: The church in a pluralistic culture*. Louisville: Westminster John Knox.

Thiemann, R. F. (1996) *Religion in public life: A dilemma for democracy*. Washington, DC: Georgetown University Press.

Tillich, P. (1951) *Systematic Theology*, vol. 1. Chicago: University of Chicago.

Tillich, P. (1959) *Theology of culture*. London: Oxford University Press.

Tracy, D. (1975) *Blessed rage for order: The new pluralism in theology*. New York: Seabury Press.

Tracy, D. (1981) *The analogical imagination: Christian theology and the culture of pluralism*. New York: Crossroad.

Tracy, D. (1983) The foundations of practical theology. In D. S. Browning (ed.), *Practical theology: The emerging field in theology, church, and world*. San Francisco: Harper & Row, 61 - 82.

Weitham, P. J., (1997) (ed). *Religion and Contemporary Liberalism*. Notre Dame: University of Notre Dame.

Wolfe, A. (1989) *Whose Keeper? Social science and Moral Obligation*. Berkeley, Calif.: Univ. of California Press.

Christian Theological Rhetoric for a Pluralist Age

Gerard V. Hall

The Pluralistic Challenge

Public theology is confronted with the task of articulating the Christian message in the 'new situation of pluralism' (Panikkar, 1979b; Panikkar, 1995).
Pluralism in the sense of religious and cultural diversity is not new. What is
new is *awareness* of the situation of radical diversity as it impinges on issues of human solidarity and even, many a tradition will say, cosmic harmony.
Modernity's historical crisis of meaning – 'Who am I?' – is replaced by the
postmodern crisis of otherness – 'Who are you?' – in which the 'other *qua*
other' becomes an *ultimate* question. [1] Politically, this is recognizable in the
increasingly audible voices of the marginalized including migrants, children,
women, indigenous peoples, victims of power politics and sexual abuse. Difference can no longer be explained away with reference to the eschatological
happy day when God, the gods, fate, destiny or development will arrive on the
historical scene to pronounce an end to chaos and multiplicity. Those days of
naïve optimism in the progress of history are behind us.

The ultimacy of pluralism is evident in the clash of religious, cultural and
political systems that harbour a not-so-hidden desire to claim the whole earth
for their heritage. While many interpretations may be complementary, the real issue of pluralism arises when we are forced to decide between mutually
exclusive, contradictory and irreconcilable views of reality. Here, there is no
middle ground or room for negotiation: either God does or does not exist; war,
racism or abortion are justifiable or indefensible; either state communism, liberal capitalism, military dictatorship or the theocratic state. Tolerance is well
and good but 'the real problem of tolerance begins with why and how to tole-
rate the intolerant' (Panikkar, 1979a: 20). Learning to love the neighbour who
espouses an opposing worldview to our own may be admirable yet, we must
say, not easily put into practice.

---

[1]   Philosopher Emmanuel Levinas develops the notion of 'being-for-other' as the essential
    human reality. Theological implications are developed by Veling (1999).

Liberal democracies face a situation in which any public discussion of
ultimacy is reduced to the political level. All voices are welcome at the
conversation-table for deciding what is humanly desirable, politically feasible or economically viable. Freedom of speech and voting rights are afforded
to all, even those who are considered ill-informed, too idealistic, a little mad
or just politically incorrect. However, majority rules. Experience shows that
democracies do not deal well with minorities who do not accept the dominant
myths of the nation-state, universal dominion of technology, modern scientific
cosmology or the capitalistic global system.

The postmodern dissolution of such western totalizing systems in favour
of unearthing repressed voices of otherness and difference marks a welcome
shift to accommodating minority viewpoints. However, too often the postmodern critique languishes into the slippery slide towards ethical relativism and
moral indifference. Nothing can be determined at the ultimate level of truth
and goodness; no interpretation of what is right and just is to be privileged. In
an age where absolutes are out of fashion, an easy tolerance of the other can be
a mask for intellectual lethargy and ethical failure. How successful has been
the Christian theological response?

Christian Responses

Mainline Christianity has responded to the contemporary challenge of pluralism with a variety of strategies. Official ecclesial rhetoric and praxis have
become more tolerant of otherness. Internally, a new appreciation of diversity
has resulted in accommodation to local churches and commitment to enculturation. There is even acknowledgement that the Eurocentric model of Church
needs to be replaced by a model more sensitive to the multicultural reality of
most Christian denominations. Externally, Christian churches have generally
replaced a conflict model with a dialogical approach to other traditions. Yet,
we must also acknowledge a neo-conservative reaction to all these trends.

At stake are a number of issues centred around Christianity's ambivalent
relationship with the European Enlightenment. Idealist theologies promoted
an openness to enlightenment culture and its secular expressions that liberal
Christianity celebrated. Rather than seeing the world and church in conflict,
Christians and secular humanists could work together for peace, justice and
human rights. [2] Freedom was the prime value espoused by all. The enlightenment and Christian projects were essentially one and the same. Here was a

---

[2]   This was essentially the perspective of Vatican II's *Pastoral Constitution of the Church in
the Modern World* (1964).

model where difference need not be divisive. Unsurprisingly, critics emerged from right and left.

Conservatives accused liberal theologies of reducing Christian faith to the level of a mere humanism. Political theologies espoused a more nuanced critique. These masters of suspicion introduced Christian theology to postmodern awareness of the other. In particular, idealist Christianity needed to become aware of its pretensions of innocence. The mystical-poetic bias of theological idealism needed to be balanced with an appreciation of the Church's own role in the history of guilt. Liberation, feminist and ecological theologies continue the thrust of unearthing Christianity's repressed prophetic-apocalyptic strain. [3] Neo-conservatives, in their rejection of enlightenment culture, however, dismiss agendas of both liberal and political theologies.

The Australian Context

In the Australian context, mainline Christian churches have learnt from each of these theological movements while continuing to be unsure of what their precise relationship to enlightenment-secular culture should be. Most Christians live happily enough with a mitigated acceptance of the values of pluralism. Never a people prone to metaphysical speculation, Australians feel happier in an ecumenical age where tolerance of otherness is not pushed to its ultimate conclusions. Unlike their European and American counterparts, Australians embrace the values of secular culture with little focus on the religious roots of that culture. They also espouse the dominant myths of the nation-state, universal technology and world capitalism with little attention to the impact of the 'western universalizing thrust' on the underclass. [4] And this despite one of the nation's founding myths of a 'fair go' for all.

The churches have not been altogether silent in raising the prophetic call of resistance and hope. Social justice issues have recently focused on the country's responsibility towards Aboriginal Australia. A conservative people, many Australians find it difficult to understand why special consideration needs to be given to Australia's indigenous population despite a disreputable colonial history in which Aboriginal people were non-citizens. It was only in 1967 that Aboriginal people were afforded citizenship on par with other Australians. The Prime Minister of the day refuses to make an official apology for the historical wrongs done to Australia's indigenous people. [5] In the midst of such official

---

3   The importance of 'mystical prophetic resistance and hope' is a repeated theme of Tracy (1994). On the continuing importance of liberation theologies, see Phan (2000a).

4   Panikkar (1995: 148) states: 'the power of the West is linked to this thrust toward universalization'.

5   John Winston Howard (PM 1996-) refuses to embrace the 'black arm-band view of history'

resistance, leaders of Christian churches are prominent among those calling for reconciliation. They have also sided with voices of resistance to current government policies on refugees, asylum seekers and the recent war in Iraq.

While the churches may be at the forefront of calls for justice, they find themselves in a compromised situation. To begin, their moral power to speak is weakened by the scandals that have beset a small but very public number of their ministers and institutions. Second, as beneficiaries of government monies in health, education and welfare, there is natural reluctance to challenge official policies. Third, with few exceptions, the churches remain European in their structures and bourgeois in their attitudes. Fourth, the mainline churches are losing numbers without, it seems, the will, commitment or imagination to meet this challenge. Fifth, as Australia itself remains uncertain of its identity and place in the world, the churches are often at a loss in developing a genuinely enculturated theology that speaks in a convincing way of Christian identity and mission. [6]

The Rhetorical Challenge

The challenge for religious rhetoric today is to articulate transcendent values in the context of the postmodern, pluralistic world. This challenge is profound because it no longer assumes that the truth-claims of religious speech can be divorced from their power to enhance transformative social praxis. In the wake of historical consciousness, which highlights the dynamic and ever-changing reality of religious belief and praxis, the question of Christian rhetoric becomes acute. In particular, the churches need to develop a discerning rhetoric of engagement with post-enlightenment, secular cultures. Evidently, many of the values espoused by these cultures stem from their Jewish and Christian roots; others appear at variance. [7] Since, in the West at least, voices that speak loudest are those based on humanist and secular philosophies, Christianity needs to uncover what it believes to be genuine and false within those philosophies. At the same time, it must allow itself to be critiqued on the basis of its own truth-claims.

This is not an appeal for a rhetoric of the lowest common denominator nor a call for some kind of vaguely Christian *ecumenical esperanto*. [8] The dia-

---

espousing instead a 'forward vision that includes all Australians'. Conservative forces in Australia believe it is un-Australian and non-egalitarian to privilege specific cultural groups.

[6]   For two recent discussions of Australian theologies and theologians, see Malone (1999) and Goosen (2000).

[7]   David Walsh (1999) argues that western culture remains profoundly Christian even in the wake of the attempts of modernity and postmodernity to deny its Christian roots.

[8]   The notion of an artificially-created universal language or *ecumenical esperanto* is promoted by Leonard Swidler (1987).

logue between Christianity and enlightenment culture is bound by these same rigours of discourse that govern interfaith encounters: there should be no attempt to minimize differences in origin, experience and understanding among traditions. Liberal Christianity is rightly critiqued on the score of its tendency to brush aside divergences and even contradictions between Christian faith and secular humanism. Equally, there is need to implore conservative Christians to recognise that sin, guilt and error are not confined to the other camp. More poignantly, there are grounds for dialogue precisely because there are shared experiences and understandings. Indeed, a shared rhetoric. [9]

The New Rhetoric

In this context, rhetoric is defined as 'discourse on the margins of thought and action' (Hariman, 1986: 51). It does not focus on the doctrinal formulation of beliefs but on the images, metaphors, gestures and partial logics associated with the communication of those beliefs (Happel, 1987: 194ff.). Theology is often critiqued for being too dry, intellectual, even sterile; spirituality is said to be more accessible to people. Good Christian rhetoric, aware of the dangers of separating the two, brings theology and spirituality together. The doctrinal expressions of Christian faith are not ignored, but their formulation takes care to address the hearers according to their cultural and spiritual worlds. Good rhetoric means effective communication.

A rhetorical approach to Christian discourse challenges us to move beyond the valuable yet narrow field of reason and argument. Religions and cultures are something more than rational thought-systems. They are total ways of life that include symbols, stories, rituals, hymns and multiple other forms of human expression. Kierkegaard's critique of 'poor little chatty Christianity' enunciates an over-valuation of the *logos* to the detriment of these other significant attributes of Christian faith. Rhetoric recognizes the role of the *mythos* as well as the *logos* in authentic dialogue. [10] Here we acknowledge the value of the other even when we disagree on purely rational grounds.

In contrast to classical rhetoric which focussed on the speaker's powers of persuasion, the new rhetoric is inherently dialogical. It emphasises the mutuality of speaker and audience in their common search for authentic values, saving truth and liberating action. In Happel's words:

---

[9]   Phan (2000b: 724f.) states the cultural heritage of the West provides a 'shared language with which ideological opponents can at least make themselves understood to one another.' This is contrasted to the situation of dialogue between Christianity and Eastern cultures.

[10]   Panikkar highlights this distinction between *mythos* and *logos*. He states that pluralism belongs to the level of myth rather than ideology: 'pluralism does not stem from the *logos* but from the *mythos*' (1979a: 102).

A new rhetoric will redescribe the interaction of speaker and audience as mutual, rather than as the conviction of the masses by a single orator. It will note the transformative character of language for the establishment of the grounds, values, and bases of community. Rather than focusing simply upon the eloquent tropes of style, it will recognize the intrinsic relationship between truth-claims and metaphors, between the authenticity of the speaker and the values preached. It will offer a critique of the biases of speaker and audience so that a transforming social praxis might be appropriated. (1987: 195).

Such a rhetoric is well disposed to a pluralistic, postmodern world in which the values and praxis of multiple traditions need to be brought together in mutual respect and critique. According to scholars of the new rhetoric, there are four major tropes of discourse: metaphor; metonymy; synecdoche; irony (Klemm, 1987: 446; White, 1978: 1 - 26). These are reviewed with an eye to their utilization in Christian theological discourse. In view of the pluralistic challenge of our age, the major focus will be on the postmodernity's use of the metaphor of otherness. Some insight into the three other major tropes of discourse will also be discussed.

Metaphor

Metaphor arises in response to a new experience we cannot comprehend. Klemm suggests the historical crisis of meaning captured the imagination of the post-war world: the crisis-metaphor. In contrast, postmodern discourse is confronted by the new challenge of otherness that asks us 'to uncover what is questionable and what is genuine in self and other, while opening self to other and allowing other to remain other' (1987: 456). It follows that the postmodern metaphor of otherness also assumes human, cultural and religious connectedness as well as acknowledging radical difference. Otherness is ultimate, but it may not be debilitating.

The other person, culture, religion or society is a revelation waiting to occur, to unsettle, to call into new ways of thinking and acting. Jesus is confronted by such a situation with the Syro-Phoenician woman (Mark 7:24 - 30). His initial reaction is one of discomfort: 'It isn't right to take the children's food and throw it to the dogs'. The woman captures Jesus unawares: 'Sir, even the dogs under the table eat the children's leftovers'. Jesus' entire attitude changes. He commends the woman, heals her daughter and commends her great faith (Matthew 15:28). Jesus does not enter into doctrinal implications of the encounter although, no doubt, these are significant. The new Christian rhetoric needs to articulate its own discomfort, enter into dialogue with other cultures and religions, and be prepared to think and act differently as a result of these encounters.

Whereas traditional Christian rhetoric relied on the authority of the Scriptures and/or Church to persuade its audience, postmodern rhetoric faces the other as a potential source of truth. 'Who are You'? 'Who are We'? In a predominantly secular culture, it is important to acknowledge the values we share in our differences. For example, secular justice and freedom may be interpreted in terms of the biblical God of grace and liberation. Christian love and forgiveness are not without meaning among socialist, egalitarian and humanistic philosophies. Equally, we need to express our concerns and challenges. Christians express alarm at a materialist philosophy that effectively denies self-transcendence. Secular culture challenges the discrepancy between the values preached and the lives lived by Christians. Both need to be open to the challenge of the other – and to change as a result of the encounter.

At the level of theological discourse, concepts such as salvation, sin and grace, may be a barrier to effective communication not only with secular society but with Christians as well. The rhetorical challenge is not to bypass the language of Scripture and tradition but to express these realities at the level of symbol and ritual – for example, through the expressive and visual arts – in ways that correlate with contemporary secular experience. The sense of the sacred is not absent in the world of theatre, film, youth culture nor in the acknowledged need for ethical principles in business and politics. [11] This is not to glorify secular culture, but to state that the churches do not have the monopoly on transcendent values. Church and State have much to learn from each other in a dialogical relationship that allows room for authentic resistance and the cry of the prophet – from either camp.

Otherness may also be a metaphor for the apparent silence of God in a time, culture and people who may be largely unaware of their call to be something other than a cog in the capitalistic machine. Otherness is also represented in the outraged voices, passive victims and sometimes profoundly wounded members of both Church and society. The otherness metaphor challenges Christian discourse to retrieve the dangerous memories of its own tradition as a catalyst for engagement with the profound inequalities of our world. [12] The doctrine of the triune God is a metaphor for the dignity and equality of all human persons. Certainly, the Christian West needs to uncover its largely repressed mystical tradition if it is to speak to the increasing numbers who no longer find the transforming presence of Christ and the Spirit in the churches.

---

[11]   Coles (1999) argues that the shift from the 'religious' to the 'scientific' mindset retains a sense of connection to the sacred.

[12]   Political theologians articulate this challenge in various ways. In his *memoria passionis* thesis, Metz (1980) highlights the 'dangerous and subversive memory of Jesus Christ'.

Metonymy, Synecdoche, Irony

Metonymy represents the movement from the universal to the particular. According to Klemm, the metonymic elements of the postmodern metaphor of otherness are dispersed according to self, other, the encompassing world and time (1987: 457). As I have argued elsewhere (Hall, 2002a: 45-49), Jacques Dupuis' Christian theology of religious pluralism (Dupuis 1997; Dupuis 2002) is an expression of metonymy according to these various elements: for Christians, saving truth is uniquely revealed in Jesus Christ (self); in other religions, the mystery of divine truth may be mediated in ways that Christians cannot know or experience (other); beyond particular religions, the universal power of the *Logos* and the unbound action of the Spirit mediate God's saving love in historically specific ways (encompassing world). Finally, for Dupuis, otherness remains ultimate since he does not presume convergence of the various traditions either in this world or at the eschaton (time).

Synecdoche is likened to a 'second metaphor' which arises from dissatisfaction with former experience and language. It appears as the inbreaking of new consciousness or a 'new revelatory experience' (Panikkar, 1979b, 195). Jesus uses synecdoche when he speaks of the 'reign of God'. Although the concept existed in the Jewish tradition, Jesus' Abba-experience transforms the concept into something more immediate and powerful. In terms of religious experience, synecdoche is less a concept than a symbol disclosing the divine mystery in a new way. A contemporary example of synecdoche is what Panikkar calls the 'cosmotheandric' vision: everything that is encapsulates the divine (freedom), human (consciousness) and cosmic (matter, space, time, energy). These are not three different aspects of universal reality, but an expression of the intrinsic, threefold relationship constituting *everything that is* (Panikkar, 1993: 54-77). Existence is *to be in relationship* whether we speak of God, the world, ourselves. This enables Panikkar to speak of secular humanism's insight into the ultimacy of the world in terms of 'sacred secularity'. He also stresses that the new revelatory experience comes as the fruit of interfaith and intercultural dialogue.

The final trope in our discussion is *irony*. Christian doctrines are nothing if not ironic: God is one and three; Christ is divine and human; Christ is the one-and-only universal saviour and God wills all to be saved; the reign of God is yet to come and already here among us. Revelation is ostensibly ironic insofar as the divine mystery is mediated symbolically or 'through what is not itself but is other than itself' (Klemm, 1987: 463). Such ironic and symbolic awareness allows us to experience the divine mystery in terms of our own tradition without excluding other possible ways in which other traditions experience and name the sacred. Biblical or doctrinal fundamentalism is adjudged inappropriate from a rhetorical perspective on account of its absence of perceived irony. Theologically, it wants to limit the reality of God to the confines of human thought processes. The parables of Jesus are saturated with irony as a means of shocking his followers into re-examining basic human prejudices, awakening possibilities of new religious experience and provoking the praxis of God's reign in the world.

The primary metaphor of otherness will dictate that non-western cultures and non-Christian traditions become central to authentic Christian self-understanding. The trope of metonymy will focus on specific and different experiences of Christian enculturation providing a genuinely pluralistic appreciation of Christian identity in the third millennium. The synecdochic inbreaking of the wholly other God will forge new expressions of the divine mystery that are consonant with Christian faith communities and other traditions. Finally, effective Christian rhetoric will be ironic and kenotic, speaking authentically of the mystery of God while being profoundly aware of the inadequacy of all human speech about God.

Interfaith and Intercultural Dialogue

Today, in face of postmodern proclamations of the death of God, the end of the human subject and the extinction of planet earth, we need a new experience of the interconnectedness of all reality. No one religion or culture has all the answers or is 'capable of rescuing humanity from its present predicament' (Panikkar, 1995: 175). However, together in relationship and eventually communion with the other, new possibilities emerge. What is needed is not some fresh theory or new doctrine, but authentic interfaith and intercultural dialogue in which religious and cultural traditions define their identities *in relationship with rather than in opposition to the other* (Hall, 2002b). Such dialogue needs to be rooted in the unique experiences and stories of each tradition (Panikkar, 1999).

This new approach to rhetoric cannot settle Christian theological claims. There is always a place for doctrinal dispute and argument. Nonetheless, Christians would do well to recall they are 'primarily a remembering and storytelling community' rather than a 'community interpreting and arguing' (Metz, 1980: 212). Jesus preached mainly through stories. In human encounter, when stories are told the threat of doctrinal dispute subsides and new understanding of the other emerges. Something of this is already occurring in cultures where indigenous peoples, the world's great story-tellers, are finally being heard. One example of the fruits of such dialogue is a renewed appreciation of the earth's sacredness leading Christian churches to re-examine the place of ecology in their own theological traditions. One hopes this will culminate in transformed ecological praxis on cultural-spiritual as well as environmental-political grounds.

We live in a pluralistic world in which no single cultural or religious perspective, neither Christianity nor the West, holds all the cards nor plays all the tunes. [13] Christians are called to live out their vocation in confident engagement with this world even as faith in their own institutional structures diminishes. Religious and cultural dialogue is a crucial need and urgent opportunity to redress postmodern fragmentation. It will also prove to be the source of imagination and vision for Christian identity and mission in the third millennium. This will go hand in hand with an emerging religious rhetoric which takes its distance from the authoritative manner of classical rhetoric since the voice of the other needs to be included in the ongoing, critical and mutual search for authenticity in religious belief and social praxis.

References

Coles, Robert (1999) *The Secular Mind*. Princeton, NJ: Princeton University Press.

Dupuis, Jacques (1997) *Toward a Christian Theology of Religious Pluralism*. Maryknoll, NY: Orbis.

Dupuis, Jacques (2002) *Christianity and the Religions: From Confrontation to Dialogue*. London: Darton, Longman and Todd.

Goosen, Gideon (2000) *Australian Theologies*. Strathfield: St Paul's Press.

Hall, Gerard (2002a) Jacques Dupuis' Christian Theology of Religious Pluralism. *Pacifica* 15/1, 37 - 50.

Hall, Gerard (2002b) 'Intercultural and Interreligious Hermeneutics: Raimon Panikkar', *Theology@McAuley* (online), 12 February 2002, available at http://www.mcauley.acu.edu.au/theology/ghall_panikkar.htm, 8pp [accessed 14 April 2002].

Happel, Stephen (1987) Religious Rhetoric and the Language of Theological Foundations. in T. Fallan and P. Riley (eds), *Religion and Culture*. Albany: Suny Press.

Hariman, Robert (1986) Status, Marginality, and Rhetorical Theory. *Quarterly Journal of Speech* 72, 38 - 54.

Klemm, David (1987) Toward a Rhetoric of Postmodern Theology. *Journal of the American Academy of Religion* 55:3, 443 - 469.

Malone, Peter (ed.) (1999) *Developing an Australian Theology*. Strathfield: St. Paul's Press.

Metz, Johan Baptist (1980) *Faith in History and Society*. New York: Seabury Press.

Panikkar, Raimon (1979a) *Myth Faith and Hermeneutics*. New York: Paulist Press.

---

[13] 'Pluralism tells us here that one should not assume for oneself (person or culture) the role of being conductor of the human and much less of the cosmic orchestra. It is enough with the music (divine), the musicians (the human) and their instruments (the cosmos)' (Panikkar, 1995: 180).

Panikkar, Raimon (1979b) The Myth of Pluralism: The Tower of Babel–A Meditation on Non-Violence. *Cross Currents* 29, 197 - 230.

Panikkar, Raimon (1993) *The Cosmotheandric Experience: Emerging Religious Consciousness.* Maryknoll, NY: Orbis.

Panikkar, Raimon (1995) *Invisible Harmony: Essays on Contemplation and Responsibility.* Minneapolis: Fortress Press.

Panikkar, Raimon (1999) *The Intra-religious Dialogue* 2nd edition. New York: Paulist Press.

Phan, Peter (2000a) Method in Liberation Theologies. *Theological Studies.* 61, 40 - 63.

Phan, Peter (2000b) Doing Theology in the Context of Mission. *Gregorianum.* 81:4, 723 - 749.

Swidler, Leonard (1987) Interreligious and Interideological Dialogue. in L. Swidler, (ed), *Toward a Universal Theology of Religion.* Maryknoll, NY: Orbis, 5 - 50.

Tracy, David (1994) *On Naming the Present: God, Hermeneutics, Church.* London: SCM Press.

Veling, Terry (1999) In the Name of Who? Levinas and the Other Side of Theology. *Pacifica* 12/3, 275 - 292.

Walsh, David (1999) *The Third Millennium: Reflections on Faith and Reason.* Washington, DC: Georgetown University Press, 1999.

White, Haydon (1978) *Tropics of Discourse.* Baltimore: John Hopkins University Press.

Reform of the House of Lords and Christian Responsibility in a Plural Society

Esther D. Reed

Bishops in the House of Lords and the question of legitimacy

The Report of the Commission on the Future of Multi-Ethnic Britain was published in October 2000. Set up by the Runnymede Trust to propose ways of countering racial discrimination and disadvantage, it recommended that the privileged position of Christianity in general and the Church of England in particular should be ended. (Other recommendations included changes in immigration and asylum policy and a Human Rights Commission to promote a human rights culture.) Later that year, the Royal Commission on reform of the House of Lords, chaired by the Rt Hon Lord Wakeham, proposed that the Church of England should continue to be represented explicitly in the upper chamber. It also proposed that 'the concept of religious representation should be broadened to embrace other Christian denominations, in all parts of the UK and other faith communities' (Wakeham 2000: recommendation 108, para. 15.9). The subsequent White Paper presented by the leader of the House of Commons, the Rt Hon. Robin Cook MP, in November 2001 suggested reducing the number of Anglican bishops from 26 to 16 in line with the Commission's proposals. It did not accept proposals for the formal representation for other denominations and religions because 'the practical obstacles are simply too great' (Cmd 5291: paras 83 - 85). One supposed obstacle was the fact that there are more denominations and faiths than could be accommodated by the number proposed, although the Appointments Committee would have been expected to give proper recognition to non-Church of England faith communities, including their lay members. Following the indecisive vote in January 2003 by Members of Parliament and Peers on seven options for reform, reform of the House of Lords remains a thorny political issue for many reasons. There is still time for Christians and members of other faiths to contribute to public debate about the kind of religious representation needed in our plural society.

The position advanced in this paper is that bishops should continue to sit in the House of Lords and should be joined by members of other faith communities. The findings of the Royal Commission are broadly upheld, with the proviso that appropriate ways should be found of representing fairly the different communities and denominations. As David Hollenbach says, 'by playing a public role in civil society and culture, religious communities can strengthen the public life of a free society in democracies' (Hollenbach, 2000:112). Religion must be allowed to strengthen public life, even at the expense of the establishment of the Church of England as we know it. Of related interest, however, is how debate about membership of the House of Lords reflects a wider discussion about what constitutes legitimate law, and the nature of Christian responsibility in a plural society.

The supposed crisis of legitimacy

In the eyes of secular, modern liberalism, the nub of the apparent crisis for the Church of England is the lack of legitimacy for established, privileged Christian involvement in law making. The old arrangements are too tied up with a system of patronage and selective privilege to be defensible in a democratic society. A Christian ethic of law cannot ignore that, for many in UK society today, history, tradition and theology have lost their power to justify privileged Christian access to, and participation in, the highest law-making body in the land. As Hugo Young observed in *The Guardian* newspaper, twenty-six senior bishops in the Church of England sitting as full voting members was seen to 'reek of falsities that have neither charm nor purpose'. No competing tradition or belief-system, including Christianity, can any longer claim *prima facie* general validity with respect to their influence on legislation. Democratic legitimacy demands that governments make possible a discursively structured legislature within which none has special privileges for arcane historical reasons.

This is not the full picture, however. The furore that surrounded the role of bishops in the House of Lords is reflective of wider social questions about what constitutes legitimate law. Where legitimacy no longer depends upon an appeal to metaphysics or even to universal conceptions of justice, individuals and governments are required to evaluate options for action according to their consequences in relation to voter-choice. Law legitimates what Max Weber called 'domination' *provided that* law is based on the agreement of the citizens of the state (Weber, 1968: Pt I, Ch. III. pp. 212ff.). Weber gave classic expression in the mid-twentieth century to modern, liberal approaches to the legitimacy of law in his analyses of the beliefs, attitudes and willingness of individuals in a given society to assume the disciplines and burdens required for membership.

Legitimate political power is that where citizens have freely consented to the exercise of such power, and is normally expressed through the ballot box. Legitimacy designates subjective attitudes and beliefs on the part of members of society rather than objective evaluation of a regime against external criteria. The legitimacy of an action is the probability that people will orient their action to it. Once attained, and when subject to the logic of reason and debate generating allegiance and loyalty, legitimacy is 'the exclusive moral right of an institution to impose on some group of persons binding duties to be obeyed by those persons, and to enforce those duties coercively (Simmons, 2001: 7).

Expanding the concept of legitimacy

The place of bishops in the House of Lords is widely unacceptable because it embodies non-democratic privilege in politically influential form. What's not exposed to question, is the very notion of legitimacy upon which this supposed unacceptability depends. The claim in this paper is that the concept of legitimate law should be expanded to include recognition of the right of Churches and religious communities to be heard in public. We must seek to redefine the right to religious freedom *away* from the 'non-interference' and 'avoidance' mentality of modern liberalism and *towards* recognition of the need for religious voices in the public forum. It is self-evidently true that modern states are legitimated by law insofar as law is legitimated by the consent of the people – or, as a skeptic might claim, by the ability of those in power to pacify the masses. The legitimacy that matters today is very different to that justified by previous generations because no single perspective can be privileged above others. Consequently, the Church tends to be associated today with hierarchies that have no place in modern democracies. The 'sacred canopy' under which Richard Hooker could claim in the sixteenth century that the church was the people and the people the church has long since gone. But the rooting of legitimacy in liberal procedures for democratic decision-making is not all that matters. Today, the important challenge for liberal, plural societies is not to keep religion out of the public forum but to ensure that the voices of minorities are heard. It is to ensure that voices from religious communities are heard in the public debates.

The needs of liberal, plural societies today are different from those of the seventeenth and eighteenth centuries when luminaries such as John Locke and Immanuel Kant were writing. We are challenged today to think about how people of different faiths, and none, can live together peaceably. Many agree that we need more than a *mere* tolerance in which we agree simply not to interfere with each other's way of life (Williams, 2000: 174; Wolterstorf and Audi, 1997: 77). The supposed neutrality of procedural approaches to the organisation of society around principles of justice can hide indifference to the differences between people and communities. This kind of neutrality is exemplified by John Rawls's notion of justice as fairness. His work has much to recommend it but asks us *deliberately to omit* religious ideas of the good life, moral precepts or beliefs from our considerations. 'The veil of ignorance secures equality by allowing strangers to ascend to a high level of abstraction' (Rosenfeld, 1998: 127). This stripping of persons culturally naked, so to speak, risks reducing us all to abstract (albeit reasoning) egos which, because we become abstract egos, are interchangeable.

Beyond mere tolerance

The pluralism of mere tolerance hides religious intolerance behind a guise of neutrality. In John Rawls's Veil of Ignorance thought experiment abstract egos are interchangeable. Consequently, the experiment does not actually facilitate dialogue but monologue. There is no universal perspective that transcends the differences of faith, social status, education, health, ethnic origin, etc. The society in which this kind of 'public reason' dominates is unable to engage practically with significant cultural differences. The pluralism of mere tolerance offers to us the self-evident benefit that the institutions of modern, liberal democracies are not interested in private morals but provide a neutral framework for political choices and practices. Where legitimacy turns only on consent, the result is split between law, ethics and morality, and a 'public square' in which values other than individual liberty and democracy (for example, Muslim values attaching to polygamy) are not recognised. Democracy serves the interests of the majority and *not* that of the people as a whole, including minority groups. The risk is that democracy becomes dictatorship by the majority.

We may illustrate with the topics of marriage, bigamy and polygamous marriage. Consider the following statement from a recent UK Immigration and Nationality Directorate Instruction (Immigration, 2000: Annex D).

All marriages which take place in the United Kingdom must, *in order to be recognised as valid*, be monogamous and must be carried out in accordance with the requirements of the Marriage Act 1949, as amended by the Marriage Acts of 1970, 1983 and 1994, the Marriage Regulations of 1986 and other related Acts (eg; the Children Act 1989).

Polygamous marriages are recognised in England and Wales only if they took place in a country which allows marriages of this kind and if both parties were legally free to marry in this way. In such cases, UK law (Social Security and Benefits Act 1992) allows for income-related benefits (income support, housing benefit) to be payable to people in polygamous marriages. [1] However, Section 2 of the Immigration Act 1988 gave effect to Parliament's decision that the formation of polygamous households in the United Kingdom should be prevented. It provided that a woman would no longer be granted entry clearance on the basis of marriage where entry clearance had previously been granted to another wife of the same man.

According to the pluralism of mere tolerance, the public square is not the place for religious beliefs and teaching. Legitimate law does not require that explicit consideration be given to religious matters, unless the majority deem it sufficiently important. What matters is whether the arguments advanced in the public square are convincing in terms of 'public reason'. In these terms, monogamy is likely to be regarded in the public square as necessary for the equality of women. The pluralism of tolerance ensures that no individual rights are infringed. The question in this paper is whether the Christian Church should fight not only for its own continued existence in the House of Lords but for the inclusion of members of other faiths also, the intention being to promote colloquial pluralism as a social and moral good. Given Christian teaching on marriage as the union of one (baptised) woman and man before God, it's debatable whether bishops would want to advance the case for polygamous marriage in the UK. Nevertheless, it's at least arguable that they should want members of other faith communities to have the freedom to advance the case on their own behalf. The issue turns on the need to recast the question of what counts as legitimate law from a rights-based consideration of individual liberties to a duties-based consideration of the common good. Questions become redefined. The question 'Does polygamous marriage violate liberal principles with respect to the equality of women and men?' is recast. It becomes 'What kinds of opportunities for good and/or the restraint of evil present themselves in society today?' If convincing, it means that the Church of England and other religious communities should not accept the removal of bishops from the House of Lords, at least without a fight.

Theological arguments

To date, arguments of a different kind have been advanced within the Anglican Communion to keep bishops in the House of Lords. For some, liberal demands for post-metaphysical vindication of reason cannot render Christian involvement in law making illegitimate because the sources of legitimacy are

---

[1] 'Under s.11d of the Matrimonial Causes Act 1973, polygamous marriages contracted abroad can only be valid in English law if the conditions outlined at 2.1 above are met. The marriage will not be valid if either party is domiciled: the UK; or in any other country whose law does not permit polygamous marriage.

not found exclusively in democratic processes. Legitimacy claims for the roles performed by the bishops were advanced on the grounds of, *inter alia*, history, tradition and theological calling. In the General Synod debate on 8 July 2002, Sheila Cameron argued that the system, inaugurated by Henry VIII in legislation dating back to 1533, reinforced by the Act of Supremacy of 1588, was too complicated and embedded to repeal. 'If we were to go ahead we would be proposing to sever one arm of the establishment and considering what effect amputation would have on the established church' (Bates: 2002). Others, for example Michael Turnbull, the bishop of Durham, claimed that changing the system would be colluding in the secularisation of Britain: 'God has called the Church of England to exercise servanthood and mission in partnership with the state. This is our unique vocation, we should not be the ones to decline that call'. His legitimacy claim was explicitly faith-based and would, consequently, be deemed by many liberal thinkers to be an unreasonable contribution to public discourse.

Others pressed for more religious representatives in the Lords on the grounds that bishops, and other representatives of faith communities, are present in 'some of the most battered parts of our country'. These community leaders have essential grass roots links with schools, drop in centres, hospital and prison chaplains, and much more, across the country. In a fascinating exchange on 29 April 2002 between the Bishop of Southwark, the Right Reverend Tom Butler, and the Labour MP Chris Bryant, the latter said he saw 'absolutely no reason why any particular part of the community should have a right, whether God-given or otherwise, to sit in the legislature' (BBC, 2002b). In response, the Bishop of Southwark did not justify his claim from an explicit faith-standpoint. Rather, he made the type of moral and practical claim that he thought would be most widely understood and accepted but claimed, in effect, that a reasonable person might accept that, on balance, the presence of bishops in the House of Lords has been a good thing. [2] Bp Butler was clearly aware that comparative justifications could be made of other Christian and religious lea-

---

[2] According to John A. Simmons, a leading political philosopher, 'justification' of the kind advanced by the Bishop of Southwark is a defensive concept that applies when the person advancing the justification feels pressed to vindicate their existence or argument against a background presumption of possible objection. The threshold of justifiability depends upon particular circumstances, personalities, and other vagaries. Essentially, however, 'justification' of this kind is a practice or strategy that shows itself to be reasonable, prudent, and morally acceptable to interested parties. It entails a willingness to rebut possible objections and to show how such a rebuttal might be achievable in practice, and attempts to meet those with whom we disagree on common ground. By contrast, legitimacy applies to legal right or status or, 'in extended use, to a right or status supported by tradition, custom, or accepted standards' (Simmons, 2001: 124). Note: Simmons writes about the 'justification and legitimacy' of the state; I re-apply his meaning in this context.

ders, not to mention humanists and liberals, whose virtues, general quality of contribution, and personalities, contribute to good law making. Given this, he argued in a manner that reached similar conclusions to those that might have been reached by those holding broadly to liberal conceptions of reason.

Alternatively, some in the Anglican communion would not object if significant numbers of senior bishops in the Church of England no longer sit as full voting members of the House of Lords and spoke on 'secular' as well as 'sacred' issues. Indeed, some leading members of the Church of England have long argued against bishops sitting in the House of Lords. Bishop Mark Santer, for example, called for an end to church-state relations in a controversial statement before his retirement in May 2003. He was reported by the BBC as calling for the withdrawal of representatives from all religions from politics. (BBC, 2002a). His stance reflected increasing disquiet at the ability of Parliament to meddle in matters concerning the Church's internal discipline, in worship and in doctrine. It also reflected an increasingly widespread hunch that the Church's mission is better performed amidst local communities around the country than, to use his words, as part of the 'fling flang' that characterises routine parliamentary life. Santer argued that the Churches make their presence felt by doing the job properly in relation to city and various communities, and that the ubiquity of the media means that the Churches' witness in public affairs would not be significantly lessened. The Church could best perform its missionary task without an established part in the law-making process but as a 'voice' engaged in lobbying and support as need arises. The legitimacy derived from speaking with and for the disempowered is what really matters.

So far, we have seen two arguments advanced for retaining bishops in the House of Lords. These are arguments from tradition and pragmatism respectively. We have also seen an argument for their removal. Each of the thinkers mentioned has more sophisticated arguments that we cannot dwell upon here, the reason being that we need a different kind of argument to meet the needs of present-day liberal, plural societies. In order to protect against discrimination, we need space in the public square for values other than individual liberty and democracy. In order to promote the common good, we need more than a pluralism of tolerance in which we agree not to interfere with each other's way of life. We need a colloquial, interactive pluralism that takes account in the public sphere of cultural and faith-based differences. This requires instantiation of the conditions for colloquy in the law making institutions of the land. It is a need based, and duty based, argument that involves the reframing of some questions. The choice is *not* between 'establishment' or 'abandonment of the public square' by Christian leaders. The Church and nation are not a single entity and every generation brings new challenges with respect to the obligations

of gospel living. The choice is not *necessarily* between 'establishment' and religious freedoms defended by human rights law. In a human rights culture, the
challenge is to redefine legitimacy *away* from the 'non-interference' and 'avoidance' mentality of modern liberalism and *towards* recognition of the right of
churches and religious communities to be heard in public. The challenge for
the Church and all faith communities is for religion to strengthen public life,
even if this costs the 'establishment' of the Church of England as we know it.

Richard Hooker's suggestion for a duty based way forward

This debate raises many more issues about the relation between law, faith and
morality than we can address here. Briefly stated, I propose a duty rather than
rights based way forward that draws upon the wisdom of the old Anglican divine, Richard Hooker (1554 - 1600). He might seem a peculiar choice of dialogue
partner given that his creative genius was a significant influence on Anglican
defences of the Elizabethan establishment. However, the claim is that he provides timely and valuable assistance in meeting challenges from secular thinkers
with respect to the meaning of legitimate law and the function of natural reason. Hooker might also seem to be an unlikely helper in these deliberations
because of his uncompromising stance against polygamy. Polygamy, he says,
is a 'corrupt and unreasonable custom' that conflicts with the law of nature and
should not be allowed to get 'the upper hand of right reason' (Hooker, [1594]
1977: Bk 1, Ch. X, § 10). Despite this unpromising start, the claim is that Hooker's method in practical theology offers surprisingly useful resources for our
debate. This claim rests on Hooker's duty-based approach to moral reasoning.

Hooker's duty-based approach to moral reasoning is as follows. *Duty to
God* is the duty of duties. This is where ethical responsiveness begins. *Duty to
others* is an appropriate moral response to a claim-possessing fact or circum-
stance. The pattern established in faith is repeated in the duty of humans to
each other. Human laws are rules that direct actions towards their appropriate
ends and the common good. Duty is a responsive claim arising from the fact
that we are all human beings before God. Moral assertions can be descriptive
and prescriptive *only because* they are also responsive to particular kinds of
claim. The moral judgement implicit in his treatments allows a certain independence to the exercise of reason. It is natural for humans to recognise their
duty towards God and other humans. It is expected that they will exercise their
judgement responsibly in whatever circumstances they find themselves. The
difficult question today is whether colloquial pluralism is an appropriate end
that pertains to the common good. If so, then it's at least arguable that Hooker
himself would allow the possibility that his position on polygamy should be
revised in the light of present-day needs.

Summary reflections

Established or not, the primary calling of the Church catholic is centred round the worship of God. This involves celebrating the sacraments and preaching the gospel, endeavouring to embody Christian truth in the world by the power of the Holy Spirit, promoting patterns of common life that are oriented towards common good, nurturing moral values and defending fundamental freedoms, praying for the coming of God's kingdom. The particular calling of the Church of England has been intricately bound up with the political life of the nation. Establishment has witnessed powerfully to the integration of faith in society and to the political implications of faith. It has facilitated a diffusion of doctrine and the sacraments into civic life, and also the public offering to God of the dynamics of government. It has yielded relatively little secular power but has provided public access to Christian faith. For example, the Church of England gives everyone, with no former partner still living, the right to get married in their, or their partner's, parish church. Today, however, the UK is a pluralist, secular society in rapid change. 'Establishment' appears to undermine the moral good of pluralism and law based on consent and the liberty of the individual. It also appears to perpetuate positions of arbitrary privilege. The question is how best to obey Jesus' commandment to love God with all our heart, soul and mind, and to love our neighbours as ourselves (Matt. 22:36 - 38). As Tom Butler, Bishop of Southwark has said, 'Frankly, it's not for the good of the Church of England that bishops are in the House of Lords' (BBC, 2002b).

References

Bates, Stephen 2002 'Church backs PM's right to choose' in *The Guardian* Tuesday July 9.

BBC 2002a 'Bishop calls for end to 'state ties'' available at http://news.bbc.co.uk/hi/english/uk/england/newsid_1866000/1866135.stm [accessed on 8 July 2002].

BBC 2002b 'Bishop defends Lords Role' available at http://news.bbc.co.uk/hi/english/uk_politics/newsid_1946000/1946699.stm [accessed on 02/07/2002].

Cmd 5291 Government White Paper Presented to Parliament by the Prime Minister 2000 *The House of Lords – Completing the Reform* London: HMSO.

Hollenbach, David 2000 *The Common Good and Christian Ethics* Cambridge: Cambridge University Press.

Hooker, Richard [1594] 1977 *The Folger Library edition of the works of Richard Hooker* Cambridge: Belknap Press of Harvard University Press

Immigration and Nationality Directorate (2000) *Immigration Directorate's Instructions: Spouses, Recognition Of Marriage And Divorce* Dec. 2000 Annex D.

Matrimonial Causes Act (1973) available at `http://www.ind.homeoffice.gov.uk/default.asp?PageId=2555` [accessed on 06 June 2003].

Rosenfeld, Michael (1998) *Just Interpretations: Law Between Ethics and Politics* Berkeley and Los Angeles, California: University of California Press.

Simmons, John A. 2001 *Justification and Legitimacy: essays on rights and obligations* Cambridge: Cambridge University Press.

Wakeham, The Rt Hon Lord DL (Chair) 2000 *A House for the Future: Royal Commission on the Reform of the House of Lords* London: HMSO, recommendation 108, para. 15.9.

Weber, Max (1968) *Economy and Society: an outline of interpretive sociology*, ed. Roth, Guenther and Wittich, Claus New York: Bedminster.

Williams, Rowan (2000) *On Christian Theology* Oxford: Blackwells.

Wolterstorff, Nicholas and AUDI, Robert (1997) *Religion in the Public Square: Convictions in Political Debate* Lanham, MD: Rowman and Littlefield Publishers.

Young, Hugo (2002) 'The church must grow up and choose its own leaders' *The Guardian* 9 July.

The Influence of Communications Technology and Mass Media in Modern Society: a Challenge for Public Theology

Wilhelm Graeb

The function of the mass media in modern societies

The mass media have gained great significance in culture and society (Keppler, 1999; Soeffner, 1998). Why this is so, and how this has come about, is what I want to outline in my paper. This will then lead to the question, what this means for the church if it wishes to remain a public church and what this means for the mission it has to 'communicate the gospel'. What are the consequences for church practice and for explicitly religious practice? But let us begin with a look at the rise to dominance of the mass media and its significance for wider culture and society.

There is general agreement in sociology and social theory that the function of the mass media consists in building, renewing, and increasing our knowledge concerning society, and in conveying that into other parts of society. Modern, functionally differentiated society cannot function without a system of mass media. For people need common, shared constructions of their social and subjective realities in functionally differentiated and pluralistic societies just as much as in others. These constructions enable them to interpret their experiences and come to grips with them in all their confusion and contingency and in their being caught up in different systems and networks of relationships. The mass media mediate, they bring us what we know about the world, about the events taking place in the world, which they make into the news which they report, and with which they entertain us. But above all – and this is, from our perspective of a theory of religion, the most significant aspect – the mass media also mediate, or convey, *meaning in a particular form*, they provide the symbolic horizons for the interpretation of our daily experiences, and they offer these forms of meaning for a verbalization of our desires, our hopes and our fears. Our everyday communications, including those concerning religion, what takes place in the worship service and the sermon, in religious instruction and pastoral care, are in fact *connecting communications*: continuing that social communication, which is being provided by the mass media, by making the connection to our daily context.

It is therefore no surprise that Practical Theology has become aware that the planning and setting up of such formal elements as a symbolic space and a ritual performance are to a remarkable degree shaped by the models found on TV, particularly in regard to the occasional services of the church. [1] The occasional services are a kind of symbolic action of the church, through which the church represents the religious culture of society in its most explicit form. In the last few years, research has shown that, for example, the TV show 'Traumhochzeit' (*Dream Wedding*) has served to establish role patterns for how people plan their own wedding (de Mol, 1992; 1993). What happens in church is supposed to correspond to what we have seen on TV (Reichertz, 1999; Hauschildt, 1999). TV provides the stage direction for the church wedding, for the wedding photographs and video. Only in this way – one may assume – are the importance of the wedding in my life and the effect of the divine blessing guaranteed on a long-term basis. In church, the wedding must be performed in such a way that the pictures taken and the video of it provide an impressive presentation. It is the media which set the stage. And the media, too, guarantee the representation of the symbolic and theological content of the event.

The mass media and the construction of reality in society

Niklas Luhmann captures it well when he says: 'What we know about our society, about the world even, in which we live, we know through the mass media.' (Luhmann, 1996, 9) What we know about society, about politics, the economy, the law, about history and nature, but finally also about an ultimate, transcendent reality and about human faith in such a reality, about religion and the religions, about the church, has been transmitted through the mass media. Social communication and with that the way we are being conscious

---

[1]   Pioneer work in regard to the media and their significance for religion and the church has been done by Horst Albrecht, *Die Religion der Massenmedien*, Stuttgart et.al. 1993; important impulse given by Hans-Joachim Benedict, *Fernsehen als Sinnsystem?*, in: Wolfram Fischer, Wolfgang Marhold (eds.), *Religionssoziologie als Wissenssoziologie*, Stuttgart 1978, 117 - 137; Hermann Pius Siller, *Bildschirmreligiosität – Thesen aus theologischer Sicht*, in: Eckhard Bieger, Wolfgang Fischer, Reinhold Jacobi, Peter Kottlorz (eds.), *zeitgeistlich. Religion und Fernsehen in den neunziger Jahren*, Köln 1994, 121 - 127; Günter Thomas, *Die Wiederverzauberung der Welt? Zu den religiösen Funktionen des Fernsehens*, in: Peter Buhmann, Petra Müller (eds.), *Die Zukunft des Fernsehens*, Stuttgart 1996, 113 - 139; Günter Thomas, *Medien, Ritual, Religion. Zur religiösen Funktion des Fernsehens*, Frankfurt a.M. 1998; and finally especially Arno Schilson, *Medienreligion. Zur Signatur der Gegenwart*, Tübingen 1997.

and aware of reality and make sense of it, rest on the mass media. Certainly, we still have personal contact and communication with others: there is socialising in families, neighbourhoods, among friends and in school. But all that is being communicated – through conversations, stories and reports, through contacts with parents, teachers, friends and acquaintances – always already follows from media communication. What knowledge parents, teachers, friends and acquainttances have about society, about nature and history, about God and the world, they have from books and newspapers, from the radio and TV and more recently also from the Internet. We do not usually take part in the mode of authentic experience, at least not in such a way that we have *been present, we ourselves*. We have everything transmitted and communicated to us through print and audio-visual media (Bausinger, 1984; Hoover and Lundby, 1997).

We have read, we have heard, we have seen images on the computer showing that the ozone hole above Antarctica has again grown larger last summer. We have not only read and heard about it, we have seen it on TV with our own eyes, just as people around the whole world became eye-witnesses of those two airplanes crashing into the World Trade Centre in New York. But in fact, we have become eyewitnesses only because there are methods of broadcasting live images which have been developed for TV by way of interposing media technology, producing a co-presence of events and news which almost completely transcends differences of time and space. Events that take place in the real world can become congruent with the reporting about them. And for how many, innumerable times has not every one of us after September 11, 2001, watched the Twin Towers collapse!

But has, what we read, see and hear through the media, *really* happened? Is it *really* true that the ozone hole above Antarctica is growing and will, in the end, endanger the whole atmosphere? Is it *really* true that on September 11, 2001, the Twin Towers in New York were hit by two passenger planes, causing them to collapse? We have heard and read about it, we have even seen the events of 9 - 11 'live' on TV. But have we been present? We have to believe the media, which in the case of live broadcasting is, no doubt, easier than with the printed word or with recorded TV reports, let alone computer simulations. But can we be sure what it is that the media present us? The media are always between us and the *images* we have of reality. We cannot get behind the media, we have no possibility to get to a real, a true reality to compare with and see the difference between true and false representations of it. To doubt the reports about the events of September 11, 2001, in New York would seem unreasonable. The media enhance our conviction that what they report is true, through various mutual agreement.

Certainly, the natural sciences are trying to discover the *truth* about the world, about society, history, nature. But their findings – equally numerous and varied – again come to our knowledge only by way of the media, even if we ourselves are part of the scientific community. There are always *methods of technical transmission* interposed between our interactions and communications. We perceive that also the sciences offer us descriptions of reality, seen from a certain perspective. For publication of their discoveries and findings, they depend on the media (Rorty, 1992; 2000). We know that we can never be sure whether the media, our source of what we know about the world, can be trusted. But knowing this changes nothing of the fact that the media have an almost transcendental function for the constitution of our knowledge. They make up the structures of our attitude towards ourselves and the world. They form part of the conditions for our being able to know anything at all.

Media society

That is why we can speak of living in a 'media society', a concept first used by Jürgen Habermas, who originally applied it to the 'structural change of public life' (Habermas, 1990), a dynamic process underway since the 18th century. [2] Beginning with the invention of printing, and then with the rise of the bourgeois middle class, the media have decisively contributed to the instigation of change in the direction of a functionally differentiated, modern society. They have shaped their own, recursive, self-supporting system, a system of knowledge about society and its world. They have then, however, in Habermas' view, played a considerable role in the 'colonialization of the life world', contributing to the destruction of the communicative structures in our interpersonal attitude towards ourselves and our world (Habermas, 1981).

The system of knowledge transmitted by way of the media has been made possible through technologies which have been interposed in the interaction between persons. Knowledge is being printed and broadcast. It is, due to compulsory education and the existence of a reading public, being read and received, listened to and watched. Yet this process of spreading knowledge about society and the world, about what we think is real, what we want to talk about with others, is possible only because of technology.

---

[2]   As an anti-critique to Habermas' critical position in regard to the media, cf. Rainer Vowe, *Medien und Öffentlichkeit*, in: Traugott Jähnichen, Wolfgang Maaser, Joachim von Soosten (eds.), *Flexible Welten. Sozialethische Herausforderungen auf dem Weg in die Informationsgesellschaft*, Münster 2002, 189 - 199.

The religious function of the mass media and the challenge of the church

What kinds of repercussions do the mass media have on people, their experiences and their way of acting? *How* are they shaping concepts of meaning, as far as this can be judged in terms of theoretical considerations? And therefore, *what kind* of influence do they have on religious consciousness? *What* challenges arise in view of this situation for the churches, if they want to keep themselves as public churches?

The media report about events. They inform us about what happens, what has changed, is different from how it was, and so on. Niklas Luhmann, following Gregory Bateson (1981, 488), defines *information* as 'any difference, which in connection with a later event will make a difference' (Luhmann, 1996, 39). This is a rather abstract description, but also a far-reaching one, at least in view of describing the mode of operation of the mass media. New is what has not been before, without which, however, there will be no reporting possible about anything happening later, anything that cannot be understood without this information. Information is what had not been known before in this particular form, and which is continued by a process of further news and reports, by the continuation of a story, and which must be continued by this in order to be understood, to make sense. Whatever is being kept in mind, over a shorter or a longer period of time, 'makes a difference'.

This constant consumption and therefore loss of information, and with it the desire for more and newer information, for news, is typical. The mass media spread information far and wide so that instantaneously everybody will count on its being known to everyone else. Just as our differentiated economy, depending on the flow of money, creates the never-ending need to replace money as soon as it has been spent, so the mass media create the need to replace information that has become redundant, that is non-information, by new information: 'fresh money and new information are the central motives of modern social dynamics.' (Luhmann, 1996, 44).

Exactly for that reason, it is the mass media – beside the money economy – which lies behind the much discussed peculiarities of our modern *time experience*. It is the mass media, which create what we call a *modernity consciousness*, the prevalence of what is new, making everything that is old look outdated and passé. In the network of global communication they stretch the co-temporality to make it cover the non-co-temporal. They make considerable use of a belief in progress still being strong in many spheres of life. The quite neurotic compulsion in the economy and in the sciences constantly to have to come up with something new has to do with the implications of the mass media in their culture-shaping capacity. The same is true for the economy, politics, humanities and the arts. This dynamics of change is built into society itself; but this has not always been the case. It is expressed in the designation society gives itself by calling itself 'modern' or 'postmodern'. What is new, permanently grows old and has to be replaced by something newer. Modern times cannot stay modern, they must overtake themselves with 'postmodernism'. This obsessive need to assess developments in itself can be said to be caused by the mass media with their stress on information on a daily basis, which gives rise to a consciousness of permanent change and constant transformation. For the dynamization of society, therefore, the mass media are a decisive factor. With Luhmann one could say: They keep society awake (Luhmann, 1996, 47). They generate a permanently renewed readiness, to expect novelty, surprises, or maybe even disturbances. In this, the mass media 'fit in' with other functional systems like the economy, the sciences or politics with their ever own, accelerating dynamics, which are continuously confronting society with new problems.

The mass media enhance the dynamization of social developments, they encourage modernization processes, but together with that they also contribute to the disintegration of traditional relationships and milieus which once provided social stability. Through permanent confrontation with the ever new, the mass media are often *too demanding*, provoking a nostalgia for what appears to be well-known and well-tried, for traditional values and a clearly structured order. Through the assessment of social processes of change, promoted and supported by the media, religion and the church may be drawn into the side of nostalgic preservation of the old, as well as to the side of a hopeful optimism looking forward to the new.

We will most likely not expect the church to stand for provoking more crises, for additional acceleration, change, disturbance, or insecurity. Sometimes the self-understanding of the church seems to let it participate in the dynamics of change produced by the mass media, without much critical reflection. The gospel is then being broadcast as (good) *news*. Men and women are being called upon the *change* their lives. The church will then present itself as a *missionary* church, announcing an unheard-of truth, which has so far not been known. Such efforts of the church do, however, not evoke much enthusiasm – understandably enough. The message of the church is not new. As such, it lacks information value. It is highly redundant, and necessarily so. *Redundancy, repetition, remembrance* can become information, through *increased attention* being paid to the old, well-known, that which in its substance cannot really be improved. What this means, is regularly demonstrated by advertising, which depends on familiarity and repetition. Adverts don't worry us with presenting something new; instead they show us the attractions of the well-known, the old, the familiar. How do they do that? By stirring our attention, by a shift in perspective, through the creation of metaphors, through eye-catching images; by way of telling stories. Creatively working with symbolic forms, advertising keeps awake the memory of what is already known.

There is potential in this method for religion, and perhaps also the church, to use this to their own advantage. It is a way, not of surprising with something new, but of settling deeper and grounding oneself in the familiar. Religion can recall the old *stories and images about life lived well,* can bring them back, call up memories and lead into their depth. Religion stands for *what is lasting in the dynamics of change, the presence of the infinite in the finite.* Proclamation as information, as announcement of a message is the wrong concept, as the whole idea of *proclamation* no longer works in the media society. Rather, the old traditions of religion are being called for, making accessible their well-tried meaning which has stood the test of time; pointing out the truth as it is present and accessible in words, forms and colours; painting images which make us stop and *tarry,* prompting high thoughts and deep feelings. This will not be accomplished through a reduction of redundancy, it calls for an *increase in resonance.* The perception of meaning offered by religion can take on a shape which the senses can grasp. Religion then works with well-known, familiar stories. Faced by our tremendously dynamic time experiences, it trusts that these stories will remind us of what is lasting. The old symbols can make possible an understanding of what it means to live in *this* time – with God going with us, at our side.

Consequences for religious communication in the church

It will then be the task of the church to tell salvation stories, not in the sense of provoking a heightened mood of crises, but helping to cope with crises and get the better of them, by way of finding reassurance about meaning in the absolute. The task will be to build a religious consciousness with the strength to put in order, being rooted in ultimate certainties of life. How can religious communication gain this ordering strength, whether in the media or inside the church?

What defines religion is that it has to do with 'ultimate concerns' (Paul Til-lich), with *the symbolization of the final, the ultimate horizons of orientation for our existence.* This *symbolization* occurs with the *telling* of deeply mea-ningful stories and with the *shaping* of symbols, which give us something to gaze at and wonder, to think about at length, which awaken and keep alive the 'sense for the infinite', the dimension of the transcendent. Religion must not try to increase the already existing complexity and dynamic of our living conditions; rather it must *transcend* them towards what is simple, steady, essential, eternal.

If, however, we want this religious communication to remain compatible with the way our modern consciousness works, we must take care not to set up the structure of a counter-culture, in a fundamentalist manner, when referring to the dimension of the absolute. We must take care that religious communication does not lose a connection to the awareness and perception of reality, as built by the media and communicated through them in society. This can be successfully done only if the shaping of our consciousness by the media is being constantly watched, and if, furthermore, we do not shrink back from acknowledging, that the media, too, are shaping religious consciousness – if mostly in non-religious language. The media, too, tell deeply meaningful stories and create symbols leading to the dimension of transcendence.

For the church, there can be only one consequence, and that is to want to do this even better, drawing on the wealth of powerful images and good stories from its tradition – and at the same time, applying a *hermeneutics*, an interpretation of present-time culture as well as of our tradition, able to *unfold meaning*. For this, we need theology.

In a media-driven society, theology must consciously reflect and consider how society functions. It will then be able to help create symbolic forms for a religious meaning perspective, which can be perceived as such, in society. Explicit religious communication, inside the church or outside, in the media, from the pulpit, on radio or TV, must always keep in mind the pressure of towards novelty on its audience. It is those experiences, specific for present-day culture, which we have in regard to ourselves, to others, to society, that call for a *religious interpretation*; through telling plausible and trustworthy stories and drawing images to make one think – as *being the word about God*.

The task of religious communication is to admit reality as presented by the media, but to *transform* it, to *analyse* it, to *reflect critically* upon it, to *interpret* it, and so to cause a shift in perspective. What is needed is *theological commentary on the times*, but in such a way that makes a marked difference to the political commentary due to the drawing out of a *religious perspective of meaning*. This perspective holds our interest and elicits thoughtfulness, not because of new stories and pictures, but because of its quite old, yet still moving stories and its thought provoking images. As a result, we may hear what Christianity has to say concerning our ambivalent experiences, our memories and expectations, which the media transmit and which are present in the deep structures of our present-day cultural consciousness. Christianity can respond to the *existential* questions triggered by the news – questions about meaning, how to make sense of catastrophes, political conflict and upheaval.

How theologians and the churches *react* to, how we *deal* with this image of reality, with the world view of the media, how we *interpret* it, and how we *understand ourselves* in it – this can become a topic of main interest for explicit religious communication within and beyond the media. It can only be a question of a theological communication continuing that of the media, a *commentary looking for a deeper meaning of a situation*, in the religious sense – with the mass media defining the situation as such. If well done, such a commentary can let us see the world *'quite differently'*.

References

Bateson, Gregory (1981) *Ökologie des Geistes: Anthropologische, psychologische und epistemologische Perspektiven*, Frankfurt a.M.

Bausinger, Hermann (1984) Media Technology and Daily Life. in *Media, Culture & Society* 6, 343 - 351.

Habermas, Jürgen (1981) *Theorie des kommunikativen Handelns*, 2 vols., Frankfurt a.M.

Habermas, Jürgen (1990) *Der Strukturwandel der Öffentlichkeit. Untersuchungen zu einer Kategorie der bürgerlichen Gesellschaft*, Frankfurt a.M . . .

Hauschildt, Eberhard (1999) Kirchliche Trauungen zwischen Magiebedürfnis und Interpretationschance. *Pastoraltheologie* 88, 24 - 28.

Hoover, Stewart M. and Lundby, Knut (1997) *Rethinking Media, Religion and Culture*, Thousand Oaks.

Keppler, Angela (1999) Mediale Erfahrung, Kunsterfahrung, religiöse Erfahrung.Über den Ort von Kunst und Religion in der Mediengesellschaft. in Anne Honer, Roland Kurt and Jo Reichertz (eds.), *Diesseitsreligion. Zur Deutung der Bedeutung moderner Kultur*, Konstanz, 183 - 200.

Luhmann, Niklas (1996) *Die Realität der Massenmedien*. Opladen.

Luhmann, Niklas (1997) *Die Gesellschaft der Gesellschaft*. Frankfurt a.M.

De Mol, Linda (1992) *Traumhochzeit: Heiraten mit Phantasie*, Düsseldorf.

De Mol, Linda (1993) *Traumhochzeit: Das Buch für den schönsten Tag im Leben*. Düsseldorf.

Reichertz, Jo (1999) 'Traumhochzeit' – magie und Religion im Fernsehen oder: Die wiederentdeckung des Religiösen. *Pastoraltheologie* 88, 2 - 15.

Rorty, Richard (1992) *Kontingenz, Ironie und Solidarität*, Frankfurt a.M.

Rorty, Richard (2000) *Wahrheit und Fortschritt*, Frankfurt a.M.

Soeffner, Hans-Georg (1998) Zum Verhältnis von Kunst und Religion in der 'Spätmoderne'. in Dieter Fritz-Assmus (ed.), *Wirtschaftsgesellschaft und Kultur*, Berlin, 239 - 255.

Christianity and Public Life in Canadian society

Solange Lefebvre

What is expressed here derives its inspiration from twelve years of experience in the media, as a columnist and an 'expert' on Christianity and religion. It is also shaped by the current situation of religion in Canada. The theme of my reflections hinges on three questions concerning the stance that religion is now granted in public life. Firstly, what have I learned from my own experience about how the sway of modernity prompts public figures to devise tactics allowing them to avoid taking a "strictly" denominational stance in public matters? Secondly, how does this attitude relate to the Christian spirituality of discretion? And, thirdly, what role are the new figures of converts and pilgrims to play as critics of this show of religious discretion in the public realm? I conclude with a discussion of modernity as a locus of paradox and tension between religion and public life. Theoretically, my paper is inspired by the works of Hannah Arendt and by the discussion between Jürgen Habermas and David Tracy.

Public religion and modernity

Today, at least in Canada, it has become difficult to take an overtly religious position in public life. This paper reflects on the fact that avoiding a strictly denominational position in the public sphere is a key part of our modern ethos: It often dictates the way public figures are expected to be, to act and to think. In *Between Past and Present*, Hannah Arendt mentions three pillars of modernity. These three pillars are doubt (Descartes and Kierkegaard), a political vision of salvation (Marx), and intra-worldliness (Nietzsche). We can think that these three pillars impose a style and content on the way Canadian religious leaders and representatives (especially theologians) speak and think about the divine when they are caught up in public debates.

Let us consider the first pillar, doubt. For academics, it has become difficult to express a clear and exclusive faith or truth in the public sphere. Seeing that theology has also come to consider itself a science, theologians feel they

must guard against adopting an openly strong evangelical or confessional tone. Secondly, in political terms, ever since Marx and Engels came up with their
scathing criticism of religion as an obstacle to human freedom and collective
accomplishment, theologians, when speaking publicly, feel they must be ethi-
cally and politically relevant: always mentioning the social dimension of faith
and testifying to their social involvement or commitment to a cause. In the
20th century, the Catholic Action Movement and the evangelical Social Gospel both had a notable influence on expressions of faith. Some scholars even
think that by insisting so exclusively on social and temporal involvement, we
have strayed from religious practices (prayer, liturgy, ritual). Finally, theological discourse now has to make room for intra-worldly dimensions such as
corporeality, sensuality, and pleasure which, it is declared, are fundamental to
human life and religious experience (Nietzsche).

Given this context, how are we to speak of religious values in the public
realm? Can a theology filtered through the paradigms of modernity – doubt,
political emancipation and intra-worldliness – still have anything theologically
meaningful to say? Habermas has reminded us that the public sphere is constituted by open conversation, plural discourses and diverse communities. Yet
in their *Habermas, Modernity, and Public Theology*, Browning and Fiorenza
point to the questions Habermas raises about the distinctiveness of the religious
contribution to the public realm. They quote the German philosopher when he
admits that: "During my time as a student, it was, above all, theologians such
as Gollwitzer and Iwand who had given morally responsible answers to the political questions that challenged us after the war. It was the Confessing Church
which at that time with its acknowledgement of guilt at least attempted a new
beginning."(1992: 228) And reflecting on the case of theology at the University of Frankfurt, Habermas notes that the more theology opens itself in general
to the discourses of the human sciences, the greater the danger that its own status will be lost in the network of alternating take-over attempts, especially in
an age of post-metaphysical thinking."(1992: 231) Habermas in a way enligh-
tens the position of the theologian in modern society: "Under the conditions
of post-metaphysical thinking, whoever puts forth a truth claim today must,
nevertheless, translate experiences that have their home in religious discourse
into the language of a scientific expert culture – and from this language retrans-
late them back into praxis." (1992: 234) Thus modern interpretations separate
social and political discourse from religious experience. Theology than risks
losing its specific status: "Faith is protected against a radical problematization
by its being rooted in cult ... Theological discourse, however, distinguishes
itself from religious experience by separating itself from ritual praxis."

Of course, other philosophical theories of language – such as, for example, the hermeneutics of Gadamer – offer a different perspective. And I agree with Tracy who takes exception to Habermas's theory of social evolution which sees history as going from myth to metaphysics, and then on to communicative rationality. Tracy reminds of opposing theories proposed in modern anthropology: in the history of religions and philosophical hermeneutics; in reflections on myth (Eliade) and symbol (Ricoeur and Kant); in metaphysics and modern theologies; in the possibilities of cross-cultural dialogue (Geertz) and in inter-religious dialogue (Panikkar), (1992: 31) But still, there is a real process of secularisation going on, particularly in the sense of an individualisation of religion which distances it from community.

Habermas points out something important: theologians who intervene in the public realm move into an interpretative mode and distance themselves from religious experience per se. They are thus no longer in a position to present themselves as witnesses who speak simply of their religious experience. In that case, their position is not so different from that of political militants who are also political experts.

A counter-hypothesis: a Christian faith governed by discretion

In a similar vein, another theological question merits consideration. According to Vatican II, the laity's most fundamental mission is "to work for the sanctification of the world from within as leaven." This mission is specifically lived out by "seeking the Kingdom of God," "managing temporal things," and "ordering them according to God's plan" (Lumen Gentium 31). These three tasks together condition Christian secular life. Seeking the Kingdom of God essentially links the world of the "here and now" to the eschatological dimension, without which the temporal world is bound to sink into secularism. The temporal world concerns our social, family, and professional life. It specifically concerns the laity. The attempt to order temporal things "according to God's plan" situates human action in the realm of Evangelical values, raising it to the level of theological ethics. The first and third aspects of the lay person's threefold secular project apply to all baptized Christians. Though those in holy orders do participate in the Church's secular affairs, they are "by reason of their particular vocation especially and professedly ordained to the sacred ministry." The Canadian laity has taken to heart this theological vision of action in the secular world. In political life and the media, Catholics feel free to adopt temporal views, leaving public discourse on religion and faith to the clergy, religious and other church authorities. [1]

---

[1]   We can find a good example of this attitude in Pierre Trudeau's life and spirituality. See John English *et al.* (eds), *The Hidden Pierre Trudeau: Faith and Politics in the Balance*, Ottawa,

At least since World War Two, Catholicism has been advocating a spirituality of discretion in secular matters. For example, Catholics see the lay apostolate as working for the world's sanctification like leaven, from within (in saeculo et ex saeculo). The metaphor of leaven is a sign that the theological discourse on temporal work has emerged from a theology of discretion, from the fact that Christians are immersed in a secular world which is more or less hostile to direct evangelization and which at some levels has severed its ties with Western Christendom. The Christian is seen as leaven: as a consequence, the accent has shifted from proselytism to silent witness, social action, and political relevance.

At the same time, this discreet Christianity which valorizes the world and its business has perhaps also hastened the decline of religious practice and the erosion of Christian communities united by worship and instruction in the faith. In some fashion, this may have given rise to Christianity espousing the forms of a modern privatized religiosity. It is actually this discretion and this silence which, since the late 1970s, have provoked the response of very faith-affirming figures: converts, media preacher, pilgrims. And specimens of such figures appear both in the Catholic denomination and in Pentecostal and Baptist churches.

Public religious celebrations as criticism of the Christianity of discretion

But, after decades of this modernity – which in Catholicism crystallised around Catholic action: discreet, worldly, tentative, respectful, and politically involved – new ways have perhaps been found to celebrate religious faith in the public sphere. There are more than a few examples of this counter-modernity movement; some that come immediately to mind are John-Paul II's World Youth Days (WYD), one of which drew hundreds of thousands of young people to Toronto (Canada) during summer 2003. Such events are powerful examples of public witness. When they were started in the late 1980s, a certain Catholic elite found such events hard to accept: they were too spiritual, too hierarchical, too noisy, and too non-political ("a waste of money and time when millions were dying of hunger and disease in the world", would say these critics). And these events still have many their critics.

After decades of discretion, unabashed witness is once more being seen and heard in public: I love Jesus; I believe in God, I love the Pope, and so on. All this adds up to a huge manifestation of popular religion. A similar trend

---

Novalis. Canada's Prime Minister for many years, Trudeau was also a 'discreet' Catholic Christian.

is seen in evangelical movements and in any others where there is a strong strain of conversions. Such movements imply lively and concrete criticism of a certain modern and urbane Christianity. Yet these modern expressions of traditional Christianity also have their modern side. For example, an attentive analysis of the Jean-Paul II's homilies will show that he offers an intra-worldly vision of Catholic life during the WYD. When he speaks of Life it is not in terms of the Hereafter; he asks young people to be missionaries of love and live here on earth, to establish on earth a Kingdom of Love, a Civilisation of Love.

Modernity: the source of new identity claims

Our last point concerns the common opponent to religious groups: a dogmatic secularity which dreams of eliminating every reference to religion from the public sphere. Here in Canada, few militants would defend this kind of secularity (the French model of "laïcité", political neutrality) and make an all-out effort to secularise the public sphere. But dogmatic secularity comes in many varieties and it can also refer to belief in a neo-evolutionist vision of modernity, in which religion inevitably "declines," becoming neither fish nor fowl nor good red herring. And this variety feeds on dialogues required to integrate the cultural and religious minorities (Muslims, Buddhists, Sikhs, etc.), which have become more numerous among us, with the waves of immigration over the last twenty years. Facing this new diversity, the majority would abandon its old denominational privileges (at school for example). Public and media milieus are deeply imbued with this neo-evolutionist vision. Around Christmas and Easter, we hear this in their comments on opinion polls; they always sound so amazed that people still have faith in God, that "religion is still alive." I always have to explain that religion is as old as the human heart! One must add that since September 11th 2001, things have changed; religious convictions have become terribly alive, even threatening.

One way of viewing the neutral stance is to look at the public sphere as the locus of a paradox. Some authors would have us understand the place of religion in democracies as inherently paradoxical, following Hobbes who holds that, in modern society, no religion should be considered as true and every variety of religion should be respected. The abstract subjectivity which underpins modern democracies incites particular inter-subjectivities to take up the locus of domination and power. It is not only a matter of survival, but the paradoxical reality of modern democracies. In a debate with Bauer, who thinks that there is no religion if there is no privileged religion, Marx replies: "Religion attains its practical universality only where no privileged religion exists." (Holy Family). The proliferation of religion occurs only in societies which are no longer religious. [2] In Marx's view, religious particularisms alienate humanity from its universal community. He sees these particularisms as obstacles to the creative forces of modern democracy, in that they separate civil society from the state.

But, in fact, particularisms are not a survival but a paradoxical stimulation of culture and religion in modern and abstract democracies. It is in this light that we can best understand religious collective demands, those of gender, class, and generations in our modern societies. This proliferation of points of view can, at the same time, weaken convictions, paralyse us with perpetual doubt or radicalise any position. This means that, in today's modern society, we can no longer be religious as men and women once were in pre-modern societies. To be religious and to speak intelligently about religion is always, in varying degrees, something of a struggle, today we live at the heart of a modern and anthropological paradox.

Conclusion

Seeking a heuristic context for practical theology, I have pondered the question of religion in public life in the light of my own experience with public debates in Canada. This experience has led me to four basic observations: First, modernity has relegated theologians to a position that makes it difficult for them to profess strongly their faith when acting as participants in public life. Second, this difficulty is not without some link to the spirituality of discretion advocated in the 20th century, notably by the Catholic Church. Third, the convert and the pilgrim have emerged as new figures to challenge the modern Christian's discretion with very public proclamations of their faith. Fourth, the liberal and rational attitudes advocated by modernity can lead to some rather paradoxical identity claims. Based on these four observations, I have come to see professions of Christian faith on today's public scene as a thing of paradox, fraught with permanent tension. This perspective reconnects with a [common and] fundamental thread running through Western history, the tension and reciprocal criticism associated with the relations between the religious and political spheres of life.

References

Arendt, Hannah [1954] *Between Past and Future: Eight Exercises in Political Thought*. New York: Viking Press, 1961.

Arendt, Hannah (1958) *The Human Condition (Condition de l'homme moderne)*. Paris: Calmann-Lévy.

---

2   See Thériault 1996 :172 - 3.

Browning, Don S. and Francis Schüssler Fiorenza (eds) (1992) *Habermas, Modernity, and Public Theology*. New York: Crossroad.

Thériault, Yvon (1996) in Mikhaël Elbaz, Andrée Fortin et Guy Laforest (eds), *Les frontières de l'identité. Modernité et postmodernisme au Québec*. Sainte-Foy : Presses de l'Université Laval/Paris: L'Harmattan.

Doing Public Theology In Africa: Trends And Challenges

Abraham A. Berinyuu

Doing public theology in Africa is an ambitious project. It also raises all sorts of expectations that I cannot meet. My intention in this paper is specific and even tentative. It is not a critical review of African theological works but rather an attempt to understand the dynamics, development, challenges and prospects of public theology in Africa with particular focus on theory, methods and praxis. I use 'understanding' here to denote a heuristic exercise in mapping and defining some of the dynamics, trends and prospects of public theology in general and African theological discourses in particular.

First and foremost, when we speak of Africa, we must ask the question, 'Which Africa are we talking about?' Mudimbe, in his book entitled *The Invention of Africa* (1988), points out how the many 'Africas' have been invented by Western scholars. This invention is predicated by ideological significations that not only distort but also permeate theological discourses in Africa. I use 'signification' in the sense that the African-American historian of religion Charles H. Long (1986) means it. It connotes the idea of pigeonholing something or somebody. It positions something or somebody at a particular social location. These significations have led not only to the distortion of African theological heritage but also dressed it up as Western theological tradition. I shall provide some examples to illustrate this point.

First, when we talk of Africa, does it include North Africa? If so, why is it that, historically, the theological discourses of the African Church Fathers such as Augustine from North Africa are often classified as Western theological traditions? The main Latin theology came not from Rome but from North Africa, from people such as Tertullian and Cyprian. Tertullian wrote *Against Praxeas*, in which he discussed the doctrines of the Trinity and the Person of Christ.

Some African theologians are beginning to question whether the West has not stolen African theologians and theologies as their ancestors and the antecedents of Western theologies. In many of the theologies we read from the West there is hardly any attempt to treat theologians such as Augustine or any of the African Church Fathers upon which many medieval and reformed theologians depended. In raising this issue I am not just being a revisionist but genuinely wondering as an African theologian whether it is possible that Augustine's theology may have influenced the theologies of Luther, Zwingli, Calvin, and Erasmus, to mention but a few. If such influences were not only possible but highly probable, then it can be assumed that African theological contributions to practical theological discourses predate modern Western practical theology.

Second, the case of practical theology from the Orthodox Churches in Africa is yet to be assessed. Until very recently, African theological discourses have been largely confined to theologies produced by and from missionary-founded Churches. The Ethiopian Orthodox Church claims its origin from the conversion of the Ethiopian eunuch. African theologians and our Western partners need to confess our sins of omission and commission and wake up from our wrong notion that Christianity is a Western religion because we only talk from the perspectives of missionary-founded Churches. On the contrary, from the perspectives of the Ethiopian Orthodox Church, there are caves and monasteries in which we will see African theological discourses that date back to periods beyond even ancestor Augustine.

Third is also the case of South Africa. It seems people have also invented an Africa without South Africa. For some South Africa with its unique history means it is not part of Africa. It is an 'Africa' within Africa. I say this because practical theology as it has been developing in the West has drawn many of their models from South Africa. For coming from South Africa are different contested public theologies of restoration, transformation, reconciliation, to mention but a few. The paradox is that while some think of it as part of the Western theological tradition, others either do not know of its existence or ignore it altogether as a genuinely African contribution. The irony is that some people in South Africa do not regard themselves as talking from an African context.

These simple but by no means simplistic descriptions may provide insights into and in some cases partially explain why some African theologians have developed various degrees of suspicion towards all kinds of Western theologians and theological associations. They ask how long it will take for African theological discourses to be recognized their due place in Christian theological discourses in history. African theological discourses clearly reflect different historical periods. There are the pre-missionary and colonial-missionary periods, African nationalistic era, and post-nationalistic and independent era. Therefore, I am of the opinion that any treatment of public theology must take these theologies occasioned by the historical realities in Africa.

The pre-missionary public theology must begin in early African Christianity in North Africa including the theological tradition of the Ethiopian Orthodox Churches. The distortions of modern geographical and historical perceptions are not adequate reasons not to credit Africa with the rich public theologies of the Early African Church Ancestors.

The colonial-missionary period may be said to have began in the late eighteenth century. Labels such as 'primitive', 'savage', and 'Dark Continent' characterize this period. In summary most of the literature on Africa about Africa was produced by mostly missionaries, colonial travelers, administrators, and scholars. Almost all of them describe Africans as having no religion, culture, or civilization. As late as 1910, the discussions of the World Missionary conference held in Edinburgh concluded that indigenous religions such as existed in Africa 'contained no preparation for Christianity' (World Missionary Conference, 1910). African ethnology and anthropology were constructed to provide colonialism with its theoretical underpinnings. Anthropology generally regarded African people, culture, and history in terms of what the French scholar Lucien Levy-Buhl called 'primitive' or 'pre-logical'. On the one hand, the White European religion and culture were regarded as superior, humane, modern, civilized, logical, and rational. On the other hand, the black African religion and culture was seen as inferior, inhumane, backward, the traditional, savagery, illogicality, irrational, and 'pagan' (Zahar, 1974, 18 - 25; Mudimbe, 1988, 64). Such racist tendencies gave rise to systematic acculturation, which aimed at eradicating African religions and culture and replacing them with European ones in order to make Africans became 'Graeco-Latin Negroes'(Sartre, 1963, 8).

Another historical milestone of signification was the Berlin conference in 1884. When the nations of Europe emerged from the conference Africa was divided up into fifty-six nation states. Consequently, its civilizations were not only partially distorted but in some cases were completely destroyed. The nation state, the principal mode of modern political organization founded in Europe, was imposed in Africa; and one cannot but wonder whether has turned out to be a curse that has over the years largely contributed to a situation in which Africa almost appears to be unable to free herself from its domination (Mazrui, 1980; Fasholé-Luke, 1975).

The encounter between the colonizers and colonized established a conversation full of arguments of words and images which led to the signifiers of the colonizing culture becoming fixed. These were seized upon by the Africans and 'sometimes refashioned, and put to symbolic and practical ends previously unforeseen, certainly unintended. Here, then, was a process in which the signifiers were set afloat, fought over, and recaptured on both sides of the colonial encounter' (Comaroff, 1994, 18). Comaroff is right when she suggests that '... a profoundly ambiguous relationship developed between the African people and their colonial invaders. A relationship in which Africans were aware that they were in danger of losing their traditional way of life.' (1994, 31)

The second stage is the period that was marked by some recognition that there is legitimate religion, culture, and civilization in Africa. The problem is that such forms were signified as bad and dangerous and in need of replacement. There was also the recognition that natural resources such as gold as well as human beings were being exploited for the economic prosperity of Western powers. The missionary ideology was greatly influenced by the colonial ideology. The missionaries also thought that with some hard intellectual work they could cleanse the African worldview of their converts so that s/he can think and act 'white'. In other words the African Christians were to become surrogate whites.

A nineteenth-century ideology of romanticism challenged the privileging of reason and objectivity and instead found value in the exotic, sensual, subjective, and non-rational. This ideology gave rise to a new attitude. Racist anthropology stopped denigrating Africa and celebrated its supposed uniqueness. Instead of characterizing Africa as essentially inferior and primitive, anthropology glorified the apparently emotional, mystical, and intuitive nature of African cultures. Encouraged by this romanticism, African intellectuals rebelled against colonialism's racial ideology (Irele, 1965; 1991).

The first truly African hermeneutic approach is similar to Tempels' method and theory approach (Tempels, 1963). This approach engages in ethnographic description and exegesis, using anthropological analysis as a model. Another group creates African philosophy in terms of Aristotelian and Thomist categories. Finally, the last group identifies a unique African philosophy by shifting through ethnographic and anthropological documentation of myths, folklore, and stories. Despite their differences, these approaches collectively contributed to the nationalistic movements as well as developing renewal, rebirth, and redefinition of a lost African essence (Kesteloot, 1974).

The post-independent stage was characterized by euphoria, excitement, naivety, and nationalistic pride. The nationalistic spirit manifested itself in three different ways. Political nationalism asserted the rights of Africans to found independent nations from colonial territories. A political agenda often included the rediscovery and reassertion of an essential cultural pride.

Therefore, political nationalism has mostly mirrored, if not intertwined with, cultural nationalism (Irele, 1965, 321). Such cultural and political nationalism formed the theoretical and methodological background of all African intellectual activity. An intellectual nationalism, throughout all academic disciplines, focused on a regained pre-colonial Africa (Wauthier, 1979, 21 - 22). Because Western intellectuals have produced almost all the knowledge about Africa, intellectual nationalism demands that the African scholar begin to control the production of knowledge about Africa and to insert an African intellectual presence international scholarship (Irele, 1991, 64). Some scholars have called this African renaissance. Indeed it was during this period that there were very bold attempt to write African literature, history, politics, and theology from the points of Africans.

Many of the theologies from Africa were attempts to address not issues, nor methods of doing theology in Africa. Rather, they were by and large attempts to address identity issues. The prolific Nigerian writer Chinua Achebe's book *Things Fall Apart* (1962) captures the sentiments, ambivalence, and contradictions of this stage. In the area of African religion, and philosophy, John Mbiti's book *African Religion and Philosophy* (1970), J.B. Danquah's book *Akan Doctrine of God* (1968), to mention but a few, were among the first attempts of African writing about religious experience by Africans. Unfortunately, many of these writings were so influenced by post-independent ideology that they portrayed the past as synonymous to paradise, perfection and unsullied by encounters with the West. Yet, as Kwame Nkrumah writes, not everything about Africa was wonderful:

The truth remains, however, that before colonization ... Africans were prepared to sell, often for no more than thirty pieces of sliver, fellow tribesmen and even members of the same 'extended' family and clan. Colonialism deserves to be blamed for many events in Africa, but surely it was not preceded by an African Golden Age or paradise. A return to the pre-colonial African society is evidently not worthy of the ingenuity and efforts of the people.(Nkrumah, 1964, 6)

My intention is not to make anyone uncomfortable, but to impress upon the scholarly community especially in the West that understanding this dynamic is very crucial to understanding the many different definitions of public theology from Africa and the North. It is also crucial to understanding the need to use different tools of analysis. In my view not to understand this dynamic is to fail to understand what constitutes public theology. Public theology in Africa is not merely dealing with issues of interest but issues of deep concerns that also are related to identity. This point is extremely important to my Western colleagues who have been involved in supervising African postgraduate students.

The point above was eloquently echoed in the final Communique of a historic Pan-African Conference of Third World Theologians held from 17th-23rd December 1977 in Accra, Ghana. It states:

We believe that African theology must be understood in the context of African life and culture and the creative attempt of African peoples to shape a new future that is different from the colonial past and the neo-colonial present. The African situation requires a new theological methodology that is different from the approaches of the dominant theologies of the West. African theology must reject, therefore, the prefabricated ideas of North Atlantic theology by defining itself according to the struggles of the people in their resistance against the structures of domination. Our task as theologians is to create a theology that arises from and is accountable to African people. (EATWOT, 1979, 193)

It is commonly held that there are two distinct public theological traditions from Africa south of the Sahara. On the one hand, South Africa has produced the theology of liberation or Black theology that specifically addressed the struggle for the social and political liberation of the conditions of inequality and oppression of apartheid South Africa (Tutu, 1987, 54). On the other hand, the other African theological tradition '... has been the theological exploration into the indigenous cultures of African peoples, with particular stress on their pre-Christian (and also pre-Islamic) religious traditions' (Tutu, 1978, 366; Idowu, 1965). In the second tradition, the main focus has been the integration between the indigenous African world-views and the Christianity as presented by Western missionaries. This tradition is best summarized thus:

African theologians have set about demonstrating that the African religious experience and heritage were not illusory, and that they should have formed the vehicle for conveying the Gospel verities to Africa... It means that we have a great store from which we can fashion new ways of speaking to and about God, and new styles of worship consistent with our new faith. (Tutu, 1978, 366)

Over the years, it has become clear that any African public theology must move beyond the two main traditions of liberation and indigenization. The simple reason is that the African reality is far more complex than the main issues that gave rise to these two traditions.

The danger I see here is the tendency to see theologies of liberation and contextualization as two different and unrelated theologies. Until very recently those who wrote on theologies of liberation thought theologies of contextualization were compromising with apartheid in particular and other forms of oppression in general in Africa. I do not think such accusations are valid. I am of the opinion that both theologies are theologies of protest and liberation. Both theologies are addressing specific forms of oppressions in their contexts. I think the relationship of white, black, and African Christian theologies are two sides of the same coin.

Sometimes, there is a wrong impression that theologies of liberation or contextualization are only limited to missionary-founded churches in Africa.

There is an interesting but very significant history of colonialization worth mentioning that developed in the Ethiopian Orthodox Church. Ethiopia was Christianized in the fourth century Common Era by two brothers from Tyre, St. Frumentius, later consecrated the first Ethiopian bishop, and Aedesius. They won the confidence of King Ezana at Aksum (a powerful kingdom in northern Ethiopia) and were allowed to evangelize. Toward the end of the 5th century, nine monks from Syria, probably Monophysites, are said to have brought monasticism to Ethiopia and encouraged the translation of the Scriptures into the Ge'ez language. The Ethiopian Church followed the Coptic Church (in Egypt) when the latter continued to adhere to the Monophysite doctrine after this doctrine had been condemned by the bishops of Rome and Constantinople at the Council of Chalcedon in AD 451.

Since the 12th century the patriarch of Alexandria had appointed the Ethiopian archbishop, known as the abuna (Arabic for 'our father'), who was always an Egyptian Coptic monk; this created a rivalry with the native *itshage* (abbot general) of the strong Ethiopian monastic community. Attempts to shake Egyptian Coptic control were made from time to time, but it was not until 1929 that a compromise was effected: an Egyptian monk was again appointed abuna, but four Ethiopian bishops were also consecrated as his auxiliaries. A native Ethiopian abuna, Basil, was finally appointed in 1950, and in 1959 an autonomous Ethiopian patriarchate was established.

There are also latter developments inside and outside Africa that must become important subjects of public theology ion Africa. AIDS, having reached epidemic proportions in Africa, 'will be the leading cause of death among adults in sub-Saharan Africa within the next 25 years… ' (Prentice, 1991). Other factors outside the continent of Africa but nevertheless impacting negatively on the economies of Africa include: developments in Eastern Europe, the breaking of the Soviet Union, wars in Iraq and Afghanistan, which seem to divert global attention from Africa. These new devastating realities do call to question the hermeneutic of yesteryears. As Theophilus Okere writes:

… the background of an African philosopher need not be the fossilized, unadulterated past. The black African philosopher is not to become a cultural historian or a curator of the ethnic museum, jealously guarding the purity of ancestral heritage and protecting it from the adulterating encroachment of time and evolution. Background for a black African philosopher certainly means traditional institutions, symbols, and values, but also the often violent culture contact that was the colonial experience and its aftermath. It means the present day reality. (Okere, 1983, 121)

Okere goes on to explain that hermeneutics as a method interprets the signs and symbols embedded in a culture's institutions and ideas to uncover the hidden meaning behind the overt symbols and signs themselves. Okere suggests,

'African cultures have their own symbols pregnant with meaning. A reflection on these symbols with a view to making the implicit meanings explicit would constitute African philosopher' (1983, 115). Similarly, Okonda Okolo argues that only hermeneutics can reappropriate African history by understanding the relationship between the past, the present, and the future. Firstly, reappropriating African history means knowing the meaning of 'tradition'. The past, never locked away in a vacuum, always creates the present, which in turn creates the future. In a sense, tradition, being a reflection of the past from the present, is an invention of the past and the present. The past can be seen only in terms of the present. Thus, Okolo describes this interplay between past, present, and future as 'a tradition-in-becoming' (Okolo, 1991, 204).

A second proposition for African hermeneutics would be that interpretation is never objective, unbiased, or neutral; it always comes out of a particular cultural, political, economic, and social situation. Anthropology especially has shown us this. It received its power to create pictures of Africa because it claimed that anthropology was a 'universal' discipline, able to present knowledge neutrally about any culture. Yet, as we have seen, anthropology could understand non-Western cultures only from within its own point of view. In this way, history is a human narrative and not an empirical fact.

Finally, African hermeneutics means understanding the practical and political role it can play in the present and concrete situation of Africa's postcolonial struggle against forms of oppression: 'Praxis unleashes the hermeneutical process and gives it an orientation. Hermeneutics, in turn, offers praxis a cultural self-identity necessary for ideological combat.' (Okolo, 1991, 208)

What is the relationship between African and Western hermeneutics? For, if Africa is an 'invention' on the part of the West and Western discourses on Africa have been largely biased and false, how can one expect that the critical use of Western philosophy will result in anything different? As V.Y. Mudimbe writes: 'The main problem concerning the being of African discourse remains one of the transference of methods and their cultural integration in Africa' (Mudimbe, 1988, 183).

In the twenty-first century, the problematic of doing public theology in Africa has been pushed to boundaries not anticipated because the context has changed. The traditional divide between liberation or black theologies and indigenized theologies have been found to inadequate in addressing current African reality because the rise of military dictators, and political and ethnic conflicts have added important factors to the agenda of doing public theology in Africa. They have dislocated families and people beyond control. These have combined to offer fertile ground for violence of various types and the spread of HIV/AIDS. Modernity and secularization have also combined to produce people who pay lip service to the major faiths in Africa. The result is that it is becoming almost impossible to talk about norms and values pertaining to any group of people. Globalization has gradually created a situation in which community farms are being replaced by modern hotels. In order to speed up the disappearance of community farms, foreign foods are becoming cheaper than local foods. Policies of the World Bank and the International Monetary Fund, coupled with World Trade Organization policies against subsidies of local foods, reinforce negative effects of globalization.

What is emerging from our search to understanding the dynamics, trends and challenges of African theology in general and doing practical theology in particular is an interplay of ambiguities and signification and the tensions that arise as to how to address them. In the light of the foresaid, the task and magnitude of doing public theology is an almost insurmountable task. For one must address the following questions. What and whose language does one use to such a theology? Whose authority does one claim to speak and for whom? Notwithstanding these challenges, doing public theology in Africa is an imperative. Fortunately, there are viable traditions set by African theologies that can be adopted and improved upon.

By the sort of agenda they have set for themselves, African theologians have achieved modest success. Though in need of further development, their methods and theories have nevertheless opened up new pathways. African Theology in general and public theology in particular has clearly succeeded in laying the foundation which has made it possible for creative, constructive and self-critical public theological discourses in Africa.

References

Achebe, Chinua (1962) *Things Fall Apart*. London: Heinemann.

Comaroff, Jean (1994) *The Body of Power, Spirit of Resilience: the Culture and History of South African People* . Chicago: University of Chicago Press.

Danquah, J. B., (1968) *The Akan Doctrine of God* . London: Frank Case and Co. Ltd.

Fasholé-Luke, E. (1975) 'The Quest for an African Christian Theology'. *The Ecumenical Review* Vol. 27, No. 3.

Idowu, Bolaji (1965) *Towards an Indigenous Church*. London: Oxford University Press.

Irele, Abiola (1991) The African Scholar. *Transition* 51, 56 - 69.

---------, (1965) 'Negritude of Black Cultural Nationalism'. *Journal of Modern African Studies* Vo. 3 No. 4, 321 - 348.

Kesteloot, Lilyan (1974) *Black Writers in French: A Literary History of Negritude*. Translated by Ellen Conroy Kennedy, Philadelphia: Temple University Press.

Long, Charles H. (1986) *Significations*. Philadelphia: Fortress Press.

Mazrui, Ali (1980) *The African Condition: A Political Diagnosis*. London: Heinemann.

Mbiti, John S, (1970) *African Religion and Philosophy*. New York: Doubleday & Company, Inc.

Mudimbe, V. Y. (1988) *The Invention of Africa: Gnosis, Philosophy, and the Order of Knowledge*. Bloomington: Indiana University Press.

Nkrumah, Kwame (1964) *Conscientism*. New York: Monthly Review Press.

Okere, Theophilus (1983) *African Philosophy: A Historic-Hermeneutical Investigation of the Conditions of its Possibility*. New York: University Press of America.

Okolo, Okondo (1991) 'Tradition and Destiny: Horizons of an African Philosophical Heremeneutics'. in Tsenay Serequeberhan (ed.), *African Philosophy: The Essential Readings*. New York: Paragon House.

Prentice, Thomson (1991) 'Birth Control vaccine tested'. *The Times*, February 18, C7.

Satre, Jean-Paul (1963) 'Preface' in Frantz Fanon, *The Wretched of the Earth*. Translated by Constance Farrington, New York: Grove Press.

Tempels, Placide (1963) *Bantu Philosophy*. Paris: Presence Africaine.

The World Missionary Conference (1910) 'The Missionary Message in Relation to Non-Christian Religions'. Edinburgh & London: Oliphant, Anderson & Ferrier.

Tutu, Desmond (1987) 'Black Theology and African Theology: Soul mates or Antagonists?' in John Parratt (ed.) *A Reader in African Christian Theology*. London: SPCK.

————— (1978) 'Whither African Theology?' in E. Fasholé-Luke et. al. (eds.) *Christianity in Independent Africa*. London: Rex Collings, p. 364 - 369.

Wauthier, Claude (1979) *The Literature and Thought of Modern Africa*. Washington,D.C.: Three Continents Press

Zahar, Renate (1974) *Frantz Fanon: Colonialism and Alienation*. Translated by Wildried F. Feuser, New York: Monthly Review Press.

Public Theology in Pop Culture

Critical Uses and Functions of The Bible in Rock Music and Metal

Jean-Guy Nadeau

One can briefly define Christian theology as reflective and critical talk [1] about God and relationships to God with regard to the Bible and a Christian world-view. As for public theology, the term would designate theology in the public realm and/or engaged with issues of public concern. Most often we hear about public theology as something that academic theologians should do in order to engage in the public conversation or have some impact on public issues. But one can see that there is already reflective and critical talk about God in the public realm of our secular culture through arts, literature, cinema, theatre, music, as well as politics. This paper will focus on public talk about God and relationship to God in rock music. But God is so ubiquitous in rock music that I will be more specific and restrict my reflection to the uses and functions of the Bible in rock music as talk about God or even a form of popular disclosure *à propos* God in the public realm and, to a lesser extent, engaged with issues of public concern.

Rock music as youth's Esperanto

Why should we study rock music when other urgent public issues confront the theologian? In the words of George Steiner (distinguished scholar in Literature and Poetry at Oxford, Harvard and Cambridge) 'rock music and heavy metal are the international *Esperanto* of today's youth' (Steiner, 2000). Rock music is everywhere: on the radio, the television, on the street, at political conventions, national celebrations, and so on. Many celebrated the fall of the Berlin Wall, discovered Amnesty International, AIDS, the famine in Africa, etc. amidst rock music. Even the Serbs *rocked* their opposition to the NATO bombings. In fact, rock music appears as everyday proof of globalization and

---

[1]   To those traits, academic theology would add that of systematic.

the relevance of public theology to young people could well be linked to its knowing this youth *Esperanto*.

Rock music, and particularly metal, manifestly displays a religious dimension (less so in pop) that could be counted as a form of 'ordinary theology' (Astley, 2002) and should be of interest to practical theologians. In an article published in the early 1990s, I pointed to the religious dimension of rock music and culture for today's youth (Nadeau, 1994). I have since discovered the large presence of the Bible in rock music, the importance of which, brought up and living in a French-speaking environment, I had been unaware of. Rock music frequently borrows biblical images and filters them through a mixer of dissonant guitars and clamouring voices. Looking at this violence inflicted on the biblical text, many see attacks against the Bible and God. But one can also find in rock legitimate uses of the biblical text. Isn't God proclaimed as 'the *rock* of the faithful'?

With rock music, the biblical text escapes the religious institutions that control it and its interpretation, and resides in popular culture. Subverting the usual discursive expectations of biblical interpretation, the irreverence of rock music, punk and heavy metal (Beaudoin, 1998) allows some distance from the sacred text; it demolishes the fictitious obviousness of the assertions, ideas, images or beliefs that are attached to it. Thus, it opens the door to discursive and hermeneutic experimentation, allowing experimentation with biblical ideas and images in the public realm of the media as well as in the private realm of the listener. So doing, it allows new appropriations of the biblical text into a *mélange* where, just as in theology, it is combined with religious traditions and contemporary issues and language. This can be called doing theology in public culture.

The following reflection is based on rock songs that contain one or more biblical quotations, excluding biblical based movie soundtracks or musicals (like *Jesus Christ Superstar*) as well as Contemporary Christian Music developed to confront pop, rock and heavy metal on their own ground. My aim is to address music from well-known groups and singers, many of them played on the radio or on MTV in the early years of the twenty-first century and, witnessing to their popularity, nominated for or receiving a Grammy or MTV Music Award. These choices come from the desire to join the discussion within the arena of youth music, an arena that constitutes the basis of many contemporary secular liturgies.

Some functions of biblical citation in rock music

One might argue that rock and metal songs use the biblical text for commercial aims, feeding on youth estrangement and rebellion. And this might sometimes be the case. But it seems to me that, despite their frequent irreverence, rock and metal songs grant to the biblical text functions similar to those that they have in preaching, prayer and theology. I have drawn up a tentative list of the functions of the biblical text in rock music and divided them between religious and sociopolitical functions. Quite often though, as will become apparent below, both types are combined. Hence the hazards of the following distinction. I will use Ricoeur's types of biblical discourse (Ricoeur, 1977) to categorize roughly the uses and functions to which I want to draw attention.

Religious uses and functions

In the prophetic genre, we find attempts to wake up sleeping Christians (see Bono below) to the tragedies of the world; criticisms (and rejections) of religion, church and religious education (by the likes of Gary Newman, Bad Religion, Ministry, Slayer, and many metal bands); critics of false preachers or false prophets. We will come back to this theme.

The hymnic genre disputes first place with the prophetic. Bible quotations are used as lyrics of lament, despair, request, thanksgiving, hope, anger, or even dispute as in *Dear God* by XTC. They are often taken from the *Book of Psalms*, Psalm 23:4 being the most quoted, although rarely in a spirit of hope, from the title of a Marilyn Manson song to U2's *40* (all the song being a quotation of Psalm 40) or *Love Rescue Me*, Bad Religion's *Heaven is Falling*, or the rap *Gangsta Paradise*:

> As I walk through the valley of the shadow of death
> I take a look at my life and realize there's nuthin' left
> 'Cuz I've been blasting and laughing so long, that
> Even my mama thinks that my mind is gone
>
> Coolio, *Gangsta Paradise*

Jesus' cross and Mark 15:32 are often present in rock, as in *Chop Suey!* by the Australian nu-metal group System of A Down, popular enough to be nominated for a 2002 Grammy Award:

> Father into your hands, I commend my spirit
> Father into your hands, (why have you forsaken me?)
> In your eyes (forsaken me)
> In your thoughts (forsaken me)
> In your heart (forsaken me)
>
> System of a Down, *Chop Suey!*

The following by Bad Religion sounds itself like a Psalm, although a punk Psalm:

> Father can you hear me?
> How have I let you down?
> I curse the day that I was born
> and all the sorrow in this world
> Let me take you to the herding ground
> where all good men are trampled down
> Just to settle a bet that could not be won
> between a prideful father and his son
> Will you guide me now for I can't see a reason
> for the suffering and this long misery
> What if every living soul could be upright and strong?
> Well then I do imagine
> There will be (sorrow)
> Yeah there will be (sorrow)
> And there will be sorrow no more
> When all soldiers lay their weapons down
> or when all kings and all queens relinquish their crowns
> Or when the only true messiah rescues us from ourselves
> It's easy to imagine
> There will be (sorrow)
> Yeah there will be (sorrow)
> And there will be sorrow no more (repeat x4)
>
> Bad Religion, *Sorrow*

The words of *God is Love* by Lenny Kravitz seem to come straight out of a hymn book:

> God loves everyone
> That's why He gave His son, oh yeah
> And you should feel His pain
> Yet He gave us everything
>
> Lenny Kravitz, *God is Love*

The *Wisdom* genre is present, in reflections or questions about the meaning or the absurdity of life. As was the case with the following excerpt, it also witnesses to the biblical culture of those musicians and their ability to blend different books. In the following one by metal group Godkiller, *Job* (one of the most quoted Bible book) acts as a counterpoint to the Beatitudes.

> Blessed are the poor in spirit
> Blessed are the sick
> Blessed are the starving
> Blessed are the merciful
> Blessed I am not
> But cursed from birth...
> ... and for eternity
>
> Godkiller, *Waste of Time*

Sometimes, Biblical passages in songs have (pastoral) functions of con-solation, support in suffering, hope building, and such as we saw in *Sorrow*, quoted above with its melodious and unforgettable chorus 'there will be sor-row/ there will be sorrow/ there will be sorrow NO MORE.'

Theological reflection is quite apparent within these genres. In some rock songs, biblical excerpts are use to reject not only religion but the Bible and God himself while contrasting His promises with the state of the world. Reflection on and contestation of God's might and goodness are often present in rock and metal songs like *Darkness of Christ* and *Disciple* by Slayer, *God's Song* by Randy Newman, *Amen* by Jewel, *Dear God* by XTC, and so on. Hence, the song *The Land of Rape and Honey* by metal group, Ministry, ends with 'In the land of rape and honey, you prey' (sic).

> Cain slew Abel, Seth knew not why
> For if the children of Israel were to multiply
> Why must any of the children
> Why must they die?
> So he asked the Lord
> And the Lord said:
> Man means nothing, he means less to me
> Than the lowliest cactus flower
> Or the humblest Yucca tree
> He chases round this desert
> 'Cause he thinks that's where I'll be
> That's why I love mankind
>
> ...

Lord, if you won't take care of us
Won't you please, please let us be?'
And the Lord said
And the Lord said
I burn down your cities – how blind you must be
I take from you your children and you say how blessed are we
You all must be crazy to put your faith in me
That's why I love mankind
You really need me
That's why I love mankind

Randy Newman, *God's Song (That's Why I Love Mankind)*

I don't know what stopped
Jesus Christ from turning
every hungry stone into bread
and I don't remember hearing
how Moses reacted
when the innocent first born sons
lay dead
Well I guess
God was a lot more demonstrative
back when he
flamboyantly parted the sea
now everybody's praying
Don't prey on me (sic)

Bad Religion, *Don't pray on me*

Torn from their families
Mothers go hungry
To feed their children
But children go hungry
There are so many big men
They're out making millions
When poverty's profits
Just blame the children
If there's a God in heaven

What's he waiting for
If He can't hear the children
Then he must see the war
But it seems to me
That he leads his lambs
To the slaughter house
And not the promised land . . .

> Elton John, *If there is a God in Heaven (What's He Waiting For?)*

Sociopolitical uses and functions

The Prophetic genre of discourse is quite predominant among biblical uses that have primarily social functions in rock. But let's first note two other genres, narrative and legislative.

On the *narrative* front, biblical passages are used in order to identify the singer or his/her group or to reinforce such identification as is the case in many reggae songs (arguably outside of the rock tradition, which is the reason why I don't quote them here, but now closer to it). In the following, we have a good example of such use of the Beatitudes and the Book of Daniel for identification purposes from the Beastie Boys, three white Jewish New Yorkers doing rap at a time when rap was exclusively black territory.

> Who shall inherit the earth the meek shall
>
> . . .
> We're just 3 M.C.'s and we're on the go
> SHADRACH MESACH ABEDNAGO (sic, repeat x4)
>
> Beastie Boys, *Shadrach*

There are very few instances of what could be called *legislative uses* of the Bible in rock. Another interesting example is the retrieval of the Creation story to demand the legalization of marijuana:

> Take a look in Genesis a mi seh book number one
> Jah mek di herb seed fi de human
> Dat was di time when di weed bum some
> So Jah mek di herb, give it unto Adam
>
> Rocker T, *Tru Ganjaman*

The *prophetic genre* is much more common, biblical passages and the Bible itself being used in social and moral strategies of denunciation and critique as in *Jeremy* by Pearl Jam, *Song of Isaac* by Leonard Cohen, and in a large number of reggae songs, *Southern Man* by Neil Young or *Rain on the Scarecrow* by John Mellancamp.

> I heard screamin' and bullwhips cracking
> How long? How long?
> Southern man better keep your head
> Don't forget what your good book said
> Southern change gonna come at last
> Now your crosses are burning fast
> Neil Young, *Southern Man*
> And grandma's on the front porch swing with a Bible in her hand
> Sometimes I hear her singing 'Take me to the Promised Land'
> When you take away a man's dignity he can't work his fields and
>   cows
>
> John Mellancamp, *Rain on the Scarecrow*

Jesus Christ, a folk song recently introduced into the rock realm by U2 also offers further examples of this:

> Jesus Christ was a man who travelled through the land
> Hard working man and brave
> He said to the rich, 'Give your goods to the poor.'
> So they laid Jesus Christ in his grave.
> . . .
> He went to the sick, he went to the poor
> And he went to the hungry and the lame
> Said that the poor would one day win this world
> So they laid Jesus Christ in his grave
> . . .
> When the love of the poor shall one day turn to hate
> When the patience of the workers gives away
> 'Would be better for you rich if you never had been born'
> So they laid Jesus Christ in his grave . . .
>
> Woody Guthrie, *Jesus Christ*

Finally, biblical quotations also serve *a poetic function* that can act for the sake of the beauty of the song or serve the previous functions, enhancing the romanticism, the drama or the critical power of the song. Examples such as *Adam Raised a Cain, Leap of Faith* and *Lion's Den* by Bruce Springsteen, *Here it is* by Leonard Cohen, *Hallelujah* also by Leonard Cohen recently covered by Rufus Wainwright in the film *Shrek*; *Jesus Christ Pose* by Soundgarden, *One* by U2, come to mind. In the video clip of *Jeremy*, by Pearl Jam, the words 'The serpent was subtle' and later 'Gen 3:6' go through the screen. Allow me to quote from *Leap of Faith* by Bruce Springsteen where references to the Bible are quite direct, though without quotations – well, he was raised a Catholic!

> Now your legs were heaven your breasts were the altar
> Your body was the holy land
>
> ...
>
> Now you were the Red Sea, I was Moses
> I kissed you and slipped into a bed of roses
> The waters parted and love rushed inside
> I was Jesus' son sanctified
> It takes a leap of faith to get things going
> It takes a leap of faith you gotta show some guts
> It takes a leap of faith to get things going
> In your heart you must trust
>
> Bruce Springsteen, *Leap of Faith*

Religious confrontation with suffering and evil

I will restrict myself to a few words about two uses of the biblical text that strike me as most prevalent in rock and appear particularly interesting as far as public theology is concerned: religious confrontation with suffering and evil and social, ecclesiastical and political critique.

In an interview, Bono of the group U2 spoke of a problem that he has with religious persons:

They refuse to stare into the face of the world we're living in [...] They're not attempting to understand the darkness in the world, or to get into it and describe it from the inside so people can really get a sense of what you're talking about. (Bono, 1993)

Most rock musicians would probably endorse such a statement. Rock has a major preoccupation with suffering and evil and it is no coincidence that Psalm

23:4; Mk 15:32 and Job are arguably the most quoted biblical passages in rock and metal songs. But rock musicians are no theodicists, so they are much less subtle about their approach to evil, although they are arguably closer to what most Christians are living through. They shout and yell about evil because it lives with us… and within us. And it is done not without excess be it in lyrics, distortion or decibels. To many, especially teenagers, rock appears as a way, often the only one (with or without drugs), of facing an intolerable life. Through the catharsis of yells and decibels, its lyrics, beats and trances, rock allows for some kind of liberation. It signals a triumph, be it momentary, over an intolerable situation or one lived as such. It succeeds in articulating sadness, melancholy, isolation, desire to live, rage, communion, joy, and freedom. At times, it is the melancholy, loneliness or distress that triumphs. At times it is joy or communion. Most often it is energy or rage, some feeling of staying alive despite of or in the face of evil (to use the terms of Barth and Ricoeur).

The principal function of the biblical quotation within this framework is not only to speak and cry out about suffering and evil, but to question a religious discourse no longer affected by the cohabitation of God and evil. It is also to question God Godself as we saw above. Such a confrontation is clearly on religious and theological grounds. Reflecting on the question of evil, theologian Adolphe Gesché has asked whether God must not take the place of the adversary in this formidable question of evil, suggesting that humanity, in its need, has the right to strike the innocent God. A God, however, much less innocent in the eyes of rockers than in those of theologians, as we saw above. Gesché goes on to ask, 'if a large part of the unbelief does not come from the fact that believers do not sufficiently take upon themselves […] the dispute with God' (Gesché, 1986). That appears to be what rock musicians are doing. Sure, their dispute has excessive accents. But don't also religion, theology, metaphysics with their claims about God? And are we not beyond measure or on the edge, trying to talk about God after and through Auschwitz, Ayacucho (Gutiérrez, 1990), Rwanda? How can we talk about God at a time when Christians and Bible peddlers enrich themselves on the back and the souls of the masses? We might ask Bad Religion, Ministry, Dead Kennedys, Jello Biafra and others. Which brings us to our second point.

Social, ecclesial, and political critique in context

The second function I will address briefly is partly connected with the preceding debate. It is the sociopolitical, even prophetic use of the Bible in rock for the purpose of denouncing the political Right, particularly as it relates to fundamentalist churches and televangelists. One could talk of rock and metal music against the Bible Belt. Most of the songs I quoted from are American (we don't find such dynamics in French rock) and one could say that some rock and metal groups are at war against churches from which they sprout, a war in which the Bible is at stake as much as it is a weapon.

> You call yourself the Moral Majority
> We call ourselves the people in the real world
> Trying to rub us out, but we're going to survive
> God must be dead if you're alive
> You say, 'God loves you. Come and buy the Good News'
>
> Dead Kennedys, *Moral Majority*

> It took three days for him to die
> The born again to buy the serial rights
> Lamb of God have mercy on us
>
> Marilyn Manson, *Lamb of God*

> I reject all the biblical views of the truth
> Dismiss it as the folklore of the times
> I won't be force fed prophecies
> From a book of untruths for the weakest mind
>
> Slayer, *New Faith*

Certain songs or rock videos are scandalous to many, and not without reason. To better grasp their meaning, it is important to look at their religious and cultural context. It seems to me that many of rock and metal music excesses towards God, the Bible or Christianity, are produced by people coming from Christian backgrounds and mostly with direct experiences of fundamentalist churches (for example, Marilyn Manson, Axl Rose, Slayer). An interesting fact is that most of them are still somewhat possessed by the question of God. So one is not astonished that metal groups appear to be as fundamentalist as those they denounce.

Fortunately, one could say, the critic is not always violent and can respond to violence with humour, as Bruce Springsteen's following barb at the creationists demonstrates:

They prosecuted some poor sucker in these United States
For teaching that man descended from the apes
They coulda settled that case without a fuss or fight
If they'd seen me chasin' you, sugar, through the jungle last night

…

Well did God make man in a breath of holy fire
Or did he crawl on up out of the muck and mire
Well the man on the street believes what the bible tells him so
Well you can ask me, mister, because I know
Tell them soul-suckin' preachers to come on down and see
Part man, part monkey, baby that's me.

Bruce Springsteen, *Part man, part monkey*

Still, violence and excess characterize rock and metal critiques. A visit to some web sites in the wake of 9/11 proved to be rich in lessons on the use of the Bible in rock and by the American right. For example, the latest album by Slayer (a group nominated for a 2002 Grammy), released on 9/11, is titled *God Hates Us All*. When one opens their web site (`www.slayer.net`) a dagger embedded in a bled-on Bible appears. The booklet with the CD is composed of pages of the Book of Job over which are printed the lyrics of Slayer's album. Band singer Araya is less harsh when he says in an interview: 'The whole idea behind God is love. At some point in our lives everyone gets tested, and that's when we hate Him. That's the test. You either hate Him for the rest of your life, or you learn to forgive Him' (Patriquin, 2002). Still, Slayer's web site opens with 'God Hates Us All' and has no trace of these remarks that would also fit well in our previous paragraph about suffering and evil.

Shocking as it is, the troubling affirmation that 'God Hates Us All' is hardly new. One can even compare the verbal violence of rock and metal music with that of biblical passages as well as of some churches, preachers, self-proclaimed representatives of the Gospel and even Gospel Lords. It comes from a long line of pastors and Christian groups claiming, Bible in hand, that God hates sinners and not only sin, that He hates fags, abortionists, secularists, evolutionists who, with their advocates, will bear His wrath.[2] They say that God hates America because of such sins and their acceptance by the Supreme Court and the government. So it is that, according to Pat Robertson and Jerry Falwell, God lifted His protection over America on 9/11 for 'the sins of an unbelieving culture' (Falwell, 2001; GLAAD, 2001).

---

[2] See, for example, `www.jayforrest.org/godhates`; `www.godhatesfags.com`; `www.wherethetruthhurts.org/godhatessinners`; `www.godhatesamerica.com`.

So rock music is well embedded in culture and engaged in ongoing debate with it: in this case a religious debate not without value. Rock is concerned with religion, the Bible and most of all with God. It appears as a contemporary practice through which many pray, question God or walk on their spiritual journey (Stockman, 2001), and we might consider rock music as a type of revelatory discourse or practice. With its strong presence in youth media, culture and celebrations, rock sometimes appears as a form of pre-existing public theology that practical theologians should not ignore.

References

Astley, Jeff (2002) *Ordinary Theology*. Aldershot (England): Ashgate.
Beaudoin, Tom (1998) *Virtual Faith: The Irreverent Spiritual Quest of Generation X.* San Francisco: Jossey-Bass.
Bono (1993) 'Interview'. *Musician*, August.
Falwell, Jerry (2001) 'Why I said what I Said'. *National Liberty Journal*. Sept. 2001, www.nljonline.com/why.htm [last accessed on 15 July 2003].
Gesché, Adolphe (1986) ùTopiques de la question du malù. *Revue Théologique de Louvain* 17 (1986), 393-418. Reprinted in Adolphe Gesché, *Dieu pour penser. 1. Le mal*. Paris: Cerf.
Glaad [Gay and Lesbian Alliance against Defamation] (2001) Timeline: Jerry Falwell & Pat Robertson's Anti-Gay Remarks. 21 September, available at http://www.glaad.org/publications/resource_doc_detail.php?id=2802& [last accessed on 15 July 2003].
Gutiérrez, Gustavo (1990) 'How Can God be Discussed from the Perspective of Ayacucho?' *Concilium*. 1990:1,103-114.
Nadeau, Jean-Guy (1994) Evangelization and Youth Culture seen from French Canada. *Concilium*. 251, 87-97.
Patriquin, Martin (2002), 'Two Decades of Aggression'. *Hour*, Montreal, January 24.
Ricoeur, Paul (January-April 1977). Toward a Hermeneutic of the Idea of Revelation. *Harvard Theological Review* 70. 1-37.
Steiner, George (2000) *Entretiens*. Paris: 10/18.
Stockman, Steve (2001) *Walk On: The Spiritual Journey of U2*. Lake Merry (Florida): Relevant Books.

PART III: TRADITION AND METHOD IN PUBLIC THEOLOGY

In this section, we examine some of the sources and norms for articulating public theology, and in particular how experience and context can be informed by tradition, and vice versa.

How do we construe and locate the public sphere and how do we understand the role of the church in such a public sphere? Will Storrar begins his account of a renewed Christian humanist practical theology by exploring these complex questions. Preferring the more precise offering of Jürgen Habermas to David Tracy he pursues an answer to these questions by suggesting a communicative, participatory and pluralist public sphere aware of its rootedness in a third wave of globalisation. Storrar argues that the possibility of such a public sphere involves a reconfiguration of the boundaries between public and private so that the voices of religious traditions may be offered as both critique and reconstruction for contemporary global society. Acknowledging that such a hopeful vision poses key questions for Practical Theology, Storrar seeks to retrieve new insights from history, evoking the figure of Erasmus of Rotterdam. For Storrar, Erasmus offers a pre-Schleiermachian 'neglected taproot' of Practical Theology in the form of his Christian humanist homeletics. This grounds Storrar's claim for a renewed Practical Theology as a 'moral cartography of God and neighbour'.

Examining the credentials of 'fundamental practical theology', Robert Mager offers a two-fold critique of the remaining deductive emphasis of much practical theology and the problematic concept of action which seems to underlie this emphasis. He highlights a critical question for practical and public theologies: the (late) modern assertion of both pluralism and autonomy for an understanding of truth. Pluralism allows us to 'propose' truth, although hopefully in a conversational mode. Autonomy makes the more radical demand that theologies articulate truth from human experience, from practice itself. However, Mager notes that there is a tension for Christian theology between the claims of autonomy and the concept of action which it invokes. Autonomy is tied to an understanding of action as 'fabrication'. For those seeking a theologically disclosive practice this will be problematic. Employing a reading of

Hannah Arendt's work on human practice he suggests the outlines of a relational (yet still dialectical) theological ethic of practice which is focussed upon
meaning rather than product. Mager finishes by offering a vision of practical
theology's "search for God in human experience, not as the One who is known,
tried and tested, but as What is ever to be discovered and revered in common".

Etienne Grieu highlights the impossibility of 'speaking about God in public' in a secular society. But as with the secularisation debate in general, the
question should be asked whether this is a crisis of faith *per se* or more a dis-
trust in religious institutions. Grieu's own research amongst activist believers
suggests that they possess powerful stories which are imbued with qualities of
what he terms 'speaking from God' in which the task is to enact and narrate the
ways in which they have experienced themselves as coming to full subjectivity
by virtue of the life-giving reality of the divine at work. The stories of such
witnesses of faith stand as the most powerful forms of practical theology.

Klaus Wegenast argues that the notion of 'tradition' in practical theology
needs redefinition, so that theology is not something received passively as an
unchanging dogma but as something which animates contemporary practice.
Tradition only comes alive – and demonstrates its value – when the insights of
the past are appropriated anew in order to interpret the present. Wegenast calls
for the communicative and transformative function of tradition and argues that
inculturation – of recontextualising the tradition – is not the betrayal of faith
but the very task of making the Word become flesh.

Chris Hermans analyses the shifting ground of practical theology, arguing
that the conscious move away from a highly clerical and narrowly ecclesial paradigm raises significant methodological and metaphysical questions. Echoing
Elaine Graham's concern with a practical theology legitimated both *ad intra*
and *ad extra*, he argues for Piercian pragmatism as an alternative grounding
for a renewed and broadened 'scientific' practical theology.

Terence Kennedy's chapter explores initiates a conversation between practical theology and natural law. He highlights key issues in the debate about
historicity and universality in morality and ethics, weaving the tense relation
between Judeo-Christian religion and modernity into the heart of this debate. Despite insisting that a careful, historical reading of natural law discourse
leads to reflection on the incommensurability of recent natural law thinking,
he concludes by alluding to a dynamic, historically attentive, suggestively *pe-
richoretic* understanding of natural law as befitting the early 21st century.

In his paper on Naming God in a (Post) Modern World, Gerrit Immink eva-
luates recent trends in practical theology in relation to the significance of naming God. Re-opening a pathway between the claims of practical theology as
empirical theology, and practical theology as a 'theory of religion', Immink of-

fers a critique of the anti-metaphysical stance implicit in each account. Whilst accepting the fragmentary nature of our theological knowledge and the social, relational nature of that knowledge Immink pushes at the boundaries between experience of God and the reality of God too firmly drawn by advocates of practical theological 'moderate conceptual realism'. He concludes by drawing on Plantinga to suggest a meaningful correspondence between our experience and concepts of God and the properties of God.

Locating Public Theology

Practical Theology as the Christian humanist discipline of moral cartography

William F. Storrar

How are we to locate public theology, both in the contemporary world and historically? Let me start not with yet another definition of public theology, at least not yet, but with a familiar piece of advice on how to do public theology. Karl Barth famously remarked that theology should be done with the daily newspaper in one hand and the Bible in the other. So let's do that.

On Monday the 7th of April 2003, at the start of this week, the following headline appeared in the London *Times*:

Archbishop in Qatar strictly for theology

In fact, the Anglican Archbishop of Canterbury, Rowan Williams, was meeting in the Gulf state of Qatar with other Christian and Muslim religious leaders for what was called a 'Building Bridges' conference. Despite his publicly stated opposition with other church leaders to the Iraqi war, Williams apparently did not intend to make any statement on the conflict during his three day stay in Qatar this week. This led to *The Times* headline and the journalist's comment in the accompanying article: 'It is feared that any further comments on the war would distract from the more esoteric purpose of the conference, at which Dr Williams and other scholars of the Bible and the Koran will wrestle with scripture and explore the theological parallels between the faiths.' There we have it. Here is the media's perception of theology: conceived rightly as a wrestling with scripture and as a critical and comparative reflection on the faith and practice of living religious traditions, but also as an esoteric discourse without significance for public affairs in a divided world of war and conflict.

Of course, that is not how Rowan Williams or his Christian and Muslim colleagues would have perceived their theological work in Qatar this week. Such inter-faith conversations are integral to any critical Christian theological engagement with the public sphere in the contemporary world. Williams' earlier public opposition to the Gulf war and subsequent participation in the Qatar conference after its outbreak is perhaps a contemporary example of Barth's daring approach in the 1930s to doing public theology: on the one hand risking all by immersing himself in public affairs and challenging a totalitarian regime, as in the *Barmen Declaration*, and on the other hand, working away at the *Church Dogmatics* as if oblivious to the surrounding political context of violence and oppression. Such a bold approach to public theology, embracing *both* the risky solidarity of critical public engagement *and* the disciplined distancing and dialogue necessary for critical theological reflection, is beyond the comprehension of even the most informed branches of the British media. However, this newspaper story does give us an opening clue as to the location of public theology.

Locating Public Theology in the Public Sphere

Public theology is to be located first in the public sphere, the place of public communication and argumentation. If, with Habermas, we agree that the public sphere is, 'a domain of our social life in which public opinion can be formed', where any and all citizens can gather freely and without coercion to consider matters of general interest, then a public theology must be a discourse that circulates in this public sphere and both informs and is informed by public opinion on public issues (Habermas, 1989, p. 231). Clearly, for *The Times* newspaper, the Archbishop only participates in the public sphere when he makes public comments about the war in Iraq, condemning it as 'illegal and immoral', but not when he engages in inter-faith dialogue on sacred scriptures and shared understandings of the nature of God between Christians and Muslims. And so the archbishop is perceived as being in Qatar strictly for the esoteric purpose of doing theology. Here, theology is located far from the public sphere, in a 'reservation of the spirit', as David Tracy has aptly described this fate.

While Tracy has written insightfully and influentially of theology's three publics in church, academy and society, and the notion of public life embraces the wide range of public institutions, activities and issues reflected in our conference seminar programme, I want us at the outset to locate public theology within a more precise notion of the public, in what Habermas has called the public sphere. For Habermas, with his theory of communicative action, the public sphere is a social space between civil society, with its associations and movements rooted in what he calls the lifeworld, and the systems of the state and the market economy:

The public sphere can best be described as a network for communicating information and points of view (i.e., opinions expressing affirmative and negative attitudes); the streams of communication are, in the process, filtered and processed in such a way that they coalesce into topically specific *public* opinions ... the public sphere ... refers ... to the *social space* generated by communicative action. (Habermas 1996, p. 360)

I am particularly interested in the critical reception and re-appropriation of Habermasian notions of the public sphere by feminist political and social theorists. The political philosopher Iris Marion Young, for example, has described Habermas' idea of the public sphere 'as a process through which the problems of a whole society are discussed, processed, and finally brought to influence the formation of ... law and public policy' (Young, 2000: 170). For Young:

The public sphere is the primary connector between people and power. We should judge the health of a public sphere by how well it functions as a space of opposition and accountability, on the one hand, and policy influence, on the other. In the public sphere political actors raise issues, publish information, opinions, and aesthetic expression, criticize actions and policies, and propose new policies and practices. When widely discussed and disseminated, these issues, criticisms, images and proposals sometimes provoke political and social change. (Young, 200: 173 - 4)

Iris Young is also concerned to see the public sphere as a site of inclusive diversity where people can express their views in a variety of modes of expression and from a diversity of backgrounds and interests. While she recognises the importance of rhetorical skill to persuade others in the public sphere, Young also makes a case for including other forms of inclusive political communication:

... a radical injustice can occur when those who suffer a wrongful harm or oppression lack the terms to express a claim of injustice within the prevailing normative discourse. Those who suffer this wrong are excluded ... Lyotard calls this situation the *differend*. How can a group that suffers a particular harm or oppression move from a situation of total silencing and exclusion with respect to this suffering to its public expression? Storytelling is often an important bridge in such experiences between the mute experience of being wronged and political arguments about justice. (Young, 2000: 72)

The public sphere is therefore a welcome site of pluralism, and many forms of communicative reason, where differences should be affirmed and attended to, not excluded. For Iris Young:

A public consists of a plurality of different individual and collective experiences, histories, commitments, ideals, interests, and goals that face one another to discuss collective problems under a common set of procedures. When members of such a public speak to one another, they know they are answerable to that plurality of others; this access that others have to their point of view makes them careful about expressing themselves. This plural public-speaking context requires participants to express themselves in ways accountable to all those plural others. They must try to explain their particular background experiences, interests, or proposals in ways that others can understand, and they must express reasons for their claims in ways that others recognise could be accepted, even if they disagree with the claims and reason ... they speak with the reflective idea that third parties could be listening. (Young, 2000: 25)

Young's feminist account of the meaning of the public sphere helps us to locate those theologies that are truly public in this communicative, participative and pluralist sense and to identify some of the key issues for such truly public theologies today.

Not all social and political theologies recognise or welcome the public sphere as depicted in these terms. Gary Simpson has described what he calls two historically dominant models of civil society and the public sphere that such theologies may hold. First, there is the *agonistic* view of civil society, in which the public space is seen as the site of competitive struggle to demonstrate the self-sufficient superiority of a particular tradition. Simpson sees sectarian Christian movements as promoting such an elitist and totalising view of civil society, with their tendency to apocalyptic rhetoric, stereotyping and Manichaean scenarios, with 'a single agenda of personal and communal virtue along with diminution, assimilation, or outright elimination of rival communal traditions.'(Simpson, 2002: 137) Second, there is the liberal view of civil society, with its 'repressive tolerance' that seeks to exclude theological traditions from bringing their private moral concerns into the public forum to avoid incommensurable public moral disagreements. By way of contrast, for Simpson a communicative model of civil society as advocated by Habermas, with his paradigm shift to communicative rationality, allows for elements of both agonistic conviction and liberal tolerance to characterise the public sphere:

A communicative civil society shares certain features with the dominant models. Like the agonistic model, and unlike the liberal model, it welcomes, and indeed accentuates questions of moral truth. Unlike the agonistic ethos, with its characteristic practices of elitist moral display and purist moral trumping, communicative civil society holds that claims to practical moral truth must be redeemed critically through participatory practices ... a communicative civil society anticipates ... overlapping moral insights. This anticipation depends on thick moral traditions becoming socially embodied and mutually engaging according to communicative procedures and by means of communicative practices. (Simpson, 2002: 139)

Such a communicative civil society is open to what he calls the prophetic vocation of congregations, exercised in their role as 'public companions in the public sphere' rather than heroic individualists, reminding civil society of the fallibilist character of every moral consensus within a Christian eschatological horizon of the 'not yet'.

From the perspective of different models of Christian identity and theologies of revelation, rather than of civil society, the Australian Catholic theologian Robert Gascoigne also suggests that certain theologies of narrative and self-contained tradition find it difficult if not impossible to engage in the public forum in ways that would recognise moral insight or common ground with those outside the church in a communicative rationality. Gascoigne argues for an understanding of Christian identity where encounter with the other in the public sphere of liberal societies is necessary to recall the church to a more faithful discipleship; and for a theology of mediation, that affirms both the particularity and uniqueness of God's revelation in Christ in history and the universal import of that revelation for a world created by God, where the Spirit is at work:

The task of a theology of mediation is to preserve the identity of Christian faith in a way which is the same time an affirmation of its openness to the work of the Spirit in the world. Because of this, a theology of mediation is predicated on the possibility of mutual comprehension and dialogue between Christian faith and other worlds of meaning. (Gascoigne, 2001: 137)

So, how one construes and locates the public sphere, in agonistic or communicative terms, and how one understands the church's role in the public forum, as an exclusive social ethic and alternative social world, or as an inclusive dialogue partner in Christian need of the Spirit's insight from the other, determines whether one can locate a theology as truly *public* or not.

It has still been demanding and difficult for some theologies that do embrace the public sphere of democratic societies to accept its constraints and responsibilities, as well as its opportunities. Even those social and political theologies of liberation that have entered the public sphere of societies open to democratic reconstruction and renewal in recent years, have found the public sphere a challenging arena requiring new skills. Robert Schreiter has suggested that theologies of liberation must now take on a wider range of public and political tasks, moving from resistance, denunciation and critique to advocacy and the responsibilities of reconstruction of their communities. (Schreiter, 1997: 109, 110) To engage in effective advocacy and reconstruction, theologies of liberation would have to place greater emphasis on inter-disciplinarity and be open to developing ethical middle axioms in order to make concrete proposals for reform in the public forum. This shift of emphasis and context for theologies of resistance entering a new democratic era in the public sphere is also found in John de Gruchy's reflections on the post-apartheid situation for public theology in South Africa. De Gruchy has identified several shifts in South African public life that require new approaches from Christian theologians and churches: including the realities of a multi-faith rather than Christian society, the move from a liberation struggle to a focus on 'democratic transformation and within that the enormous challenge of inequality and poverty' and HIV-AIDS, and accepting a democratic government's invitation to the faith communities to participate in the task of nation-building, truth-telling and reconciliation. (De Gruchy, 2004)

The task is daunting. Writing in a collection of essays on the problems and potentials in South African civil society as it faced issues of sameness and difference after the end of the apartheid regime but not its deadly legacy, Denise Ackermann identifies the relevance of the biblical tradition of laments for those who have suffered. But, she notes, 'We have no public forums for lament.' (Ackermann, 2000: 232) When we remember that Iris Marion Young argues for the importance of story-telling and the need to affirm other forms of expression for those silenced and excluded from the public sphere, in order that they can name their injustice publicly and seek public redress, we realise that the needs of public theology and the public sphere to find new forms of inclusive communication are not dissimilar. The two came together in 1999, when Rebecca Chopp spoke at a public conference on the Multi-nature of South Africa in 1999, and drew on black and feminist theology to advocate modes of public theological discourse that included 'the phronesis of empathy': 'the ability to identify with and understand someone different than oneself especially when listening to their stories and testimonies, fosters the cultivating of compassion within the public space.' (Koopman, 2002:6)

If location in a feminist-critiqued Habermasian public sphere helps us to identify truly public theologies in contemporary society, and some of the key issues that these public theologies must increasingly address, where do we locate public theology historically and in relation to Practical Theology? If these first thoughts on locating public theology came out of reading a headline in this week's newspaper, what reflections are sparked by reading the Bible in our other hand?

Locating Public Theology in Globalization

Here is a familiar artistic image inspired by the Gospel narrative. At least, it seems very familiar. It is the well-known Mother and Child nativity scene that has shaped the Christian consciousness of the incarnation of God for two thousand years. On closer inspection, the figures in the scene are wearing Near Eastern clothing from the medieval period. Is this the devotional artwork of the Eastern churches of Syria and the Middle East? No, this is a Muslim

depiction of the birth of the Prophet Mohammed, adapted from the standard compositions of the Nativity in Christian illustrated books of the time, by artists working in the Mongul Ilkhanate empire in Western Asia, modern-day Iraq, Iran and Syria. The illustration appears in Rashid al-Din's *Compendium of Chronicles*, his history of the world, written in the early 14th century of the Common Era. Rashid al-Din was the Vizier, the senior government official in the Ilkhanate empire, based in its capital city of Tabriz in modern-day Iran, described by scholars today as 'perhaps the major metropolis of the contemporary world [of its time], a multicultural, multiconfessional, political, and commercial center that served as a bridge between Europe and East Asia.' This painting represents the religious and cultural diversity and officially-fostered pluralism of 'the Ilkhanids during the period of their rule in Iran and Iraq, from the mid-thirteenth to the mid-fourteenth century.' (Komaroff and Carboni, 2002: 105 - 112)

I hope the Archbishop and his Muslim colleagues were locating their 'esoteric theological discussions' in Qatar in this historical context. It is the context of what I would call, 'globalization.' With the Australian historian Robbie Robertson, I wish to argue that globalization does not begin in the later twentieth century, with the aftermath of the Second World War, the collapse of communism and the total spread of global capitalism and communication technologies. With Robertson I would define globalization fundamentally as the inter-connectedness of human communities and cultures around the globe. As Robertson argues:

> ... globalization is is more than just McWorld or Westernization. It is about human interconnections that have assumed global proportions and transformed themselves. If we focus on globalization simply as a modern strategy for power, we will miss its historical and social depths. Indeed the origins of globalization lie in interconnections that have slowly enveloped humans since the earliest times, as they globalized themselves. In this sense, globalization as a human dynamic has always been with us, even if we have been unaware of its embrace until recently. Instead we have viewed the world more narrowly through the spectacles of religion, civilization, nation or race. Today these old constructs continue to frustrate the development of a global consciousness of human interconnections and their dynamism. (Robertson, 2003: 3)

Robertson argues that while human social, economic and cultural interconnectedness has been a feature of human history on this planet from the primal origins of the human species, we can identify three distinctive waves of this interconnectedness that have a global quality and a global consciousness. For Robertson, the first wave starts in the 16th century and is linked to European voyages of discovery, expanding commercial trade networks and strategies of conquest in the Americas, Africa, Asia and finally Australasia. But the first wave of globalization is also the story of the dominance of China in Asia as the most advanced trading and technological power in the world in this period. The second wave begins in the 19th century with Western industrialization and colonial expansion through imperial conquest and trade in the non-Western world but it is inseparably linked to the resistance to such developments, for example by China in the 19th century Opium Wars or by the nations of Africa and Asia in the 20th century anti-colonial independence movements. The third wave is upon us today, with the development of new international political and trade institutions after 1945, the end of the Cold War, the spread of global communication technologies compressing time and space, and the expansion of global markets from the later 20th century.

I wish to argue that as we address the issue of theology's voice in our contemporary public life, with all its pluralism, we remember at the outset the long history of globalization as human interconnectedness, symbolised by this Christian-Muslim painting of the birth of the Prophet, from 14th century Iran-Iraq. We must shift our perspective on public theology from the recent Western debates about the public domain in modernity and post-modernity, and re-locate it historically in these three waves of globalization, with its key concept of the human dynamic of interconnectedness. In other words, the public sphere has for centuries before the modern era been a pluralist one of complex human interconnections, multiple identities and many voices mixing together and influencing one another. This has two consequences for our understanding of the recent history of public theology.

First, there is no such thing as a global public theology but only local, contextual public theologies. However, these local public theologies have been and are profoundly interconnected with one another around the world. Reflecting on 'Theology After Auschwitz in Germany', Jurgen Moltmann has recently written of the ways in which European political theologies, responding to the pain of the Holocaust, were in turn challenged by Latin American liberation theologies, with their *locus theologicus* in the misery of the poor. In turn these public theologies have been influenced by feminist and ecological theologies:

The road leads from political theology to economic theology, and from economic theology to ecological theology. In a theology of life which comprehends God and the earth, the different contextual theologies, with their diverse contributions, can find themselves once more. (Moltmann, 2004: 41 - 2)

Secondly, these local public theologies may be generating a new kind of global public theology in the 21st century. Robert Schreiter has called this interconnecting of local contextual theologies the 'new catholicity', in which four main 'global theological flows' circulate around the world and interact with local contexts: theologies of liberation, ecology, feminism and human rights. (Schreiter, 1997: 114, 115) For Schreiter, this now means doing contextual theology in a new way, between the local and the global:

Globalization is ... both enticing in its promises and abhorrent in some of its consequences. The local situation can seldom keep globalizing forces out altogether ... and so it is inevitabily changed by the encounter. The local situation may indeed fell itself overwhelmed by the global ... But local situations are not powerless either ... the important point for cultural (and theological) production becomes the line of encounter between the local and the global, where the two come up against each other. Roland Robertson describes this encounter of the local and the global as 'glocalization' ... some of the most salient features in religion and theology today can best be described from the vantage point of the glocal. (Schreiter, 1997: 12)

To Schreiter's four global theological flows, I would add a fifth, the notion of public theology itself, rooted as it is in the local American context and experience of the 20th century, and named by Martin Marty to describe the distinctive public life and theological work of Reinhold Niebuhr and the American tradition in which he stands, alongside Catholic public theologians like John Courtney Murray (Koopman, 2002; Anderson, 1996). So, we must locate public theology not only in the communicative public sphere but in the interconnecting waves of globalization, with their global theological flows and cross-currents of liberation, feminism human rights, environmental sustainability and publicity itself. But where, in closing, does that leave Practical Theology, in relation to these two locations for public theology? We must look at one last news headline.

Locating Public Theology within Practical Theology

Picture the situation we are in. From America we have heard news of terrible atrocities and acts of terrorism committed in the name of God. From the Middle East, there is daily news of war between so-called Christian and Muslim states. And into this situation of global conflict in the public life of West and East, another headline appears:

Orbis minima pars est Europa … Quotidie regiones hactenus incognitae reperiuntur

The dateline is 1535, not September 11, 2001. The author is Desiderius Erasmus of Rotterdam, not Rowan Williams of Canterbury.

The headline reads:

Europe is a very small part of the world … Every day unknown lands are being discovered

Erasmus in 1535 was referring to the geopolitical situation of his day. In the East, in the former Christian heartlands of Asia and North Africa, the Christian nations of little Europe were at war with the larger Muslim world of 'the Turks'. And in the West, after Columbus' voyage to what he thought were the Indies in 1492, their Catholic majesties of Spain, Ferdinand and Isabella, were now conquering the recently unknown lands of the Americas, after their defeat of the Muslim Moors and expulsion of the Jews of Spain in the same fateful year of 1492.

Some forty years later, Erasmus writes with the combined eloquence of evangelical anger and humanist irony about Christian Europe's public role in the contemporary global situation, with wars of conquest and acts of terror being reported daily in both the Muslim East and the recently discovered Americas:

But what am I to say of those whose fleets daily sail past unknown shores and who loot and lay waste cities that expected no hostile act? Under what description shall deeds of this sort be celebrated? They are called victories. Yet such victories never earned praise even among the pagans, when peoples are suddenly attacked upon whom war has not been declared. "Ah, but they supported the Turk", they say. This is in fact the excuse offered for the overthrow of towns. If they themselves will accept such an excuse, should the Turk take the opportunity to lay waste a city and claim, "It supported the Christians." I do not know. There is a very great difference between banditry and Christian warfare, between the one who advances the Kingdom of faith and the one who furthers the tyranny of this world, between the one who seeks the salvation of souls and the one who hunts the spoils of Mammon. From lands that have been discovered there is fetched gold and precious stones, but a much more worthy reason for triumph would have been to bring to that place that Christian wisdom which is more precious than gold and that gospel pearl which well bears comparison with all merchandise. (Erasmus, 1535)

Written in 1535, these remarks by Erasmus could have been written to address our global situation today, in the early 21st century. In fact, the occasion for his geopolitical framework and searing critique of Christian Europe's role in the wider world is twofold.

First, Erasmus is writing from the core of his being as a Christian humanist thinker. Erasmus the greatest Christian humanist of the Northern Renaissance in the early 16th century, is addressing a central and recurring theme in his life and work: condemnation of the violence and war used by the European Christian powers for centuries against the Muslim Turks and now against the indigenous peoples of the Americas, in the name of the Gospel of Jesus Christ. He is reminding his readers that the Christendom of his day was restricted to Europe and that Europe was a very small part of a much larger world, with its expanding global consciousness through its cross-cultural encounter with other lands. As he wrote, *orbis minima pars est Europa ... quotidie regiones hactenus incognitae reperiuntur*. If those Christians engaged in statecraft and mission in little Europe were to be faithful to their calling, argued Erasmus, then they must abandon violence against their non-Christian neighbours in this expanding world and share the wisdom of the Gospel alone, through the persuasive power of peaceful witness and non-oppressive Christian practice.

But second, the particular occasion which prompts Erasmus to make this analysis of the contemporary world situation is an extraordinary one – an extraordinary one for practical theologians concerned with this theme of theology and public life in a pluralist era and the relationship between public theology and practical theology. These statements from Erasmus on global public affairs, which I have deliberately quoted at some length to bring home their quality of extensive argumentation rather than incidental comment, occur in his final major work, published in 1535, the year before his death: *Ecclesiastes sive De Ratione Concionandi*, his *Handbook for Preachers*. In four books, Erasmus the Renaissance Christian humanist scholar teaches the preacher to draw on both the theory and practice of the Greek and Roman *art of rhetoric*, and the exposition of the original biblical text in order to proclaim the Gospel faithfully and effectively. Now Erasmus' handbook on preaching stands in a long medieval tradition of this genre of preaching handbooks. Richard Osmer has rightly recognised this body of medieval homiletical literature as one of the pre-modern roots of the modern discipline of Practical Theology (Osmer, 1999: 113 - 139). But here something of historical moment happens. Unlike the many authors on preaching before him, Erasmus, the most brilliant linguist of his age, takes a global turn, and situates his theory and practice of preaching in the political context of the contemporary pluralist world as well as in the scholarly context of rhetoric and biblical studies and the ecclesial context of a church in need of reform.

Suddenly, in the midst of his exposition of how the art of classical rhetoric might be brought into the service of the sacred rhetoric of preaching, and while addressing the particular need for suitable missionary preachers to take the Gospel to lands beyond Christian Europe, Erasmus pulls aside the curtain of his humanist scholarship – as in the famous Hans Holbein portrait of Erasmus in the Louvre (see below), where he sits writing at his desk, with a rich curtain behind him – and opens a window onto the contemporary world. What a terrifying and all-too familiar scene meets his eyes.

In 1492, when Christian Europe sailed across the Atlantic the Carib population of Hispaniola was eight million people. In 1535, the year in which Erasmus made these statements on global mission and politics in his book on preaching, the Carib population had fallen to zero. *Zero*. The entire population of eight million human beings had been wiped out within Erasmus' lifetime. (Robertson, 2003: 74)

Erasmus was writing about a situation of genocide from first-hand reports: 'If travellers of these regions speak truly, the very Christian princes who have taken possession of the people in question oppose the arrival of any teachers of the Gospel, fearing lest if their subjects gain a little wisdom they may cast off the heavy yoke that oppresses them. Those "satraps" prefer to govern asses than people.' (Erasmus, 1535) On the island of Hispaniola in 1535, that was all their Catholic majesties were left to govern, animals. There were no Caribs left to rule or oppress, after the Christian conquest of this part of the Americas brought with it the killer diseases that were to wipe out an estimated 95% of the indigenous peoples of the Americas. (Robertson, 2003: 74)

Why tell this story of Erasmus at such length? Because this is where we must start in locating the history of public theology as we recognise it in the 21st century. This is where and when we must begin to locate theology and public life historically in a pluralist age. I wish to argue, with globalization scholars like Robbie Robertson, that the period from 1492 to 1535, marks the beginning of the modern era of globalization. It is here, with Erasmus and his Christian humanist contemporaries, that we see Christian thought and practice being challenged profoundly in its self-understanding and its public engagement by what Robertson has called 'the first wave of globalization' and its defining interconnection with the other. Erasmus' response as a practical theologian is to address the public sphere, in this handbook on preaching, as in so many of his other writings. But in his work on preaching he makes a practical theological critique of colonial conquest in the guise of Christian mission that will make a profound impact on public opinion in the literate public of Europe, debating as it was in his day the legality of the Conquest in terms of the humanity of the peoples of the Americas, and among the proto-liberationist priests of the Americas like Bartolome de Las Casas. (Rivera, 1992: 249)

If we are to locate public theology today in the context of what Robertson calls the latest and third wave of globalization, then we must begin at the source, *ad fontes*, as the humanist Erasmus would have put it: in the emerging global era of Erasmus in the 16th century, with terrorism in the Americas and Christian-Muslim conflict in the East, and with this seminal European encounter with the other in the first wave of globalisation.

However, this is also where we must *re-locate* our discipline of Practical Theology, its history and self-understanding. In my judgement, this story of the Christian humanist Erasmus making his global turn in the midst of a handbook on preaching is the beginning of Practical Theology as the discipline which we recognise and serve today: concerned as it is with the critical and contextual study of the theory of religious practice in the contemporary world. If we can say that the publication of Schleiermacher's *Brief Outline of the Study of Theology* in 1810 marks the Protestant Pietist birth of Practical Theology as a separate ecclesial discipline within the academy, with its accompanying linguistic turn in hermeneutics, then I wish to argue that Erasmus' *Handbook on Preaching* in 1535 marks the Christian humanist birth of Practical Theology as a critical public discipline within society, with its accompanying global turn in public ethics.

This other, neglected taproot of Practical Theology in Erasmian Christian humanist homiletics is inseparably inter-twined with the umbilical cord of public theology in a global era, the Erasmian strand of Christian humanist critique of European conquest and oppression of the non-European world, the boundaries of which were expanding in European global consciousness by the later 15th and early 16th centuries. Both root and chord and their inter-weaving development as practical and public theology are inseparable from their public context in the rise of globalisation. Both are inseparably interconnected in the public sphere. And so as practical theologians we are here to do theology, strictly *public* theology. For me, that means re-locating the origins of Practical Theology in time, beginning with the Northern Renaissance and the first wave of globalization in the early modern period of 16th century humanism (Toulmin, 1990); and re-conceiving the discipline in spatial terms, as the moral cartography of God and neighbour in the Christian humanist tradition of Erasmus of Rotterdam and the world.

References

Denise Ackermann (2000) 'Lamenting Tragedy from "The Other Side", in James R. Cochrane, Bastienne Klein, eds., *Sameness and Difference: problems and potentials in South African civil society* (Washington DC: Council for Research in Values and Philosophy,), 213 - 241.

Victor Anderson (1996) 'The Search for Public Theology in the United States', in Thomas G Long, Edward Farley, eds., *Preaching as a Theological Task* (Louisville, KY: Westminster John Knox Press), 19 - 31.

Desiderius Erasmus (1535) *Ecclesiastes Sive De Ratione Concionandi* (Basel, Johannes Froben), forthcoming in English, *Complete Works of Erasmus*, Vols. 70 - 75, Spiritualia and Pastoralia (Toronto: University of Toronto Press).

Robert Gascoigne (2001) *The Public Forum and Christian Ethics* (Cambridge: Cambridge University Press).

John de Gruchy (2004) 'From Political to Public Theologies: the role of theology in public life in South Africa', in W. Storrar and A. Morton, eds., *Public Theology for the 21st Century* (London: T&T Clark International/Continuum), 45 - 62.

Jurgen Habermas (1996) *Between Facts and Norms: contributions to a discourse theory of law and democracy*, transl. W. Rehg (Cambridge, MA: MIT Press).

Jurgen Habermas (1989) 'The Public Sphere', in Steven Seidman, ed., *Jurgen Habermas on Society and Politics* (Boston, MA: Beacon Press, 231 - 6.

Linda Komaroff and Stefano Carboni, (2002) eds., *The Legacy of Genghis Khan: courtly art and culture in Western Asia, 1256 - 1353* (Yale, CT: Yale University Press).

Nico Koopman (2002) 'Public Theology in South Africa Today', unpublished paper delivered at the Centre for Theology and Public Issues, University of Edinburgh, 2002.

Jurgen Moltmann (2004) 'Political Theology in Germany after Auschwitz', in W. Storrar, A. Morton, eds., *Public Theology for the 21st Century* (London: T&T Clark International Continuum), 37 - 43.

Richard Osmer (1999) 'Practical Theology as Argument, Rhetoric and Conversation', in Friedrich Schweitzer, Johannes A. van der Ven, eds., *Practical Theology: International Perspectives* (Frankfurt: Peter Lang), 113 - 139.

Luis N. Rivera (1992) *A Violent Evangelism: the political and religious conquest of the Americas* (Louisville, KY: WJK Press).

Robbie Robertson (2003) *The Three Waves of Globalization: a history of a developing global consciousness* (London: Zed Books).

Robert Schreiter (1997) *The New Catholicity theology between the global and the local* (Maryknoll, NY: Orbis Press).

Gary M. Simpson (2002) *Critical Social Theory: prophetic reason, civil society and Christian imagination* (Minneapolis, MN: Fortress Press).

William F Storrar (1995) 'Marrying Wisdom and Witness: a new foundation for Practical Theology', in Alan Main, ed., *But Where Shall Wisdom Be Found?* (Aberdeen: Aberdeen University Press).

Stephen Toulmin (1990) *Cosmopolis: the hidden agenda of modernity* (New York, NY: Free Press).

Iris Marion Young (2000) *Inclusion and Democracy* (Oxford: Oxford University Press).

Do We Learn to Know God from What We Do?

A Plea for a Relational Concept of Action.

Robert Mager

Practical theologians may be convinced that theology can play an important social role, and a public one at that. But it is an understatement to say that the credibility of practical theology within the public realm and its relevance for public debate are yet to be established. At least in Quebec, but in many other Western countries as well, theology as a whole is still widely perceived as a dogmatic and authoritarian discourse that can be tolerated, at best, when it remains within the boundaries of theory and moral principles, but that must be kept in check when practical matters are at stake.

Perceptions can be overcome, however, and practical theologians may feel that their constant emphasis on practice, experience, facts, context and the like, has laid ground for a different, nondogmatic, empirical and inductive theology, which can fruitfully participate in public debate and progressively gain recognition. My first contention here is that, as a rule, this inductive theology is not yet fully in place, and that a deductive frame of mind, deeply rooted in Christian tradition, hampers its development. My second contention is that a theoretical obstacle must be overcome for the theological conversion to take place, which has to do with the way practical theology conceives *action*. I intend to suggest how a different, relational concept of action, based on the views of the German-American political philosopher Hannah Arendt (1906 - 1975), could challenge the current pragmatic concept and open new horizons for practical theology.

The following reflections pertain to the field of *fundamental practical theology* (Audinet, 1995, p. 254; Viau, 2000, p. 324), a label which seems to be an elegant way of escaping the practical ground, but which is actually based on the conviction that practice involves fundamental assumptions that gain to be reflected upon for the sake of action itself, if one does not want to be trapped in a "naive relationship" to practice or an "arbitrary subjectivity that cannot or does not want to account for its statements" (Audinet, 1995, p. 107).

Inductive theology?

The dialectical relationship between theology and practice has become sort of a dogma in practical theology (cf. diagram1).

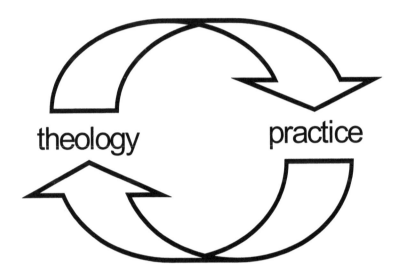

It is expressed in different terms: bipolar unity of tension (Greinacher, 1974), conversation (Browning, 1990), correlation (Donzé, 1989), dialog, and the like. But many practical theologies, though they confess reciprocity, do not put an actual dialectical relationship into place.

For example, in his masterwork *Theory and Practice*, Clodovis Boff pleads explicitly in favour of a dialectical relationship between theology and practice, "so that theological truth may be practiced in History, and political practice may be a true one" (1990, p. 52). This statement is structured reciprocally, but it is not open to the possibility that "theological truth" be *questioned* or *shaped* by practice. In a similar manner, Marc Donzé argues for a "critical correlati- on between the reality of ecclesial practice and its references"; he dismisses explicitly an understanding of this correlation as "a question-answer system, whereby the world of the reference would answer the questions of practice" (1989, p. 185). Nevertheless, a few pages later, correlation is detailed in the- se very terms: "The correlation is reciprocal: the present time asks questions that are new or original in their context, while both Gospel and History keep a permanent capacity of challenging today's achievements" (p. 189). Following in the footsteps of the Seeing-Judging-Acting model, his method refers prac- tice to "criteria stemming from the Gospel, as well as from Tradition and Ma- gisterium" (1995, p. 297). In this theological process, in spite of the author's cautions, the "world of the reference" is never challenged by practice.

Other examples should be called to the stand, but these will suffice to indicate that more often than not, the relationship between theology and practice still goes essentially one-way. The authors clearly expect theology to *have an impact* on practice. Admittedly, practice must *inform* theology but most of the time, this means to provide data so that theology might adjust to reality. No real, significant impact on theology itself is envisioned: all in all, deduction still reigns. A sign of this can be found in the way authors often invoke the theme of Incarnation to support their call for theology to reach practice; the opposite theme, divinisation (*theosis*), is never used in this context (cf. diagram 2).

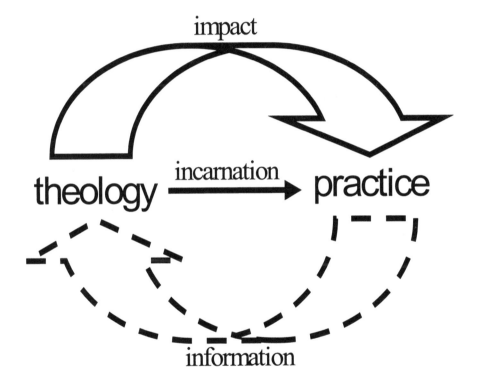

To put it in a blunt way: human practice is hardly understood as a *locus theologicus* in the full sense of the phrase, that is, as a God-revealing process. Rather, it is there to be questioned by God's revelation, as if revelation were somehow given beforehand. And in a real sense, it is: the biblical times have a special status in Christianity, as the foundational and referential times of the Christian historical experience. Catholic theology, among others, holds that Revelation ended with the formation of the canon of Scriptures. But biblical studies have demonstrated how the Bible itself locates God's revelation within human experience, as a practical process of liberation and interpretation.

It is as though this insight had not yet overcome centuries of another theological mindset, much influenced by the Greek understanding of (eternal) truth and its relationship to (fleeting) human practices. Theology (and even practical theology) still draws heavily upon a theoretical approach to truth, as a matter of contemplation (or theoretical reflection), while the Bible tends to envision truth as something to be "done" (John 3:21).

This theological issue is admittedly a difficult and much debated one; it is crucial for practical theology as public theology. Modern debates rely on a few basic assumptions. One of them is *pluralism*, which allows for different points of view to engage discussion; it can be invoked by theology to justify its voice in the debate. But another one, and a decisive one at that, is *autonomy* (as opposed to heteronomy): modern thought expects truth to be derived from human experience (through reason), and not imposed on it (by authority or tradition). *The issue, therein, is to know if practical theology can elaborate significant truth out of practice itself*, and not only "propose" it, however cleverly, empathically and dialogically it may do so[1].

But the difficulty to let practice shape theology does not come only from our cultural tradition. It is enforced by a view of action that prevails in modernity, whereby action is seen essentially as a fabrication process, as a way of pursuing goals and choosing means, with an emphasis on mastery and efficiency. Such a view supports the deeply rooted tendency of theology to see itself as the goal provider (criteria, references, values, vision, meaning, purpose) and to simply ask practice for advice about the appropriate means (tools, strategies, plans, methods, steps) to achieve these goals. Hannah Arendt argued forcefully against this model of action, in favour of a relational model centred on the disclosure of meaning. This needs further exploration and explanation.

Action as fabrication

Arendt writes in *The Human Condition*:

[...] the division between knowing and acting, so alien to the realm of action, whose validity and meaningfulness are destroyed the moment thought and action part company, is an everyday experience in fabrication, whose processes obviously fall into two parts: first, perceiving the image or shape (*eidos*) of the product-to-be, and then organizing the means and starting the execution. (1958, p. 225)

---

[1]   According to Audinet, empirical practical theologies tend to consider theological references as self-evident (1995, p. 249), instead of opening them to discussion, exploration, even contradiction. David Tracy, by contrast, sees the importance of considering institutionalised Christianity as a practice dealing with its references: "Here, the word practice does not refer to empirical action, but to the operation by which action is analysed, theorized, formulated, and elaborates its own criteria." (Audinet, 1995, p. 253)

This distinction between action and fabrication is central in Arendt's under-standing of human practice in general, and of political action in particular. It is not obvious in common language, or in practical theology. For most peo-ple, action refers to what we *do*, without much distinction between doing and making. In French (*faire*) and in Spanish (*hacer*), one word encompasses a large range of activities, without distinction. This tends to fuel a very fuzzy usage of the concept of action and, as consequence, of the notion of practice. Reading different essays in practical theology, one comes rapidly to the con-clusion, with Jacques Audinet, that "the same word 'practice' hardly points to anything identical" (1995, p. 103) and that "[here] is a word that must always be defined" (p. 258).

Arendt's distinction between acting and making is grounded in her philo-sophical anthropology (1958). She contends that human existence, considered from the point of view of activity in general, has three basic dimensions: it is grounded in nature, it evolves in a world of things, it takes shape in a web of human relationships. To these three dimensions correspond three basic activi-ties, that she calls labour (in relation to nature), work (in relation to the world of things), and action (in relation to human relationships). These three dimen-sions and their corresponding activities constitute three realms of human exis-tence, each realm with its inner laws and logic. The realm of action, to which the universe of speech belongs, must thus be distinguished from the realm of work, even though both realms are integrated in human existence itself:

Action and speech go on between men, as they are directed toward them, and they retain their agent-revealing capacity even if their content is exclusively "objective", concerned with the matters of the world of things in which men move, which phy-sically lies between them and out of which arise their specific, objective worldly in-terests. These interests constitute, in the word's most literal significance, something which *inter-est*, which lies between people and therefore can relate and bind them to-gether. Most action and speech is concerned with this in-between, which varies with each group of people, so that most words and deeds are about some worldly objective reality in addition to being a disclosure of the acting and speaking agent. Since this disclosure of the subject is an integral part of all, even the most "objective" intercour-se, the physical, worldly, in-between along with its interests is overlaid and, as it were, overgrown with an altogether different in-between which consists of deeds and words and owes its origin exclusively to men's acting and speaking directly to one another. This second, subjective in-between is not tangible, since there are no tangible objects into which it could solidify; the process of acting and speaking could leave behind no such results and end products. But for all its intangibility, this in-between is no less re-al than the world of things we visibly have in common. We call this reality the "web" of human relationships, indicating by the metaphor its somewhat intangible quality. (Arendt 1958, p. 182 - 183)

Though the different realms of existence overlap, human beings get in trouble when they try to function in one realm with the laws and logic of another realm. In particular, Arendt insists on the way we tend to understand action in terms of work, that is, of fabrication. In a world of inanimate things, work operates entirely within the laws and logic of causality. This allows to forge plans and to realize them in a precise manner, in order to obtain the desired results. Mastery is an important value here, which can be perfected and developed systematically, hazard being tracked and trapped along the way. But action does not operate primarily with objects; it deals with human beings capable of reacting in their own way, independently, or relatively so, of the motivations and goals of the one who initiated the action. Action is creative; it basically means initiative, the capacity to initiate something new, something unexpected, that cannot simply be deducted from a previous state of affair. Experienced in the midst of the human community, action is closely related to speech; it engenders stories that capture the meaning of the action.

The creativity of action and the boundlessness of its effects in the web of human relationships are such that unpredictability of the outcome, irreversibility of the effects and anonymity of the author are the three main characteristics of action as opposed to work, to fabrication. Action tries to compensate for the unpredictability of the outcome by relying on *promise* (commitment, engagement, alliance, treaty, testament, law), while work relies on mastery of the process. Action tries to compensate for the irreversibility of the effects by relying on *forgiveness* (magnanimity, oblivion, amnesty), while work can always reverse the process, undo what was purposefully fabricated. Action tries to compensate for the anonymity of the author by inspiring *history*, that is, stories capturing the meaning of the action and recollecting the greatness or meanness of its actors, while work inscribes the name of the maker on the deed itself.

Action is not centred on the things of the world as much as on the people who inhabit it. Action is *interaction*, through which human beings both *reveal* and *realize* themselves publicly: "In acting and speaking, men show who they are, reveal actively their unique personal identities and thus make their appearance in the human world" (Arendt, 1958, p. 179). Action is a *performing art*, not *tekhnê*, nor *poiesis*, but *praxis* [2]. Its specific "product" is stories;

---

[2] "It is this insistence on the living deed and the spoken word as the greatest achievements of which human beings are capable that was conceptualized in Aristotle's notion of *energeia* ('actuality'), with which he designated all activities that do not pursue an end (are *ateleis*) and leave no work behind (no *par' autas erga*), but exhaust their full meaning in the performance itself. It is from the experience of this full actuality that the paradoxical 'end in itself' derives its original meaning; for in these instances of action and speech the end (*telos*) is not pursued but lies in the activity itself which therefore becomes an *entelecheia*, and the work

action "'produces' stories with or without intention as naturally as fabrication produces tangible things" (p. 184). It is a matter of *meaning* rather than one of end results.

The point is, human beings have often been worried by the weaknesses, risks and uncertainties of human action, and thus been tempted to replace action by the comforting all-controlled process of work, of fabrication. Action has thus been modelled on "an activity where one man, isolated from all others, remains master of his doings from beginning to end" (Arendt, 1958, p. 220). It has been led by "the delusion that we can 'make' something in the realm of human affairs – 'make' institutions or laws, for instance, as we make tables and chairs, or make men 'better' or 'worse'" (p. 188). Action, conceived as fabrication of history, is made apparent when it is presented as if it were dealing with things that obey the laws and logics of causality, when it makes systematic use of the categories of means and ends, or when insistence is put on mastering the process of intervention.

The very essence of human action is at stake here. By systematically insisting on causality, on means and ends, on mastery of the process or on efficiency, action conceived as fabrication operates as if it were not dealing with people engaged, by their very existence, in the process of becoming *free*. Admittedly, this is a process and human beings are never "absolutely free" (and maybe not mainly free); thus there are causal patterns in human behaviour, which support "interventions" aimed at modifying behaviours. But the issue here is to affirm the *possibility* of freedom, and the importance of its *actualisation*. This is the main "purpose" of action, its meaning, a meaning that does not pre-exist action but that can only be "enacted".

Obviously, such perspectives challenge openly the concept of action at the basis of many practical theologies. To give only one example, C. Boff writes: "By Praxis we mean *all practices aiming at transforming Society* or *producing History*" (1990, p. 32). He adds in a footnote:

[...] we adopt, including for our understanding of 'theological practice', the definition of '*practice* in general' given by L. Althusser: 'Any process by which some given raw materials are *transformed* into a given *product*, the transformation being done by given human work using given means of production'[3].

The Marxian line of thought is explicit here. But it need not be there for action to be conceived along the lines of the fabrication process. Actually, we find such views on action in mainstream modern social theories of action, on which practical theologies often rely. In his article published in the venerable

---

is not what follows and extinguishes the process, but is imbedded in it; the performance is the work, is *energeia*." (Arendt, 1958, p. 206)

[3] Boff, 1990, p. 32, note 11, quoting Althusser's *Pour Marx*, p. 167.

Encyclopaedia Universalis, R. Daval describes action as "making" something, without taking the subject and his environment into account: "in the broadest sense, action is defined as the search for means and their arrangement to realise an end"; consequently, praxeology aims at determining the most efficient means to reach given ends (1972, p. 873). This allows for the results of action to be "predicted" and the process to be properly engineered.

Practical theologies are not necessarily geared towards such social engineering and can be very attentive to issues pertaining properly to the realm of action (Nadeau, 1993, p. 92). But many put a strong emphasis on the means and the goals of action, on the mastery of its process and on its efficiency, at the expense of its essential dynamics, which do not have as much to do with "results" as with the *meaning* that is enacted and with the way the participants both *reveal* and *actualise* themselves in the course of action. Briefly stated: action may have *results*, but its essence is to be *meaningful*. It has to do with *revelation*: revelation of who people are, something that can only be told retrospectively, from the point of view of those who witnessed the action and who can capture its meaning into words and texts. In such a relational model of action, where action is seen as initiative and interaction, neither practice nor theology can totally be predetermined and mastered, because the unfolding of meaning takes form in action itself. Theology and practice are then necessarily in a dialectical relationship, as speech and action are always, in any true practice (cf. diagram 3).

Action as revelation

The very dynamics of the biblical revelation can be perceived in those last sentences. The Bible often refers to God's "works", but the prevailing vision, even with regard to creation, is thoroughly praxeological. The biblical narrative is centred on the relationship between God and His/Her people, on liberation acts and their meaning, on the revelation of God through history, and on who the believers become in return. It relates a few chapters of the emergence of human freedom, in action and speech, through specific events. N. Greinacher thus writes that the Christian God "is a 'God in the World', a God that reveals himself in history and society. [...] And because it is so, all Christian theologies, as theological theories, are fundamentally related to praxis"[4].

Gracefulness is central to this biblical journey, as it is to human relationships in general (Godbout and Caillé, 1998). Both creation and salvation are presented as free gifts, undeserved. The Kingdom is promised to "happen" without warning; the early Christians see the death and resurrection of Christ as a grace to which they respond in gratitude, by offering their own lives in return. Faith is a participation in this threefold experience of receiving, praising and giving.[5]

Action conceived as work, as fabrication, has lead to view God's action in terms of fabrication: the "maker of heaven and earth" has become the "maker of history". Insistence is then put on God's "plan", a plan He/She realises in human lives and history. This vision unfolds in invitations to "build the Kingdom", to collaborate with God, to work in His/Her field, to "practice" the commandments. These expressions, however legitimate, can mask the essential dynamics of faith, by which the important aspect of the process is not so much what is done but what happens and who we become in the doing.

And maybe *who God Him/Herself becomes*. Theology enters new grounds the moment the action of God is conceived in relational terms, as a process of revelation and of self-realization taking place in the web of human relationships. Then Incarnation takes a whole new dimension. God does not engage in history to transform it into eternity, or to rescue human beings from temporality, but to be "personally" involved in the human journey and fate. God's revelation through love, as outlined in Johannine literature, implies God's realisation in human history.

In this realm of action where gratuitousness prevails, neither the gift nor its consequences can be foreseen or controlled. Its meaning unfolds in experience itself, which means that the biblical times do not so much *contain* revelati-

---

[4]   Greinacher, 1990, p. 244, quoted in Audinet, 1995, p. 244.
[5]   Zulehner, 1996, p. 1020. These three aspects evoke the three fundamental concepts of Metz' practical fundamental theology: memory, story and solidarity (Metz, 1980).

on than *testify* to its dynamics in human history, which remains open to new experiences. That perspective invites to let go of a concept of Revelation confining it to the past, and to envision something like a "praxeological relationship to Revelation" (Nadeau, 1993, p. 92). Practical theology is accustomed to approach practices in a theological way; it still has to learn, or to learn better, how to approach God in a practical way, which does not mean "to put God into practice", so to speak, but to discover God in practice.

Such a shift in perspective means to let go of long-held certainties about God and God's ways. It also means to trust practice's ability to produce meaning, that is, stories in which what is worthy ("glorious") and what is unworthy ("sinful") may come to light. There lies, potentially, the specific contribution of practical theologies to public debates: its ongoing meditation on God's coming through our own public becoming. Practical theologies search for God in human experience, not as the One who is known, tried and tested, but as What is ever to be discovered and revered in common, as long as there is life on Earth. Under these conditions, practical theologies could become a public companion in the common quest for an authentic and meaningful humanity.

References

(Translation of the English quotations of French texts by Robert Mager.)

Arendt, Hannah (1958) *The Human Condition*. Chicago: The University of Chicago Press.

Audinet, Jacques (1995) *Écrits de théologie pratique*. Paris: Cerf; Montréal: Novalis; Bruxelles: Lumen Vitae; Genève: Labor et Fides.

Boff, Clodovis (1990) *Théorie et pratique*. Cogitatio Fidei, 157. Paris: Cerf, 1990. (I quoted the French version, but an English translation exists: *Theology and Praxis: epistemological foundations*. Maryknoll: Orbis, 1987.)

Browning, Don (1990) Methods and Foundations for Pastoral Studies in the University. In A. Visscher (ed.) *Pastoral Studies in the University Setting*. Ottawa: University of Ottawa Press.

Daval, Roger (1972) Praxéologie. In *Encyclopaedia Universalis: corpus*. 8, 873 - 874.

Donzé, Marc (1989) La théologie pratique entre corrélation et prophétie. In S. Amler et al., *Pratique et théologie*. Genève: Labor et Fides, 183 - 90.

Donzé, Marc (1995) Objectifs et tâches de la théologie pratique. *Revue des sciences religieuses*. 69/3, 292 - 302.

Godbout, Jacques T. and CAILLÉ, Alain (coll.) (1998) *The World of the Gift*. Montreal: McGill-Queen's University Press.

Greinacher, Norbert (1974) Das Theorie-Praxis-Verhältnis in der Praktischen Theologie. In F. Klostermann (ed.) *Praktische Theologie heute*. München: Kaiser, 103 - 118.

Greinacher, Norbert (1990) La théologie pratique en tant que théorie critique de la praxis ecclésiale dans la société. In A. Visscher (ed.) *Pastoral Studies in the University Setting*. Ottawa: University of Ottawa Press.

Marlé, René (1979) *Le projet de théologie pratique*. Le point théologique, 32. Paris: Beauchesne.

Metz, Johannes Baptist (1980) *Faith in History and Society: toward a practical fundamental theology*. New York: Seabury Press.

Nadeau, Jean-Guy (1993) La praxéologie pastorale: faire théologie selon un paradigme praxéologique. *Théologiques* 1/1, 79 - 100.

Viau, Marcel (2000) Postface. In A. Binz, R. Moldo and A. L. Roy (ed.), *Former des adultes en Église*, St-Maurice (Suisse): Éd. Saint-Augustin, 317 - 327.

Zulehner, Paul M. (1996) Théologie pratique. In P. Eicher (ed.), *Nouveau dictionnaire de théologie*. Paris: Cerf, 1018 - 23.

Speaking *of* God and speaking *from* God

Inquiry into a virtuous circle

Etienne Grieu

God: not suitable for the public domain?

My first point is an assessment of the difficulty of speaking about God in a highly secularised society such as France, especially in the public arena. In my country, it is practically impossible to pronounce the word 'God' in the public sphere, except, of course, in the specific context of a debate about religions, or in a documentary about spirituality or religious movements. This kind of interest could be compared to an ethnographic study in which the discourse about God is observed from outside. But if someone, in the public arena, mentions God as an important reference or support, it casts a chill: people think 'he is a crank' or 'he is trying to claim authority by referring to a transcendence'; in short, *God is not suitable for the public domain: the word sounds either violent or strange.*

The question, then, is: why is this so in my country? As an answer, I think there are two hypotheses:

– the first would say that the very idea of God sounds offensive: in a democratic country and in a pluralistic culture, this concept of God tries to reduce diversity into a unity which is, moreover, protected against all criticism by its transcendence. To refer to this Being signifies an attack on pluralism and otherness. This Being, God, when introduced into the public arena, hampers the nature of the public domain [1].

– the second hypothesis would say that it is less the idea of God that is suspect, than the attitude of the Church (I speak here in the singular because I refer

---

[1] This radical incompatibility between the public and religious domains can be understood if we follow Habermas when he defines the public arena as being mostly a forum for debate. For, when we introduce a religious argument into the debate, it can't be considered rationally, because by definition, it is an indisputable statement. See J. Habermas, *Le discours philosophique de la modernité, (Der philosophische Diskurs der Moderne, zwölf Vorlesungen*, 1985), translation R. Rochlitz, Gallimard, Paris 1988, chapter XII.

essentially to the Catholic Church). The Church is still seen as an institution that is both authoritarian and not courageous. Speaking of God, in our catholic culture, will always bring immediately to mind this institution and its image which is a very bad model for democracy. Here, we share the point of view of Johann Baptist Metz, when he says that the crisis of Christianity is not the crisis of the faith, but the crisis of the institutions that are in charge of the faith, whose shape and style are not coherent with their messages (Metz, 1979). He would say that the idea of God is impossible to accept – and difficult even to hear – because of the churches who are the bearers of this idea.

Maybe these two factors fuel one another with the result that *the word 'God' is spontaneously understood as the keystone in a structure of hierarchical subordination.* That is why, I think, the culture of my country is reluctant to accept this idea, especially when it is introduced in the public sphere.

Then what? How might this situation change? In the field of theology two possibilities have been explored. Firstly, to consider understanding the God of Jesus Christ, by opposing him to the God of theism (here, we could think about anti-theistic theologies of the Cross; the most significant contributions in this field being *The Crucified God*, by J. Moltmann; *God as mystery of the world*, by E. Jüngel, and in France, *L'homme qui venait de Dieu*, by J. Moingt). These works are necessary, but I guess it will take a very long time before this new vision of God is widely accepted. The other attempt focuses on the churches, asking them to change, to become communities which give reality to the way opened up by Christ. But, of course, institutions, like churches, are not as easy to change as theories!

Of course, we must not abandon these two approaches: we must continue to ask ourselves who is the God we praise, and involve ourselves in the life of our Church. But I think that a third possibility could be explored by theologians, by listening to how faith can give life, freedom and creativity, how God gives believers – and communities the ability to speak and to act. Then it would be a question of what we could call 'speaking *from* God', if we recognise that God – precisely the Holy Spirit – can shape faith attitudes, is able to open the mouth of those who are mute and to free prisoners. My thesis is that '*speaking of God' has no chance of being heard if the listener cannot correlate it with such a 'speaking from God'*, in other words, with accounts which recognise God's ability to call speechless beings to become subjects. [2]

---

[2] I understand by "becoming subject" the process of being able to speak, to act and to relate in one's own style, that testify to my unique way of being engaged in the world. Of course, this is always in process, never achieved, except when I die. And it is always also a struggle (which is equally a spiritual struggle) to escape the powers that try to diminish this freedom that comes from God.

Then two questions arise:
- what exactly is 'speaking from God', how could we characterise and recognise it?
- how could speaking from God be correlated to speaking of God?

The first question is very large. Of course I cannot give here a complete and definitive answer. I will just give an example of the kind of work we can do to study this way of 'speaking from God' and try to analyse some of its features. For my doctoral thesis [3] I asked around thirty people to tell their faith stories. I chose to question people who recognise themselves as Christian believers and who were recognised as such by their communities. Furthermore, they were volunteers – in organisations, unions or political parties. I wanted to meet believers who were really engaged in the world. Firstly, I was surprised by the ease with which the majority of these people spoke, as if it were just what they were waiting for; secondly, when we studied – in a group – these stories, we noticed the singularity of each one in their structure and in the style that each story displayed; we noticed also a sort of joy in their speaking, expressed by the creativity of their language (the use of metaphors, for example). But did this language necessarily speak from God? Of course all creative speech isn't necessarily inspired by God; we can engage in great linguistic acrobatics to show how great we are! But, intuitively, I could feel that, at least some of these stories sounded like the Gospel and of what I knew of the God of Jesus Christ. Then I tried to analyse them to see how we could recognise in them some of the features of what we know of the divine life. To embark on such a reading of these narratives required also a discernment; I had to engage myself as a believer, of course [4].

I studied these stories through the phenomenon of 'subject-becoming': how do they speak of the emergence of a being able to speak, to act and to relate singularly ? I have identified three features that kept occurring in some of these stories:
- people insisted on recounting what they had received from others in their life; they revealed their lives as founded on gifts and promises which they enjoyed. And they often made a parallel between these gifts and promises, and what the Lord had done for them.
- one can recognise also in many of these stories, a specific way of speaking about the persons with whom they mix. They don't escape conflicts and

---

[3] Forthcoming under the title *'Nés de Dieu', Itinéraires de chrétiens engagés, essai de lecture théologique*, Le Cerf Paris September 2003.

[4] This is the point from where my research can be considered a theological work. It is a practical theology that is seen as a discernment: by organising a sort of echo between commentaries of such faith stories and biblical texts, I tried to elaborate a theological discourse to give an account of the faith experience and of the divine life in the context where I live.

struggles, but they fight with the confidence that conflict won't have the final word in their lives: they speak as if they know that a new communion will be possible again. This hope is often related – explicitly or implicitly – to God's promise.

– when these people speak about what they do, they present themselves as engaged – naturally, because I questioned people who are volunteers. But they are engaged not only for a specific activity or cause; they look forward also to another reality in the future: through their attitude they call for new voices, they wait actively for new subjects or relationships to "become" in the world; they know that they may not see the fruits of their efforts, but this fact doesn't discourage them: their engagement is, in a way, non-conditional.

Their efforts contribute to giving reality – at least in their stories, but maybe also in their way of being – to a specific way of considering life: not as action whose inspiration is myself; not as a struggle where I have to defend or to promote myself; not as a calculating game where I act only to receive a remuneration, but as a participation in what we could call a 'an economy of grace'; in other words, a way of receiving and of giving life, a way of welcoming it and a way of letting go of it. *This way of engaging oneself in the world is much broader than what we usually call religious experience. But I think that is has to do with faith experience*[5].

This economy looks like God's way of proceeding as revealed in Jesus Christ, and as expressed by the metaphor of divine filiation: Jesus revealed himself as a man who comes from God his father, who looks for a brother or sister in all human beings, and who engages himself totally for a future reconciled with God and between all people. The way of Jesus Christ is now opened up for his disciples, who can be called 'adoptive sons and daughters of God', in Christ. I think that some of the features of the faith stories I collected give examples of what it could mean 'to be a son or daughter of God'. These people born from God display in the world something that comes from God and speaks from God.

This does not mean, of course, that these people are any better than others. It means only that they read their stories in the light of the dynamics of Revelation (to put it briefly). Of course we could ask: what, then, is the difference if it lies only in the way one reads reality? But we know, because we have heard about hermeneutics, that the way we read reality is anything but neutral. In

---

5   After the reflexion of Paul Tillich (*Dynamics of Faith*, Harper and Row, New York 1957, French translation 1967) and Karl Rahner (*Traité fondamental de la foi*, 1973, French translation 1983) and the following debates, it is now generally accepted that faith experience is much broader than the explicitly religious one (see also Juan Luis Segundo, *Jesus de Nazareth, La historia perdida y recuperada*, chapters I-III or Marcel Viau, *Practical Theology : a new approach*, part III)

fact, it really contains the possibility of changing reality (Ricoeur, 1983; 1986; 1990; see also Delory-Momberger, 2000).

This 'speaking from God' is always provocative with regard the usual way of living, and always disturbs the peace of the civil society, because the rules of the society aren't gracious: they are obliged to calculate, to make contracts, to punish and to remunerate; the economy that speaks from God has another logic which is revolutionary.

This does not mean that the economy of grace should be opposed to what we could call an 'economy of calculation'. The economy of grace can never be found purely but is always mixed with other interests, calculations, struggles, needs, etc. That is why the reality is always ambiguous, and we need discernment. But despite and because of this ambiguity, the economy of grace can operate in the public space, and works within a culture and its rules [6]. This is only an example of an attempt to consider what this 'speaking from God' might mean.

Correlation between 'speaking from God' and 'speaking of God'

Then comes the second question: how such 'speaking from God' could be related to 'speaking of God'? I think that it is this point which is precisely the difficulty which prevents many of my contemporaries from hearing something about the Lord. These two sorts of discourses (speaking of God and speaking from God) are developed into symbolic fields that can no longer communicate. When someone sees a believer and appreciates their way of life, they don't make any connection with their faith and the divine life. They think only: 'this is a nice guy'. That is probably what happened in France with the worker priests: they were perfectly accepted as colleagues and friends, as men in whom we could trust, but their behaviour was rarely related to something that could speak of God (Pousset, 1980). Another example would be the pastoral tradition of "Action Catholique" in France. These movements didn't really succeed in elaborating a way of correlating a language of engagement in civil society with a faith language: the only articulation between these two contexts lies mostly in the realm of morality: 'I act so, because I am Christian' (or 'because of my values, that come from my Christian faith). The problem is in the 'because': the style of life is separated from its source by a logical link that

---

[6] For example, societies generally give a place to people who are not 'profitable' for them (children, ill people, elders, disabled people, etc.). However, while each law institutes the possibility of calculating or of evaluating something, they contain some factors that are not subject to the pure logic of calculation.

can be no more inhabited by the believer; God is sent back to his position as keystone of an order, master of a law. [7]

One of the most important tasks of practical theology – at least in a country like France – is, I think, to contribute to filling this gap between two languages which seem to be mutually impenetrable. I don't want to elaborate a sort of programme; I would like only to underline a few points:

– Ultimately, the correlation between 'speaking of God' and 'speaking from God' occurs in the head – and the heart – of Christians. It would be dangerous and illusory to try to control from beginning to end this phenomenon. We could speak about this correlation as *a game* that will last as long as the believer lives and believes. So, nobody can do it in the place of the Christian, and nobody can oblige someone to enter into this relation; but we can help in this task.

– The correlation between 'speaking of God' and 'speaking from God' needs *a mediation*. In the Gospels we can also see this: Jesus speaks sometimes of God (with the metaphor of the father, his father), but not so much; He does act in a way totally new, that indicates another way of seeing life and the world: this is 'speaking from God'; but he speaks also about the Kingdom of God. I think that this is the mediation he chose to relate the 'speaking of God' to the 'speaking from God'. *This mediation offers the listeners the possibility of recognising the work of the God they know, in their ordinary lives and in their experience of community.* We could call it *'expression of the experience of faith'*, or more precisely, *'symbols of faith experience'*. [8] What could help us today in such an approach? The 'speaking of God' represents now a huge treasure that only specialists can visit; the 'speaking from God' does still create miracles among Christians, but they hardly know how to share this – except the few who take part in groups of spirituality.

– As theologians, we can help the churches and Christians to find new ways of expressing how God lives in them. This aim will be achieved with difficulty if we don't allow people to tell their life and their faith experiences, it means helping people to express this 'speaking from God' that they experience. In the catholic culture, the community is not so much a space to speak: it is first of all a place to listen. But the pernicious effect is that our language

---

[7]   The language of morality creates, by definition, a distance between words and actions. Of course, I don't mean by this that we should banish ethics or moral reflection from all faith language. But if morality is the only way of making a bridge between faith and acts, then there will be no possibility of opening the door of the faith experience of those we meet. To allow this door to be opened, we need expressions that are not so distant from the experience, like narratives, poetry, gestures, proclamations, prayers, etc. Cf. Ladrière, 1984.

[8]   Symbols express significations that cannot be related by a conceptual language without losing the performative strength they contain. See Ladrière, 1984.

for expressing faith experiences is now very poor. In addition, the relationship between 'speaking of God' and 'speaking from God' must not remain
simply at the level of discourse: it is also a symbolical language that we can
find in poetry, art, liturgy. If not, the dynamics of creativity that shape this
'speaking from God' will disappear (Viau, 2002).

– Of course, the elaboration of expressions of faith experience won't be achieved in one moment. It is a discernment that is never finished. We could compare it to a Brownian movement that mobilises all Christians and the different dimensions of the life of the Christian community (*koinonia, diakonia,
  martyria*, and also *leiturgia*). This expression of faith experience has always
  to be adjusted to the new aspects of the 'speaking from God' that appear, and
  to the changes in language. Expression of this faith experience will 'speak'
  if it gives rise to a rich echo between the discourse and the experience.

– This work of finding a discourse of Christian experience leads the theologian
  to remain in the position of assistant. The theologian, then, is no more the
  master of the discourse, but only a facilitator. He helps the believers and the
  community to become conscious of the grace they enjoy, and to find ways
  of expressing what they are experiencing.

– This theological task doesn't replace the more classical tasks of theology
  which I mentioned earlier, namely, that of elaborating ever new ways of
  speaking of God, and of examining critically the direction of the churches.
  But maybe these tasks would gain greatly if they were nourished by this
  form of practical theology that I have tried to present here.

We could represent this process in triangular form with three elements
which should be distinguished, but which are inseparable: faith experience,
symbolic expressions of faith (i.e.: a symbolical way of expressing faith experience and of sharing it) and theology (i.e.: a conceptual way of accounting for,
and debating the faith and the contents of the faith).

These three elements inter-relate with one another; it means that, in the same movement, they both feed and criticise each other. The theological pole is
shaped by the heritage of theological thought from the past, by the contemporary research of new formulas from theologians, and also by 'ordinary theology'
(Astley, 2003) that is diffused in the popular culture: it is a complex relationship. Symbolic expressions of faith belong both to "speaking from God" (without which the faith experience could not at all be expressed or even emerge
in the consciousness of the person) and to "speaking of God" (for the symbolic
expressions create a certain distance from the immediate experience.).

If we agree with this representation, the split between 'speaking of God'
and 'speaking from God', which is especially deep in my culture, will only be
reduced through a multi-lateral approach which mainly involves the construc-

tion of new symbolic ways of expressing the faith experience, and as a result of this work, new ways of working out theological discourses with regard to the faith. It is only in this way that we might hope once again to speak of God in the public arena in my country.

References

Christine Delory-Momberger (2000) *Les histoires de vie, De l'invention de soi au projet de formation*. Anthropos, Paris.

E. Jüngel (1983) *Dieu mystère du monde*. (French translation, Le Cerf Paris 1983).

Johann Baptist Metz (1977) *La foi dans l'histoire et dans la société, Essai de théologie fondamentale pratique*. (Mainz, French translation Le Cerf, Paris 1979).

J. Moltmann (1972) *Le Dieu crucifié*. (München, French translation Le Cerf Paris 1974).

J. Moingt (1993) *L'homme qui venait de Dieu*. Le Cerf, Paris.

Paul Ricoeur (1985) *Temps et Récits*. Le Seuil, Paris.

————— (1990) *Soi même comme un autre*. Le Seuil, Paris.

————— (1986) *Du texte à l'action* Le Seuil, Paris.

Edouard Pousset (1980) *Aujourd'hui l'Eglise*. Texte polycopié, Association Roche Colombe, Paris.

Marcel Viau (2002) *L'univers esthétique de la théologie*. Mediaspaul, coll. "Brèches théologiques", Montréal.

Tradition and Spirit

Remarks on the relationship between the early witness of faith and the modern world as problem of practical theology

Klaus A. Wegenast

Preliminary remarks

Since the time of Friedrich Schleiermacher, the task of practical theology (as the theorisation of the practice of the Gospel in society) is to think about and to clarify the relationship between the theology which embodies the received tradition of Christianity and the actual practice of faith in the context of a given life situation. From a scientific-theoretical perspective, therefore, practical theology defines itself as mediator between attempts to approach and engage with tradition and the effects of the historical and systematic endeavours of theology, and the actual practice of faith under the conditions of a particular culture: its language, cultural imagination, concrete societal structures, specific milieus and their questions, hopes and fears. As far as religious education is concerned, this entails not only intensive attention to societal and common anthropological conditions, but also developmental-psychological aspects of human experience (Wegenast, 1997, 706 - 714).

It is evident, if you look at the description of the tasks of practical theology, that the model cherished still today by many – a one-way street between exegesis and systematics on the one hand and the lowlands of practice on the other – is no longer useful. It has to give way to a model of theology which moves *between* questioning and answering, and practises a close cooperation with original scientific attempts foreign to theology. As far as the practice of the Gospel in society and its practical theology are concerned, there is now no longer a dispute about the fact that today's responsibility to the faith as tradition of the Gospel is not fulfilled by passing on contents that have always been fixed.

Rather, tradition is an interactive process, in which the existence of the basic sources stands open to question just like the individual interpreter, be he/she a historian, systematician, practitioner or one who listens, for example to a sermon. Furthermore, tradition as transmission of something understood is not simply the responsibility of one individual, but always an action within a group, that shows a relationship between partners only seen as meaningful when the message answers to certain questions and needs (Wegenast, 2002, 224 - 232). Again and again in the process of transmission of the faith, do we have a dialectic of tradition and reception. The people living in a given life situation, for example, the preachers and the listeners, are not something like an empty river bed, but the result of certain past and present with specific questions, fears and hopes. These people are touched by that which was done once and for all times through Jesus Christ and by its promise, but they interpret tradition and understand it for themselves. Without these questioning people, the original proclamation of the faith would only be a document of, possibly, historical interest. If, however, it is true that interpretation of Holy Scripture is not intended merely to draw us back to the horizon of the past, but to challenge its readers and interpreters to find an answer to the question of how God's future correlates with the present of our world, then the objective of today's public responsibility for Christian faith in society can only be to address the people who ask questions of meaning, to help them grasp the faith message in a reflexive way – or even to critically reject it – in any case: to be subjects of their own life histories. In short, an objectively given truth does not exist, but only the momentary truth experienced each time anew on the basis of a given tradition in the action of interpretation *ubi et quando visum est deo.*

Only when present reality, now directed through word and deed, is interpreted and newly understood in the light of the Gospel, does tradition come alive: people are challenged, obligation is present, faith occurs. The obligation and authority of tradition are elements of a communication event, by which new understandings take the place of the old. Tradition and life situation interpret one another, in that they interlace with one another in a process of discussion with reality. Therefore, next to the task of a critical-constructive acknowledgement of the many ways of interpretation of scripture, it is also important for all disciplines of practical theology carefully to analyse all aspects of the present human context, its language and symbols. This means that every transmitter of tradition, be s/he preacher, teacher or pastoral counsellor, must see the necessity of thorough engagement with the human and social sciences, with the goal of using them critically and with a willingness to learn their contribution towards enhancing the theological competence of pastoral practitioners in the manifold fields of church and society.

Gospel and culture

Gerhard Besier, a historian of Church history at the University of Heidelberg, laments that many theologians do without all normative claims and understand themselves as social science-oriented scientists of culture, or historically scientists of the arts. Here, to speak of faith and revelation in Jesus Christ is seen as being unscientific. Against this spirit of their theological teachers, students of theology often lose their orientation and would extract from the fragments of the Bible and tradition only what they could still accept as 'constructive theology' (Besier, 2002, 28).

Unfortunately, the reader is not being informed what Besier really understands when he uses terms like 'faith' and 'revelation'. Nevertheless, a problem comes into view which needs to be considered, namely the problem of the relationship between the theory and practice of the Gospel to the given culture as life situation and system of communication (Rodi, Graf and Tanner, 1990; Schwoebel, 1996; Biehl and Wegenast 2000). It is evident that the definitions of dialectical theology, in which culture and faith were seen as exclusive alternatives to one another, can no longer be seen as being of help (Graeb, 2002). This holds true in a similar manner for the relationship between the Christian proclamation to the fast-changing life situations. A relationship that does full justice to faith and culture is to be preferred to, and sought beyond, a simple adaptation of faith to the surrounding life situation as well as to the antipathy between of faith and culture, already identified. In this search it can be helpful to remember that the original document of the faith, the Holy Scriptures, did not 'fall from heaven', but is a collection of literature dependent on culture, in other words, the result of a successful inculturation of the faith of Israel and of the early Christian congregation in the context of the old orient, Judaism and the so called late Hellenism of the first century after Christ (Biehl and Wegenast, 2000, 55 - 68). Only in this way did faith have the power to direct its message, to win people of different life situations, to have a future and to become the source not only for a 'ever new' proclamation of the church, but also for plural cultures which did not understand themselves as being Christian (Schmidinger, 1999; Wegenast, 1999; Brinkmann, 1999; Schwarze, 1997; Fermor, 1999). A short look into literature, and also into contemporary popular culture, shows this clearly.

Of interest in this context is a contribution by Christoph Bizer, who describes the relationship of religion and culture with reference to Jeremiah 29 in a phenomenological way and would like to understand religion as an action of 'cultivation' (Bizer, 2000, 141 - 164). According to him, this can be seen especially in the orientation of the Church's service to the needs of its cultural surroundings, but also in its adoption of certain cultural forms, in its special

use of the language and not least in the situational nature of the interpretation of Scripture. In short, evidently the Christian faith without cultural form,
without style, is not viable; but it develops, however, at the same time a consciousness of its need to resist mere assimilation to a given 'ideology of the
present'. A new inculturation is not a betrayal of the faith, but the prerequisite
for its possibility to ever anew become practical in the context of socio-cultural
and ideal-historical situations and changes.

How does St. Paul write to the congregation of Corinth? He would like
to be 'a Jew to the Jews' and to those, 'who are outside the law, to become
one outside the law' (1 Corinthians 9:20); for he has become all things to all
people, so that he can save them all in the name of the Gospel. For him it is not
a program without character or a cringing servility without direction, but the
basis for his mission: to understand the other – its questions and convictions –
as a partner to be taken seriously; to take the culture of his audience seriously
in view of the proclamation of salvation.

Religious Education as an example of practical-theological theory and responsible practice of faith and its tradition in the context of the public domain

I would like to use the rest of this paper to make some remarks from my subject
area, religious education, to the problem of the responsibility of the Gospel in
the context of religious education and teaching. This is not the place to sketch
the still ongoing strong tendencies of differentiation in public life (Steck, 2002,
168 - 185), but a chance to point to the fact that the public sphere is highly
segregated and compartmentalised in terms of language and behaviour patterns, sets of regulations and rationalities. Politics, economics and religion, to
mention only a few important sub-systems of our societies, demand *rebus sic
stantibus* societal autonomy. As far as the impact of religion on public life
is concerned, things are even more complex, because organized Christianity
and the institutional churches are no longer so dominant, as was the case for
centuries. Furthermore, as far as organized Christianity is concerned, we must
differentiate between a private, public and church Christianity.

For practical theology this means examining these different appearances of
the Christian religion each for its own sake, but also in view of that which they
have in common. In doing so, one needs to assume that individualized Christianity does certainly carry syncretistic aspects, which make it hardly possible
to gain important empirical data. However, a limitation of practical theology
to formal church practice would mean to lose from sight the complexity of real lived experience in many aspects of the Christian religion. It is likely that

the Christian religion under the conditions of modern societies presents something like an ensemble of different contoured religious life forms, which are manifold and interwoven with one another and with given cultural forms in the realm of one society. This ensemble is, for example, in Swiss society an ever present power everywhere, even though at the same time one has to notice that 'constitutional' religion – the official profile of churches within the modern nation-state – finds itself unable to penetrate society from a religious centre and thus to structure the everyday life of the masses. Is this not a signal, especially for practical theology, to explain the religious heritage anew, in order to open a possibility for a 'symbolic reassurance' of human life, articulated in Christian language, in faith? The alternative to this under the conditions of modernity is a self-chosen ghetto of an introverted religious culture for churchly socialized people opposed to the 'world' with its more or less autonomous subsystems.

With this we arrive at religious education, whose objective since the beginning of the 20th century has been to transmit to each new generation the Christian tradition in the context of the public school system. An important attempt in this direction was in the 1960s the so-called hermeneutical Religious Education, whose objective was to define religious education and teaching no longer only from the church or theology, but rather also in relationship with the actual educational reality of the public school system and in recognition of pupils' own questioning about the nature of existence, meaning and reality.

Here, instead of working in a normative-deductive way from tradition to experience, the demands were seen to emerge, almost in a reverse gear, from certain phenomena of the present and then to explore the sources of the Christian tradition. The criterion for successful instruction was the best possible gain for the social, personal and intellectual welfare of the students. Problematic still, however, was the fragmentary recognition of the role of the social sciences, of educational and psychological research into the life situation, the ability to understand and illuminate the questions posed by young people. At this point the so-called problem-oriented religious didactic brought improvement, because more than ever before it accepted the task to reflect the tradition in view of the personal, interpersonal and also social 'problems' of the students in their surrounding society and culture, and attempted to assist them in their search for identity. Still, with reference to this new way of religious-educational theory and practice, one needs to say that it remained a largely cognitive understanding and interpretation of tradition, overlooking in many ways, for example, the role of affective or subjective 'experience' in the productive search of individuals and groups (Meyer-Drawe, 2001).

At this stage the attempts at new methods, such as the biblio-dramatic-

movement or the discussion of religious language in popular music, were more innovative, as far as the intention was to bring about an entirely new and
fundamental interaction between culture and tradition. In the 1980's then came the so-called symbol-didactic, a development of both hermeneutical and
also problem-oriented Religious Education. If we look closely, we can see that
also this attempt was based on societal conditions, for example, the loss of
self-understanding of Christianity and its meaning for life in society, but also the discovery of distinctive symbolic systems amongst children and young
people. Thus it attempted, for example, under the given conditions of a secular
society, to relate religious aspects and important experiences of life with one
another, acknowledging that symbols may need to emerge which express the
relationship between life practice and religious aspects in new ways.

The results of these attempts can best be seen in the methodical structure
of the symbol-didactic work, in which the basic insights of the interaction between the symbolizing self of the student, the symbol of tradition which was
to be interpreted, and the reality symbolized, received attention throughout. At
the beginning there stands the symbol, for example, a wooden cross. Through
the focussing effect of the symbol, experiences of present life, certain basic
experiences and also certain historical events may be reflected. The insights
gained through such learning processes are then 'lifted up' in a still further
process by means of a creative task or symbolic action and thereby rendered
valid.

In all of the three mentioned models of Christian religious education we
have to do with tradition and its interpretation in the context of society, for
which religion only functions as a sub-system. There is also the task of enab-
ling a self-responsible faith to develop, as opposed to a simple execution of
churchly-given models of interpretation. The problem of all models is evident:
how can the different didactic models of explanation of tradition in the context
of our society transmit the origins, for example, of Holy Scripture, to children
and youngsters, to whom we owe assistance on their way through life, as a signal for encouragement and confidence and a model of humane practice? What
contribution can our attempts in Religious Education give, especially in terms
of an awareness of tradition amidst a culture fixated on immediacy, experience
and novelty, to which the individual is often exposed without defence? Initial
answers to these questions hint at one strong point of our tradition, which is
that it does not just connect practical ethos with normative teaching. In a message of justification it relates the individual's hopes and aspirations, including
the hope for a successful life, with the commitment for the dignity of the other
(Junker-Kenny, 2002).

Because of this, I hold tradition as it is given us for explanation, for example in the Old and New Testaments of the Bible, not as something which is to be overcome as soon as possible in the interest of a free self-articulation of the subject. I know, however, as well that tradition is not necessarily first encountered in cognitive mediated learning processes, but shows its strength best in certain other milieus, such as the parental home, in groups and in corporate worship and generally in the life of the congregation as a fellowship of remembrance and narrative. It was Hans Martin Gutmann who opened in a remarkable way a bridge between church, school and popular culture to teach religion, a bridge between the church as fellowship of remembrance and narrative, and popular culture and its symbols (Gutmann, 2000, 11 - 19, 28, 176 - 179, 191 - 200, 227 - 230). He did this in that he tried to show to what extent religious symbols are present in popular culture. He concluded from this that it is evidently impossible to deal with central experiences and conflicts of life – love, hate, longing death, loneliness, freedom and liberation – without using the symbols of the religious tradition. From this fact Gutmann concludes, also with regard to the ability of the life and function of culture, that it is necessary to cherish and form religious tradition in the realm of the church, for example, in the narration of the biblical tradition in service and in the social and political engagement of the congregation. As far as religious education is concerned, he defines its task and objective as:

realising the factual power of symbols and rituals and to work with pupils in building up helpful inner pictures, especially the mighty narrative of God's bond of friendship with people and their fears and uncertainties, with the search for life perspectives and the hopes, also with the production of symbols of children and youth, to bring them in such a way into contact with one another, that the symbols of the Jewish-Christian tradition can become helpful inner pictures. (Gutmann, 2000, 17).

We could say much more about this model of Religious Education, but these remarks should have shown that Religious Education should not just signal loyalty to tradition, but make possible also a new interpretation and a new inculturation in critical dialogue, for example, with popular culture in its manifold form and its fascination. Only then we could again speak of a living tradition and thus of an effective cooperation between tradition and spirit, as all 'productive' phases of church history were characterized. We began with an excursion to the essence of tradition in its relationship to its interpretation in the context of continuing history, dealt then in a fragmentary way with the relationship of the Gospel and culture, in order then to sketch the relationship of tradition and interpretation in the area of religious education on the background of post-modern relationships, to show how only change can guarantee the identity of tradition.

References

Besier, Gerhard (2002) Die Amtskirchen verwässern das Christentum. *Die Welt* December 13, 28.

Biehl, Peter and Wegenast, Klaus A. (eds) (2000) *Religionspädagogik und Kultur*. Neukirchen-Vluyn: Neukirchener Verlag.

Bizer, Christoph (2000) Gottesdienst und Kultur. in P.Biehl and K.A.Wegenast (eds), *Religionspädagogik und Kultur*. Neukirchen-Vluyn: Neukirchener Verlag, 141-164.

Brinkmann, Frank T. (1999) *Comics und Religion*. (Praktische Theologie heute 46), Stuttgart: W. Kohlhammer.

Fermor, Gotthard (1999) *Ekstasis*. (Praktische Theologie heute 46), Stuttgart: W. Kohlhammer.

Graeb, Wilhelm (2002) Praktische Theologie als Praxistheorie protestantischer Kultur. in W. Graeb and B. Weyel (eds), *Praktische Theologie und protestantische Kultur*. Gütersloh: C. Kaiser Gütersloher Verlagshaus, 35-51.

Gutmann, Hans M. (2000) *Der Herr der Heerscharen, die Prinzessin der Herzen und der König der Löwen. Religion lehren zwischen Kirche, Schule und populärer Kultur*. Gütersloh: C. Kaiser Gütersloher Verlagshaus.

Junker-Kenny, Maureen (2002) Religion und Öffentlichkeit am Beispiel der Schule. in W. Graeb and B. Weyel (eds), *Praktische Theologie und protestantische Kultur*. Gütersloh: C. Kaiser Gütersloher Verlagshaus.

Meyer-Drawe, Käte (2001) *Leiblichkeit und Sozialität*. Wilhelm Fink München.

Rodi, Frithjof, Graf, Friedrich W. and Tanner, Klaus (1990), Art. Kultur I/II. in *Theologische Realenzyklopädie* vol 20, Berlin and New York: Walter de Gruyter, 176-204.

Schmidinger, Heinrich (ed) (1999) *Die Bibel in der deutschsprachigen Literatur im 20. Jahrhundert*. 2 vols., Mainz: Matthias Grünewald Verlag.

Schwarze, Bernd (1997) *Die Religion der Rock- und Popmusik*. (Praktische Theologie heute 28), Stuttgart: W. Kohlhammer.

Schwoebel, Christoph (1996) Glaube und Kultur. *Neue Zeitschrift für systematische Theologie 38*, 137-154.

Steck, Wolfgang (2002) Praktische Theologie als Topographie des zeitgenössischen Christentums. *Pastoraltheologie 91*, 168-185.

Wegenast, Klaus A. (1997) Art. Religionspädagogik. *Theologische Realenzyklopädie* 28, Berlin and New York: Walter de Gruyter, 699-730.

Wegenast, Klaus A. (2000) Kultur und Bibel – Bibel und Kultur. in P. Biehl and K. A. Wegenast (eds), *Religionspädagogik und Kultur*. Neukirchen-Vluyn: Neukirchener Verlag, 55-68.

Wegenast, Klaus A. (2002) Art. Tradition VII. Praktisch-theologisch. *Theologische Realenzyklopädie* 33, Berlin and New York: 224-232.

Wegenast, Philipp (1999) Die neunte Kunst und die Bibel. in G. Adam and Rainer Lachmann (eds), *Kinder- und Schulbibeln: Probleme ihrer Erforschung*. Göttingen: Vandenhoeck und Ruprecht, 135-157.

A pragmatic practical theology as public theology

Chris A.M. Hermans

Introduction

Practical theology has broadened the coordinates in which it operates: from the actions of the pastor within religious institutions, to Church (or religious institutions) and society, and to (Christian) religion within society. There is a general consensus among practical theologians about such an enlargement of the scope of practical theology (Schweitzer & Van der Ven, 1999). The consequence of this development is that practical theology has inherently become a public theology that is not only involved with a theological legitimation *ad intra*, but also *ad extra*. In this external legitimation of academic theology, there is a dilemma. On the one hand one needs to be truthful to the normative claims of a religious community and tradition; but on the other hand one needs to be involved in an open dialogue with persons who do not share the metaphysical ground of this claim. How can one sail between Scylla of being publicly irrelevant but strongly distinct and Charybdis of being relevant but to relinquish its distinct truth claim?

In this chapter I will follow the suggestion of Victor Anderson (1998) that pragmatism can offer a ground for theology to enter the public arena. On the one hand, academic theology has no meaning for the public debate on moral issues with regard to our society unless it is truthful to the religious community and the tradition to which it is affiliated (Anderson 1998, 6). But on the other hand, academic theology cannot be a source feeding public debate if it remains a function of church dogmatics and professional ministerial education. I will turn to one of the classic authors of American pragmatism, Charles Sanders Peirce, to find a way out of this dilemma. First, I turn to the question of inquiry in practical theology. According to Peirce, all thought starts with the irritation of doubt, or a surprising fact. This irritation ceases when belief is attained. Peirce distinguishes four different methods of belief fixation: the method of tenacity: the method of authority; the a priori method and the method of scientific inquiry (Peirce, [1877](1992). I will argue in the second part

of this paper that only through the latter method can practical theology be relevant to public debate. Following from this assertion, I will turn to the object
of scientific inquiry in practical theology. In the third section of this paper, I
argue that practical theology is the scientific inquiry into the integrity of the
beliefs of people engaged in religious practices. Through this inquiry practical theology contributes to the public debate about the relevance of a religious
tradition or community to moral issues of human fulfilment.

Four methods of inquiry in practical theology

Pragmatism can offer a way for practical theology to enter the public arena.
It can make the cognitive claims of practical theology communicable and intelligible in relation to other disciplines within the academy. But what method
of inquiry should practical theology use in order to meet this claim of com-
municability and intelligibility? I will reflect on this with the help of a critical
appropriation of Charles S. Peirce's differentiated methods of inquiry.

What is inquiry? For Peirce, 'the irritation of doubt causes a struggle to
attain a state of belief' (Peirce, [1877]1992, 114). Without doubt there is no
struggle, and with the cessation of doubt this struggle ends. Peirce puts great
stress on the difference between belief and doubt. They both have positive
effects on us, though different ones. 'Belief does not make us act at once, but
puts us in a certain condition that we shall behave in a certain way, when the
occasion arises' (Peirce, [1877]1992, 114). A belief is a rule of action, or, as
Peirce would prefer to say, the nature of a belief is 'habit of the mind'. Doubt
does not have this effect but stimulates us to inquiry until it is destroyed. Apart
from this practical difference, there is also an affective difference.

Doubt is an uneasy and dissatisfied state from which we struggle to free ourselves and
pass into a state of belief; while the latter is a calm and satisfactory state which we
do not wish to avoid, or to change into a belief in something else (Peirce, [1877]1992,
115).

We cling tenaciously to what we believe. But a belief is not the same as an
opinion. A belief is a tested opinion, for example, the result of a process of
reasoning which produces true conclusions from true premises. The sole end
of inquiry is the settlement of opinion. For Peirce, this is the core presumption
in a pragmatic theory of inquiry. Before discussing four methods of inquiry,
Peirce rejects three erroneous conceptions of proof. The first is the view that
one can start an inquiry with a question instead of a doubt. 'The mere putting
of a proposition into the interrogative form does not stimulate the mind to only
struggle after belief. There must be a real and living doubt, and without this all
discussion is idle' (Peirce, [1877]1992, 115). In order to have an inquiry, one

really must take interest in what one is doubting. The second conception is that reasoning should only take place from absolute indubitable propositions. This claim is too strong: it suffices if propositions are free from actual doubt. The third conception is that there is a point beyond which a doubt is settled. But doubting beyond the point after all the world is fully convinced of, is without purpose. There is no proof beyond proof.

Peirce differentiates between four methods aimed at the settlement of opinion. The first method of fixing belief is called the *method of tenacity*. It consists of 'taking any answer to a question which we may fancy, and constantly reiterating it to ourselves, dwelling on all which may conduce to that belief, and learning to turn with contempt and hatred from anything which might disturb it' (Peirce, [1877]1992, 115). This method of settling an opinion systematically keeps out of view anything that might change this opinion. By simply not reflecting on alternative ideas, one tries to keep a form of 'calm belief'. How would this work out for inquiry in practical theology? People who prefer this method of inquiry have an instinctive dislike of an undecided state of mind. Religious belief is a matter of certainty, and to question belief is seen as a lack of strength. Reason is made problematic by viewing it as weak and illusive. In this way, this method is made insusceptible to doubt. Practical theology which follows this method, is a form of confessional theology. It is poorly fitted for public debate, because it does not allow other views to challenge its own opinion. It is a form of thinking 'in which the conception of truth as something public is not yet developed' (Peirce, [1877]1992, 120). It only confesses what it believes. It will only convince the followers of a religion or religious movement (*ad intra*) but nobody outside their confession (*ad extra*). Peirce stresses the attraction of this method of tenacity. 'Men who pursue it are distinguished for their decision of character' (Peirce, [1877]1992, 122). There is only one problem which this method faces, and that is the fact that in the social world we live in, we are confronted with people who have different opinions. It will only be a matter of time before this person suggests to him-/herself that their opinions may be quite as good as their own belief and this will shake one's belief. The method of tenacity only works in a social world in which no alternatives arrive on the horizon.

The second method of fixing belief is the *method of authority*. When inquiry is directed to this method, the aim is 'to keep correct doctrines before attention of the people, to reiterate them perpetually, and to teach them to the young' (Peirce, [1877]1992, 117). The method of authority only functions with the help of coercion. A necessary condition for this method to work is the existence of an institution which has the power to prevent contrary doctrines from being taught, advocated or expressed. Within most of the Christian churches

and movements, one will find an institutional body which has the task of upholding the correct theological and political doctrine. Practical theology which
follows this method, is a form of church discipline. The fixation of belief rests
on the authority of Scripture, a doctrine of church, or a combination of both.
Many questions may be raised in practical theological reflection on personal or
societal issues, but there will never be doubt. Questions are rhetorical, that is,
the correct answers are already known. The method of authority is very strong
in upholding the religious community. Practical theologians can adopt this method for different reasons. The first is a negative reason: because they are afraid
of the potential professional consequences involved in challenging a 'correct'
theological doctrine. But there can also be a positive reason, namely born of
a sense of responsibility for the religious community to which they belong.
There is a natural social feeling behind this responsibility, as Peirce stresses. A
practical theologian who belongs to a specific religious community, will feel
responsible for the unity of the community. With regard to public debate, this
method of authority is ill fitted. In the dilemma outlined by Anderson, it remains within the confines of church dogmatics, which are not translated into
language that open up communication and critical debate. This makes it irrelevant for public debate concerning personal and societal issues. According to
Peirce, this position is opened up as soon as people begin to think that there
is no reason to rate their own beliefs higher than those of other people. Peirce
calls this 'a wider social feeling' in comparison to the 'parochial' social feeling
mentioned above. This feeling will give rise to doubts, and as soon as doubt
arises, a person wants to break with this method of authority.

The third method of fixing belief is the *a priori method*. This method of
settling opinions does 'not only produce an impulse to believe, but shall also decide what proposition it is which is to be believed' (Peirce, [1877]1992,
118). Beliefs are accepted on the basis of what is 'agreeable to reason'. This
method is far more intellectual than the method of tenacity and authority, as it
is based on open discourse and free exchange of ideas. Now, what does 'agreeable to reason' imply? 'It does not mean that which agrees with experience, but
that which we find ourselves inclined to believe' (Peirce, [1877] 1992, 119).
According to Peirce this method resembles some conceptions of art in which
the artist starts from an intuition instead of the observed facts.

Take, for example, the doctrine that man only acts selfishly – that is, from the consideration that acting in one way will afford him more pleasure than acting in another.
This rests on no fact in the world, but it has had a wide acceptance as being the only
reasonable theory (idem).

The *a priori* method leads to transcendental thinking within theology in which
one reasons about the conditions in human nature for religious experience.

How can we think of religion as something reasonable within human nature? Within practical theology this method can be used in a public debate in order to make the contribution of religion(s) reasonable. After all, it is the aim of the a priori method to lead to universal reasons and to deliver our opinions from what is accidental and capricious. This method will work as long as people do not challenge the intuitions on which it is based. But, as Peirce underlines, this is exactly what has happened throughout history [1]. But more fundamentally, the a priori method can never close the gap with facts. As soon as a person understands, that a belief is determined extraneous to the facts, from that moment on this person will experience a real doubt. Is this belief true or false? As a consequence this belief ceases to be a belief (Peirce, [1877]1992, 120). The a priori method is a stronger method than the method of tenacity and authority, because it is based on a free exchange of ideas in order to make a belief intelligible. But is cannot solve the problem of doubt [2].

The fourth method of fixing belief is the *method of scientific inquiry*. This method also rests on a community, namely a community of inquiry. This community of inquiry is open to everyone. It is not a community of doctrine in the sense that is committed to any particular set of beliefs. The community of scientific inquiry is committed to the integrity of belief. It's aim is not preserving the worthiness of ideas by practicing a method of inquiry that can produce beliefs that coincide with the facts. Beliefs are tested against reality, that is the essence of scientific inquiry. The method of inquiry is superior to the methods mentioned before in the sense that it is self-corrective. If a rule of action (or habit of the mind) is not reflected in reality, this belief has to be rejected. The members of the community of scientific inquiry are committed to follow the rules of the inquiry. 'The test of whether I am truly following the method is not an immediate appeal to my feelings and purposes, but, on the contrary, itself involves the application of the method' (Peirce, [1877]1992, 121). This is the major difference compared with the other methods of fixing beliefs. They depend on something outside the method, namely the will to believe (see the method of tenacity); social feeling or the need to obey (see the method of authority) or intellectual intuition (see the a priori method). The method of scientific inquiry recognizes that truth is public and available to all who inquire properly. Practical theology which seeks to incorporate this method of

---

[1]   No one will now agree with Plato that 'the distances of the celestial spheres from one another should be proportional to the different lengths of strings which produce harmonious chords' (Peirce, 1992, 119).

[2]   Riposa points to the fact that the latter Peirce (after 1900) was more positive about intuitions (Riposa, 1989, 99). He is surely right about this, but even than Peirce would speak about critical testing of intuitions. He speaks of 'critical common sensism' in his article 'Issues of pragmaticism' (1905). Critical testing brings in the method of scientific inquiry.

inquiry, is according to pragmatic standards, more suited for the public debate than a practical theology which applies one of the methods mentioned before. Practical theology needs to bring in the moral ideas of the specific religious community and the tradition which it is committed to. Do the ideas and practices of this community contribute to human fulfilment, both on a personal and societal level? The integrity of belief which the method of scientific inquiry aims at, presupposes doubt. Only through doubt one can reach truth. In accordance with the pragmatic maxim, truth implies that 'if acted on it will carry us to the point we aim and not astray' (Peirce, [1877]1992, 123).

Religious practices as object of scientific inquiry

What is the object of scientific inquiry within practical theology? In the previous section I have settled on the method of scientific inquiry through which practical theology can contribute to public debate on moral issues about human fulfilment (both personal and societal). This solves one element of the problem raised by Anderson, namely that academic practical theology can only contribute to this public debate if it is not just a function of church dogmatics and professional ministerial education. On the one hand, according to Anderson, academic theology has no meaning for public debate on moral issues unless it is truthful to the religious community and the tradition to which it is affiliated. What do religions offer to moral issues which exist in society with regard to life and death, issues of the union between persons, the emancipation of women, questions of ethnic identity, environmental problems, and so forth? It is the aim of practical theology to show what religious traditions and religious communities contributes (actually) or can contribute (possibly) to these public issues. [3]

Practical theology is the scientific inquiry of the integrity of the beliefs of people within religious practices. Through this inquiry practical theology contributes to the public debate about the meaning of a religious tradition or community for moral issues of human fulfilment (or happiness). In this section I will define religious practices as a specific type of cultural institutions. Practices are social constructions based on a dual ontology, namely neurobiological processes imbedded in the human body, and a system of meaning imbedded in skills, habits, practices and other human activities. How are the two ontologies related? Harré (1998, 44) solves this problem by means of what he calls a tool/task distinction. Human activities are performed with the aid of tools.

---

[3]   I do not restrict scientific inquiry of practical theology only to the religion to which the researcher or the institution in which he works is affiliated to. I skip this debate because it is not essential for my line of argument of grounding practical theology on pragmaticism in order to make it fit for public debate on moral issues.

Social and institutional activities are inconceivable without such tools. For example, the baptism of a child as a religious practice is only conceivable in terms of all sorts of tools associated with it: certain objects (water, a font, oil, salt, special vestments), the set pattern of the baptismal ritual, certain actors (priest, parents, child, godfather, godmother), religious symbols and a religious system of meaning which, on the basis of a tradition, interprets this as a religious practice. The human body, too (especially the brain and central nervous system), may be regarded as a tool that is requisite for action. One can make a distinction between neurobiological and cultural bases of behaviour, but they should not be separated as the basis of human activities. Hence although there is a dual ontology, there is no dualism. A given task presupposes both tools in close interaction.

What are religious practices? (Hermans, 2003, chapter 3)

Religious practices consist of collective intentionalities
which are grounded on the authority of a tradition
grant a religious status-function
to certain matters (objects, persons, situations, time and spaces)
from the perspective transcendence and immanence
as influenced by religious regimes.

In principle, there is no limit to religious practices. All human practices could become religious if religious meaning is attributed to it. But then, on what ground do we call a human action a religious practice? [4]

1. A religious practice is a form of rule-governed or intentional action, with the rules creating an institutional fact. They constitute a particular practice, hence they are called constitutive rules (Searle, 1995). On the basis of a constitutive rule water *counts as* "baptismal water", a book *counts as* "a sacred book", a person *counts as* "a holy person" and an action *counts as* "a religious action". In the absence of such a rule there would still be water, a collection of stories and a person, but they would not have the same status that is ascribed to them in a religious practice. A religious status is ascribed in rule-governed or intentional human actions. A story only becomes a religious story if people reading that story ascribe a status function to it. Such ascription of meaning is crucial in a culture-oriented approach to religious practices.

---

[4]   For an elaborate account of religious practices, see Hermans, 2003. Here I give also a theological evaluation of this concept based on three theological criteria: tradition, marginality, and the relation between transcendence and immanence.

2. The rule-governed behaviour is shared by a group of people (a collective). A practice is always a social fact. Individuals participating in the same practice must share their rule-governed behaviour with other people. Collective intentionality has to be differentiated from individual intentionality. Collective intentionality is structured as *"we intend* to do Y". Even when a person prays a certain prayer in solitude, it could still be called a religious practice if the person realizes that he or she is sharing this activity with other people. Participation in a practice makes people part of a community. Without a community there can be no practice. According to culture-oriented institutional theory, however, a community cannot be defined without reference to practices. Thus we speak of a community of practice (Wenger, 1999). In practices individual persons act with a specific intentionality which is embodied in the practice – that is, as members of a community.

3. Tradition plays a major role in religious practices, specifically as regards the recognition or non-recognition of a status function. A collection of texts is given the status of a sacred book on the authority of tradition. The authority of the tradition does not have to be recognized before the practice can be performed. Participation in the practice implicitly and simultaneously recognizes that authority. Such participation presupposes sharing a common purpose (collective intentionality) in the activity. By acting on the basis of collective intentionality an individual accepts the authority of a tradition that ascribes a particular status function to an object, person or action. By participating in a baptismal service, for instance, we accept the authority of the tradition that ascribes the status function of baptismal water to the water in the font. It is not necessary to recognize the authority of the tradition prior to the practice. By taking part in this collective activity one recognizes the authority of the tradition that calls this practice "baptism".

4. The collective intentionality with which an activity is performed makes a religious practice meaningful. Without that meaning there is no practice. But practices must not be reduced to mental activities (intentions). Intentions cause actions, but practices are also characterized by a particular structure and sequence, a context, agents and means (cultural tools used in the activity). Thus we speak of mediated action, implying both the intentionality of the agents and the religious "tools" that are used. Tools can be everything included in the performance of the action: object, persons, action-patterns, times and spaces.

5. Religious practices differ from other cultural practices in that the status function ascribed to them is associated with transcendence. A particular action (prayer, Bible reading, meditation, singing, fasting) puts the person in contact with God. The exact meaning of transcendence, and how it rela-

tes to immanence, is determined by the tradition. We refer, cautiously, to a working hypothesis (following N. Luhmann): religions assign meaning to practices according to the binary code of transcendence versus immanence.

6. Religion as practice is defined at the micro level of social practices. [5] The micro level is not separate from the macro level of society at large; religious institutions form part of the public order. This public order is evident in practices that are performed in society to promote religion. Even though we approach religious practices from a cultural perspective, we cannot ignore the structural dimension. In dealing with the structural dimension I use the concept of religious regimes. A religious regime may be defined as a totality of inter-institutional relations of dependency which are more or less formalized and legitimised by religious experts (Hermans, 2003). This definition has two main elements. First, a religious regime is a constellation of power inasmuch as it determines which practices are beneficial to the religion and which are deviant or anomalous. Secondly, the constellation of power has an ideological base. This not only indicates the significance of religious practices, but also provides strategies for retaining and entrenching power ("how to fight and how to win"). Religious regimes are constantly in development within society. Three dynamics influence this development: (1) the relation of a religious regime to a public regime; (2) the relation to other religious regimes, and (3) internal relations within a religion between the dominant regime and counter-regimes.

References

Anderson, V. (1998) *Pragmatic theology. Negotiating the Intersections of an American Philosophy of Religion and Public Theology*. Albany: Un. of New York Press.

Harré, R. (1998) *The singular self. An introduction to the psychology of personhood*. London: Sage Publications.

Hermans, C.A.M. (2003) *Participatory Learning. Religious Education in a Globalizing Society*. Leiden: Brill.

Peirce, C.S. [1877] (1992) The Fixation of Belief. In Peirce, C.S. *The Essential Peirce. Volume 1 (1867 - 1893)* (ed. by N.Hauser and Chr.Koesel). Bloomington: Indiana Un.Press.

Raposa, M. (1989) *Peirce's Philosophy of Religion*. Bloomington: Indiana Un.Press.

Searle, J.R. (1995) *The Construction of Social Reality*. New York: The Free Press.

---

[5]   I agree with Tuomela, that social practices are conceptual prerequisite for macro processes (Tuomela, 2002). This is a major reason why I give preference to an analysis of religions on a micro level. But this does not exclude the fact that religious practices on a micro level are influenced by macro processes. On the contrary. That is why I include the structural component in my cultural institutional definition of religious practices (see Hermans, 2003, section 3.4.1. sub F).

Schweitzer, F. and Van der Ven, J.A (eds.) (1999) *Practical theology – International perspectives*. Frankfurt a.m.: Peter Lang

Tuomela, R. (2002) *The philosophy of social practices. A Collective Acceptance View.* Cambridge: Cambridge U.P.

Wenger, E. (1999) *Communities of Practice. Learning, Meaning, and Identity.* Cambridge: Cambridge U.P.

Can Natural Law still address Civil Society?

Terence G. Kennedy

Understanding natural law is like explaining a recurring decimal. In the history of ideas it just keeps reappearing apparently without reason. An illusion, neither legal nor natural to its opponents: its advocates accuse them of forever stealing the wrong corpse for burial. In general the public finds insurmountable difficulty making sense of it.

Traditionally it justified the foundations of both law and morality by insight into authentic humanity. Although rarely discussed in practical theology it is often presumed because of its foundational function for social institutions and human action. It is particularly relevant to a public theology because it proposes a way of addressing the public square in terms of law and ethics as rational discourse. Historically it has used to channel the Church's teaching, particularly its social thought, to a wider world. Natural law is usually taken to mean that a comprehensive definition of human nature generates the principles from which law and morality flow automatically as total systems. Seen from this ahistorical perspective, an Archimedean point outside the world, natural law traverses time uncontaminated by history. Naturalism reinforced this strikingly rationalist mentality by inducing laws from facts, thereby collapsing law into science.

Romans 2: 14-5 suggests that the moral order can be "read off" human nature where the Creator addresses conscience personally, writing his imperatives on the human heart. Such unmediated knowledge seems to short-circuit the workings of experience as it labouriously gains insight into humanity. Despite the Enlightenment's confidence in reason we enjoy no facile access to human nature and its definition as MacIntyre (MacIntyre, 1984) has demonstrated. Theory can only be properly understood through history's mediation, its universal claims not being absorbed without trace by historical conditions. Although it cannot be divorced from the language in which it is formulated, it is translatable into another culture setting by entering a dialectical relationship with it. Natural law belongs with happiness, virtue, law and justice to the classic notions of ethics that have a history of continuity and discontinuity. Might it not better be addressed as a set of traditions than as a single monolithic mental construct?

Natural Law and History

It is a wonder that nobody has used Kuhn's *The Structure of Scientific Revolutions* (Kuhn, 1970) to describe the natural law's history as a series of paradigm shifts. MacIntyre (1988) has done this successfully for virtue, practical reason and justice. Why should it not be done for natural law? A.P. d'Entreves (d'Entreves, 1951) delivers a bifocal reading of legal history that emphasises its philosophical worth less than its power to sustain social institutions in their historical settings. Its first focus is the medieval synthesis achieved through Justinian's *Codex Iuris Civilis* and Gratian's *Decretum*. The Middle Age chose the rational morality embedded in Scripture over Platonism's image of an organism and feudalism's notion of hierarchy as the way to structure society. The second is the Enlightenment's derivation of natural rights from natural law. "The Rights of Man" overturned unjust regimes in the American and French revolutions. Individuals could now enforce their rights against the state. Bills of Rights concretised the rationalist ideal of embracing the whole of law and morality in a comprehensive set of norms.

This system imploded when the importance of history which undermined the pretensions of so many "immutable institutions" was recognised. Bernard Williams calls "*relativism*, the anthropologist's heresy" (Williams, 1972: 20) which is overcome when people reach out over cultural barriers to acknowledge others as human. The Enlightenment so inflated natural law's possibilities that it created a totalising theory derived from clear and distinct ideas. No rule however trivial escaped its survey. Despite the current revival of natural law thinking from classic, medieval and Enlightenment sources we have not fully recovered from the nineteenth century's opprobrium for this absolutist approach.

For M. B. Crowe (Crowe, 1977) its history is less one of unmitigated progress than of tensions unresolved over centuries. It yields no full portrait, but only a profile glimpsed from age to age like Wittgenstein's family resemblance. Nevertheless, Crowe perceives a pattern of growth, climax and decline, a common reading of history as drama. Thomas Aquinas is the obvious benchmark who climaxed this story by integrating it into *sacra doctrina*.

Citing Aquinas's axiom *Natura humana mutabilis est* Crowe refutes the idea of a rigidly immutable natural law. In the *ordo scientiae* or of explanation it guides action because human nature generates human activity. But from our point of view we only come to understand our nature in the *ordo inventionis* through doing, through seeking to realise the good that fulfils us. In this sense metaphysics follows ethics even though possessing greater dignity. For Aquinas natural law provides the rational base for a community's morality, being the plan that God as law-giver created in human reason. Although applying only metaphorically to the physical and biological world it shows human persons their place in the community of the whole universe. Reason is infused into human nature at creation rendering it capable of distinguishing good and evil. The light of reason, as Augustine acknowledged, shares in God's eternal law as the basic rule of human conduct.

William of Ockham began the disintegration of Aquinas's synthesis. It was dismembered in the never really resolved titanic struggle between intellectualism and voluntarism (Bastit, 1990). Francisco Suarez attempted to balance will and intellect as alternative sources of law. There are intrinsically good and evil acts but the obligation to perform or abstain from them flowed from their being imposed by God's will. Although his synthesis proved unstable this way of seeing natural law persists If Aquinas sets the criteria for natural law then those who succeed him are rather disadvantaged.

Pauline Westerman (Westerman, 1998) neither puts Aquinas aside nor succumbs to historicism in her sympathetic treatment of Suarez, Grotius, and Pufendorf. She allows that theory from another period might be objectively superior to the original ideas they invented to rebut contemporary objections. Suarez responded to the accusation that intellectualists were blaspheming against God. He thus posited obligation as dependence on God's will irrespective of an action's intrinsic worth. Grotius's "perfidious hypothesis" was not intentionally irreligious. It affirmed a new ethical rationality on which all could agree so as to bring the wars of religion to an end. Natural law could be saved only in the form of a theory of human rights. Pufendorf propounded that natural law's internal consistency undergirded not a collection of human rights but positive and civil law. By reconciling Hobbes' pragmatism about state authority with Grotius's rather idealistic account he pushed natural law thinking toward rationalism. With Aquinas's ideas so distorted it was easy for Hume to pronounce the final death sentence. Grisez and Finnis accept Hume's challenge, proceeding on the premise that a good theory of natural law should be independent of historical contingencies.

Three Alternatives

Natural law can relate to history in three possible modes.

A Historicist. Natural law theory cannot transcend its historical context with universally valid transcultural claims. Instead it explains in a useful manner what particular cultures think is irreducibly human.

B Ahistorical. Natural law is valid because of its *per se* self evident principles established independently of historical circumstances. Radically
it is constituted by a set of logical relations untouched by historical conditions.

C Dialectical. This approach provides a method for untangling, in a logical
way, knotted points of tension within history. It releases natural law to
become a force forming social institutions. This nuanced position calls
for some clarification. It copes with pluralism by applying Aristotelian
dialectics to the opinions of groups opposed in debate. It distinguishes
the comparative strengths and weaknesses of traditions in conflict. From
their confrontation the best possible explanation on the basis of available
evidence should result. Natural law theory elevates dialectics method to
treat of principles. First principles cannot be proved syllogistically nor
can they be denied without contradiction. Thus good is to be done and
evil avoided. Other principles included in this first principle are perceived in its light, not being deduced by logical necessity. This approach
does not pretend to enforce consensus but allows that one explanation
might be decisively more probative than another. Its first principles yield
insights articulated by human wisdom into our essential inclinations toward fulfilment. It employs a type of situated, non-historicist rationality
that consults basic moral experience to decide between conflicting universal claims and their interpretation. Its conclusions are progressively
subject to change and error as they distance themselves from first principles. This means that natural law is not the whole of morality because
it needs to be complemented by the virtues particularly prudence which
mediates it to particular situations.

These three interpretations all resonate in contemporary discussions. Historicism, here in the form of legal positivism, upholds the thesis that law has
validity solely from being rightly posited according to the rules of jurisprudence and promulgated by appropriate authority. Legal system are autonomous
and so independent of morality, a view firmly advanced by Kant. Each legal
system has to be interpreted in its own terms which may include its historical
justification. Historicism in the law led to the tragic disasters of the totalitarian
Nazi and Communist regimes. Their ideologies never permitted the possibility
of dissent against unjust legislation. When these regimes fell their leaders had
to be prosecuted for the massive woes they had wrought on humanity. But they
had broken no law in the criminal codes formulated by themselves. Yet people
spontaneously judged them guilty of crimes against humanity. To bring charges
at the Nuremberg trials and after the collapse of the East German Communist

regime lawyers were forced to have recourse not to positive but to unwritten natural law as binding all humanity.

Lawyers dislike such a situation. They tend to resist appeals to an unwritten law not sanctioned through custom or usage. A law not clearly promulgated by legal authority lacks the certainty necessary to bind. How can a law "above" all civil laws and codes truly be law? Some sources in the tradition might help here. Firstly, Aristotle's statement, "Now to political justice. There are two forms of it, the natural and the conventional." (1955: 157) To reduce all law to the conventional or posited is a denial of natural justice, a vacuum at the heart of the *polis*. Augustine says that if civil law does not sanction natural law then it lacks force as law and becomes null and void. Natural law is perceived to be active in the deep values inerent to law itself. Lawyers do not have to refer to it always since it is tacitly present in all valid law. Ironically, law forms an autonomous system inseparable from the moral values which support it.

After World War II natural law thinking blossomed as a critique of totalitarianism and legal positivism. Among refugees who fled to America from persecution in Europe Leo Strauss (Strauss, 1953) had a lasting impact on moral and legal thinking. He refuted the accusation that natural law contravenes the fact-value distinction and Max Weber's contention that the social sciences were by definition incapable of making definitive value judgements although they were essentially about such values. Weber foresaw that they would breed a value -free world that reduced natural law to a matter of purely private opinion. Strauss argued that we need the tradition of natural right to ward off scepticism in the practice of social science and to prevent nihilism from becoming the predominant cultural force.

The Grisez-Finnis New Natural Law Theory

Many defenders of natural law were calling for a new rationale, its refoundation in fact. Germain Grisez and John Finnis took up the challenge to rework the foundations of ethics in a way that incorporated Hume's is-ought distinction. Grisez examined Aquinas' text in S.T. I-II. 94. 2 and concluded that far from falling foul of this distinction it implicitly observed it with surprisingly different results. Finnis carried Grisez's results into law and jurisprudence, and restored natural law's credibility in the English speaking world, particularly the universities(Finnis,1980). By rehabilitating Aquinas he aimed to develop a convincing ethical theory for the Catholic Church at the time of the contraception controversy.

Finnis constructed his theory at two levels, the basic goods and the modes of responsibility. The first principles of natural law are not inferred from facts.

Finnis counts seven basic human goods:life, knowledge, play, aesthetic experience, friendship, practical reasonableness and religion. The basic practical principles are concerned with those goods that are fundamental to all action and are irreducible to one another. They are intrinsic goods desirable for their own sakes. Other goods are combinations or ways of pursuing them. He claims that these basic goods correspond to the natural inclinations. Taken together they constitute "the good life," the basic forms of human flourishing.

These methodological principles of practical reasonableness or responsibility are also practical principles and are validated in the same way. Grisez thinks they are principles of practical reasonableness and not just of moral behaviour. Natural law is thus a law of reason and not of nature in any physical or biological sense. In chapter five of his book Finnis produces the following list. 1. A coherent plan of life. 2. No arbitrary preference among values. 3. No arbitrary preference between persons. 4. Detachment from all the specific and limited projects. 5. Never abandon commitments lightly. 6. Use efficient actions for reasonable purposes. 7. "Respect every basic good in every act." 8. "Favour and foster the common good of one's communities." 9. Act in accordance with conscience.

These principles belong to the deep structure of practical reasoning. The Grisez-Finnis theory is presently considered the most coherent account of natural law among English speaking intellectuals. It posits a shift from human nature to the basic goods as foundational to moral and legal thinking. As a lawyer Finnis does not deride legal positivism but counters worries about historicism by invoking a logic that is eternally true. Secular thinkers tend to consider this theory as just another player on the field. Its advantage is that it makes a religious morality intelligible to a wide public and so can be licensed for the secular arena. Scholars wonder, however, that its results are so wonderfully in line with Catholic teaching. Elaborated as a defence of a Catholic position its purpose can be said to be basically apologetic. On the other hand it is a conspicuous example of the recent growth of the school known as analytic Thomism, whose goal is to bringing natural law within the purview of Anglo-Saxon linguistic and analytic philosophy. It tends to put aside historical arguments and appeal to strictly logical notions that must always be true.

Faith and History

The tension between historicity and universality meet in religious faith. The Judeo-Christian tradition's confrontation with modernity emerged in this context. David Novak (Novak, 1998) highlights the principle that Jewish Covenant morality is reasonable and so can be made intelligible to people of good will. Faith and reason do not work against each other but function to bring a com-

munity to an historical understanding of itself. Even before the Mosaic revelation natural law was present in people's spontaneous awareness of right and
wrong given at creation without previous instruction. Noahide law ensured the
minimum conditions of human existence and conviviality, now best expressed
as human rights. Novak summarises his position in five theses. 1. The Torah
presupposes natural law as a requirement of human nature, 2. Its normative
requirements are common to all the other nations of the earth, 3. A commo-
nality immediately evident in certain basic norms held in common, 4. Which
other historical communities have accepted for themselves ... 5. Israel has so
completely accepted natural law in her own unique Covenantal law as to be in
a special position to teach the world about it.

What follows for Novak is a kind of Jewish formulation of the *ius gentium*,
whose features one finds formulated in all societies as basic to humanity. It is
an internal limit on personal and communal pretentions. Natural law has a part
in the political process, particularly as regards the inherent ends at which that
process aims.

In Judaism, these ends are covenantal... Hence natural law does not function as the
normative whole of which positive law is the applied part thereof. Positive law is not
deduced from natural law, but is only explained and guided by it. Its function then is
essentially heuristic. (1988: 157)

Among Christian intellectuals Karl Barth withstood any incorporation of natural law into theology. He objected to the Catholic view as a latent deism that
creates an autonomous morality completely separate from God's revelation in
Jesus Christ. He accused Lutheran theologians of replacing the *lex creationis*
with the *lex naturalis*. Barth's attack on natural law was so vehement that after
World War II Christian ethics slid down the slippery slope of situation ethics.
Catholic scholars responded by pointing out that revelation confirmed natural
law's essential rationality and that it had been personalised by assumption into
the law of Christ. [1]

Cultural Wars over Natural Law

Russell Hittinger (Cromartie, 1997) has clarified Catholic moralists' core difficulty in interpreting natural law. Two schools of opinion divide on whether
it is established by reason, or discovered as a God-given law of reason. Are
its first principles dependent on knowledge of divine providence, or are they

---

[1] See B. Häring's, "Dynamism and Continuity in a Personalistic Approach to Natural Law",
    in (1968) *Norm and Context in Christian Ethics*. edited by G. H. Outka and P. Ramsey. New
    York: Scribner's Sons.

posited by autonomous reason? He highlights John Paul II's conception of "participated theonomy," (Cromartie, 1997: 24) in *Veritatis Splendor*. But how can reason be truly autonomous while remaining open to God? Jacques Maritain's thesis (Maritain, 1951) is that natural law lays the foundation for human rights and the international order as proposed by the United Nations. As Catholics began dialoguing with other political movements, liberation theologians in South America, Maritain's influence faded. But theological accounts faithful to Aquinas's inspiration continue dialoguing with current philosophy, law and politics. The tension between moral autonomy and the Gospel's universal call to salvation is reflected in Eberhard Schockenhoff (Schockenhoff, 1996) and Martin Rhonheimer (Rhonheimer, 2000). Without a doubt the best informed commentary on Aqinas is Otto Herman Pesch's *Das Gesetz* (Aquin, 1977) which leads us to see the law of the Spirit as the highpoint of Aquinas synthesis on law.

A staple feature in Catholic tradition is the premise that civil institutions are founded on natural law. After World War II Maritain and John Courtney Murray (Murray 1960) seized the moment to make natural law once more tenable as a basis for the social order, phrasing it in terms of human dignity and natural rights. It is difficult to assess this project's successes and failures. The teaching authority of the Catholic Church has taken a long-term view of natural law's fortune a manner indicative of its current importance.

Cardinal Roy (Cromartie, 1997) expressed what has been a standard position in his remarks addressed to Pope Paul VI for the tenth anniversary of the encyclical *Pacem in Terris*.

Although the term "nature" does not in fact lend itself to serious misunderstandings, the reality intended has lost nothing of its forcefulness when it is replaced by modern synonyms... Such synonyms are: man, human being, human person, dignity, the rights of man or the rights of peoples, conscience, humaneness (in conduct), the struggle for justice, and more recently "the duty of being," the "quality of life." Could they not all be summarised in the concept of "values," which is very much used today. (Cromartie, 1997: 13)

Contrast that with John Paul II's statement in *Evangelium Vitae* where he observes that the tradition of natural law that in fact founded human rights is being widely rejected:

A long historical process is reaching a turning-point. The process that once led to the discovering of the idea of "human rights" – rights inherent in every person and prior to any Constitution and State legislation – is today marked by a surprising contradiction. Precisely in an age when the inviolable rights of the person are solemnly proclaimed and the value of life is publicly affirmed, the very right to life is being denied and trampled upon, especially at the more significant moments of existence: the moment of birth and the moment of death (§ 18).

This situation is typical of the "cultural wars" dividing Western societies at the moment. By employing rights' language the Pope is implicitly invoking a natural law philosophy. His stance has a double valency: *ad intra* the encyclical *Veritatis Splendor* repeats the definition of natural law as a participation in God's eternal law and providence; *ad extra* the Church's mission is to be a consensus-builder among the peoples and the nations. Its educational mission is to teach the precepts of the moral order that are in principle accessible to the human mind. The Scripture are invoked to throw faith's light on natural law so that the Church may show her true countenance as an authentically human community of believers.

Fergus Kerr (Kerr, 2002) sums up the situation with a chapter entitled, "Natural Law: Incommensurable Readings." This is the only reasonable judgement to be given on its recent history. It does not mean that there is no consistent theory to be had nor that such a theory is only accessible to ecclesiastic authority. Scholars still need to put traditional concepts in dialectical confrontation with contemporary philosophies to illustrate natural law's capacity to fashion civil institutions to a truly human measure for a postmodern world. Natural law has inspired Michael Keeling (Keeling, 1995) to seek a "Protestant Christian theological basis" from which to "define mandates for the whole of humanity." He believes that natural law far from being "the discovery of a set of rules for putting a plan into effect" is really "a dance... As the Greek fathers said, life is a *perichoresis*, a dance of the universe led by Christ the Lord of Creation, towards a fulfilment that is not jet seen." (Keeling, 1995: 203)

References

Aquin, Thomas von (1977) *Das Gesetz*. Kommentiert von Otto Hermann Pesch, Wien: Styria.

Aristotle (1955) *Ethics of Aristotle*. translated by J.A.K. Thomson, Harmonsworth: Penguin.

Bastit, Michel (1990) *Naissance de la Loi Moderne*. Paris: Presses Universitaires de France.

Cromartie, Michael (1997) (ed.) *A Preserving Grace: protestants, catholics and natural law*. Grand Rapids, MI: William B. Eerdman.

Crowe, Michael Bertram (1977) *The Changing Profile of Natural Law*. The Hague: Martinus Nijhoff.

d'Entreves, A.P. (1951) *Natural Law: an introduction to legal philosophy*. London: Hutchinson.

Finnis, John (1980) *Natural Law and Natural Rights*. Oxford: Clarendon.

Keeling, Michael (1995) *The Mandate of Heaven: the divine command and the natural order*. Edinburgh: T. and T. Clark.

Kuhn, Thomas (1970) *The Structure of Scientific Revolutions*. Chicago: University of Chicago Press.

Macintyre, Alasdair (1984) *After Virtue: a study in moral theory*. Notre Dame, IN: University of Notre Dame Press.

————————————— (1988) *Whose Justice? Which Rationality?* Notre Dame IN: University of Notre Dame Press.

Maritain, Jacques (1951) *Man and the State*. Chicago: Chicago University Press.

Murray, John Courtney (1960) *We Hold These Truths: Catholic reflections on the American proposition*. New York: Sheed and Ward.

Novak, David (1998) *Natural Law in Judaism*. Cambridge: Cambridge University Press.

Kerr, Fergus (2002) *After Aquinas: versions of Thomism*, Oxford: Blackwell.

Rhonheimer, Martin (2000) *Natural Law and Practical Reason: A Thomistc view of moral autonomy*. New York: Fordham University Press.

Schockenhoff, Eberhard (1996) *Naturrecht und Menschenwürde: Universale Ethik in einer geschichlichen Welt*. Mainz: Grünewald.

Strauss, Leo (1953) *Natural Right and History*. Chicago: Chicago University Press.

Westerman, Pauline C. (1998) *The Disintegration of Natural Law Theory: Aquinas to Finnis*. Leiden: Brill.

Williams, Bernard (1972) *Morality*. Cambridge: Cambridge University Press.

Naming God in a (post)modern world

F. Gerrit Immink

Specifying the question

Who is God? Is God a subsistent personal being? A subject of speech and action, a person whom we address? Or should we consider God to be an immanent force within the world, a symbol of an ultimate liberating creativity in the historical cultural process, according to Gordon Kaufman 'an ultimate tendency or power, which is working itself out in an evolutionary process'?(Kaufman, 1995: 43)

Let me first present in an introductory way two theological positions. In some circles of modern theology it is fashionably to speak about God in a non-referential way. "God" is dealt with from within the "hermeneutics of suspicion" and the idea is that we cannot make truth claims about God. However, this does not necessarily lead to atheism or to a cynical agnosticism. Religion is still in vogue, but now as a human construction of reality and not as a description of God. Religion remains very useful, for it 'indirectly opens us to what is beyond our present world, opens us to that which we do not yet know but which will be creative for our future'.(Kaufman, 1989: 44) "God" has a practical function for human life and gives us proper orientation.

In more orthodox circles God-language is primarily related to the notion of divine revelation. The idea is that our knowledge of God and our God-language originates in God's *self disclosure*. 'God has taken the initiative and has freely made known the divine identity and purpose.' (Migliore, 1994: 20) In this model God receives priority in the divine-human encounter, and consequently God is depicted as a subject of speech and action. According to Karl Barth 'knowledge of God can be understood only as the bestowal and reception of this free grace of God.'(Barth, 1957: 29) God is the primary subject and has the initiative and human faith is a response (comes *nachher*). This structure is deeply rooted in the Protestant tradition. Notions like *word, promise, revelation, covenant* and *divine election* emphasize this divine a priori. This is especially true for the notion of justification of the sinner, as it presupposes the priority of

God's judgement of grace. In this vein Ronald Thiemannn observes that 'promise provides a category within which the notions of relation and priority can be held in a dialectical balance.'(Thiemann, 1985: 151)

Naming God is neither an abstract nor an indifferent human act. On the contrary, it is about that which concerns us ultimately. It expresses what we believe about our human life and what we hope for. *Naming God* is an activity which has moral and religious implications in the human realm. Perhaps these dimensions are in the Christian tradition well expressed in the concept of salvation. I hold that "God" and "salvation" are terms or names that come in a pair: when we speak about God, we speak about justice, love, mercy, et cetera. These are qualities which determine what a good life is like. We speak about these qualities religiously, when we relate them to the name of God.

Here is my point: if we name God, then this naming is somehow connected with events, processes and states of affairs in the human realm. And yet, God is not *identical* with these events, processes, et cetera. With respect to the human realm God is transcendental, be it understood in a metaphysical or eschatological way. So there is a discontinuity between God and humankind, an incongruity, an ontological divergence, a distinctness of quality and majesty. Suppose we agree on this non-identity. Or, to put it differently, suppose we agree 'formally' on a non-identity between God and humanity. Personally I think that, once we believe in God, we accept this non-identity. It is intrinsically related. Then still the question is: how do we construe the relation between God and humanity? Or, put in practical theological terminology: how do we speak about God? What is our God-language like? What do we mean by God?

I will deal with these questions by describing shortly two positions adopted by contemporary practical theologians: Wilhelm Gräb and Hans Van der Ven. Then I will discuss the theme in a more systematic way. In order to understand the current debate, let me first make a more structural comment. Since the nineties there is a new turn toward the concept of religion in Practical Theology. Modernity is no longer considered to be the end of religion, although in (post)modernity religion appears in a new shape. Consequently Gräb argues that Practical Theology is a *theory of religion*. And religion, in turn, is understood as *Sinndeutung*; it is part of the human search for meaning. This turn also implies that a theistic approach to religion is not currently favoured. According to John Hick the 'displacement of "God" by "religion" as the focus of the wide realm of discourse has brought a change in the character of the questions that are most persistently asked in this area.'(Hick, 1973: 79 - 80) These questions are not typically about God, but about the human subject. This coincides with the practical theological turn to faith-as-it-is-lived, to the *gelebte Religion*.

Gräb's ultimate meaning

In recent Practical Theology there is a strong emphasis on subjective religion. In Germany Henning Luther constructed a theology of the subject in which personal biography and the fragmentation of life are key concepts.(Luther, 1992) Wilhelm Gräb starts from the subjective search for meaning. (Gräb, 1998) His idea is that religion originates in the personal search for meaning, and that subjective religion is fortunately free from external coercion and institutional authority. The freedom of the individual person and the needs of the situation are considered to be essential to religion. As I see it, a positive characteristic of this approach is that the human subject receives full attention. We cannot explain religion apart from our mental functions and apart from our psycho-social life.

But what happens to the God-language? We can imagine that God is not primarily depicted as a speaking and acting God. After all, the human subject is the focal point. Perhaps it is fair to say this: God is mentioned indirectly. If I try to formulate it in a positive way: if there is God-language at all, it is about *our awareness of God*.

How should we construe Gräb's argument? He starts with the human condition, or, perhaps better: in human destiny, that destiny is to live in freedom. But can we as mere human beings accomplish that? Aren't we too ambivalent? Indeed, so Gräb argues, we endure anguish and we live with doubts. At this point religion comes in, and Gräb argues that religion consists in a *feeling of basic trust (Gefühl unseres absoluten Gegründetseins)*.(Gräb, 1998: 67) This is a subjective awareness (*frömmigkeit*), a feeling of the heart, beyond all conceptualisation. In this ultimate concern we come to a limit where our search for meaning finally rests.

So far, there is not much explicit God-language. There is a feeling of basic trust, but can we answer the question: What are you trusting in? Whom are you trusting? Tell me, what is this unconditioned condition? As a good Lutheran theologian Gräb comes up with a theological foundation, namely the old doctrine of the *justification of the sinner.* We are accepted by God and we experience that when we encounter unconditional love of other people.

This approach has the characteristics of what Lindbeck once called the *expressive-experiential model.* God is the ultimate point of reference, a religious symbol, a metaphor embedded in a social-cultural network.

Whatever the variations, thinkers of this tradition all locate ultimately significant contact with whatever is finally important to religion in the prereflective experiential depths of the self and regard the public or outer features of religion as expressive and evocative objectifications (i.e. nondiscursive symbols) of internal experience.(Lindbeck, 1984: 21)

The human self appears as the nursery of religion. As a reaction to the critique of the Enlightenment tradition, especially in its Kantian judgement that we cannot know God as an 'external object', theologians intend to focus on human experiences as a subjective awareness of things divine. I think that Schleiermacher is the founding father of this model and I guess that Schleiermacher is also Gräb's favourite teacher.

Van der Ven's empirical theology

Van der Ven unfolds practical theology as empirical theology. More precisely, it is a theological discipline that uses methods that originate in empirical sciences. What is the effect of this approach on our theme: naming God? Do the theological concepts refer to God or is God by definition excluded because He does not belong to the empirical realm? In his development of theoretical insights van der Ven is indeed strongly influenced by the empirical tradition. This prejudice, however, does not lead him to a reductionist view of religion. As a matter of fact religion concerns the reality of God. However, from an empirical perspective we only have access to religious experiences, religious language and religious acts. But then my question becomes: how is God related to such empirical data? And what is the nature of this data? For example, are religious experiences experiences of God? Or should we say that are manifestations of God? Or should we take one more step and talk about the God who manifests himself in these experiences?

Van der Ven frankly argues that the object of practical theology is faith and not God. So the object is something in the human realm, namely, the religion of human beings. Not God. God may be the object of faith, but not the object of Practical Theology. What we investigate is what human beings perceive of God. Their reception in religious experience, their response in prayer and liturgy and their reaction in social conduct, that's what we investigate.

Only in and through these multiple forms of reception, response and reaction and not outside of them is God indirectly accessible to theological research. The assumption is nonetheless that through this reception, response and reaction one at least draws nearer to God, that God's healing presence can be fragmentarily touched through them. These three elements can be empirically investigated... (van der Ven, 1993: 104)

So in an indirect way we refer to God. He is in the perspective of our human experience; we see fragments of the divine. The human realm is not devoid of God, and God is not wholly transcendent. Even in empirical research we come across signs of God. God is not a mystic blank, but something that makes a difference in our human situation. Only, we cannot directly point to him.

How should we evaluate this approach? The theological argument runs, I think, as follows.

(1) Events and actions in the human realm can, under certain conditions, become a sign of God's salfivic presence. Social interaction, if it is liberating and salfivic, can be seen as a *sign* of God's kingdom. Further (2), there is a connection between "sign" and "denotatum" (that what is signified). At least the human being as an interpreter of life may see certain events as a sign of God's salfivic action. (3) We can interpret life-experiences this way if we are familiar with the conventions or codes of a religious tradition. (van der Ven, 1993: 100)

In this argument God is named indirectly: events in the human realm refer to God, that is, God can be thought of from the *perspective* of events in the empirical world. What we name, however, is not God as a *subject* of predication. For our predicates only apply to the empirical world. However, our empirical world is not devoid of God. He is partially present, in fragments. It seems that van der Ven assumes an *aspectual* identity between sign and signified.

Theological motives and theoretical foundations

Naming God is an act of faith, performed by human beings. Since it is a human act, we can specify three *anthropological* reflections. (1) As I already observed, God is related to fundamental characteristics of human existence, expressed in qualities like justice, freedom, compassion, et cetera. There is, so to say, an analogy between naming God and naming the qualities of life. Perhaps there is even more involved than a formal analogy, for when we name God, we name an effective, worldtransforming presence-among-us. (2) In addition, naming God presupposes the intentionality and spirituality of the human subject. As John Searle observes, the human mind is *intentionally* directed toward the world in which we live.(Searle, 1999: 85) Consequently, I hold that, when we name God, then the human being is subjectively involved: he or she has an awareness of God, knows and experiences God, et cetera. So, the act of naming implies all kinds of mental and communicative functions.

(3) Naming God is, according to Niebuhr, also a *social* act.(Niebuhr, 1989: 34) It has to do with a relation between *subjects*, with a personal encounter. Trust and trustworthiness are fundamental characteristics in a relation. Consequently, the act of naming God is embedded in the psycho-social structure of our human condition.

When we name God, we intentionally relate to the Other. How to understand this "otherness" of God? Here we come to the *metaphysical* aspect of naming God. My thesis is: God is the *object* of faith and a *subject* whom we encounter. Just a few remarks on these aspects. Faith has, as I see it, propositional content. We believe certain things about God, for example, that He is merciful and just (*fides quae*). Believers will answer the question: who is the God you trust? Further, God is also understood as someone with whom we speak (prayer), as a person whom we encounter, as a subject of speech and action. That means, God is depicted as a centre of consciousness and action (as an active presence).

Therefore, naming God brings forth a metaphysical worldview. And as theologians we should be aware of the theoretical implications of religious speech. Roughly speaking, there are two distinct models through which theologians deal with these problems. (1) The perspective of revelation. God encounters humankind, and this encounter is God's own work. God makes himself *gegenständlich*, so Barth argues. 'God speaks; He claims; He promises; He acts... Take away the objectivity of this He, and faith collapses, even as love, trust and obedience.' (Barth, 1957: 13) God makes himself known and He is the *unaufhebbares Subject*. (2) An anthropocentric perspective: God is beyond the reach of our human capacities of knowing and naming. Consequently, God is a symbol of a different order and our religious language is by definition limit-language. In this vein Schleiermacher observes that 'brooding over the existence of a god before and outside the world may be good and necessary in metaphysics, in religion that becomes only empty mythology'.

Default positions

I hold that faith is best understood in terms of a bipolar relation. It is an intersubjective encounter, a mutual contact or engagement. In the act of faith we trust God and we share in his love. We get involved in his life-transforming presence. I think both Gräb and van der Ven, be it in different ways, overlook the metaphysical structure of our God-language. Let me shortly illustrate that.

Gräb

Gräb narrows faith down to an anthropological phenomenon. Theology turns into a theory of religion with a Protestant flavour. Consider the doctrine of justification. It is interpreted as a postulate of human freedom. I hold that in Protestantism the notion of the justification of the sinner implies the *external* judgement of God. The kernel idea is not the human awareness of the divine grace, but the divine *imputation* of grace. Salvation and grace are bestowed upon us, it is the disclosure of a new reality, it is a gift-like quality. It arises *extra nos*. The sinner is accepted only on the basis of an extraneous justice. Jüngel: *allein aufgrund der ihm ganz und gar fremden Gerechtigkeit Gottes.*

(Jüngel, 1999: 175) At this point there is a fundamental difference with Gräb. In his view "Sinndeutung" is a human act: it is *we* who construct meaning. Perhaps that is the pitfall of a hermeneutical approach. But in the Protestant understanding of faith there is a deep conviction of the priority of God in the divine-human relationship. New life, salvation and the kingdom of God are enacted as liberating acts of God.

That makes the *identity* of God the fundamental issue in the praxis of faith. Revelation as God's *self-disclosure*. When we name God, we identify Him in a specific way. That identity determines what we expect our human life to be and what we live for.

Van der Ven

Van der Ven holds that we name God indirectly: God is in perspective of experiences of and events in our human world. Let me elaborate on his view a little bit more. Van der Ven is neither denying the mystery of God, nor the presence of God in our world. He seems to think, however, that we don't have access to God. The interesting thing is that here philosophical insights and theological reflection coincide. What is the point? Van der Ven is aware of the fact that our human concepts on the one hand and reality (that what is the case) on the other hand are not one and the same thing. And he rightly thinks so. The issue at stake is the relation between concept and reality. Van der Ven defends a "moderate conceptual realism". If I understand him correctly, he uses this distinction to distinguish between faith on the one hand and God on the other hand. Human faith is one thing and God another. But of course we cannot totally separate our concept of God and God. That is the "moderate" part. Our experiences et cetera are somehow related to God; they tell us *aspectual* about God.

A philosophical problem is lurking behind this theological statement. The way in which we understand "naming God" coincides with our construction of the relationship between the human mind and the real world. In our Western philosophical tradition we construe that linkage in different metaphysical models: (a) conceptualism, (b) external realism and (c) social constructionism (or perspectivism). Roughly speaking we can say that conceptualism holds that we ourselves are the architects of the world. The emphasis is on the *ideas*, on our state of consciousness. (Searle, 1999; Plantinga, 1990: 14) In its Kantian form conceptualisation – and thus knowledge – is a structural feature of our human condition. The basic idea is that reality is structured by our human conceptual activity. Reality is ultimately not something existing independently of our perceptions, but rather constituted by our perception. External realism takes a different stand. Here the idea is that indeed there is a world existing independently of us and our interests, that there is an objective way that things are, and that we have epistemic access to that world. Finally, in Postmodern circles not only realism, but also conceptualism has been rejected. Human concepts are not based on a common structure of the human mind, they are just social artefacts, 'products of historically and culturally situated interchanges among people'. (Gergen, 1994: 49) Here the conceptual structure is not universal, but based on conventions.

These models interfere with our reconstruction of our God-language. When we name God, what do we name? Are we referring to our images of God, to our mental concepts, to social artefacts, or are we in fact naming *God*? Or should we say that God is beyond our knowledge and understanding? A (post)modern voice, Sallie McFague:

> God is and remains a mystery. We really do not know: the hints and clues we have of the way things are – whether we call them experiences, revelation, or whatever – are too fragile, too little (and more often than not, too negative) for much more than a hypothesis, a guess, a projection of a possibility that, although it can be comprehensive and illuminating, may not be true.(McFague, 1987: 192)

Here the idea is that our concept of God is precisely that – *our concept* of God – and not God. But, I think, we still should ask: what is the relation between our concept of God and the referent of the term "God"?

In my view both conceptualism and constructionism fail with respect to the *referential* aspect of naming God. It indeed makes sense to differentiate between concepts of God and the referent of the term "God". But what is wrong with the idea that having a concept of God as a loving God, is just this that we grasp that *God is loving!* Of course, concepts have subjective connotation, but they also function as a *link*, they constitute the connection with an external reality. Isn't what we grasp in faith precisely that – the *love of God?* Having a concept of God's love, isn't that precisely this, that we understand what it means that God loves us? Having a concept is, I would say, apprehending a property. We have concepts corresponding to those properties we grasp or apprehend. (Plantinga, 17-21) Here some distinctions may be relevant and others not. It makes sense to say that we have limited or fragmentary knowledge of God. Our knowledge may be miniscule in comparison with what we do not know; furthermore, there may be much of which we have no conception at all. Or, and may be this is more relevant, our knowledge is a knowledge by degrees. Our apprehending of qualities like goodness, justice and benevolence may be such that we have *some* knowledge of it, just a small portion. So, it makes sense to say that our knowledge of God is partial and fragmentary. But nonetheless, this is knowledge *of God*.

References

Barth, Karl (1957) *Church Dogmatics*. II.1, Edinburgh: T & T Clark.

Gergen, Kenneth (1994) *Realities and Relationships. Soundings in social construction*. Cambridge London: Harvard University Press

Gräb, Wilhelm (1998) *Lebensgeschichten, Lebensentwürfe, Sinndeutungen. Eine praktische Theologie gelebter Religion*. Gütersloh: Chr. Kaiser.

Hick, John (1973) *Philosophy of Religion*. Englewood Cliffs: Prentice-Hall.

Jüngel, Eberhard (1999) *Das Evangelium von der Rechtfertigung des Gottlosen als Zentrum des Christlichen Glaubens*. Tübingen: J.C.B. Mohr.

Kaufman, Gordon D. (1985) *Theology For A Nuclear Age*. Manchester: Manchester University Press.

Kaufman, Gordon D. (1989) Evidentialism. A Theologian's Response. *Faith and Philosophy* 6, 35 - 46.

Luther, Henning (1992) *Religion und Alltag. Bausteine zu einer Praktischen Theologie des Subjects*. Stuttgart: Radius Bücher.

McFague Sallie (1987) *Models of God. Theology for an Ecological, Nuclear Age*. London: SCM Press.

Migliore, Daniel L. (1994) *Faith Seeking Understanding*. Grand Rapids: Eerdmans.

Niebuhr, H. Richard (1989) *Faith on Earth. An Inquiry into the Structure of Human Faith*. New Haven: Yale University Press

Plantinga, Alvin (1980) *Does God Have A Nature?* Milwaukee: Marquette University Press.

Plantinga, Alvin (1990) *The Twin Pillars of Christian Scholarship*. Grand Rapids: Calvin College and Seminary.

Searle, John R. (1999) *Mind, Language and Society. Philosophy in the Real World*. New York:Basic Books.

Ven, Johannes A. van der (1993) *Practical Theology. An Empirical Approach*. Kampen: Kok.

Ven, Johannes A. van der (1993) *Ecclesiologie in context*. Kampen: Kok.

PART IV: SPIRITUALITY AND FORMATION IN AN AGE OF PLURALISM

The final section relates questions of theology as public discourse, and theology in the public domain, to issues of personal formation, autobiography and spirituality. It also explores the territory of the resources of spirituality and liturgy for the formation of the Church's public witness.

The city may be a metaphor for human community but is it necessarily a city without God? Daniel Louw asks what abiding images and values should inform our understandings of 'church' in an urban, pluralist society such as South Africa. Christian theology full of images of heavenly city in which the presence and promise of God in the world is given concrete shape and expression in human community. 'Being church' in contemporary city is not simply an intra-ecclesial issue, therefore, but a public matter, involving healing, reconciliation, partnership, empowerment and justice as practical forms of 'speaking of God in public'.

Ottmar Fuchs is concerned to ask, what is meant by 'mission' today? After Gutiérrez, Fuchs argues it is not a question of requiring people to believe certain truths but of inviting them to see how God offers full humanity to those dehumanized by oppression and poverty. Mission is a self-emptying on the part of the faithful community as a radical identification with the suffering of the incarnate God, as well as a solidarity with all creation in the name of the universality of the creator God: so to speak of God in public is to participate in the source of unconditional grace and compassion alongside those who suffer.

Karl-Ernst Nipkow's paper combines autobiography and analysis to form a powerful synthesis of the personal and the political. He asks what it means for the Church to be a public reality, offering illustrations from different historical and political German settings in the twentieth century to the present day. He finds models of church as *diakonia*, expressing a concern for the sick; as *confessing church*, in resistance to the Nazis; and as new social movements, concerned for human rights, ecology and peace. Nipkow then discusses the challenges posed by the contemporary context – particularly the existence of new generations of 'unchurched' youth – and the implications for religious education for both Church and State. In this new, secular society, the Church is called once more to live out a different way of 'being public', through its educational outreach. However, the churches' educational public impact must always be closely linked to convincing forms of 'lived faith' as social witness, and informed by vigorous theological criteria.

The marginalization of religious and theological discourse in the public domain is not only a challenge to the churches, but presents challenges to many aspects of our society, in terms of the values, meanings and symbols by which people live their lives. Using sociological analysis and primary empirical research into the religiosity of young people, Hans-Georg Ziebertz develops a typology of patterns of religious understandings, and suggests that young people still engage in theological speculation, although they tend to rely on personal experience rather than official teaching. He poses the question whether practical theology is equipped to deal adequately with such conditions, or whether the gulf between institutional faith and everyday 'talk about God' will continue to widen.

Eberhard Hauschildt's paper deals with the challenges and opportunities of locating practical theology in the secular academy, and tells of the success of an inter-disciplinary programme in Social Services Administration hosted by his theology faculty in Bonn. In the process, it is possible for faith-based values and ethical considerations to take their place alongside themes of leadership, social analysis, economics and psychology, thereby offering one paradigm of 'theology in public'. Yet Hauschildt also emphasises the ways in which the very approach to theology itself has undergone transformation: surrendering any claim to a privileged position, nor simply seeking to 'baptise' the perspectives of other disciplines, theology operates as both 'external' and 'internal' discourse, mediating between the world of shared values and the specific values of faith. In such a process of dialogue, participants may find themselves both enriched by other traditions and encouraged to dig more deeply into their own convictions, offering a model of good practice for other instances of public theology.

Exploring different forms and types of metaphor, Cas Vos offers a reflection on the relation between spirituality and the public realm. For Vos any public and practical theology needs to be attentive to the 'art' of liturgy in which metaphor is used to 'blow' the liturgy in a similar manner to the artistic work of a glass blower breathing his object into life. She advocates the creation of rich, imaginative spaces for engagement with the divine, which whilst drawing on a Hauerwasian communitarian ethics, offers itself in the service of a broader 'public becoming'.

Church within the city or city within the Church?

Urbanisation as a public challenge to the *communio sanctorum*

Daniël J. Louw

The Urban Way of Life

The basic presupposition of this paper is that 'the city' is a corporate identity. It is more than merely an 'urban setting'. City symbolizes a very specific fabric of human life; it refers to a way of life, a mode of being. 'The city is corporate human power in positive self-assertion and activity' (Willmer, 1989:33). In my view, the city symbolises the way people live together in a global world so that they are able to achieve significant control over their environment and cultural context. Therefore, one can view the 'global village' as a worldwide web and space that incorporates some view of humanity in its workings and operations. The city today shapes people's humanity and determines human wellbeing. It becomes a network of moral issues and therefore a moral concretisation of responsible or irresponsible humanity.

Wirth (1962:21 - 34) sees urbanism as a way of life. This description coincides with the view of Harvey Cox, 'Urbanization means a structure of common life in which diversity and disintegration of tradition are paramount. It means a type of impersonality in which functional relationships multiply. It means that a degree of tolerance and anonymity replaces traditional moral sanctions and longterm acquaintanceships.'(1967[3]:4)

The technological metropolis of the urban context projects a 'secular style' where the place of God and Christian faith is questioned anew. Cox divides the *manière d'être* of the secular city into its *shape* (anonymity and mobility as the social component), and its *style* (pragmatism and profanity as the cultural aspect). However, during the past three decades the 'secular city' of Cox has developed into the 'global village' of computer technology and the website of international communication and cyberspace. Both shape and style is determined by globalisation as a process of moulding human beings into a new species of human community.

To summarize, one can say that 'city' is the epitome of:

- A *mentality* and *attitude* of our being human in a global society.
- A *systemic network* of relationships determined by communication techno-logy.
- An indication of a qualitative rather than a quantative state of mind and being.
- An experience of space where architecture and structure projects pragma-tism and consumerism as well as a simulation of existence where digital communication projects a new species of being human, namely the cyber-space of cyberpunk culture.

City as a metaphor

The basic problem for the paper is a practical theological and ecclesiologi-cal one, namely how should the *communio sanctorum* be structured and how should our understanding of our being the church in a global society be ref-ramed in order to communicate the gospel in an appropriate way within the lifestyle of the urban website? What is meant by an ecclesiology for the ci-ty and how do global forces impact on people living in a very unique urban structure, the so-called townships of South Africa?

It is indeed true that city could represent many images. For example, *Je-rusalem* represents the *eschatological model* for citizens who view themselves as strangers and pilgrims with no abiding city (see also Fritz, 1995). In this 'theistic' understanding of city, the question at stake is whether God's pre-sence means anything for our largely secularised politics. How could the grace of God be embodied in social relationships so that city becomes a space for rediscovering human dignity? How should the Church meet the dangers of a possible dehumanised society?

Secondly, *Athens* represents *citizenship* as active participation in the affairs of the political community. This metaphor challenges a practical theological ecclesiology to take the notion of public theology, justice and human dignity seriously. On the other hand, *Calcutta* represents the *social predicament* of people exposed to poverty and structural violence. It refers to the impact of globalisation on local issues such as life within slum areas and squatter camps.

This paper is therefore an attempt to make an analysis of the features and characteristics of city life within the processes of globalisation and urbanisa-tion. Its main objective is to reflect on what it means to be the church in a context which demands a more public and inclusive approach to different life issues rather than a church-/official-centred and exclusive approach.

The first part explores the culture of the global village; the second part deals with contextuality and discusses the interplay between global forces and township life; the third part gives attention to an ecclesiology for the city.

Urbanisation: the metropolitan mentality of the global village

It is difficult to define postmodernity. To a certain extent postmodernity could be viewed as a philosophical stance which tries to sum up the current mode of thinking and being in the global village. It is even more difficult to distinguish between modernity and postmodernity. As linked to globalisation, postmodernity can be defined as a process wherein modernity (the critique of reason) has been expanded into relativity and deconstruction due to an intensified experience of translocation. Thus the following description of globalisation by Waters (1995:3): 'A social process in which the constraints of geography on social and cultural arrangements recede and in which people become increasingly aware that they are receding'.

Part and parcel of this ongoing process is what Waters calls processes of exchange. He divides it into three processes: (a) a local process of material exchanges: material exchanges localise; (b) political exchanges of support and networking: political exchanges internationalise; (c) symbolic exchanges by means of communication and electronic technology: symbolic exchanges globalise (1995:8 - 9).

Waters' further argument is that one cannot understand the global village without reckoning with the dominating force of *capitalism*. 'Capitalism encompasses two major processes which tend to increase the level of societal inclusion. First it is driven by a logic of accumulation that depends on progressively increasing the scale of production. Second it is driven by a logic of commodification or marketisation which drives it towards an increasing scale of consumption (Waters, 1995:36).

The global village: a new state and mode of being

The following features of a global mindset and mode of being can be identified:
- An *experience of disembeddedness* where local needs are daily moulded by a process of transnational internationalisation. Everyone is assessed in terms of the illusion of sameness.
- An *experience of the concentration of time and space*. This can be called a phenomenology of space concentration. It coincides with the shrinking of our planet; the annihilation of distance; the elimination of space and the generalisation of time.
- The *impact of managerial systems* and big companies on local businesses.
- The new *imperialism of the unknown*: trust in the incalculable and unpredictable forces of a market driven economy. One can even call the floating finance of stock exchanges as the economical exploitation of the 'capitalistic' beyond.

- *Fordism*: utilisation, standardisation and mechanisation in terms of mass production: 'It aims to reduce the cost per item by intensive mechanisation and by economics of scale in the utilisation of capital equipment' (Waters 1995:80).
- The *migration of labour*. Due to a *Gästarbeiter*-mentality (developed countries profit from the predicament of those in developing countries), temporary migration all over the globe takes place. People move temporarily according to booming economies.
- *Efficiency and McDonaldisation*. Due to the monopoly of consumerism, people develop a drive-through service mentality, geared towards instant satisfaction. 'McDonaldisation represents a reordering of consumption as well as production, a rationalisation of previously informal domestic practices, that pushes the world in the direction of greater conformity' (Waters 1995:144).
- The *idol of leisure and pleasure*: globetrotters and jetsetters within the global sport morale of *Sanssouci* (the coolness of indifference and the moral of fitness and leisure/recreation). Public activity or 'work' becomes more separated in time from domestic activity which means that to the extent that the latter is becoming undemanding, and could be defined as leisure. Leisure is not anymore restricted to feasts or holy days. It becomes a universal and general expectation. The *homo faber* becomes a tourist; the idea of travel for the sake of leisure and pleasure.
- The *digital expansion of place into cyberspace*. In his book, *The secular city*, H Cox refers to urbanisation as life in the 'secular city'. Due to globalisation and digitalisation, the concept of the '*secular city*' developed into the concept of the '*cyber city*'. Through virtual reality it is possible to simulate an existence in cyberspace, that is, to simulate a body and a space that can be varied by design and thus by choice. The citizens of the 'cyber city' live by the infinite variations of simulated existence and virtual realities.

Burning issues for urban ministry

The above mentioned features highlights the need to identify basic issues at stake which the church should take into consideration in designing a pastoral model for 'urban ministry'. (Bakke, 1997; Conn, 1997; Carle & DeCaro, 1997; Green, 1996; Northcott, 1998; Ortiz, 1996). The important burning issues and needs for an urban or cyber ministry which result from the previous exposition are:
- The culture of *achievement ethics*. Behind this issue lurks the need for a reassessment of norms and values which can address the important component of human dignity and identity within the global village.

– The culture of *detachment and the need for intimacy*, i.e. the need to be accepted unconditionally without the fear of rejection.
– *Disembeddedness* and the need for *intimacy and belonging*.

In terms of a practical theological ecclesiology for the cyber city, ministry should deal with these issues. In dealing with them, the Church should be aware of the importance of a *pastoral hermeneutics*: the art (empathy) of understanding the mentality of human beings within the global village/cyber city. Due to this pastoral hermeneutics, the Church has a new calling and vocation: not to move into the city, but to let the city be part of the liturgy of the Church. This is what we call a new stance: *city within the Church*; namely an understanding of existential issues which are at stake within a metropolitan mentality and a mode of *koinonia* wherein fellowship reflects current social and contextual realities as determined by an urban and global lifestyle.

Subcultures

Before we design a ministerial model for urban ministry (the Church in the city), the Church should become identified with the needs and mentality of 'cyber punks' (and 'website citizens'). In order to do this, a pastoral and ministerial hermeneutics must reckon with the following *subcultures* which are developing alongside the culture of the metropolis:

– *Glocalisation*: understanding the impact of globalisation on the development or on the hampering of local resources.
– *Fundamentalism*: the revival of oppressed sentiments within local, cultural regions.
– *Transpostmodernity*: within the processes of deconstruction and relativisation, the urgent need for reconstruction and reintegration is surfacing. This need touches the area of an integrative spirituality and wholeness.
– *Postglobalisation*: the process of 'housing' cyberspace with virtues and values that develop the capabilities of humans in order to cope with life. We can call this coping with life, the rearrangement of basic human capabilities or liberties as it reckons with development and maintenance of local cultural identity as well as global networking.

According to Martha Nussbaum, the focal point for developing human dignity in 'postglobalisation' and 'transpostmodernity', is the language of *capabilities*, rather than rights, liberties or functioning. 'The capabilities approach asks concretely, what people are *able* to do and to be' (Nussbaum, quoted in Lebaqz, 2001:119). Alongside key capabilities such as *affiliation* and *'friendship'*, basic Christian virtues like *compassion* and *'sacrifice'* are becoming of paramount importance.

The quest for intimacy and the need for capabilities bring us back to another question: If these are the basic virtues or capabilities required to live in the cyber city, how do these processes of globalisation and urbanisation impact on cultural contexts, such as the African context?

The impact on Africa: township life as sandwiched in between city and village

The predicament in South Africa is that the country is being forced to move rapidly from a rural setting to an urban environment (see Moolman, 1990). This movement occurred without the long process of *Aufklärung* as in the case of Europe.

Electronic and digital revolutions, along with rapid processes of political transformation, social changes and the democratisation of traditional policies, have meant that many countries in Africa were forced to move from a communal system to an individualised system; from a rural approach to an urban approach. (See Maasdorp & Humphreys, 1975:1 - 60). Due to financial and economic demands, people migrated to cities. The urban setting becomes the place for hope and job creation.

In South Africa, the policy of apartheid contributed to the fact that slums and squatter camps developed, the so-called townships. (For township development, see *Commission of inquiry*, 1984:3 - 7). *Townships* in South Africa could be described as the sandwiched in situation of people situated between urban consumerism and existential crises such as unemployment and poverty caused *inter alia* by the policy of apartheid. (See Becker, 1974:123 - 255). A township is a very unique place of location. Due to class and race discrimination, townships are located at the edge of the city. It became the marginalized place between the urban environment of consumption and the rural setting of traditional communality (the village).

A *village* can be described as a more rural setting determined by tribal system and traditional values. Its basic features are:
- Structural interconnectedness;
- Cultural communality and sense of belonging;
- Animated cosmology determined by spiritual forces;
- Interplay between ritual, life, play and tradition;
- Intimacy: support system of the extended family as embedded within the hierarchy of positions (discipline and respect).

The important point in understanding the South African context of township life is that people are caught between the bygone image of the romantic rural setting and the materialistic dreams of consumarised urban values. On the one hand, one cannot romanticize Africa anymore. On the other hand, the rhythm of urban life is replacing traditional values and forces people to live according to achievement ethics where identity is not determined by position, but measured by functions.

The *township* is a settlement where permanent structures (buildings) and informal structures (squatter camps) determine one another. Townships are located on the edge of the city and are subjected to the taxi-movement between inner city (industrial areas) and private life. People living in the townships become commuters between the darkness before sunrise and the darkness after sundown. People are therefore moulded into a lifestyle of commuting; they develop an attitude of impermanence and temporary commitment; they develop a wait and see stance where indifference replaces commitment. Black people are therefore forced into what can be called the continuous switching of roles, from being the humble garden boy for the madam to that of a dignified laypreacher, '... it remains a shuttle process between two worlds' (Hagg, 1990:20).

As a result, township mentality implies the in between of:

– The *illusion of wealth*: within the reality of chronic poverty and unemployment.
– The *flux of migration*: the in between of urban relationships and rural relationship.
– *Survival through violence*. Within the reality of crime and gangsterism, the slogan for life is not the survival of the fittest, but the survival of the criminal/the gangster; life is on a daily basis being determined by the in between of survival and violence.
– *Moral confusion*. Due to the Aids pandemic, and the fragmentation of life, morality is in turmoil; the in between of traditional values and secularisation.
– *Structural violence and destabilisation*. Due to a lack of appropriate health services, support system and educational institutions, people are exposed to confusion on a daily basis; the in between of permanency and temporariness.

In order to understand urbanisation in Africa, one needs to understand how urbanisation changed kinship patterns and customs. Berry (1998:29) refers to the fact that at the same time that the kinship system is in some ways narrowed down to the nuclear family system, it is also expanded in the urban context. This phenomenon is called 'tribalism', i.e. tribal allegiance and the expansion of the kinship system in order to survive. However, the important point to understand is that urbanisation has led to a deterioration of societal moral values which does not only impact on the family system, but on urban youth and their search for identity (see Mbuga, 1998:35).

Existential issues in township life

In terms of the objective of this paper, namely the design of a practical, theological ecclesiology for people living in both the cyber city and the township, the following basic existential problems can be identified: *aggressive behaviour; emotional suppression, and the coping mechanism of escapism* (for example, drugs and substance dependency). These existential problems should be assessed and understood within the culture of *ubunthu* where the basic rules are: the restoration of a sense of communality, rootedness and respect for authority.

These existential issues should force the Church to reflect anew on urban or township ministry. Due to the previous analyses, our basic thesis is that in order to design an appropriate, ministerial approach, three basic needs for restoring the human dignity of people living in urban settings should be addressed: the quest for intimacy (to be accepted unconditionally without the fear of rejection); the sense for belongingness (where being functions are more important than knowing and doing functions); the need for communality (interrelatedness).

Our exposition thus far poses the following question: how is the Christian Church going to respond to the challenges which have been put forth by processes of urbanisation and globalisation? What should the strategy and shape of ministry be within township life?

A ministerial approach: an ecclesiology for urban ministry

Basic human needs

Within the paradigm of urban ministry, the following basic human needs should be addressed: the need for embracement (grace and human dignity); the need for intimacy (unconditional love); spiritual direction (commitment to the ultimate and sound values); hope and meaning (imagination/vision and anticipation/future).

It is one of the theses of Geyer (1993:336) that theory formation and praxis should be oriented towards the needs of people living in the megapolis. In terms of the above mentioned basic needs, such as intimacy, belonging and communality, different routes for urban ministry should be explored.

Different routes for urban ministry

− The development of a *theology of communication and liberation*: It should be the prophetic task of the Church to voice the needs of the voiceless and to speak out against oppressive structures which deprive people from their basic rights. In this regard, a theology of liberation is appropriate.

- *Acts of service and community development* which embody and enflesh a compassionate *diakonia*;
- A *reframing of God-images*: Instead of an official and institutionalised God – the God of hierarchy – urban ministry needs a compassionate God. Within a pastoral assessment, pastoral ministry should consider God-images that portray the Partnership and Friendship of a living God.
- *Social competency*: The church should display a deep concern for social issues. Ministry should therefore focus on real social needs as related to poverty, violence and Aids. The social competency of the Church must re-present the engagement of God with public life (see Koch, 1991:69).
- *Developing a liturgy of the street*: The Church should become the open place and space where people with diverse cultural backgrounds and needs, meet. The Church and congregation must become an open space where diversity is being experienced as an enriching and stimulating event.
- *Church as a family*: The *communio sanctorum* should be structured accor- ding to the basic principles of fellowship and *koinonia*. The idea of the church as a family necessitates a small group approach. This model im- plies interaction and sharing. In order to apply this model, there should be a presence of the church beyond the so-called 'official paradigm'. Lay people should therefore be equipped in order to make contact with people in their homes and working places. It is becoming the task of the Church in urban ministry to start with networking: the bringing together of different cultural groups and diverse needs within local settings. Lindner (2000:240) refers in this regard to the interconnectedness of above and below.
- *Plurality of congregational structures*: In order to minister to diversity and plurality, several different congregational structures and models should be in place. There is not anymore 'one approach' possible. If the Church is going to be relevant to urban life, different approaches and model should be designed. There is not 'one strategy' which can really address the needs of people living in the megapolis (see Löwe, 1999:446).

Conclusion

In the light of the different features of urban life and the characteristics of the cyber city, a design for a practical theological ecclesiology should reckon with the following dynamic ecclesial movements:

- From formal institution to a more informed space of grace (*soteria*): the congregation (a small group approach) as a place of healing and a space of spiritual retraite. (Silence and solitude; experiencing the presence of God). (For a multidimensional healing of the city, see Ellison, 1999:38 - 42).

– From communication to *communio* (fellowship, *koinonia*): the small group approach. (Home visitation; marriage and family enrichment). The principle of *koinonia* implies another paradigm shift: from polarised thinking in township life, towards synergistic cooperation (see Fritz, 1998:17).
– From entertainment to worship and mutual sharing (*sacramentum*): narrative preaching, participation of members, sharing through prayers. (Utilising the eucharist for a celebration of healing).
– From *kerygma*/pulpit to a liturgy of care (*leitourgia*): developing a caring congregation/community. (Equipment of layworkers; grief groups; hospital care; prison care; visiting the sick' terminal care and the Aids pandemic).
– From dogma to charisma (*marturia*): the sacrificial life stance of reaching out. (Cellgroup approach in flats and the townships).
– From office (hierarchical authority) to service (*diakonia*): community development. (Overnight shelters and food kitchens).
– From church building to family worship, (family-/marriage-/relationship-enrichment) *oikodomein*: (Projects focusing on prevention, the empowerment of people and the enrichment of family life).
– From formal catechism (Youth education, the accent on rational knowledge and church dogmatics) to life learning (*didache*). (Youth education and the development of life skills; the integration of faith and life).
– From denomination to corporate unity (*oikumene*): Ecumenical cooperation. (Cooperative and joint ecumenical projects).
– From management/bureaucratic administration to care (*parakalein*): Developing the church as a caring community. (Pastoral identity: pastor as soul friend, guide to and interpreter of life).

References

Bakke, R. (1997) *A theology as big as the city*. Downers Grove: InterVarsity Press.

Becker, P. (1974) *Tribe to township*. St Albans: Panther Books.

Berry, E. (1998) Family support and the African city. *Urban Mission* 16(2), 27 - 33.

Carle, R. & Decaro, L (Jr) (eds) (1997) *Signs of hope in the city: ministries of community renewal*. Valley Forge: Judson Press.

Commission of Inquiry. (1984) *Commission of inquiry into township establishment and related matters*. Pretoria: Staatsdrukker.

Conn, H. (ed) (1997) *Planting and growing urban churches: from dream to reality*. Grand Rapids: Baker Books.

Cox, H. (1967³) *The secular city*. London: SCM Press.

Ellison, C. (1999) Healing in the city. *Urban Mission*, 16(3), 38 - 42, March.

Fritz, V. (1995) *The city in ancient Israel*. Sheffield: Sheffield Academic Press.

Fritz, P.J. (1998) African decision-making styles: urban and rural. *Urban Mission*, 16(2), 15 - 25.

Geyer, C. (1993) Forderung und These. in C. Bäumler (ed.) *Menchlich leben in der verstäderten Gesellshachaft. Kirchliche Praxis zwischen Öffenlichkeit und Privatheit*. Gütersloh: Chr. Kaiser/Gütersloher Verlagshaus, 336 - 346.

Green, C.J. (1996) (ed) *Churches, cities, and human community: urban ministry in the United States, 1945 - 1985*. Grand Rapids: William B. Eerdmans.

Hagg, G. (1990) A window on township art. in G-M. Van der Waal & G. Hagg (eds) *Venster op die stad / A window on township art*. Potchefstroom: Instituut vir Reformatoriese Studie.

Koch, T. (1991) Wofür die Kirche gut sein könnte. in H.W. Dannowski et al. *Kirche in der Stadt*. Hamburg: Steinmann & Steinmann, 63 - 73.

Lebacqz, K. (2001) Faith, globalisation, the economy, the earth and fullness of life. *Reformed World* 51(3), 116 - 122.

Lindner, H. (2000) *Kirche am Ort. Ein Entwicklungsprogramm für Ort Gemeinde*. Stuttgart: Kohlhammer.

Löwe, F.W. (1999) *Das Problem der Citykirchen unter dem Aspekt der urbanen Gemeindestruktur*. Münster: Lit Verlag.

Maasdorp, G. & Humphreys, A.S.B. (eds) (1975) *From Shantytown to township: an economic study of African poverty and rehousing in a South African city*. Cape Town: Juta.

Mbuga, L.G. (1998) Understanding African urban youth. *Urban Mission* 16(2), 34 - 43, December.

Moolman, M. (1990) *From town to township: regional services councils assessed*. Johannesburg: South African Institute of Race Relations.

Mutunga, S. (1998) Africa's urban search for identity. *Urban Mission* 16(2), 7 - 13 December.

Northcott, M.S. (ed) (1998) *Urban theology: a reader*. Herndon: Cassell.

Ortiz, M. (1996) *One new People: models for developing a multiethnic Church*. Downers Grove: InterVarsity Press.

Waters, M. (1995) *Globalization*. London/New York: Routledge.

Watson, P. (2002[3]) *A terrible beauty. The people and ideas that shaped the modern mind*. London: Phoenix Press.

Wilmer, H. (1989) Images of the city and the shaping of humanity. in A. Harvey (ed.) *Theology in the city*. London: SPCK, 32 - 46.

Wirth, L. (1962) Urbanism as a way of life. in R. Lee (ed.) *Cities and churches*. Philadelphia: Westminister.

Christian Mission in a Pluralistic, Unjust and Violent World

Ottmar Fuchs

The example of a missionary

My thesis is this: it is my opinion that, in the light of the present situation in Western society and globally, the mission of the Church has become more necessary than ever. I start with a very concrete reflection, with a kind of human personal 'artefact' on our topic, and shall from there arrive step by step at the basic structures of Christian mission and its implications for public theology.

I would like to tell the story of Father Rudolf Lunkenbein. We find this Salesian Father in 1970 in Merúri with the Bororo-Indians in the Amazon area of Mato Grosso. He has been given the order to evangelise this tribe. Soon he realises: the whole tribe faces extinction. And this is not nature's doing but has been caused by people. In the background is the clash with the white landowners and settlers who penetrate deeper and deeper into the territory of the indigenous people, and are close to distributing everything among themselves. Because the former have gradually lost the basis of their way of life, the rain forest, they have given up. Since the mid-sixties they have stopped building new huts, and have even stopped caring for their own language. The women drink the juice of a forest plant which inhibits conception. For six years no children have been born. The whole tribe has resigned itself to die. It is this situation into which Fr. Lunkenbein enters as a missionary with the order to preach the gospel to them.

But how to bring the message of a living God for people to whom the right to life is jeopardised from outside, and who cannot be revived inwardly, to whom death is wished and who are seeking death themselves? In this situation the priest realises very quickly: one cannot talk about the message of life if opportunities for living are not created simultaneously. One cannot speak of God's redemption without talking at the same time about liberation from injustice and the borders of death, without fighting for *this* kind of plurality: that this tribe remains in the plurality of life. He thus writes: 'First it is necessary to help these people to find the way back to life … , to show them what they have in themselves, what inner strengths they neglect, what magnificent traditions they let go waste. I have supported them, I have defended their rights' (Roehrig, 1978). Against this background, one understands how happy Fr. Lunkenbein was about the first baptism, not only because children were re-born into God's grace but because they were born at all.

On 15th July 1976, however, Fr. Lunkenbein and the local chief were shot dead by white settlers in the court-yard of the mission station. The settlers were angry about the revival of the tribe they believed was finished, and wanted revenge for the fact that, with the help of Rudolf Lunkenbein, a land survey in favour of the Bororo Indians had taken place.

Initially Fr. Lunkenbein wanted to become a missionary in the old sense of the word, namely to bring the faith to the 'unbelievers'. But then he entered into a situation which first demanded a totally different missionary testimony, namely to give up one's life in the fight for life and survival of these people. This connection developed its own dynamism, because at some time he must have recognised the choice before him: to get more involved or to get out? He could have got out, the more so as there were *confrères* in his own congregation who preferred a certain neutrality and non-interference, who understood mission in the old restricted sense of spreading religious faith which does not enter very much into the conflicts of the world.

In Fr. Lunkenbein I see a model for that process concerning the *prior* recognition of *all* people as 'God's children' within the horizon of God's universal grace, in which spreading the Gospel and practising solidarity universalise and radicalise each other. Universalisation applies insofar as the Gospel message which proclaims salvation in the form of human solidarity is granted, awarded and given to all people; radicalisation as a motif which can pull one into a dynamism which 'finally' also risks self-abandon in history for this gift of God, something which can never be ordered but only enabled in the context of a relationship with God whereby this relationship attains the quality of adoring devotion and devoted adoration. This devotion to God (as confidence in God's power over life, justice and reconciliation in history, beyond history and beyond death) deepens the devotion in favour of people and vice versa. The acknowledgment and sheltering of plurality needs solidarity.

Mission as the universalisation of Christian and Church pro-existence (the 'external' aspect)

Firstly I would emphasise the universal responsibility to express in the form of 'be-ing' human with and for the people (co- and pro-existence) the fact that God loves all people even before they have changed. Christianity can refer to its own long history of misinterpreting God's universality which has cost millions of people the possibilities of living, freedom and finally life itself. Religion inhibits solidarity whenever it restricts God's love to an exclusive area and considers all those who don't belong to that particular faith, hardly or not at all worthy of solidarity. On the other hand religion always accelerates solidarity if it grants God's love to all people and experiences one's own area as a learning field where one's inwardly-directed solidarity turns towards the outside (Fuchs, 1993). Every religious chauvinism applies God's mercy only *to itself*, and thus renders itself universal in relation to others, thereby losing sight completely of God's mercy for all creatures. Universalistic and thus integralistic strategies form the sharpest contradiction to resistance to the only existing universality, namely God himself. However, this imposes a specific challenge to Christian experience, not simply to render itself universal but to detect God's grace in the world and to help to shape it. The problem of 'inward-outward' has never stopped being a problem. The letter of the Bible alone does not protect us from a religiously-motivated withdrawal of solidarity; only the spirit and the intention respectively with which the Bible is read, namely that dynamism towards a more merciful God and a more universal inter-human solidarity (Fuchs, 1998). The Christian creed thus coincides with human rights (Sander, 1999). This is necessarily a missionary dynamism. Everything depends on a 'globalised' understanding of grace within the horizon of a radical theology of justification. For only within it can God's grace relate to all people in such a way that solidarity with all people is possible for those who believe in this God.

In our world-historical context it is absolutely necessary to promote this missionary dynamism as a globalisation of solidarity. The neo-liberal and capitalist globalisation which has already pushed more than one billion people below the poverty line and into absolute misery, and which has not only sharpened the gulf between North and South but also between the poorest and the richest in any society, has to be countered by all powers of good will, namely the globalisation of a solidarity which embraces all people and all nations. It will have to be a solidarity which is not based on egotism but includes also the renunciation of one's own advantages. This global solidarity has to be implemented in time before wars of drought and famine will force rich countries to respond; or what is more probable, before states with military and economic strength fall into the terrible temptation to close their borders, exposing millions and most likely billions of people to death from thirst and hunger. Whoever does not want to share now will have to kill later on!

In order to motivate towards this global solidarity, and to open people's view, one needs relevant fields where solidarity is experienced within the more comprehensible area of local social forms and societal life. Unless it is learned there it will not be realised towards the outside. But the opposite is also valid. Where people in missionary institutions, in missionary congregations, third-world groups and partnerships care for the poor and distressed in the countries of the Southern hemisphere, they learn to consider also more critically their own contexts and to meet the local victims of the situation with greater solidarity. For the sake of the universal option for the poor a mutual global networking of solidarity [1] is needed between inside and outside, between near and far. Structurally this would have to be realised in stronger networking between relevant institutions and initiatives. [2]

Mission as radicalisation of Christian and Church existence (the internal aspect)

Mission by 'martyrium'

Whoever transmits in word and deed God's grace, and thus God's justice, to the people knows that they will never fall out of this grace but knows also that this handing over of God's and the people's justice and charity may cost them dearly in ungraceful and graceless contexts. It is an integral part of the experience of God's grace that human witness to God's grace approaches powerlessness and thus carries the risk of long- as well as short-term martyrdom, be it the 'martyrium fidei', or the 'martyrium caritatis'. In the face of a threatening lack of meaning and success, faith preaches that it is never in vain to spend oneself in justice and mercy even if it does not seem to make sense. The Gospel contains the eschatological message that nothing but mercy and justice are the realities which fulfil God's kingdom on earth, and will find eternal realisation in God's kingdom. The option for the poor is not a programme of success but provokes additional experiences of powerlessness and failure for those who take it seriously. To be able to believe that God (in the meaning of Roman 8:26) is not indifferent to this suffering, especially bearing such powerlessness in the crucified Christ, is at the core of the Christian message which strengthens action and perseverance.

From the early beginning of Christendom there existed something like the epistemological axiom that the identity of Christian and Church existence can

---

[1]   Regarding this 'new Catholicity' between globality and locality, see Schreiter, 1997.

[2]   Regarding the relationship between Christian faith, networking in parity and solidarity with those far away see Zulehner, 1996, 215. This paper proves in examples that fundamentalist-exclusive concepts of faith and social forms (such as those which regionalise God's grace to their own area) are not able to develop solidarity with those far away. On the other hand, religiosity which breathes the freedom of God's universal grace forms the seed-bed for that solidarity to those near *and* far which is so decisive for our society, for the survival of democracy and the whole globe.

be decisively learnt from the men and women martyrs of the Church. In his texts at the turning of the millennium, John Paul II called the Church not to abandon the remembrance of global and local martyrs but to deepen and shape it. In 'Incarnationis Mysterium' he says: 'The faithful who has seriously considered his Christian calling for which martyrdom is a possibility already announced in the revelation cannot exclude this perspective from the horizon of his life.' (Jean Paul II, 1998) If Christians are not to give up on God's mercy in a merciless world but preach and realise it, the coming century will mean for them the way of the cross. Jesus has not paid back with his own coin, 'the mendacious judgement and the violent attack but turned the intensified evil and gave it back as doubled love' (Schwager, 1990, 146). One should not fool oneself and others: every step towards a solidarity which extends beyond present borders, and towards further poor and discriminated ones brings massive structural and individual counter-forces into the arena. The declaration of a limitless mercy of God cannot do without meeting these borders *and* penetrating through them. It is then a special mercy of God in history if people accept risks for this.

On account of the self-commitment to solidarity there was and always is also the self-commitment for the sake of this faith. At first sight there seems to be less claim for this martyrdom out of faithfulness to Christ in a world with a plurality of religions. Martyrdom remains nevertheless a real possibility within the context of fundamentalist and theocratic forms of religion which are more likely to increase than to decrease in numbers. In the so-called postmodern societies too, lack of understanding and possibly also disadvantage are growing for those who, in the face of people with different views and different beliefs, stand up in an non-egalitarian manner for the claim that their own faith is truth. Altogether, a hard battle is necessary to counter the religious trends towards trivialisation and banality, the super-quick fulfilment and thus the obstruction of transcendental yearning.

It is the relationship with Christ which breaks through any effort to remove plausibility from martyrdom even if it is well meant and justified by charity. At any time, and even today, there would have been reasons to stifle such radical over-exertion with soothing arguments. The charitable removal of plausibility from martyrdom is not new,[3] but is met already in the story told by Mark 14: 3 - 9 immediately prior to Jesus' passion. Jesus is sitting at table in Simon's house. A woman enters with costly oil in a precious alabaster vessel, breaks the vessel and pours the oil over Jesus' head. Some of his disciples are displeased

---

[3] Incidentally as little as the removal of pastoral plausibility from eschatological dynamism; see Fuchs, 2002. It cannot be discussed in detail here in how far the dynamism of mission and that of eschatology belong together.

and find an argument to rationalise their indignation by quoting Jesus' charitable teaching. What a luxury: one could have given the money which was spent for these precious objects to the poor. But Jesus, who always supports the poor, protects the woman and states that she has done a good deed, and justifies it thus: 'The poor are always with you, and you can always do good to them as often as you want but you do not have me always.' In this moment he stands up in favour of the wasteful instead of the charitable action; and we have here a precious epiphany of a deep encounter and commitment which will not return and should not be gambled away. Such moments of giving oneself away without doing any calculations whatsoever are not at the expense of the poor and do not want to put them to shame, but are the experience of that depth of life in which people learn that sensibility and receive that strength which render them unconditionally capable to exert themselves for others.

All this is not so dramatic in our present situation in Western Europe. Yet as the term 'martyrium' (testimony) implies, even the smallest testimonial to dramatic martyrdom is concerned with 'bearing witness' to the Gospel. Everything, even martyrdom, originates in 'its small coin', or to use a biblical picture, in the form of a small mustard seed which can reach full maturity very quickly. This may happen in the readiness to confess to a merciful and just God; in the readiness for action in the context of assistance to and solidarity with the troubled near-by and far-away; and, in particular for the readiness to risk not abandoning such actions if own disadvantages and discriminations have to be accepted.

In their commitment to the lives of others, Christians in many countries go so far that this 'overstepping of borders' costs them their lives. Faith without remembering them is like preaching resurrection without the cross. These martyrs, women and men, are an example that the ultimate consequence of Christian life can be to receive from God and to be dispossessed by people (Weckel, 1998). Whoever stands for God's de-limiting justice for the sake of those who are excluded must be prepared to sacrifice their own life-chances.

Mission in un-fanatical devotion

Thus, from the perspective of normal rationalisation, each act of extreme testimony is perceived as not at all understandable and as utterly unnecessary. And yet, the affected know what is needed in that very moment even though they are often not able rationally to apprehend the need. It is what Dietrich Bonhoeffer experienced in 1939 in New York. Without being able to explain to his friends and even to himself but out of an existential evidence which is finally unfathomable, he feels compelled to leave the USA through the depth of his faith and to return back to Germany,[4] although previous plans had actually been quite different. After having refused to stay on in New York, Dietrich Bonhoeffer writes on 20th July 1939: 'For me this has probably more meaning at the moment than I am able to see clearly. God alone knows. It is strange, in all my decisions I am not really clear about the motives. Is this a sign of lack of clarity, inner untruthfulness or is it a sign of the fact that we are led beyond our knowledge or is it both? In the end one is more likely to act from a level which remains hidden. ... At the end of the day I can only pray that God judges this day and all decisions mercifully. It is now in his hand' (Bonhoeffer, 1958).

God's 'transcendence' experienced in history means an unconditional challenge which in the end can neither be caught through argument nor calculation. Bonhoeffer could have found good ethical arguments, justifiable in Christian faith, for remaining in New York, but an existential decision was needed which, having weighed up the argument at a rational level, finally puts its appreciation of the truth with confidence into God's hand. Dietrich Bonhoeffer exposed himself to that process, and without thinking that he could model his life self-determinedly, subordinated it to his availability to do God's will.

Something peculiar, totally anti-fundamentalist presents itself here, namely the strict connection between absolute self-devotion and non-claimed absolute truth regarding this decision which totally affects one's own self. Bonhoeffer hoped that his decision was the right one, but did not know if it was, neither as regards intellectual capacity nor his relationship with God. He put the validity of the truth of his ultimate decision in God's hand. Such a relationship with God leaves it to God to judge the validity of one's own decision even if this decision is ultimate for one's own existence. It also protects against fatalism and fanaticism, which often manifest themselves in the temptation to claim for oneself and for others God's ultimate truth in the quality of the finality of a decision which affects one's own existence. Bonhoeffer makes it very clear. In no decision, even one of great consequence regarding his own Christian identity, does he claim God's absolute truth. Otherwise, even in this moment, the great temptation would be to make God an idol through one's own divinisation based on the claim of a radical self-devotion.

Result and outlook

Based on these reflections one can develop something like a critical hermeneutic of Christian 'martyrium', in particular within the present actual context in

---

[4]   In his Christology Bonhoeffer so develops that Christ's presence in those who suffer which renders compassion to be the decisive sense organ of Christian doing; see Kallen, 1997, 158 - 164.

which the term martyrdom is publicly mainly used in connection with suicidal terrorists. Not in the least from that latter aspect, a new and also theological, debate about Christian martyrdom is needed. The criteria are clear. The debate must not take place against people but only for them, and in principle for all of them, for justice towards them, and for their redemption from poverty and suppression. It must not become dissociated from these criteria of the Gospel. Longing for death alone is not martyrdom, which can ever only happen as a consequence of a life and an identity measured against the life of Jesus of Nazareth who did not sacrifice others but himself. Christian martyrdom must not get tempted to claim divinity for itself as if this unconditional self-abandon would entitle one to unconditional access to God's will. Even in martyrdom the human being remains what he or she is, needing redemption and being sinful.

If Fr. Lunkenbein committed his own life for the Indians, then this act of service may end in a total loss of life, but also in an encounter with life in its fullness. What he considers absolute in his own existence (because it is the will of the Absolute – God – to be on the side of the poor), is at the root of his testimonial. After centuries of Church mission during which Christianity's claim to absoluteness often went against those it subordinated and excluded, with disastrous effects, Fr. Lunkenbein puts this claim of self-abnegation on himself. There is no other form of mission for spreading the Gospel.

Thus, Christianity somehow takes seriously the polemic request from the Berlin philosopher, Herbert Schnaedelbach (2000), to step down from history's stage and to dissolve itself. This means in our perspective to step down from history in a very particular form, namely the hitherto used form of 'blanket coverage' approach to spreading the faith, with the simultaneous risk of hurting people's dignity, and to replace it by a new way of being which is much nearer to the core of Christianity's identity. This means that the old way of being is replaced by one in which Christianity exerts itself for the sake of human dignity, the dignity of all people. Plurality is an ambivalent word, if there is not a power which shelters those who are potentially dispossessed by their difference from those who have all the resources and power to define the identity of these 'others'.

References

Bonhoeffer, Dietrich (1958) *Gesammelte Schriften I*. München: Huber.

Fuchs, Ottmar (1993) *God's People: Instruments of Healing*. Berne: Peter Lang.

Fuchs, Ottmar (1998) Kriterien gegen den Missbrauch der Bibel. *Jahrbuch für Biblische Theologie* 12, 243-274.

Fuchs, Ottmar (2002) New ways for pastoral eschatology, in J. S. Dreyer and J. A. van der Ven (eds), *Divine Justice – Human Justice*. Pretoria: Unisa, 19-38.

Johannes Paul II (1998) Incarnationis Mysterium. *Verlautbarungen des Apostolischen Stuhls* Nr. 136. Bonn.

Roehrig, H.-G. (1978) *Lasst uns leben. Ermordet für die Rechte der Indianer*. Bamberg: Otto.

Sander, Hans-Joachim (1999) *Macht in der Ohnmacht. Eine Theologie der Menschenrechte*. Freiburg/Br.: Herder.

Schnaedelbach, Herbert (2000) Der Fluch des Christentums. *Die Zeit* 20 (11. Mai 2000) 41 - 42.

Schreiter, Robert J. (1997) *Die neue Katholizität. Globalisierung und die Theologie*. Frankfurt/M.: Patmos.

Schwager, Raymund (1990) *Jesus im Heilsdrama. Entwurf einer biblischen Erlösungslehre*. Innsbruck: Tyrolia.

Weckel, L. (1998) *Um des Lebens willen. Zu einer Theologie des Martyriums aus befreiungstheologischer Sicht*. Mainz: Matthias Grünewald.

Zulehner, Paul M. (1996) *Solidarität. Option für die Modernisierungsverlierer*. Innsbruck: Tyrolia.

Meeting the Public Church in my Life

Experiences, observations, conclusions

Karl Ernst Nipkow

For Konrad

Initial theoretical outlines

The following is not an academic analysis, but a biographically-tinged essay, glimpses of how I experienced a public church in very different situations. Nevertheless, my argument will be devoid neither of theoretical background (see this introduction) nor systematic conclusions (see summary).

Explicitly speaking of a 'public church' indicates that today we are about to regain something that has been lost. It is *the loss of the taken-for-granted nature of the church as a powerful public reality*. One hundred years ago, 'the worlds of work, school, and worship intertwined in ways that allowed children to learn the same values from the same people in all spheres of their lives' (Osmer and Schweitzer, 2000, 36). In those days, the church didn't *speak* about itself as a public church, it simply *acted* as the omnipresent public body. In their brilliant analysis, Richard Osmer and Friedrich Schweitzer have recently described how the process of modernization, which in its heart is one of *functional differentiation*, was to displace religion from its traditional role as 'sacred canopy' (Berger, 1967), leaving it 'as merely one subsystem among others' with a puzzling 'role uncertainty' (Osmer and Schweitzer, 2000, 43) and 'diminished social support' (p. 44) at that.

A second introductory remark is to be addressed to the *church* itself. *Does the church really want to regain a public role* if this will inevitably mean being exposed to the tempests of our time with its competing pluralism and postmodern relativism? My response is given in a quote from Parker J. Palmer:

The public expression of great religious truths gives us our best chance to find the framework of love and justice within which true pluralism can thrive ... Perhaps we resist true public worship because worship in private allows us to emphazise that which makes us different, that which divides us, rather than that which unites. In private, in the company of 'our kind', we can find our uniqueness and even denigrate others without being checked against reality, without being called to account. But public expression is accountable. Under the pressure of accountability religious discourse may be forced to reach for the essentials which unite us. (Palmer, 1986, 138)

My third remark wants to clarify *terminology*. There are three spheres to be distinguished, the private, the political and the public sphere. [1] I would define a 'public church' as a church that directly or indirectly contributes to public issues according to the mandate of the church. The 'public sphere' is not identical with the 'sphere of polity' which covers the field of political administration and parties. The 'public sphere' is related to democracy as a 'civil society' which encompasses all citizens and social institutions, today in a global scope.

Eventually, within this framework, my specific interest is to go in for a *broad concept* of public church activities, preferably at the grassroots level. It is this focus on a greater variety in different historical contexts and on events that have taken place that has prompted me to look at my own life as a point of departure, no more.

The public church as a caring church – the von Bodelschwingh institutions

I was born in December 1928 in Bethel, a small community of Christian charity in the north-western part of Germany, now belonging to Bielefeld, a middle-sized city. Bethel has become famous for the von Bodelschwingh institutions, a large assemblage of homes and hospitals for disabled, ill and disadvantaged people, in particular epileptics and persons with multiple disabilities, and founded in the 1860s. Now, altogether 26,000 people live either in Bethel itself or in other affiliated sites in Germany, almost half of them being patients or others in receipt of treatment, the other half employees in various fields of medicine and therapy, including different schools and training centres. The institutions are the biggest of their kind in Europe, and exemplify the idea of *a public church as a caring church*.

Although my parents didn't live in Bethel itself, I saw and learned to know what it meant to take care of extremely disabled persons. Later my future wife worked in one of the Bethel schools. Bethel stands for the Christian commitment in the field of *diakonia*. For the von Bodelschwingh institutions, a living diaconate means 'preaching through the hands'.

---

[1]   Among others see R. J. Neuhaus (1986) *The Naked Public Square: Religion and Democracy in America*, Grand Rapids, Michigan: W. B. Eerdmans, 2nd ed., p. 141.

A central New Testament story as a spiritual resource of the daily work is the one about a father who brings his epileptic son to Jesus (Mk 9: 14 - 29). He tells Jesus what's the matter when a crowd had gathered:

'Teacher, I brought you my son. The boy has a spirit that makes him unable to speak, and whenever it seizes him, it dashes him down; and he foams and grinds his teeth and becomes rigid.' (Mk 9: 17 - 18)

The Christians in Bethel are passionate dreamers. They envisage the Kingdom of God as something that is about to throw the divine light and the power of God's love and care on their work here on earth. For them it is imperative to embody God's overwhelming goodness by living with the sick in sensitivity, compassion, and patience. Bethel is a place of Christian and humanitarian care without which the world would be an ugly place.

The public church as a critically intervening and resisting church – health service policy and euthanasia

There are times when this kind of Christian caring has to be accompanied by *public interventions*, by raising the voice for those who are 'unable to speak' (see Mk 9: 17). One such situation at present is the strangulating *public health service policy*. Germany, a country with an admittedly high standard in this field, is nevertheless facing growing social and medical disparities. Curtailing the budgets is about to lead to unequal burdens, much more at the cost of the poor than of the rich, more to the benefit of the pharmaceutical companies than to the maintenance of an equal and careful treatment of all sick people independent of their status and financial resources. Acute analyses stimulated by a humanitarian and Christian ethos see the deteriorating development creeping through the hospitals, turning care into dehumanizing routines, thus subtly eroding the medical ethos of the clinical personnel. The hospital staff is being squeezed 'between economy, technology, and humanity' (Goerg, 2001). The worst perspective is the idea of denying people beyond the age of 75 medical help without which they would be unable to live (as in the case, for example, of kidney dialysis patients). This shockingly reminds me of the following historical crime.

In 1910, the Revd Fritz von Bodelschwingh, the youngest son of Friedrich von Bodelschwingh (the major founder) became the head of the Bethel institutions. During the Nazi regime he successfully resisted the delivery of his mentally-ill patients to the *mass euthanasia executions* ordered by Hitler, a brave example of public resistance, whilst almost all the other German asylums obeyed the instructions of the Nazi authorities.

In contrast to academic theology, the practical work of Christians in caring institutions earns the highest public appreciation, and this in an astonishing historical continuity. The caring church is an expression of 'doing theology' for the benefit of people independently of their social status and religious affiliation. Its strength lies in its encompassing openness without any exclusion. It represents a universalist moral and religious ethos rooted in the particularity of a living specific faith tradition,not in an abstract concept which so often leaves behind the ways of 'an ethic enacted in life' (Osmer and Schweitzer, 2000, 54).

The public church as the prophetically remembering and confessing church – the Ernst Kaesemann case

Two months before my tenth birthday, in the night of the 9th of November 1938, all over Germany hundreds of synagogues were set on fire by special forces of the National Socialist state party (NSDAP). They also smashed the windows of innumerable Jewish shops, looting them and attacking the owners, quite a few of whom were killed.

At the Sunday following this so-called *Reichs Kristallnacht* ('Crystal Night'), to use the euphemistic national jargon, the Lutheran minister Ernst Kaesemann held his service in his parish in one of the industrial towns in the Ruhr area. He belonged to the 'Confessing Church' (*Bekennende Kirche*) which opposed the regime in important respects. Kaesemann had chosen a reading from the prophet Isaiah, the same one chosen for his own funeral service which I attended as one of his colleagues much later in Tuebingen, where he was to teach as a famous New Testament scholar.

> O LORD our God,
> other Lords besides you have
> ruled over us,
> but we acknowledge your name
> alone.
> (Isaiah 26: 13)

Kaesemann's congregation understood. He himself knew that he was being watched by secret agents, members of the notorious GESTAPO (Secret State Police). Shortly afterwards he was arrested and imprisoned. This is an example of the church as a public church in the field of *preaching* – now becoming a public church of *warning, remembering and awakening* the conscience. However, the majority of German ministers and parishes kept silent, many of them in those years harbouring anti-Semitic feelings.

We hit upon the sad fact that the church *does* play a public role anyway, even when, ostrich-like it puts its head in the sand, dodging public responsibility. A neutral position is no excuse, since neutrality implies keeping silent, a compliance which indirectly assists the existing power structures. There is no escape. I am not in any way denying the paralyzing character of a dictatorship with its systematic pressure on free opinion, a conformist state press, the climate of denunciation and a wide-spread fear in the population, where even in one's own family parents could not be sure of not being blamed and denunciated by their children. We grew up in those days under the influence of constant ideological indoctrination and military manipulation. The regime knew about the most effective means of suppressing the mind and colonising the soul to produce a destructive potential of deep-rooted structural militant inclinations.

In July 1944, after the invasion of the allied troops at the coast of France, one of our teachers came to us in our anti-aircraft site at the fringes of our town – we were then just 15 years old – in order to continue the poor amount of schooling we were receiving. When we asked him about the chances of the invasion of the allied troops in France, he frankly uttered his doubts about the final victory of the German forces, whereupon we had a debate among ourselves whether to or not to tell the authorities. I am still happy that we did not.

Individual Christians representing the public church – the case of Johann K.

In the 1930s, under the Nazis, my wife's father belonged to the rural police in East Prussia. In 1934, one year after Adolf Hitler had taken over, he was attending a service one Sunday morning, dressed as usual in his uniform. Suddenly, members of the special forces of the state party rushed in and arrested the minister from the pulpit. It was an incredible, unprecedented scene. My father-in-law, Johann K., rose, protested, took the names, and reported to his office; he considered the action as clearly illegal. The ensuing case, however, was against him, not against the law-breakers. The case was packed with a lot of false accusations. Witnesses were sought to rake up incriminating evidence against him: once he had indeed said, 'The Nazis are our greatest enemies'. Witnesses in his defence were not permitted. He was found guilty, fined and given another post of minor status in another place. He had acted in a threefold way, as a citizen, as a guardian of the legal order, and as a Christian, a member of the local congregation.

Yet an individual public Christian commitment was possible in more ways than the German population was prepared to imagine, the congregations included. The famous studies of the Anglo-Jewish historian Martin Gilbert have revealed the actions of Christians and of Church institutions to assist in the protection and rescue of Jews throughout Nazi-occupied Europe. In Germany, these actions were much more limited in numbers, because the vast majority of people believed in Hitler. At that time they had not yet undergone any thoroughgoing democratic education. The Weimarian conservative national elite, including leading theologians, had been busy in systematically delegitimizing the new democratic constitution (Tanner, 1989). In that dreadful period of German history, protest was theoretically an option, but a risky one in public with risky and shameful results.

I shall never forget the moment when two state youth leaders in uniform were standing in our sitting-room in threatening postures pressing my parents to let me become a member in the state youth organisation. Recruiting started early, at the age of ten, in order to rally boys around the flag of the regime at an age which we all know to be susceptible to ideological seduction by the grandeur of the national scheme. My parents felt obliged to give in.

A public church's dynamics in new social movements – the peaceful revolution 1989 and other examples

After the Second World War it took me some time to cleanse myself of what the Nazi propaganda had left as a subtle poison in my soul and an ugly imprint on my mind. In this process my next discovery was a *public church embodied in Christian groups, associations and movements*. First I became a member of a voluntary Lay Bible Group of friends of mine at my age, second of a Christian-Jewish Association in my home town, the aims and goals of which were gradually to renew mutual understanding and reconciliation between Church and Synagogue. At University I became a member of the Student Christian Movement, and later I encountered adherents of the Taizé community. From 1968 to 1983 I served in commissions of the World Council of Churches and learned about the ecumenical movement intimately. After the Fifth Assembly of the WCC in Nairobi in 1975, my wife and I joined an ecological organization. Let me use these examples for a more generalized observation concerning public theology and pressure groups and movements.

Today, the public church is no longer identical with the structures of the official church. On the one hand, many younger Christians and non-Christians miss the vitality of religious (and political) movements, while, on the other hand, they are willing to initiate projects and join campaigns provided they get the chance of participation in a way that allows for actively shaping the outcomes through their own commitment. Thus, in the last decades, young Christians have engaged in tackling many burning issues. Together with others they now form a vital segment of secular movements like human rights movements

('Amnesty International'), social movements, feminist movements, ecological movements ('Greenpeace'), the peace movement, and the anti-globalization movement ('ATTAC'). All of them are more or less inspired by the specific Christian dynamics of faith and hope for humanity according to God's promises.

There are three intriguing characteristics here:
– These movements share a greater interest in achieving common goals than in the strict preservation of doctrinal Christian identity;
– They show no anxieties about co-operating with secular political groups and non-religious humanitarian campaigns;
– They live by a fresh reading of the Bible where messages for today are being discovered.

In relation to ecological issues, for example, they learn to look after the planet as a 'garden' in order 'to till it and keep it' (Gen 2:15), not primarily to 'fill the earth and subdue it' and exercise 'domination' (Gen 1: 28). With regard to war and peace in the world, in both the German Democratic Republic and the Federal Republic of Germany, Christians in congregations and other groups prophetically quote the famous sentences in Isaiah chapter 2, the description of the messianic kingdom:

> For out of Zion shall go forth instruction,
> and the word of the LORD from Jerusalem.
> He shall judge between the nations,
> and shall arbitrate for many peoples;
> they shall beat their swords into plowshares,
> and their spears into pruning hooks;
> nation shall not lift up sword against nation,
> neither shall they learn war any more. (Isaiah 2: 3 - 4)

In Germany the greatest success of *collaboration between local congregations and new social movements* was the 'peaceful revolution' in East Germany. In 1989 freedom was achieved without bloodshed. The famous Friday evening prayers of Christians and others in the big city churches in East Germany, with gatherings and demonstrations after the services outside in the light of thousands of candles, added to the transformation of the society, until the processions of peacefully marching people made the military forces helpless. At the end, the powerful resigned and left the public square to the spiritual power of the weak. Surely, the wisdom of political leaders like Michael Gorbatschov, the courage of other East European countries (such as Hungary in opening its borders), and the approval of Western neighbour states also helped to bring it all about.

While to some extent local congregations supported the demonstrations, the reaction of the official church was different. For a rather long time in the pre-revolutionary months in the late 80s, the church authorities in the GDR were afraid of jeopardizing the small free space left to them. They had achieved some restricted liberties from the government provided that church members would not escape the control of the church authorities. Church leaders feared that independent Christian groups might discredit the church in the eyes of the leading communist party. On the one hand, one must understand this. On the other hand, churches and congregations have to find to a new estimation of the different forms of Christian witness in the public domain. In the future the church will have to learn much more intensively than before from the experiences of young church members in groups and movements.

Church schools, Religious Education and Christian adult education as expressions of a public church: the Christian voice in the German educational system

In Europe the institutional church is an organisation of dwindling public recognition. The intellectual elites indulge in ironical remarks on its obsoleteness. In her recent detective novel, 'Death in Holy Orders', P. D. James, introduces a rich Lord, head of a Corporation, who believes that his adopted son's wish to become an Anglican priest to be absolutely futile:

'Of course it wasn't what I wanted. A job with no future. The C of E [2] will be defunct in twenty years if the present decline continues. Or it'll be an eccentric sect concerned with maintaining old superstitions and ancient churches – that is if the State hasn't taken them over as national monuments.' (James, 2001, 26)

When I was 26, I started my professional career as a teacher at a state school teaching RE together with two other subjects. Afterwards I moved into a University as an educator and teacher of theology. [3] In 1919, the separation of state and church in Germany had taken place not in a rigid ('laicist'), but a 'mild', constructive way. The churches were given the opportunity to co-operate with the state within the public educational system. Today this co-operation covers a very wide range of work, state-supported denominational elementary institutions ('Kindergarten'), confessional Religious Education (RE) in state schools,

---

[2]   Church of England.

[3]   For the following see also my contribution to the Festschrift for James W. Fowler: Public Church and Public School Systems in Pluralistic Contexts: a European perspective, in R. Osmer and F. Schweitzer (eds) (2003) *Faith Development Theory and Public Life*. Chalice Press.

church schools, state-sponsored institutions of adult education and theological faculties at state universities.

The churches welcome these opportunities of *sharing* public responsibility, not of dominating the school. We look to the functions of RE not for reasons of mission or for directly recruiting new church members. In numbers church membership is in decline; but we are apt to draw a historical conclusion from the irreversible loss of religious consciousness among about 80 per cent of the German population in the territories of the former GDR. The complete lack of RE in schools, accompanied by persistent atheist propaganda between 1945 and 1989 has resulted in universal indifference to religion. In the former West Germany we wouldn't be Christians in still considerable numbers if it hadn't been for those institutionalized offers to the younger generation to learn about Christianity. I am not saying that RE in schools is sufficient on its own to awaken or preserve faith; its functions belong to something more preparatory, namely to learn about religion as a potentially meaningful option in life.

What happened in those 40 years was not only a fundamental erosion of church membership, but moreover a collapse of religious consciousness and culture as such. It was not a matter of maintaining or losing Christian faith only, but a matter of *cultural impoverishment*. Let me illustrate this point by two examples. After Germany had regained its national unity, church historians were invited by University fine arts departments to lecture on the European Christian cultural heritage. Undergraduates in fine arts were unable to decipher paintings with religious themes. They asked questions like, 'Who is that woman with a baby in her lap?' It was the same with young people. One story stands for many: on a hot summer's day, when a group of socialist teenagers entered a church building for refreshments, one of them asked: 'Who is the man hanging there on the beam?'

Summary

1. A public church expresses itself in *a variety of forms*, first and foremost in those local congregations which leave their cosy pious isolation and open up to common issues. On principle, each Christian service is theoretically open to all people, following in the steps of Jesus who spoke to everyone in the open. Still today, however, the language of the church often implicitly excludes the unchurched, the young people and the religiously disappointed.

2. A public church serves in hospitals and schools, in the diaconical and educational sphere, through church policy and study work, by synods and declarations. These are the more traditional means; but increasingly the public

church is being transformed into, and mobilized by, Christian groups, lay initiatives, new social movements, and individual lay persons.

3. A public church is challenged to act under *different political conditions in differing ways*. In a hostile context it is challenged in other ways than in a friendly context; in a majority status there are other issues at stake than in a minority status. The future will probably bring about a growing importance of the public witness of the individual Christian and the commitment of Christian groups. Will this be unwelcome to church authorities or assisted by them?

4. A public church is also *present in the private sphere* such as family life. Under the GDR regime, Christian families felt responsible to educate their children alongside their Christian convictions in a sort of counter-strategy. I have friends in East Germany who, as young Christians, were refused the normal school career which was the door to academic studies. It became a matter of public record whether they believed in Jesus Christ more than the officially propagated and inculcated atheism. Thus private life became a witness of the public mandate of the church.

5. Public activity can *divide church membership*. One part of the membership may engage in social and feminist issues, race relations and inter-faith dialogue, whereas the other part rather wants to satisfy their craving for old beautiful liturgy. In dogmatic and moral issues of public weight the one side will look at themselves as the indomitable sentinels against the steadily-advancing enemies of true faith and satanic evil in the world, whereas the other side will go on dropping doctrines because of their obsoleteness, as it seems to them, and share liberal moral values. Speaking of a public church will remain in constant need of theological criteria.

6. In my view, there is one fundamental *Christian guideline* that public actions of the church should be decided by. Do they contribute to public reconciliation or not, in particular in the new 'global public'? Christians are called after Jesus Christ, and he embodies God's unconditional revelation of love meant for all creatures. This perspective is undermined and betrayed if Christian camps cling to dualist thought patterns by separating the chosen from the condemned, or fall prey to simplistic distinctions between good and evil. As there is no distinction in sin there is no exclusion in God's grace (cf. Rom 3, 23f.). A public church has to be a mediating and reconciling church.

References

Berger, P. (1967) *The Sacred Canopy: Elements of a Sociological Theory of Religion.* Garden City, N. Y.: Doubleday.

Goerg, Konrad (2001) Wandel um jeden Preis? Klinikaerzte im Spannungsfeld zwischen Oekonomie, Technik und Menschlichkeit. *Deutsches Aerzteblatt* 98: 1172-1176.

James, P.D. (2001) *Death in Holy Orders.* London: Penguin.

Osmer, R. R. and Schweitzer, F. (2000) *Religious Education between Modernization and Globalization: New Perspectives on the United States and Germany.* Grand Rapids, Michigan: W. B. Eerdmans.

Palmer, P. J. (1986) *The Company of Strangers: Christians and the Renewal of America's Public Life.* New York: Crossroad.

Tanner, Klaus (1989) *Die fromme Verstaatlichung des Gewissens. Zur Auseinandersetzung um die Legitimität der Weimarer Reichsverfassung in Staatswissenschaft und Theologie der Zwanziger Jahre.* Goettingen: Vandenhoeck & Ruprecht.

The Presence or Disappearance of God

A quantitative empirical study among Youth in Germany [1]

Hans-Georg Ziebertz

The Disappearance of God in Modern Culture?

The issue of God(s) has always figured in the history of the human race, no matter what era or culture we speak of. 'God' is considered the core from which religious beliefs and denominations stem and from which they maintain their credibility. In Christianity the idea of God is inseparably connected to that of Jesus Christ. God is transcendental, but insofar as he showed himself in Jesus Christ to the world, so he has become a complete human being. The Christian idea of God further assumes that God is not an anonymous power, but is addressed personally or as one would a friend. God has a personal character, although this character is not to be confused with an anthropomorphic perception, which for example finds expression in paintings of 'the old man with the beard,' as often found in the vaults of baroque churches. Yet nevertheless, within the Christian tradition, there is also an abundance of abstract concepts used to characterise God: power, energy, breath, storm, light, love and so on.

The Christian idea of God is part of Western culture; it has both influenced people and shaped people's world perceptions, and has permeated the symbolic universe (Ziebertz, 2001a; Ziebertz, Schweitzer, Häring and Browning, 2000). The disappearance of God, or more generally, a widespread loss of transcendence, is increasingly the topic of theological-philosophical discourse. The Dutch theologian Anton Houtepen (1999) questions whether the gradual disappearance of God from people's thinking will lead to an entirely new definition of the world and the self. The disappearance of God is not merely a 'matter for the Church,' but it is also important in areas such as behaviour, visions, rituals and symbols, all the things that give colour to life. It concerns how we deal with illness, suffering and death, as well as disciplines such as

---

[1]   An extended version of this paper appears in Hermans, C.A.M. and Moore, M.E. (eds.) (2003) *Hermeneutics and Empirical Research in Practical Theology*. Leiden: Brill.

language, art, academic teaching and writing, and worldviews which have always acted as cultural mechanisms for the guidance in life of people and for the socialisation of future generations. The German theologian Michael Welker (1995) sees the ending of the classical theism in the modern world. For him, theism is the core of the Christian faith, and thus with the disappearance of belief in a supernatural God, Christianity will disintegrate and firm contents of beliefs disappear. Will this bring about a dramatic change in people's thinking patterns; changes regarding the control of private and public morals, regarding the question of the meaning of life and changes in coping with contingency? It could be argued that as long as such questions are being posed, perhaps the issue of God has not yet been completely forgotten in public discourse. Perhaps the question of God still has public currency, and not merely for theologians and church representatives.

The present situation and the recognisable changes in the role of religion are without doubt characteristic features of social, cultural and religious change, but can they be seen as indicating a process of secularisation as a whole? Does one come to a different conclusion if the changes are examined from a pluralist perspective, which takes the structural change of society into account? What characterises this change, what meanings accompany the change, do we find only religion's inevitable decay, or is there also evidence of growing diversity? There is a fundamental difference in perspective between these two positions. Within the secularisation theory, it is assumed that there was a culturally developed form of the presence of God that was mediated by society and culture, and it is the process of modernisation which is the factor that has undermined this view of God. The alternative, pluralist view has a different understanding of culture. Culture is seen as an ever-evolving, complex interaction structure, that has both a surface layer and inner layers, and tradition plays a role in both.

In recent years a field of research has been established which in cultural-ethnographic terms goes beyond the assessment of empirical findings. One basic assumption is that besides the neurological basis of memory (or brain hardware), there is a *cultural* memory that is fed through deliberate and unintended interaction. Derrida speaks of an 'archive' (Derrida 1997). This archive contains the decay of traditions, the return of long lost traditions, and the emergence of new traditions; and thus the entire continuity and discontinuity throughout the course of history. This archive accommodates what has been forgotten as much as what has been remembered. It has a narrative linguistic dimension in which what is learned and memorable is accessible because it is brought together with implications. By interpreting what they have experienced, people are feeding the narrative linguistic archive. A second part of the archive is dubbed the visual scenic memory, which reaches down into lower levels of consciousness of the personality. Above all, it is developed through the emotional consciousness of impressions. Just as the individual memory gives the inner life of a person some kind of structure, so culture is the structure of the social and societal life. Structure is memory, but not merely memory in words, but also memory through non-verbal records: buildings and construction works (such as the architecture of religious buildings), pictures and symbols (Tintoretto's scene of Jesus' passion in the entrance portal of Notre Dame Cathedral; representations of the Cross), Feast days (Easter, Pentecost, Christmas), norms and values (charity and compassion), music (religious music and the religious content of popular music), religious content in the media, western Christian principles in legal systems, alternative forms of religion, special places of pilgrimage (Lourdes, Taizé, Santiago di Compostella and so on), the aesthetics of religious art, to name but a few. Apart from these areas there are specific endeavours in which Christianity is handed down through the catechism, preaching and religious education. These many direct and indirect elements form memories and hand them on. They do not stand isolated from one another, but are connected to one another through a varied exchange process.

Daniele Hervieu-Leger (2000) and Grace Davie (2000) have labelled the European societies as 'amnestic' societies. They deal with memory in a complex way (Davie 2000, 30). Other further differentiations are possible. Memory is not, for example, carried by all people equally. A minority can keep a memory alive, so that it is potentially available for the majority at another point in time. Moreover, memories are not static; they can change with time; different memories can be formed that conflict with one another; certain memory strands can be erased, others can be rediscovered. An example of that is the former East Germany, which was atheist for 40 years. It is difficult for us to ascertain where this application of memory is heading. The one certainty is that the store of religious memory continues to grow and change. Moreover, memories are not only handed down personally, they remain symbolically and collectively. The German theologian Karl-Fritz Daiber (1996) also maintains in this sense that there are hardly any Christianity-free religions in the western European countries. There is no common language with which religion can be discussed, without helping oneself considerably to the Christian vocabulary, and there are no religious rituals which are not essentially connected with the Christian cult. Whoever thinks of God thinks of images and subjects that are connected to Christian roots.

With these reflections the thesis which holds that the religious subject matter and symbols of different cultures on which people inevitably come to rely are exhausted, can be called into question. Such reflection gives evidence of how the material-orientated perception can be complemented by a processional perception, which understands the change not merely as a loss of substance. Even if, to use an image from Hans-Georg Gadamer, Christian connotations are not present on the direct thematic level, they still indirectly reflect the cultural horizon (cf. Ziebertz 1999, 63ff). This horizon functions as a source of special discussion of a subject. The challenge of theological research is the possibility that religion and God can be present thematically and as a horizon, to include generally epistemology. The second challenge is to grasp hermeneutically the contours of religion and belief in God, and to prove them empirically.

Empirical Analysis

Data for the empirical analysis in this paper will be taken from a survey carried out in Southern Germany in 2000. Just under 800 school pupils at a selective school aged sixteen and seventeen were interviewed, and 729 surveys were incorporated into the following analysis (for the publication of the entire empirical analysis see Ziebertz, Kalbheim and Riegel, 2003).

The measuring instrument was constructed as follows (see also Figure 1). Firstly, terms were used in which God is spoken of in *Biblical terminology*; secondly, concepts which suppose a *humanistic* discussion of God, in which the divine transcendent is attributed to the people themselves. God's *immanent presence* marks a third area and a fourth perception of God has *deistic* features. Fifthly, a *cosmological* interpretation of God and of the divine respectively, distinguished by their holistic character, is used. A sixth conception is labelled as *meta-theism*. In this conception the transcendent divinity stands in the centre, because of which nothing further about God can be said. In a seventh conception the figure of God is understood as an *instrument of delusion*, and eighthly, in an *atheistic*-perspective the interpretation is advanced categorically that there is no God. Lastly, in the *agnostic* position the doubt is expressed as to whether there is or can be a God. This conceptualisation is held to reflect empirically the common perceptions of God of those interviewed. After trial runs a scale with 25 items in total remained, which was applied to the following analysis. Those interviewed could give the following answers: strongly agree, agree, neither agree nor disagree, disagree, disagree strongly (5-point scale).

Frequencies

On the basis of the individual items it should first be examined how the young people we interviewed reacted to the statements. Of the 25 statements, 11 fell into the positive half of the scale and 14 into the negative half.

In the positive half, three items from the meta-theistic group, three from the immanent group, and three from the deistic group, one from the cosmological and one from the agnostic group can be found. Which ideas of God convey to us these responses? In the eyes of young people God can only be described and understood with difficulty. In the statements scoring positively, God appears as an insinuation and as an abstraction respectively. God escapes our definitional clutches, and what the religions say about God are each specific attempts of language to describe semantically the indescribable. God is a higher power throughout the entire universe, and at the same time this God is in each individual person. At the same time there is the uncertainty of whether there actually can be a God or something divine. Altogether the representations of God of the interviewees comprise three features: the word 'God' and 'the divine' respectively are one, a mystery and indefinable; God/the divine is anthropologically-immanent; the person and the divine higher power are connected to each other in the universe.

In the negative half of the scale images with biblical connotations are found. These items belong to the group of judged as inconclusively-related items. Two atheistic statements and that critical of religion rank among the negatively scoring statements about God. There was no agreement with the items 'there is no higher power' or 'there is no God'. The interviewees answered as a result that they believe in the existence of God or a higher power. However the acknowledgement of the existence of God, as far as the content is concerned for them, is not so easily synonymous with the God of the bible and the God whose kingdom will come respectively.

We can conclude from the findings that the majority of those interviewed think 'anti-a-theistically,' that is to say they reject the negative statements about God or a higher power. Concepts with statements about God which are classically considered as Christian-theological connotations meet with little or no approval. If therefore, statements critical of religion, in the same way as critical negative statements, are judged as statements with classical Christian contents, it poses the question of what representations of God consist in the final analysis. It is certainly noteworthy that God is not held as an outdated world view, as represented by the view critical of religion, which spoke of God as a representation of a false consciousness (Marx), as an invention, projection or illusion (Freud), or as a construction or mirror image of the self (Feuerbach). Only a minority of those interviewed agreed with such ideas, and they are considered rather as a counter foil for a positive religious worldview. Whilst ideas in which 'God as in the God of the Bible,' as the father of Jesus Christ and as an personal friend come up, they are less popular perceptions of the idea of God. Both areas (Christian God versus Atheism) have dominated the theological-philosophical debate up until the 1960s. This polarity is today however hardly even important.

Dimensions of the representations of God

The question is now whether the theoretically accepted structure can be empirically or at least partly confirmed, or whether the theoretical construction must be changed against the background of the empirical findings. The result is as follows (see Fig. 1): three concepts prove statistically weak and must be left out of any further analysis (HUM, ATH, AGN). Otherwise three concepts remain unchanged after the factor analysis (BIBL, IMM, CRI). Beyond that, a new concept has been formed which combines aspects from three other concepts (COSM, DEI, META). This new concept shall be labelled 'cosmodeistic,' since such a term best describes the semantic aspects of the items.

Fig. 1: Theoretical and empirical dimensions of concepts of God

Scale (theoretical)		Scale (empirical)
Biblical	BIBL	Biblical (Bibl)
Humanistic	HUM	Non applicable
Immanent	IMM	Immanent (Imm)
Cosmological	COSM	Cosmodeistic (Code)
Deistic	DEI	
Meta-theistic	META	
Critical	CRI	Critical (Cri)
Atheistic	ATH	Non applicable
Agnostic	AGN	Non applicable

(The basic of the graphics is a factor analysis with Oblimin-Rotation; Eigenvalue $\geq$ 1; Factor-loading $\geq$ .50; second loading $\geq$.25)

Whilst theoretically ten dimensions were originally conceptualised in construction of the questionnaire, the statistical analysis of the empirical responses shows that it must be adapted to a four dimensional structure. From the perceptions of the young people interviewed there are four semantic centres through which the different statements are put together. These centres function as a system which was not previously visible. Firstly, the statements in which God is represented as the God of the Bible prove particularly stable. When this dimension is labelled 'Biblical' from here on, use of biblical terminology is meant and not that these items can only be interpreted in a Christian biblical sense. Just as stable are the statements about the immanent presence (of God), namely that God is in every person, every person is a part of God. And finally the statements that are critical of religion and critical of God form a stable dimension in which the idea, 'there can be a God,' is 'unmasked.' This focus of statements does not combine with the agnostic or atheistic items respectively. The new compound, deistic dimension contains firstly statements about the existence of a transcendent impersonal God; secondly statements about the symbiosis of the idea of God with the universe as a whole; and lastly statements about the indescribability of God on the one hand, and of the contingency of human perception, human thinking and human speech on the other.

Correlations between the dimensions and evaluation

Are these four dimensions to be understood as pure types, that is, can it be assumed that the representations of God in the eyes of the interviewees correspond exactly to the critical, biblical, cosmodeistic or immanent concepts? Is the rejection of each of the three others linked to the endorsement of a particular concept? The analysis of the connection between the four dimensions (cf. Fig. 2) shows that the last presumption can in no way be borne out. Rather the opposite holds true, apart from a few exceptions. Three concepts correlate with one another, with the strongest connection between biblical and immanent ideas of God. The second strongest connection exists between immanent statements and cosmodeistic statements. In terms of the content, this boils down to the position that God is considered a transcendent higher power and force, and at the same time is quite immanently present in individuals. The weakest positive connection exists between cosmodeistic and biblical statements, thus between ideas where God is understood as (a) 'power,' and as a biblically conveyed 'personal friend.' But this connection is also positive, and thus a conceptual triangle can be spoken of, in which the immanent concept is in the best position, connecting the others to it.

Fig. 2 (a) Correlations between the concepts of God

	Biblical	Immanent	Cosmo-deist	Critical
Biblical	—	.38	.29	− .38
Immanent		—	.16	− .22
Cosmo-deist			—	Ns.
Critical				—
Pearson Correlation; $p = .000$				

(b) Evaluation

	Mean	S.D.
Biblical	2.55	.92
Immanent	3.37	.86
Cosmo-deist	3.35	.81
Critical	2.55	.92

Legend: 1=negative; 3=middle; 5=positive

Discussion

Seen theologically, the correlation between the biblical and immanent concepts is unproblematic. In Christian understanding the transcendent God is immanently present, because God has bound himself through Jesus Christ, to the
world; many reports of Christian mystics describe individual inner experiences
of God; God himself has become human. The positive relationship to the cosmodeistic ideas is theologically more difficult to convey. Is the cosmodeistic
understanding a philosophically-motivated alternative doctrine to Christianity
for the young people interviewed? In-depth interviews, which were carried out
in addition, but which cannot be addressed here, go against such a view (Prokopf and Ziebertz, 2001). Rather it appears that the young people are making
an attempt to understand the transcendence of God generally and put it into
words; their attempts at verbalisation are firstly not directed against an existing religious tradition, for example Christian tradition, but rather a document
of their individual ways of understanding.

  Thus the empirical findings which are shown in the correlations are also related to theology. This triangle is positioned clearly opposite the fourth concept
('critical') by the interviewees. The strongest contrast is produced between the
biblical and critical statements about God, that is, one either follows the one or
the other model – there is no synthesis. The same is also true, albeit somewhat
weaker for the critical and immanent representations of God. If God is seen
as an immanent power, it is not plausible to pass off the existence of God as
a human construction or to evaluate the discussion of God as a power play of
interests, for example, of the church. On the contrary, whoever represents the
latter will not want to understand God as an immanent reality. Only between
the critical and cosmodeistic statements is there no significant connection. This
finding means in practical terms that no comment can be made over any of the
connections; or more precisely, that no secure statement about probability is
possible, as both concepts integrate with the interviewees. The result therefore virtually means that both ideas are compatible with each other, without
unforeseeably mutually influencing each other.

Theology as a whole has tried for some time to deal contextually with questions of the passing on of faith. It is concerned with the consequences of religious pluralism against the backdrop of the modern age. Inevitably its perception has broadened, as well as its arsenal of methods. Practical theology aims to perceive reality and connect theologically to the religion of everyday life (Prokopf and Ziebertz, 2001; Riegel and Ziebertz, 2001; Kalbheim and Ziebertz, 2001). The problem of perception has a reflexive hermeneutical dimension and it is a question of empirical research method. With regard to the diversity of the images of God, an inevitable degeneration is no longer diagnosed today. The variety is considered as an expression of the diversity of God himself. God himself is a community: Father, Son and Holy Spirit (De Lange 1995). Correspondingly the biblical-Christian tradition knows a wealth of discussion of God (cf. Lang and Hülz 1988, 16). It has fatal consequences when modern pluralism is suppressed. If this happens, there are no new insights. The multiplicity of images cannot simply be labelled as post-Christian. Could it not also be the starting point for a type of religious evolution, in which the construction of the specific symbolic order falls back reflexively on archaic and traditional forms (see Green, 1998; Holm and Bowker, 1994; Mertens and Boeve, 1994; Shanks 2000; Ward 1997)?

It is an open question whether perhaps the tendency towards more abstract representations of God is a result of secularisation, or whether it reflects an evolutionary process of a growing connection with God to the person. To consider these conditions of modern religiousness is not only the task of practical theology; here it is above all to contemplate systematic and biblical theology.

References

Daiber, K.-F. (1996) Religiöse Gruppenbildung als Reaktionsmuster gesellschaftlicher Individualisierungsprozesse. in Gabriel, K. (ed.), *Religiöse Individualisierung oder Säkularisierung?* Gütersloh: Gütersloher Verlag, 86-104.

Davie, G. (2000) *Religion in modern Europe. A Memory mutates.* Oxford: Oxford University Press.

Derrida, J. (1997) *Dem Archiv verschrieben.* Berlin: Akademie.

Dohmen, C., Englert, R. and Sternberg,T... (1988) In der Bilderflut ertrinken?; in *Katechetische Blätter* 115.(1988), 4-15. München: Kösel.

Green, G. (1998) *Imagining God: Theology and the Religious Imagination.* Grand Rapids/Cambridge: Eerdmans.

Hervieu-Leger, D. (2000) *Religion as a Chain of Memory.* Cambridge/Oxford: Polity Press.

Holm, J.and Bowker, J. (1994) (eds.), *Picturing God.* London: Pinter.

Houtepen, A. (1999) *Gott – eine offene Frage*, Gütersloh: Gütersloher Verlag.

Kalbheim, B. and Ziebertz, H.-G. (2001) God in Creation? An empirical survey among Dutch adults. in: Ziebertz H.-G. (ed.), *Imagining God. Empirical Explorations from an International Perspective.* Münster: Lit-Verlag, 145 - 157.

Lang H and Hülz, M., Von Gott in Bildern sprechen?; in: *Katechetische Blätter* 115.(1988) 16 - 22, München: Kösel.

Lange de F. (1995) *'Legio is mijn naam'. Het plurale zelf als thema in de theologie,* Kampen: Kok Pharos.

Mertens, H.-E. and Boeve, L. (1994) (eds), *Naming God today.* Leuven: Peeters.

Prokopf, A. and Ziebertz H-G. (2001) Images of God among young Germans; in Ziebertz, H.-G. (ed) *Imagining God – Disappearance or Change?* Münster: Lit-Verlag, 35 - 53.

Riegel, U. and Ziebertz H-G. (2001) Images of God in a Gender Perspective: an empirical typology. in Ziebertz H.-G. (ed.), *Imagining God. Empirical Explorations from an International Perspective,* Münster: Lit-Verlag, 229 - 244.

Shanks, A. (2000) *God and Modernity.* London/New York: Routledge.

Ward, G. (1997) (ed.), *The Postmodern God.* Oxford: Blackwell.

Welker, M. (1995) *Kirche im Pluralismus.* Gütersloh: Gütersloher Verlag.

Ziebertz H.-G. (1999) Religion, Christentum und Moderne. Veränderte Religionspräsenz als Herausforderung, Stuttgart: Kohlhammer.

Ziebertz H-G. (2001a) (ed.) *Imagining God. Empirical Explorations from an International Perspective,* Münster: Lit-Verlag.

Ziebertz H-G. (2001b) (ed.), *Religious Individualization and Christian Religious Semantics,* Münster: Lit-Verlag.

Ziebertz H-G, Kalbheim, B. and Riegel, U.(eds) (2003) *Religiöse Signaturen heute. Ein religionspädagogischer Beitrag zur empirischen Jugendforschung,* Gütersloh/Freiburg: Gütersloher Verlag/Herder.

Ziebertz, H.-G., Schweitzer, F., Häring, H. and Browning, D.S. (2000) (eds), *The Human Image of God,* Leiden: Brill.

Public Theology in the Market of Academic Education

Reflections on the Involvement of Practical Theology in the Master of Arts in Social Services Administration Programme at the University of Bonn

Eberhard K. Hauschildt

Theological Academia in the Market

Theology today finds itself placed in the market of academic education. In Germany this is a relatively new situation. Academic theology used to be state protected and to a lesser degree is still a state protected science. I mean by this: academic theology in Germany is – with only a handful of exceptions – taught at state universities and academic teachers of theology are paid by the state. On the other hand: the faculties in which they teach are neverless confessional in nature – either protestant or catholic. Church and state influence is put into a balance: the faculties themselves select candidates for a professor's position. The Protestant or Catholic Church then approves the decision of the faculty before the State Ministry of Education will employ the person.

This way of organising academic theology reflects a situation in which the vast majority (more than 90 per cent) of the German population are either members of the Catholic Church or of the regional Protestant Church. Today however, in East Germany only 30 per cent of the population are members of Christian churches and in the inner cities in West Gemany the tendency is somewhat similar. In the city of Hamburg for example, church members account for only about 50 per cent of the population. And there is another change, felt very much in the theological faculties:the numbers of theology students have dropped in the past 15 years, mainly as a reaction to a surplus of pastoral candidates. Most likely the number will not return to former heights – for demographic reasons. And as a result of a decrease in church finances because of decreased church tax income, the church will not be able to afford more than today's low numbers of new pastors.

In such a situation the theological departments are put under pressure. They have to justify themselves anew. Why should non-church members pay for them via state taxes? And why should universities not radically cut down the finances for theological faculties and the number of professors? State and universities nowadays expect faculties to increase the percentage of funding from business sources. Thus, the faculties have to take the initiative and find out for which research there is interest in the market.

A new interdisciplinary masters' programme in Bonn

This is the background from which a considerable change in academic theology is necessary and indeed is starting to take place. The Protestant Theological Faculty at the University of Bonn is among the first in Germany, which has taken a new step towards a new kind of theology on the market. We have started, in cooperation with a large social work company, an independent non-profit organisation which runs three hospitals and 20 to 30 homes for the elderly and for the mentally disabled. The name of this company is "Theodor Fliedner Werk", because it has grown out of the work of the Protestant pastor Theodor Fliedner who in the middle of the nineteenth century – so to speak – "invented" the profession of the celibate Protestant Church nurse. These Christian nurses were the backbone of protestant social work in Germany up to the 1960s. Nowadays they hardly exist.

The Fliedner Werk is the financer of a small Institute of Interdisciplinary and Applied Science of Protestant Social Welfare (Institut für Interdisziplinäre und Angewandte Diakoniewissenschaften) at the University of Bonn. This institue has organised a number of scientific symposia in the past years. And in the fall of 2001 in cooperation with the theologial department it has started a Master of Arts in Social Services Administration Programme.(Hartmann, 2003) It offers a masters' degree for leading personnel of social services (be it doctors, theologians, educators or other professionals from other backgrounds). Today in the top positions interdisciplinary knowledge and competence is necessary in order to run a business of social service sucessfully in the social market. Therefore courses of this masters programme are grouped in four different columns: non-profit organisation, social services, business leadership, value orientation of social work. Courses are taught by professors of economics and business administration, law, psychology, sociology, medicine and also theology. The perspectives of law and economics, social politics and sociology, psychology, ethics and theology are employed. The teachers from the different faculties also come together regularly to discuss among themselves the topics they teach. I myself can say that I have benefitted quite a bit from these discussions.

So it is the theological faculty which offers this masters programme in weekend courses, taught by professors from the different faculties of the University of Bonn. The students – in contrast to the education usually offered by the universities in Germany – have to pay tuition (€5,000) for this two year course, or the institution which sends them pays. From this tuition fee all expenses of this programme have to be paid.

We found that there is a market for this programme. In the first year there were twice as many applicants as places. And also in the second year we could not accept all applicants. There are also catholic students, and students who work in state organisations or social organisations related to the workers' movement involved in the programme. In the student group which started in 2002 there is also a Muslim student.

We think this programme is quite unique in two ways. Firstly, we differ from traditional theology in the fact that we have a strictly interdisciplinary curriculum. Secondly, we differ from from other institutions which offer a master of arts in social services administration by the fact that in terms of its world-view, religion and ethics is an integral part of the curriculum. Social services are viewed as embedded in cultures of compassion and help. By integrating this perspective we want to be not only different but simply better than other programmes on the market. Better than other programmes which for example are offered by faculties of business administration and do not include the religious perspective.

Internal and external theology as public theology

A new practice of a theological faculty is also an opportunity for new reflection about theology. What kind of theology is it we are doing? It obviously wants to be public theology, that is theology not simply for a sector of society, not simply for the churched, but also for the unchurched. Theology not separated from other faculties, but integrated into a task we want to achieve together: to convey knowledge and competence for leadership in the area of social services. This theology does not simply serve the church and does not simply serve society through the church, but adresses society directly.

If you do something new, you have to watch out that the practice does not fall back into old outdated models. And you have to ensure that theory will reflect the change. Today, theology in public, theology for the university as a whole and for the society is theology in a pluralistic age. What we need is a theology which neither overstates nor minimises its position, finding a position as a partner alongside other sciences. Theology is no longer the main integrator or norm setter even though the attention to norms and values is an important topic in theology. We as theologians involved in such a master programme will not be the ones to establish right and wrong, we are not trying to convert colleagues and students into good faithful Protestants. As students and teachers from a multitude of religious backgrounds they have to be sure that they will not be indoctrinated and that other perspectives will not be neglected. I cannot guarantee quality if I simply teach the protestant culture of compassion and leave my students uninformed about catholic culture, the Jewish culture of compassion, the culture of workers' solidarity and also the culture of Muslim compassion. They need this knowledge if they are to be successful in this field.

There is also another danger: that theology lacks weight, appearing simply decorative. My colleges from other sciences or students would let me speak and endure my sermons for a while, and then afterwards would wake up from slumber and go on with the real business. Equally theology lacks weight if I simply replicate what the other sciences are already teaching. This would render irrelevant what theology has to say.

True interdisciplinarity means that theology has no automatic prerogative, but it retains its own field. It is no more and no less than a science amongst and in communication with other sciences. The hegemonic status of theology in relation to other sciences has ended. There is, however no reason to grovel.

However, a further question arises. Is this description of theology as a science alongside other sciences not in fact a concept of religious sciences? Why a confessional faculty, a decidedly Christian faculty, even a decidedly Protestant one? Of course it would also be possible, that a department of religious sciences works fruitfully in such a curriculum. However, I would like to show that the participation of the confessional faculty is involved in more than simply conforming to the German university tradition. It has certain distinctive advantages.

For one, it is simply closer to practice. In the field of religious backgrounds for compassion there is no neutrality. Religion as such does not exist, religious motives for compassion do come out of real religions and churches, and it is an abstract analytic category to speak of religiosity as such. Therefore it will be helpful if students who want to be a leader in the field of social services are trained to know about religious effects, but also to reflect on their own religious background and to learn how to communicate with others from other backgrounds. And the individual teachers and the content of teaching is no exclusion to this rule.

However, such a confessional theology is only closer to practice if it is able to act in a pluralistic situation. Theology itself has to become differentiated. Duncan Forrester in his concept of public theology states on the one hand, that public theology "claims to point to publicly acessible truth" (Forrester, 2000: 127) and on the other hand"tries to articulate in the public square its convictions about truth and goodness" (2000:128). To me it seems that Forrester's concept implies a distinction of two types of theology or a combination of the two. I shall call them external and internal theology. [1] Both of them are necessary. Internal theology draws on insights from immediate experience. It employs a logic which rests on distinctive premises of faith. Helping is understood to be motivated by Gods' love which he has shown in Christ – this is an experience which argues on the premise of the existence of God and of Jesus being the Son of God. External theology rather looks at the experience of effects and it employs a logic which rests on premises which are shared by society as a whole or by the scientific community.

The Christian motivation for social engagement in the nineteenth century used the romantic imagery of love as a model for solving problems of society and by this reached a successful coalition between more evangelistical piety and enlightenment optimism. Thus is can be compared with the advantages and disadvantages of other motivations, be it the communist by solidarity or the Jewish people through God's justice.

Both of these perspectives, internal theology and external theology, are kept together in that academic theology, which is needed for public theology. You cannot do without either the internal or the external type of theological reasoning.

The didactic concept

Let me show this by pointing towards the didactic concept of the course, which I teach in the master programme in which I want the students to become more deeply aware of the different cultures of compassion which are present in society and the different organisations of social engagement.

Gradual theology

I would like to add a last reflection. If it is true that public theology in today's plural society has to be a combination of internal and external theology, what happens to the claim of truth? When I teach public theology in such a way as described, do I still think the protestant logic of help is true, and the catholic logic of help is false, along with the Jewish logic, the socialist and the muslim logic of help? Or do I think: Well, they are basically all the same; there is no substantial difference? Or – and this would be worse – do I publically construct a pretence and behave as if the logics were the same in order not to offend

---

[1]   Sociologists have pointed out that the coexistence of the internal and the external perspective is not limited to the case of religion but a constitutive characteristic of modern societies: different ways of world perception and practice have been institutionalised in subsystems of society (e.g. politics, law, business, science, mass media). See Kaufmann, (2003).

Cultures of helping/compassion – didactical steps

LEVELS	INTERNAL THEOLO-GY	EXTERNAL THEO-LOGY
experience	**Step 1: my motives** *Aim: to realize one's own background motives* action: filling out a questionnaire about one's own motives for helping and for involvement in a social services organisation	**Step 2: the multitude of motives** *Aim: to become aware of other religious motives* action: tell your own motives to your neighbor and later tell the neighbour's story to the group
knowledge	**Step 3: finding the logic behind the motives** *Aim: to follow the internal logic* action: Intepretation of texts from different cultures of help (Protestant, Catholic, Jewish, Muslim, Social Democrat etc.)	**Step 4: comparing the advantages and disadvantages of different logics** *Aim: comparative knowledge* comparion of the different texts and a lecture about the historical development of helping and social services organisations
competence	**Step 5: cooperation with conflicting convictions** Aims: *to communicate one's own to cooperate with other conviction traditions of help* action: role plays about leadership in situations of different traditions of help in conflict (e.g. a room for prayer in a hospital; a Muslim therapist in a Christian counselling organisation; a curriculum for nourishing the spiritual competence of people working in the organisation) (elements already taught in the course on the psychology of communication are applied)	

anybody, but in my heart still think that only I am right and the others are wrong?

Is there another possibility? I think so. What I suggest here I call "gradual theology" (Hauschildt, 2002). Gradual theology means: indeed I am a Protestant of confession and I think that the Protestant logic of help and the Protestant theology which stands behind it is my preferred theological doctrine. If it were not, then I should convert to that confession which has the best doctrine. However, there are elements in other logics from other cultures of help and religions which may be superior to my own tradition. For example I have high regard for the Jewish tradition of help which argues not simply according to the motive of God's love, but strongly according to the duty of following God's justice. This I have found to be quite an enrichment to my tradition. And I hope my students from this course who are Protestant or not Protestant will benefit in two ways. They will have gotten a deeper insight into their own tradition and have been enriched by the perspectives of other traditions.

Conclusion

A simple course to be taught to a plural group of students is quite a challenge; a challenge to revise the practice and theory of our public theology. The challenge I see for public theology has been condensed into the following six statements.

1. For public theology in the market of academic education the times for ruling over the other sciences are over, but also there is no reason to grovel.
2. Public theology in a plural society consists of a combination of internal as well as external theology.
3. Internal theology draws on insights from immediate faith experience. And it employs a logic which rests on distinctive premises of faith.
4. External theology looks at (often measureable) experiences of effects of faith and it employs a logic which rests on premises which are shared by the society as a whole or by the scientific community.
5. When combining internal and external theology the position of complete absolutism (I am right and the others are wrong) as well as the position of complete relativism (everybody is right) is revealed as contradictory.
6. In gradual theology, I can express with reasons of internal as well as external theological character, the ways in which my theology is better than the world view of others, but am also open to being shown, the ways in which the world view of others has advantages over my theology.

References

Forrester, Duncan (2000) *Truthful Action*. Edinburgh: T&T Clark.

Hartmann, Klaus (2003) 'Sozialmanagement. Ein Qualifizierungskonzept für Führung und Leitung' in A. Heller and T. Krobath (eds.) *OrganisationsEthik: Entwicklung in Kirchen, Caritas und Diakonie*. Lambertus: Freiburg i.Br., 237 - 246.

Hauschildt, Eberhard K. (2002) 'Praktische Theologie – neugierig, graduell und konstruktiv: Verabschiedungen, Trends und Optionen' in: E. Hauschildt and U. Schwab (eds.) *Praktische Theologie für das 21. Jahrhundert*. Stuttgart: Kohlhammer, 79 - 99.

Kaufmann, Franz-Xaver (2003) 'Die Entwicklung von Religion in der modernen Gesellschaft' (2003) in K. D. Hildemann (ed.) *Religion – Kirche – Islam: Eine soziale und diakonischer Herausforderung*. Leipzig: Evangelische Verlagsanstalt, 21 - 37.

Liturgical Language as Metaphorical Language

A Contribution to Spirituality and the Public Realm

Casparus Vos

The argument advanced in this paper is that liturgical language functions as metaphorical language while contributing to spiritual formation and that this spiritual forming is reflected in the public domain. But our understanding of liturgical language as metaphorical language and our insight into its spiritual impact and influence depend on our ability to savour liturgical metaphor to the full.

The power of metaphors

Metaphors are sparks ignited by imagination. This is illustrated in the film *Il postino*. A postman is a conveyor of news – sometimes bad news. This is especially likely when the envelopes have windows. At other times the news may be good, as when the letter comes from a friend or loved one. One of the characters in the film is an enthusiastic postman, Mario Ruoppolo, who dutifully does his bicycle rounds, delivering mail on an Italian island, Cala di Sotto. The recipient of the mail lived on the upper slopes of a steep hill. He was the famous Chilean poet, Pablo Neruda, and in exile for political reasons. One day Mario fell in love with a beautiful girl, whose name was Beatrice Russo. He stared at her in speechless admiration. To declare his love for her he needed the poet to supply the words. Neruda taught the postman that his tongue was not simply meant for licking stamps, but also for creating metaphors. Metaphors are wings on which love is carried. Liturgical language is metaphorical language. Liturgical speech must therefore be metaphorical, otherwise we cannot speak to or about the Invisible God.

Poetic impulses for liturgics

The process of glass-blowing offers a useful metaphor for reflection on a creative liturgy. My poem, "The Glass-blower", leads us into a study of the liturgical process.

'Glass-blower'
La Rochère, 1475

His spirit looms over dark
Voids, chaos broods.
Let there be light!
In his fire-ripe oven he stokes
Molten glass incandescent and fragile.
Through his pipe he blows her heart to beating,
Suckles bubbles from her lungs.
His eyes approve the glowing curves of hips,
Her flaming form he baptises in Holy Water,
Revives her, then
Clinks her without a crack.

It is clear upon first reading that the subject of this poem is a glass-blower who is skilfully making a vase. The reference to the Creation of the earth in Genesis in the first two lines engenders a contextual framework within which the creative process of the glass-blower finds a parallel. This enables us to think afresh at various levels about the liturgy as a creative process.

The liturgist creates a liturgy that has to be carefully handled because it is extremely delicate and fragile. Even if the liturgy has been carefully shaped in advance, in the heat of the moment, when the congregation comes together in the flesh, it can break into shards. The hallmark of the liturgy, no matter how carefully it has been created by the liturgist, is no guarantee that the service will be marked by wonder and inspiration.

It is the task of the liturgist to blow life into the liturgy. The congregation must experience the liturgy as a living event. The liturgist needs to remove every possible flaw, meticulously "suckles bubbles" that could mar the beauty of the liturgy. It is the task of the liturgist to scrutinise the radiant sequence of liturgical events and ensure that the liturgy is beautiful in the eyes of the congregation, and of God. The liturgy, as designed by the liturgist, should be something of a work of art. Where the design of the liturgy differs from the making of a vase is that the liturgy provides the means by which the liturgist and the congregation raise a glass in a toast to God. In the liturgy we celebrate the glory of God. These spiritual events must find their reflection in society.

In the metaphor used here liturgical language serves as the glass-blower's pipe which brings the liturgical miracle into being. A liturgy may be said to be "blown" from metaphorical language.

The metaphor provides the mechanism used by the liturgical glassblower to perform an act of creation in miniature. All the liturgical acts and movements can be created through the metaphor. With the aid of liturgical language used as metaphorical language the liturgist can raise a glass that contains no crack or flaw. This perfection may be reflected in society.

The metaphorical landscape

Using the yardstick of logical language usage, many philosophers see the metaphor as a case of catachresis (incorrect use of words), as a necessary evil or simply as a decoration, and therefore unsuitable for the expression of proportional "truths" (Gräbe 1992:288). Even in the sixties, for example, the philospher Max Black (1962) still found it necessary to defend the use of metaphorical language in philosophical writings.

The traditional, and in fact the general view of phenomena such as metaphor, hyperbole (a figure of speech in which exaggeration is used as an expression of overpowering emotion or to make an impression), litotes (a figure of speech in which something is emphasised through negation of the opposite, or through deliberate understatement, such as, "I'm bringing out a little book" or "not too badly" (= well) and so on) is that these are rhetorical devices that belong exclusively to the world of poetry, and to imaginative works. Metaphors, and the other "figures of speech" mentioned are regarded as rhetorical devices that chiefly serve the purpose of stylistic decoration, mainly in literary texts (Carstens 1992:114, 1993:85; Van Leeuwen 2002:69).

Metaphors can never have fixed meanings, neither can their effect be predicted with any degree of accuracy. Metaphors are "unfettered language" (langage délié; Ricoeur 1975a:152 et seq): people do not consider themselves bound by the usual meanings of words; instead they mobilise hitherto undiscovered shades of meaning. The living metaphor brings renewal to language (Van Leeuwen 2002:70). This renewal and its accompanying new insights come about because a metaphor is normally a word or expression used in an unusual context. Metaphors are explosive, and their force hurls people towards new insights and blasts open new worlds. These fresh insights must be reflected in the public domain as well, allowing us to look with a new metaphorical vision at the moral foundations of our society, political decisions and institutions.

Metaphors are supremely an instrument of the "odd language" (Ramsey 1957), religious language. This does not mean that religious language is exclusively metaphorical and that all religious sentences contain verbal anomalies. In the liturgy the uninterrupted use of poetical, metaphorical language would be wearying rather than uplifting (Van Leeuwen 2002:70). Nevertheless, liturgical metaphor is not without its surprises and moments of exhiliration. Metaphors that enlighten the community of faith can enable its members to experience surprises and moments of awe in their everyday life. New light may be cast on values such as, respect, justice, peace, honesty and responsibility.

Functions of the metaphor

Aristotle distinguishes three kinds of words: strange, ordinary and metaphorical. Strange words give us headaches; ordinary words convey familiar meanings; metaphors offer us new and fresh insights (Carson 2000: 30).

Metaphors create tension

In order to appreciate the impact, newness and freshness of metaphors, we need to examine certain functions of metaphors. A metaphor helps us to begin to understand the unknown in terms of the known (Van Huyssteen 1986:159). Metaphors do more than "name": they give us access to the objects referred to (Van Huyssteen 1997:188). They create a bridge, an interaction between the "matter" and the "image". The image supplies access to the matter.

The metaphor functions through the paradox that something simultaneously *is* and *is not* (Ricoeur 1979:27). The tension inherent in a metaphor simultaneously serves to confirm and deny that something is the case. According to Ricoeur, there is an implicit negation in every positive metaphorical statement (Ricoeur 1978: 221 - 224, 255 - 256). The metaphor, God is a rock, confirms that there is a relationship between God and a rock (permanence, strength, shelter) but still retains the "and is not" element. God is not literally a rock. The real meaning emerges from the conflict between the concepts "God" and "rock" (cf Van Leeuwen 2002:69 - 70). The conceptual framework of the listener, the instrument by which he observes, gives the God-as-rock metaphor associations of permanence, strength and security. This allows new perspectives on God, and new experiences of Him in the service, all of which should be reflected in society. The metaphorical tension is maintained because God is not always experienced as "a rock" in everyday life.

What are the implications of this kind of metaphorical reflection for theology? Sometimes God is and at other times He is not! The problem with most forms of public theology is that for the most part it is the product of only one mode of thinking. Either one sticks to the perspective of the Christian faith, or one starts thinking from the viewpoint of secular debate. The first attitude never really brings us onto speaking terms with proponents of other views. The second attitude seems to reduce the content of faith to very general notions, ignoring the more radical demands of Christian morality (De Kruijf 2000).

It is my contention that, in a pluralistic context (cf Van Huyssteen 1999:235 - 286) we should not try to soften the tension between church and society, but rather accentuate it – for the sake of public life as well as for the sake of Christian life. Of course we may strive for unity by proclaiming the gospel and call for faith in it. But we should not anticipate this unity by pretending that it is already there, although "hidden". That would imply making a claim on public life that Christians themselves would not accept from other parties. So Christians must be aware that in fact their views represent those of a minority of society, and they must behave in accordance with that minority position, irrespective of the factual power of their beliefs. To accentuate the tension between Church and society is also in the interests of the identity of the Church. Christians must be aware that faith in Christ demands other things than obedience to public rules and respect for public decency. Faith in Christ is not necessarily in conflict with making moral compromises in public debate, but Christian morality certainly cannot be identified with the content of public morality (De Kruijf 2000). So Christians really are citizens of two worlds!

The metaphor links related truths

The process of metaphoric substitution draws our attention to two realities that are linked in some way. In Psalm 91:1 the psalmist declares that he is resting in the shadow of the Almighty. This is a reference to the sanctuary and protection that are the gift of God. There is a further reference in Psalm 91:4 to God's feathers and wings. These metaphors indicate God's care and protection. The question, however, is what influence these metaphors from the liturgy have on the lives of people living in the public domain.

Conventional metaphors

Figures of speech like metaphors and similes are sometimes seen as manifestations of extraordinary rather than ordinary use of language. Further, these phenomena are seen as relating to language alone, and not also to human thought and endeavour (Vos 1999: 98).

Metaphors are not confined to the liturgy, however. Like breathing, they are part of our entire lives. They permeate our thinking and actions. Our everyday conceptual system, which governs our thinking and actions, is fundamentally metaphorical in nature (Lakoff & Johnson 1980:3). This means that all language is permeated by *conventional metaphors*. By "conventional metaphors" we understand metaphors based on everyday experiences that by implication structure the way in which people think and communicate with the world. Since metaphor does not find expression in language alone, it also creates new possibilities and prospects in the areas of thought and endeavour.

The following example of a conventional metaphor from the New Testament provides an illustration (Liebenberg 2001:97). Matt 7:13 - 14: "*Enter* through the narrow *gate*. For *wide is the gate and broad is the road* that leads to destruction, and *many enter* through it. But *small is the gate and narrow the road* that leads to life, and only a few find it."

Although the author of Matthew was probably not consciously thinking of life in terms of a journey, this basic metaphor nevertheless largely colours the way he thinks about life. The basic metaphorical concept is the link through which one concept (life) is understood in terms of another (journey) (see Turner 1991:158; Liebenberg 2001:98). A metaphor acquires validity through its use in everyday language and thinking. To understand its function, one needs to be familiar with the way the metaphor is used and functions.

How can a conventional metaphor be embedded in the liturgy? In a well-known South African television advertisement the viewer is encouraged to buy a certain motor car. The jingle tells us that *life is a journey*, a metaphor from everyday life with which viewers are familiar. Life is indeed a journey and the advertisement encourages us to associate a particular motor car with a pleasant journey. The congregation at divine service is just as receptive to conventional metaphor. Such metaphors can take on another meaning and value in the service. The liturgy itself is a journey: during divine service, from the introductory prayer to the blessing, and then out into everyday life again. "*Life is a journey*": in the liturgy these words take on the value of vitality, movement, progress and joy. In fact this slogan lives in the minds of the congregation, and is echoed in their daily lives.

The metaphor as a network

Ricoeur (1977:44) pointed out that "the primary unit of meaning" is the sentence and not the word. When we refer to metaphorical language, we are referring not only to a function of *words* but also to the total co(n)text within which words (phrases) are used. By "context" we understand not only the literary aspects (ie macro structure, discourse, narrative etc), but also other co-"texts" such as the nominated subject (ie the writer or reader/ listener), including his or her sociohistorical background and literary competence. The liturgist should never lose sight of the fact that numerous metaphors are not confined to a single closed context but may be spread over the whole text.

The Lord is my shepherd

The shepherd motif plays a key part in the metaphorical dynamics of Psalm 23. This metaphor crops up frequently in the Old Testament. In many passages Jahwe is represented as the Shepherd of his flock (see for example Ps 80:2; Is. 40:11; 49:9 et seq; 63:14; Jer 23:3; Ezek 34:10; see also Ps 74:1; 79:13; Hos 4:16). The shepherd metaphor is used in the Old Testament to represent Jahwe as the shepherd of his flock or his people, but in Psalm 23 the metaphor is individualised. Here the psalmist speaks of "my" shepherd.

A metaphorical network is built up around the shepherd metaphor in Psalm 23. Structurally Psalm 23 can be divided into four stanzas, with a chiastic arrangement, namely 1b-3: confession/witness regarding Jahwe (He-I); 4: prayer expressing trust in Jahwe (I-Thou), 5: prayer expressing trust in Jahwe (Thou-I) and 6: confession/witness regarding Jahwe (I-He) (Zenger 1993:152).

Our attention is claimed by the way the shepherd metaphor occurs in the first stanza. The nominal sentence, "the Lord is my shepherd" (1b) is offered in the form of a confession (Van Uchelen 1971:160; Seybold 1996:101). The abundance offered to us by the shepherd (line 1) is illustrated in Jahwe's pastorate (lines 2 - 4). In lines 5 - 6 the pronouncement "I shall not want" is worked out (Schuman 2002:32).

The *care* of the shepherd emerges clearly in the metaphorical network. The expressions "green pastures" and "still waters" attest to the abundance of the shepherd's care (Miller 1986:114). In the context, within the framework of the shepherd metaphor, the expression in 3a implies that Jahwe restores the psalmist's strength when he is world-weary and can barely drag himself along.

The mountains of Judah are interspersed with deep, dangerous and dark valleys containing numerous caves that shelter robbers and beasts of prey. The poet uses this image to show that Jahwe, the Shepherd, is also to be found with his "flock" in "the valley of the shadow of death", in the gravest danger (Schuman 2002:47).

In the structure of Psalm 23 verse 4b serves as the hinge. This is underlined by the central position of 4b; it is exactly in the middle of the nine stiches of the psalm (Prinsloo 1991:37; Schuman 2002:31, 47). The first part of this line, "for you are with me" is an expression of faith in the presence of Jahwe.

The second part of 4b shows that the presence of Jahwe is a safeguard. The shepherd uses his "rod" to protect his sheep against wild animals. He uses the "rod" to lean on and to draw his sheep nearer and lead them (see also Van Uchelen 1971; Jüngling 1998:801; Schuman 2002:47).

A spiritual forming takes place in the liturgy. These spiritual elements of care, courage, and experience of the Lord's presence and protection in danger and in need should leave their mark on us as we wrestle with the problems of daily life.

Imagination and Images

Artists are imaginative people with imaginative wishes. Theologians can learn the art of imagination from artists. To do so theology has to take the words, paint and sculpture of artists seriously. Imagination is not something that is reserved for artists. It is open to all of us, because:

> You are like a rich man entering heaven
>
> Through the ear of a raindrop. Listen now again (Heaney 1996:1).

Imagination is something other than fantasy. Fantasy is an escape from reality, whereas imagination expands and enriches reality. Imagination is like a painter who has painted some apples. Once he has painted them they are no longer apples but patches of colour and shapes suspended in space; in passing we register them as "apples" and the next time we see "real" apples we look at them with altered expectations. It is imagination that conjures apples out of patches of colour and shapes, which we see as apples and which make us see more than apples. Imagination allows us to reach deeper layers of our inner being than we could ever access through our reason (Siertsema 1998:379).

The liturgy leaves space for imagination. In this space our relationships with God, our neighbour and the world can be creatively explored and deepened. This imagination brings people into contact with the kingdom of God where we find not soley peace but also discord, conflict and pain. The believer sees God as being present and working *within* the given, visible human reality (Jongsma-Tielema 1998:61). Imagination makes it possible for us to encounter and experience God in his different "guises" under different circumstances. A theology of imagination sees the Invisible, even if God's footprints cannot always be seen in the dusty paths of life.

Imagination also makes room for various "images" of other people. People appear in their vulnerbility, fragility, their hunger for power and fame, their vindictiveness and vengefulness, their charity, gentleness, goodness, affection and courtesy. Imagination also feeds ethical actions. It enables people to seek and discover new ways of making their interaction with other human beings meaningful and happy.

The imaginative impulses in the liturgy can grow into an imaginative life within the community. That means that the faith-community enters the public domain by concentrating on moral integrity and offering this as a contribution to public life (Stanley Hauerwas). But this contribution cannot take the form of demands. The faith-community must approach the world at large with openness and respect. Society must be convinced and persuaded that certain values make sense and give meaning to life. People must take responsibility for a more moral society by giving more thorough and concrete consideration to the consequences of their actions. The plea of Hans Jonas (1984) is that we should remember that we have the technological capacity to destroy the whole world, and then recoil from the potentially destructive consequences of our actions. (Here he is using fear as a heuristic method). Neither God nor man limits us – we are independent beings – but the fear of the future that we would create ourselves acts as a brake and guides us towards responsible and imaginative conduct.

Concluding Thoughts

Liturgical language as metaphorical language is a means of feeding spirituality. It allows us to discover the power of metaphors in everyday life. We can then think and live with imagination. And we can raise our glass in a toast to the metaphor.

References

Black, M., (1962) *Models and Metaphors. Studies in language philosophy.* Cornell University Press: Ithaca.

Carstens, A., (1992) Metonimie, polisemie en die leksikografie. *Suid-Afrikaanse Tydskrif vir Taalkunde*, 10(3), 114 - 122.

Carstens, A., (1993) In Funksionele benadering tot metonimie. *Suid-Afrikaanse Tydskrif vir Taalkunde,* 11(3), 85 - 93.

Carson, A., (2000) *Men in the off hours.* New York: Alfred A. Knopf.

de Kruif, G.G., (2000) *Noster Congres.* The Netherlands.

Gräbe, I., (1992) 'Metafoor' in Coete T.T (red.), *Literêre terme en teorieë.* Haum Literêr: Pretoria, 288 - 293.

Hauerwas, S., (1981) *A community of character.* University of Notre Dame Press: Notre Dame.

Hauerwas, S., (1983) *The peaceable kingdom.* University of Notre Dame Press: Notre Dame.

Heaney, Seamus, (1996) *The spirit Level.* Faber and Faber: London.

Johnson, M., (1987) *The body in the mind. The bodily basis of meaning imagination and reason.* University of Chicago Press: Chicago.

Jonas, H., (1984). *The imperative of responsibility.* University of Chicago Press: Chicago.

Jongsma-Tieleman, P.E., (1998) Godsdienst als speelruimte voor verbeelding. *GthT*, 98(2), 57 - 66.

Jüngling, H.W. (1998) 'Psalms 1 - 41' in Farmer, R. (ed), *The International Bible Commentary. A Catholic and Ecumenical Commentary for the Twenty-First Century.* The Liturgical Press: Collegeville.

Lakoff, G. & Johnson, M., (1980) *Metaphors we live by.* University of Chicago Press: Chicago/London.

Liebenberg, J., (2001) *The language of the Kingdom and Jesus.* Brill: Berlin.

Miller, P.D., (1986) *Interpreting the Psalms.* Fortess Press: Philadelphia.

Prinsloo, W.S., (1991) *Die psalms leef!* NG Kerkboekhandel: Halfway House.

Ramsey, I.T., (1957) *Religious Language.* SCM: London.

Ricoeur, P., (1975a) Parole et Symbole. *RevSR*, 49, 142 - 161.

Ricoeur, P., (1975b) Biblical Hermeneutics, *Semeia* 4, 29 - 145.

Ricoeur, P., (1977) *The rule of Metaphor. Multi-disciplinary studies of the creation of meaning in language.* Routledge: London.

Ricoeur, P., (1979) Naming God. *USQR*, 34(4), 15 - 27.

Schuman, N., (2002) *Pastorale. Psalm 23 in Bijbel en Liturgie verwoord en uitgebeeld.* Meinema: Zoetermeer.

Seybold, K., (1996) *Die Psalmen.* J.C.B. Mohre (Paul Siebeck): Tübingen.

Siertsema, B., 'Verbeelding in de liturgie' in Oskamp P en Schuman, N., *De weg van de liturgie.* Meinema: Zoetermeer, 379 - 387.

Turner, M., (1991) *Reading minds. The study of English in the age of cognitive science* Princeton University Press: Princeton.

van Huyssteen, J.W., (1986) *Teologie as kritiese geloofsverantwoording.* RGN-Uitgewery: Pretoria.

van Huyssteen, J.W., (1997) *Essays in Postfoundationalist Theology.* Grand Rapids, Michigan: Eerdemans.

van Huyssteen, J.W., (1999) *The Shaping of Rationality. Toward Interdisciplinarity in Theology and Science.* Grand Rapids, Michigan: Eerdemans.

van Leeuwen, M., (2002) 'De onalledaagse taal van de liturgie' in Barnard, M. en Schuman, N., *Nieuwe wegen in de liturgie.* Meinema: Zoetermeer.

van Uchelen, N.A., (1971) *Psalmen I.* Callerbach: Nijkerk.

Vos, C.J.A., (1999) 'In Raaisel in die spieël. Kantaantekeninge oor Letterkunde en Homiletiek in Lombaard, C. (ed), '... In die wêreld... '. Lewende Woorde Randse Afrikaanse Universiteit: Johannesburg, 93 - 106.

Zenger, E., (1993) *Die Psalmen I.* Herder: Freiburg/Basel/Wien.

PART V: PILGRIMS IN THE PUBLIC SQUARE

In the final contribution to this extensive volume Heather Walton demonstrates exactly the 'poetic impulse for liturgics' advocated in the preceeding article on metaphor and liturgy by Cas Vos. Walton's contribution was originally a sermon, preached during the IAPT Palm Sunday liturgy, in which the entry of Christ into Jerusalem was used as the Biblical centrepiece for an extended reflection on the nature of the Gospel's impact on the public square. As a performative piece at the heart of worship, Walton's essay operates at a number of different levels and is placed here at the end of our collection as something both very old, in the pastoral tradition of homiletics, and as something new: an aesthetic performance which in its multi-layered, lyrical-analytic style suggests new departures for 21st century practical theology. If we opened with our comments on the significance of our local context for the reflections of this conference, then we close with reflection on the intricate weaving of global and local, Biblical and experiential, historical and contemporary, and their immediate importance for a renewed public theology for our times. Walton's piece is placed here as an end which, to plunder from T.S. Eliot, might allow us to return to our (Christian) beginnings and know them anew.

This Common Road

Palm Sunday in a time of War

Heather Walton

In Matthew's gospel the road Jesus travels is from Jericho towards Jerusalem.

It is the final journey. Jesus stands in the ancient streets of Jericho and looks up at the solid city walls. Walls the old ones say once trembled and fell at the sound of a ram's horn. He says to his friends, those who will go with him, 'The rulers of the nations are tyrants. They lord it over their people. Don't let it be like that with you. Whoever wishes to be great amongst you must be the servant of all'. These are the words that Jesus spoke before he journeyed from the city of Jericho towards Jerusalem. He entered David's city gently, humbly, riding on a donkey.

I remember that in my children's picture book Bible Jesus was shown heading up a procession to the gates of Jerusalem. Before and after the road is clear. Someone must have stopped the road for this Palm Sunday parade. But those of us who have walked alongside Jesus from Jericho to Jerusalem know that this is a crowded route. Our small company tries to guide a couple of wayward donkeys – and perhaps one of us carries a ram's horn just for luck. We are jostled by the other travellers. Some of these believe the road belongs to them. The soldiers, the traders and the pilgrims would call this road their own.

The soldiers, of course, believe all the roads to all the cities are theirs to travel. Their ghost roads stretch across the deserts. In a skeleton tank a blackened warrior remains forever still and vigilant – guarding the military way.

In the darkened room the map of the city is flashed onto a bank of computer screens. Every road into the city can be traced. Each artery is visible. Every grid can be expanded. The city is x-rayed and revealed. It can be entered with surgical precision.

The soldiers are our friends. They carry in the big, flap, button-down pockets of their uniforms a folded document wrapped in plastic to protect it from sand or rain or snow. It is the road map for peace given to them by the rulers of the nations. It is not a map that we have been shown yet. But our small group cannot worry about this. We are trying to persuade these stubborn donkeys to tread the way we know we must follow.

Always with the soldiers travel the traders. They are enthusiastic about our journey. Glad that we are visiting their great city. 'The city is founded on trade' they tell us. 'Should the city fall we have, signed in our briefcases the contract for its reconstruction. The walls of Jericho stand again now stronger than before. For Jerusalem the tenders are in place'.

The traders are happy to talk for the essence of trade is communication. In the heart of the city is the market and 10,000 telephone lines link it to the world. Futures are bought and sold here. The traders have the ear of the government and a hot-line to the presidential palace. They travel along the electronic super-highway. They believe a fast road from the airport is essential. Along all this route are the billboards and the banners, the arches of triumph. Welcome, Welcome, Welcome. To the city of culture, the city of sport, heritage city, the city of the future. World city – sponsored by ...

Travel quickly along this broad, bright road the traders tell us. But we cannot travel quickly. We are the wedding party and we are the funeral procession. We move slowly because of the tender love we have for the one who travels with us. We move slowly so that other wedding guests and mourners can join us. Coming out of the narrow streets and dark alleyways now: the daughter of Jerusalem and all her children.

The pilgrims believe that before the soldiers came and surveyed this straight smooth route, before the traders came with their wayside stalls and flags and banners, there was an ancient pathway to the Holy City. 'The route was not marked by the signs we now see', they tell us, 'but the true way was known to the faithful'. Beneath the paving still lies the pilgrim way – coming up from Jericho towards Jerusalem.

The soldiers listen and say nothing. They know how the rulers of the nations authorise travel, grant safe passage and send their garrisons to guard the sacred sites. The traders smile because the number of pilgrims has been predicted to rise year on year. They contribute significantly to the national economy. They have a graph to show that this is so and shares in 47 religious broadcasting companies.

We walk beside the pilgrims for a while. Sometimes it comforts us to sing the old songs and hear the deep strong harmonies. But the pilgrims tell us that the city towards which we are travelling is not real. Only the temple is real. 'City walls tumble', they say, 'but the temple walls stand firm'. The pilgrims seem to be walking the same road as us but we realise that they are in truth following their own invisible path. Jesus asked us to walk with him from Jericho to Jerusalem. This common road.

This common road. Marked by craters. Barred by checkpoints. Which is becoming crowded now. Our small band has been swollen by lines of prisoners walking in single file. The daughter of Jerusalem clutches her baby beneath her black veils and hurries to avoid the crossfire and the curfew. Those whose limbs are shattered limp beside us. There are those whose eyes are blank because they have seen too much and children who cry and cry and cry.

I can see this road. I can see this long road between Jericho and Jerusalem. The military way, the trade route, the pilgrim path and the road trod by all those others who chose, or who did not choose, to accompany Jesus on his journey.

It is the road that I have seen on my television screen for the past month now crowded with tanks and refugees. It is the road to hell and the long road to freedom. It is the road we all travel each holy week when we take in our hands the palms that will become ashes. It is the road of my life for I have been compelled to join the wedding party/funeral procession as it winds its way up the hillside to the city walls. It is probably me who is carrying the ram's horn (just for luck). I slap the side of the donkey when it stops dead in the road. I can see myself, I can see us, I can see all of us as we enter the city. We are there just on the threshold when the miracle takes place.

Jesus travelled from Jericho to Jerusalem. As he entered the city the huge walls trembled and the stones broke into song. The trees flung down their branches. The prisoners tore off their uniforms to lay them on his path – and their guards did also. The eyes that had been blind could see again and the lame could dance. The children cried. Hosanna, Hosanna. Behold daughter of Zion your lord is coming to you. Gentle, humble, riding on a donkey.

I can see that moment as we enter the city and everything and everyone rejoices. This is my vision – our common vision. It has been given to us as a sign.

It is a sign that not in some other place but right here in this city God comes to us in gentleness and humility but with a transforming power that makes the stones tremble and the trees clap their hands. Look around and catch the glimpses of a mystery that surrounds us. It can be seen. It can be felt.

It is a sign that not amongst some other people but right here amongst us the sweetness of God enters – not to overcome or subdue but to empower. It is the daughter of Zion who raises her head to see who enters. It is the little ones we have seen crying on the road who raise their palms and sing Hosanna. Our heads are raised and our mouths are full of praise. We have witnessed that this can happen.

It is a sign that not at some other time but right now we must join the procession. Affirm that in this manner of coming amongst us God is most welcome. In this way of peace, that reclaims the ghost roads, that turns the tables of the traders and topples the temple – God is welcome amongst us. In the carnival chaos our weaknesses turned to strength and we are filled with joy.

It is a sign that you must keep before you as we continue on our way through this week. The helicopter gun ships are now patrolling the streets and the daughter of Jerusalem is calling for her children. It is a sign you will need when the soldiers come to make their arrest, when he is traded for twelve pieces of silver and the pilgrims call for their sacrifice. It is the sign you will need as you follow the procession on the road that leads outside the city.

Raise your head and look. It is the sign you have been given.

Contributors

John Atherton, Manchester Cathedral, Manchester, UK
Abraham Berinyuu, Department of African and General Studies, University for Development Studies, Tamale, Ghana
Chris Baker, William Temple Foundation, Manchester, UK
Riet Bons-Storm, University of Groningen, The Netherlands
Duncan Forrester, New College, University of Edinburgh, UK
Ottmar Fuchs, Eberhard-Karls-University, Tübingen, Germany
Wilhelm Graeb, Humboldt University, Germany
Etienne Grieu, Centre Sèvres, Facultés Jésuites de Paris, France
Elaine Graham, The University of Manchester, UK
Gerard V. Hall, Australian Catholic University (Brisbane Campus), Australia
Chris A.M. Hermans, Catholic University of Nijmegen, The Netherlands
Eberhardt K. Hauschildt, University of Bonn, Germany
F. Gerrit Immink, Faculty of Theology, Utrecht University, The Netherlands
Terence Kennedy, Accademia Alfonsiana, Rome, Italy
Solange Lefebvre, Faculty of Theology, University of Montreal, Canada
Daniel Louw, Stellenbosch University, Republic of South Africa
Robert Mager, Université du Québec à Trois-Rivières, Canada
Bonnie Miller-McLemore, Vanderbilt University Divinity School, USA
Jean-Guy Nadeau, Université de Montréal, Canada
Karl Ernst Nipkow, University of Tübingen, Germany
Esther D. Reed, St Mary's College, University of St Andrews, UK
Anna Rowlands, Westcott House, Cambridge Theological Federation, UK
Friedrich Schweitzer, Faculty of Evangelical Theology, University of Tübingen, Germany
Will Storrar, New College, University of Edinburgh, UK
Marcel Viau, Faculty of Theology and Religious Sciences, Laval University, Quebec City, Canada
Casparus Vos, University of Pretoria, Republic of South Africa
Heather Walton, University of Glasgow, UK
Raymond Webb, University of Saint Mary of the Lake, Mundelein, Illinois U.S.A.
Klaus Wegenast, University of Bern, Switzerland
Hans-Georg Ziebertz, University of Würzburg, Germany

Jahrbuch Politische Theologie

hrsg. von Torsten Habbel, Hans-Gerd Janßen, Ottmar John, Jürgen Manemann, Michael J. Rainer, Claus Urban, Bernd Wacker und José A. Zamora

Jürgen Manemann (Hrsg.)
Demokratiefähigkeit
Den vorliegenden Band I "Demokratiefähigkeit" eröffnen Statements zur Frage "Was heißt eigentlich politisch?" Beteiligt sind der Verfassungsrichter *Ernst-Wolfgang Böckenförde*, die Politiker *Peter Hintze* (CDU), *Freimut Duve* (SPD) und *Winfried Kretschmann* (Bündnis 90/Die Grünen) sowie mit theologischer Perspektive *Jürgen Moltmann*, *Dorothee Sölle* und *Edna Brocke*. Beiträge von *Tiemo R. Peters*, *Johann Baptist Metz*, *Ottmar John*, *Michael J. Rainer*, *Willi Oelmüller*, *Jürgen Manemann*, *Edmund Arens*, *Kuno Füssel* und *Michael Ramminger* vertiefen den grundlegenden Zusammenhang zwischen Monotheismus, Theodizee und moderner demokratischer Gesellschaft. *Debatte* – diesmal um die "Politik der Anerkennung der Anderen" (mit Thesen von Günter P. Suess und Kommentaren von Walter Lesch, Matthias Möhring-Hesse und Peter Rottländer), *Rezensionen* (zur aktuellen C. Schmitt-Diskussion) und Portraits einschlägiger *Institute/Projekte* (Fritz Bauer Institut, Frankfurt a. M.; Institut für Theologie und Politik, Münster) zeigen weitere Dimensionen politisch-theologischer Arbeit.
Bd. 1, 2. Aufl. 2000, 272 S., 17,90 €, br.,
ISBN 3-8258-2227-3

Michael J. Rainer; Hans-Gerd Janßen (Hg.)
Bilderverbot
Dieser Band stellt mit "Bilderverbot" ein ungewöhnliches, aber theologisch zentrales Thema in den Mittelpunkt. Im Blick auf häufig undurchschaute Querverbindungen z. B. in Kunst und Medien, verweist das Jahrbuch auf neue und alte "unsichtbare Mächte".
Es untersucht fragwürdige Profile politischer Ästhetik und kritisiert mitunter verdeckte Ansprüche auf universale Gültigkeit seitens bildloser Machtsysteme. Die ursprünglich in den Religionen gestellte Problem der "Abbildbarkeit des Unvorstellbaren" gewinnt über die aktuelle Denkmaldebatte neue Brisanz. Mit Beiträgen von: Bischof Pedro Casadaliga, Rita Burrichter, Franz Hinkelammert und Bob Brecher, Hanna Gekle, Agnes Heller, José A. Zamora, Saskia Wendel, Torsten Habbel, Jürgen Ebach, Jürgen Goldstein, Ottmar John, Hans-Gerd Janßen, Jürgen Manemann, Wolfgang Mantl, Jürgen Werbick und Johann Baptist Metz.
Bd. 2/1997, 1997, 344 S., 20,90 €, br.,
ISBN 3-8258-2795-x

Jürgen Manemann (Hg.)
Befristete Zeit
In Band 3 wird der Zeitindex der Theologie diskursorisch herausgearbeitet: "Wer christlich zu denken glaubt und dies ohne Frist zu denken glaubt, ist schwachsinnig." (J. Taubes). Zeit als Frist denken – das ist der Theologie aufgegeben. Eine apokalyptisch angeschärfte Gottesrede verweigert sich der bloßen Faktizität, indem sie ihren Herrschaftscharakter zu enthüllen und einen Horizont aufzubrechen versucht, von dem aus Geschichte in ihrer Herrschafts- und Unterwerfungsstruktur entlarvt und in ihrer subjekthaft erfahrenen Leidens- und Hoffnungsstruktur erkennbar wird. Ein solcher Entwurf provoziert eine kontroverse Diskussion im Zeitalter der Beschleunigungen und der Zeitvergessenheit. Zu dieser Diskussion im Konzert mit anderen Disziplinen (Soziologie, Philosophie, Politologie, Ästhetik u. a.) herauszufordern, ist die Aufgabe des 3. Bandes. Mit Statements von U. H. J. Körtner, F. Rest, C. Wulf, U. Lüke. Textbeiträge u. a. von J. Habermas, N. Bolz, K.-H. Brodbeck, M. L. Lamb, J. B. Metz, T. R. Peters, J. Reikerstorfer, C. Türcke, J. Werbick, J. A. Zamora.
Bd. 3, 1999, 280 S., 20,90 €, br., ISBN 3-8258-3957-5

Jürgen Manemann (Hg.)
Monotheismus
Dieser Band schaltet sich in den gegenwärtigen Diskurs über den Monotheismus ein. Mit dieser Thematik steht das Zentrum politisch-theologischen Denkens zur Debatte. Das Jahrbuch setzt an mit der Frage nach dem Zusammenhang von Ethik und Monotheismus und fokussiert die Kritik des ethischen Monotheismus im ausgehenden 20. Jahrhundert. Der Band enthält Analysen gegenwärtiger Anti-Monotheismen in der (post-)modernen Gesellschaft und in christlichen trinitätstheologischen Auslegungen. Zur Debatte steht im besonderen das Monotheismus-Verständnis, das Jan Assmann in seinen Studien entworfen hat und sein Versuch, die dem Monotheismus inhärenten Feindbilder, nämlich Ägypten und den Polytheismus, zu rehabilitieren. Neben einer ausführlichen Rezension über die populärwissenschaftlichen Angriffe gegen den biblischen Monotheismus werden Projekte vorgestellt, die hier angerissene Problemzusammenhänge gesellschaftspolitisch umzusetzen versuchen. AutorInnen dieses Bandes sind u. a.: Jan Assmann, Richard Faber, Thomas Freyer, Alois Halbmayr, Ottmar John, Otto Kallscheuer, Daniel Krochmalnik, Gottfried Küenzlen, Jürgen Manemann, David Patterson, Johann Reikerstorfer, Thomas Ruster, Dieter Schellong, Heinz-Günther Stobbe, Marie-Theres Wacker, Erich Zenger.
Bd. 4, 2002, 200 S., 20,90 €, br., ISBN 3-8258-4426-9

LIT Verlag Münster – Berlin – Hamburg – London – Wien
Grevener Str./Fresnostr. 2 48159 Münster
Tel.: 0251 – 62 032 22 – Fax: 0251 – 23 19 72
e-Mail: vertrieb@lit-verlag.de – http://www.lit-verlag.de